ZEROKILLER™

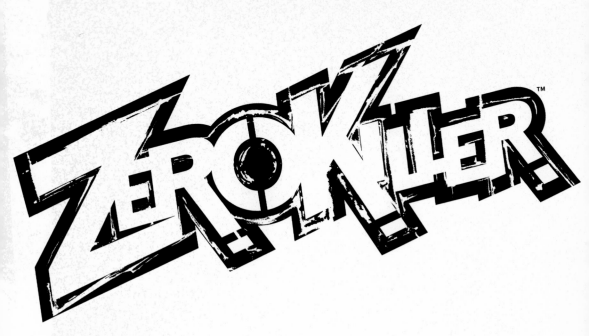

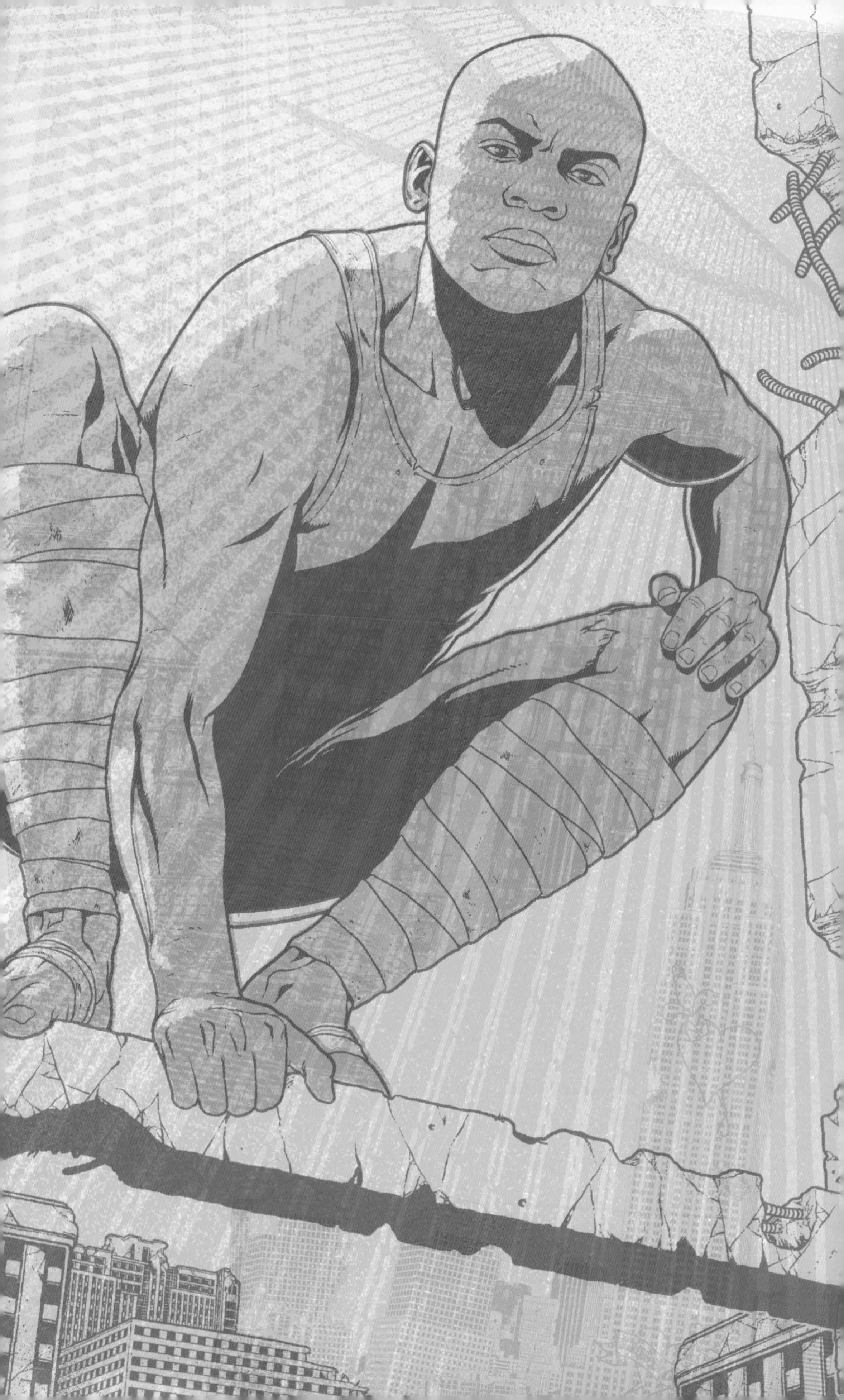

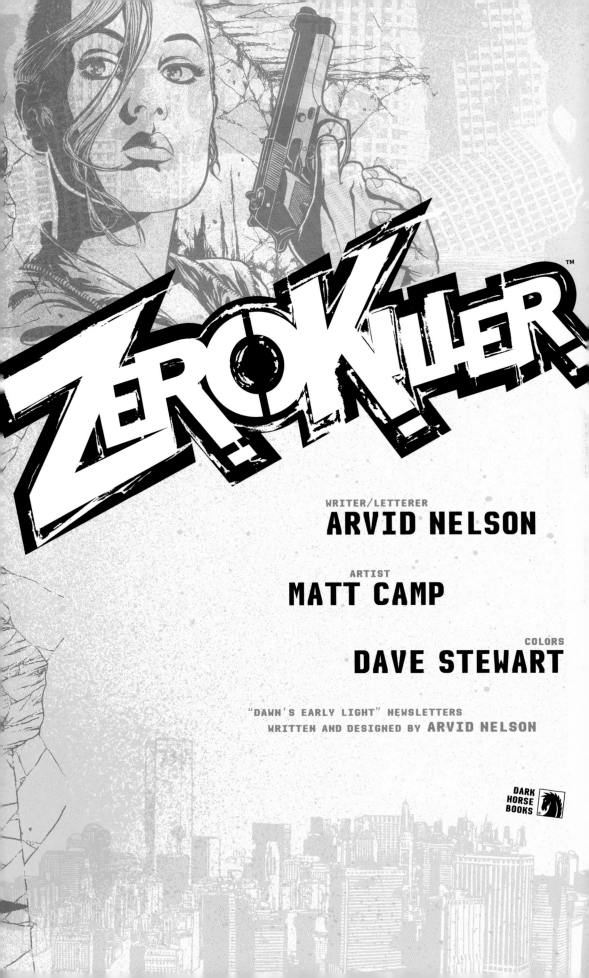

Zero Killer ™

WRITER/LETTERER
ARVID NELSON

ARTIST
MATT CAMP

COLORS
DAVE STEWART

"DAWN'S EARLY LIGHT" NEWSLETTERS
WRITTEN AND DESIGNED BY ARVID NELSON

DARK
HORSE
BOOKS

Publisher **MIKE RICHARDSON**
Editor **PHILIP R. SIMON**
Consulting Editor **SCOTT ALLIE**
Assistant Editors **RYAN JORGENSEN** and **PATRICK THORPE**
Editorial Assistant **JOHN SCHORK**
Book / Logo Design **JOSH ELLIOTT**
Digital Production **MATT DRYER**

This volume collects issues #1–#6 of the Zero Killer comic-book series, and the
short story "Zero Killer: Catch a Joker by the Throat" from Free Comic Book Day 2007.

Published by
Dark Horse Books
A division of Dark Horse Comics, Inc.
10956 SE Main Street
Milwaukie, OR 97222

zerokiller.com
darkhorse.com

To find a comics shop in your area, call the
Comic Shop Locator Service toll-free at 1-888-266-4226

First edition: August 2010
ISBN 978-1-59582-531-5

10 9 8 7 6 5 4 3 2 1

Printed at Midas Printing International, Ltd., Huizhou, China

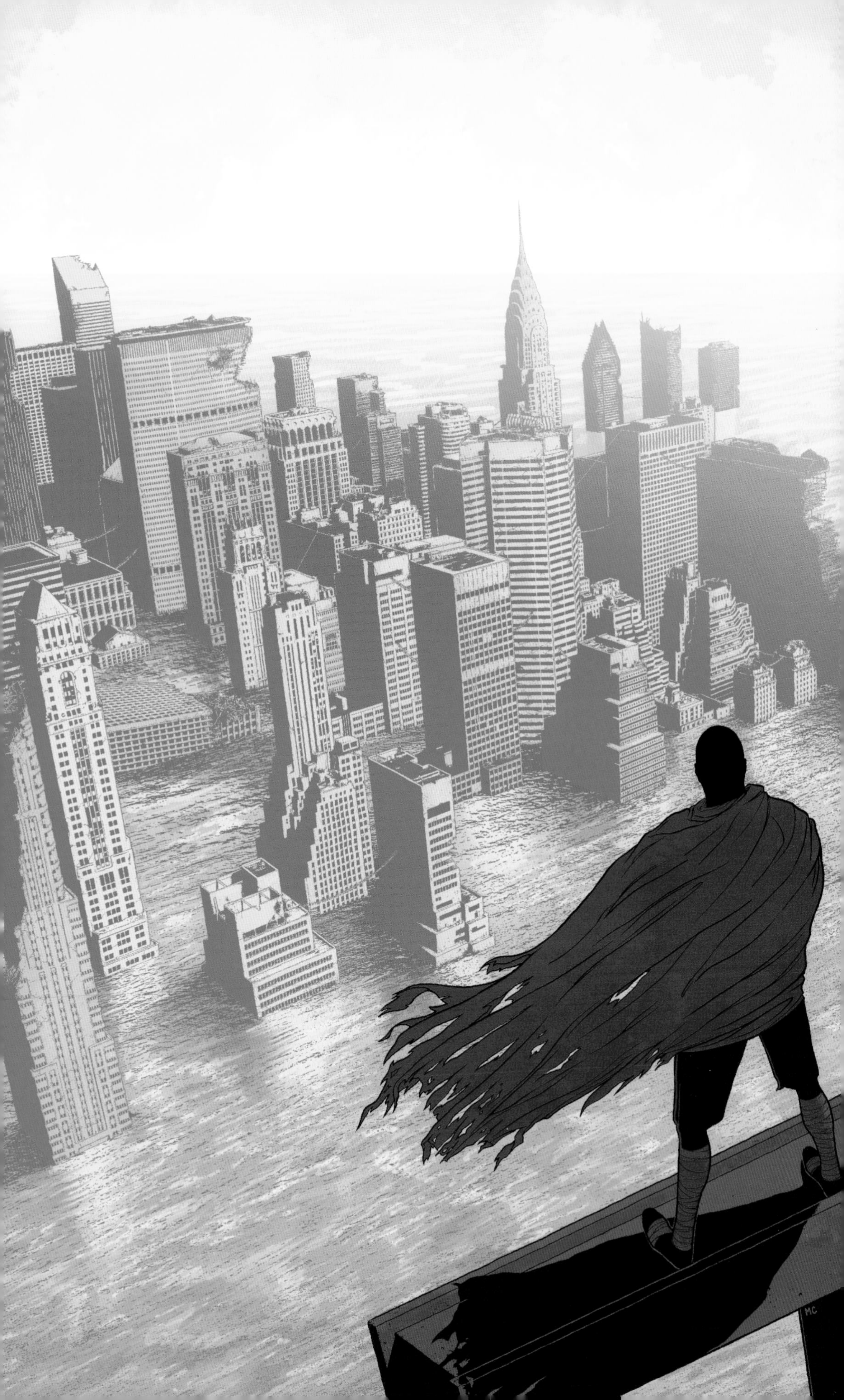

CHAPTER 1
LIVE AT THE WINTER GARDEN

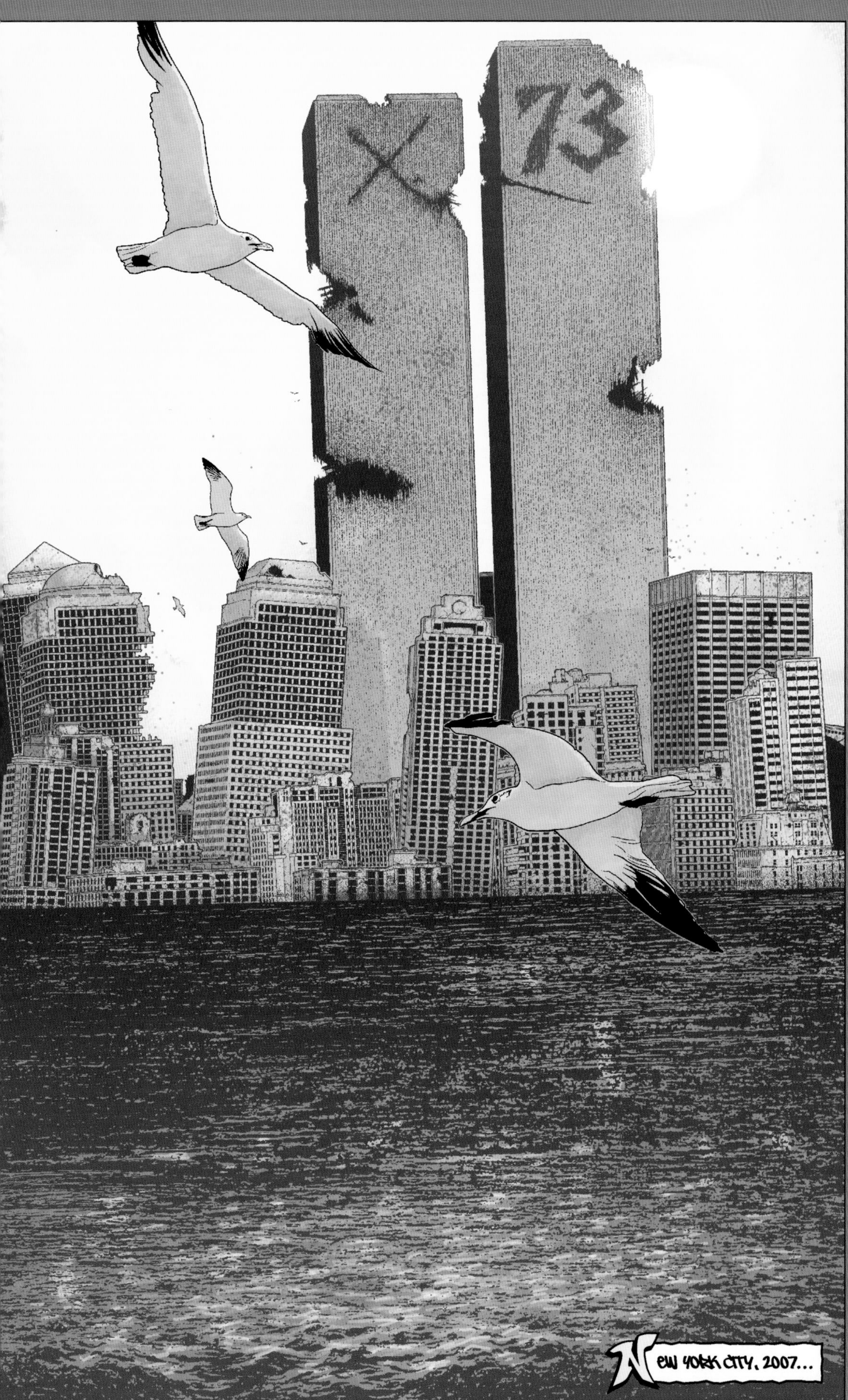

73
New York City, 2007...

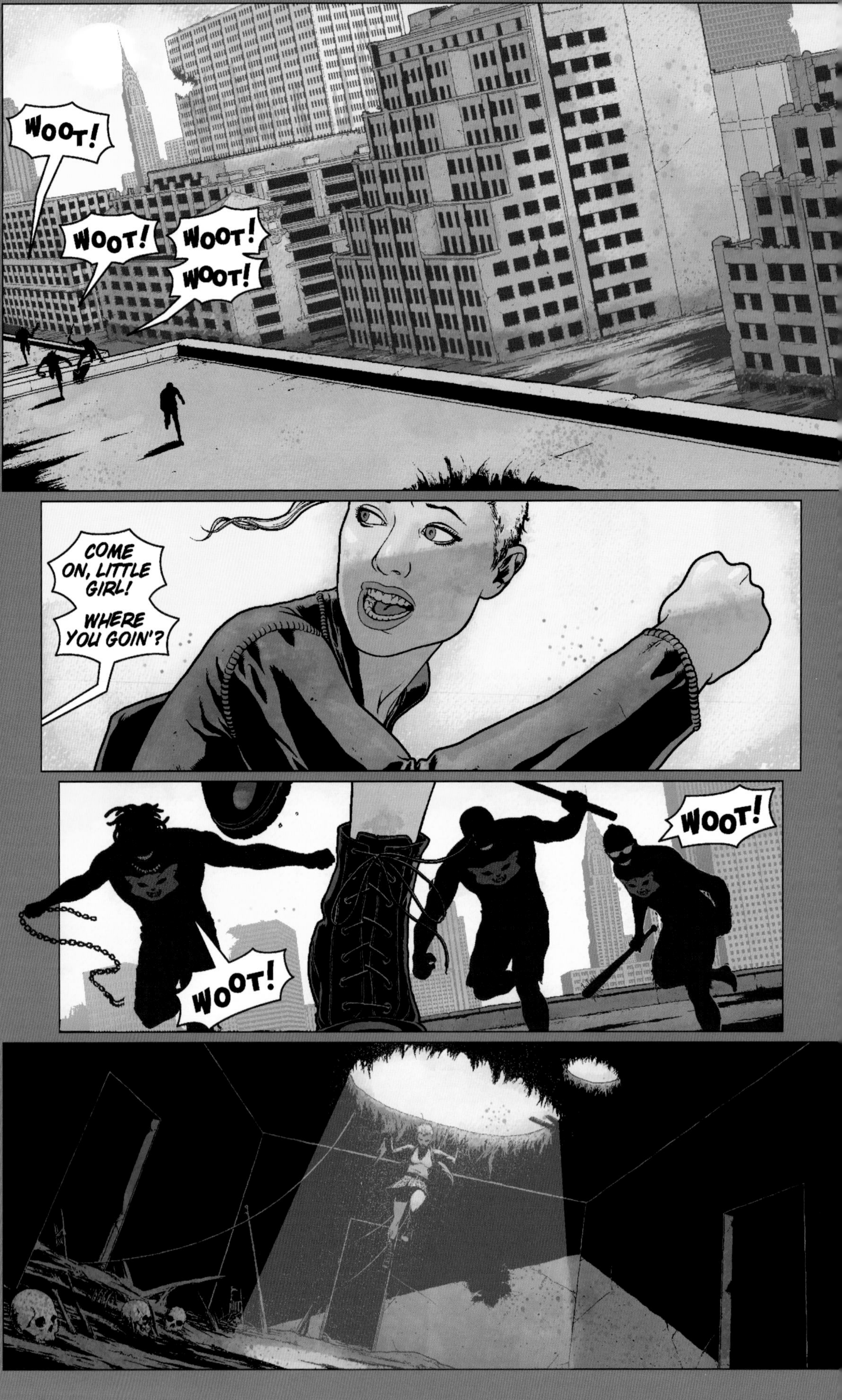
WOOT!
WOOT!
WOOT!
WOOT!
COME ON, LITTLE GIRL!
WHERE YOU GOIN'?
WOOT!
WOOT!

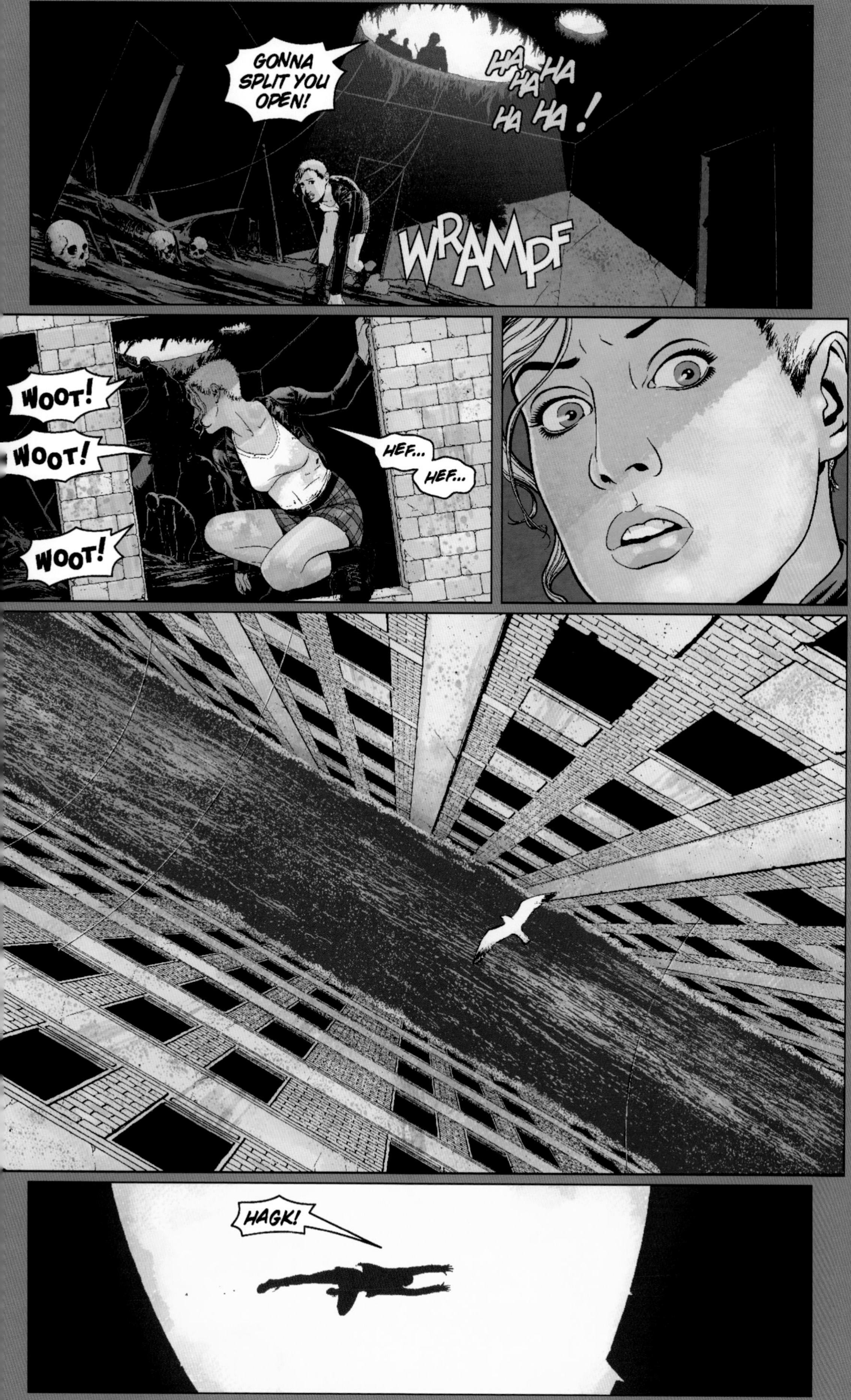
GONNA SPLIT YOU OPEN!
HA HA HA HA HA!
WRAMPF
WOOT!
WOOT!
WOOT!
HEF...
HEF...
HAGK!

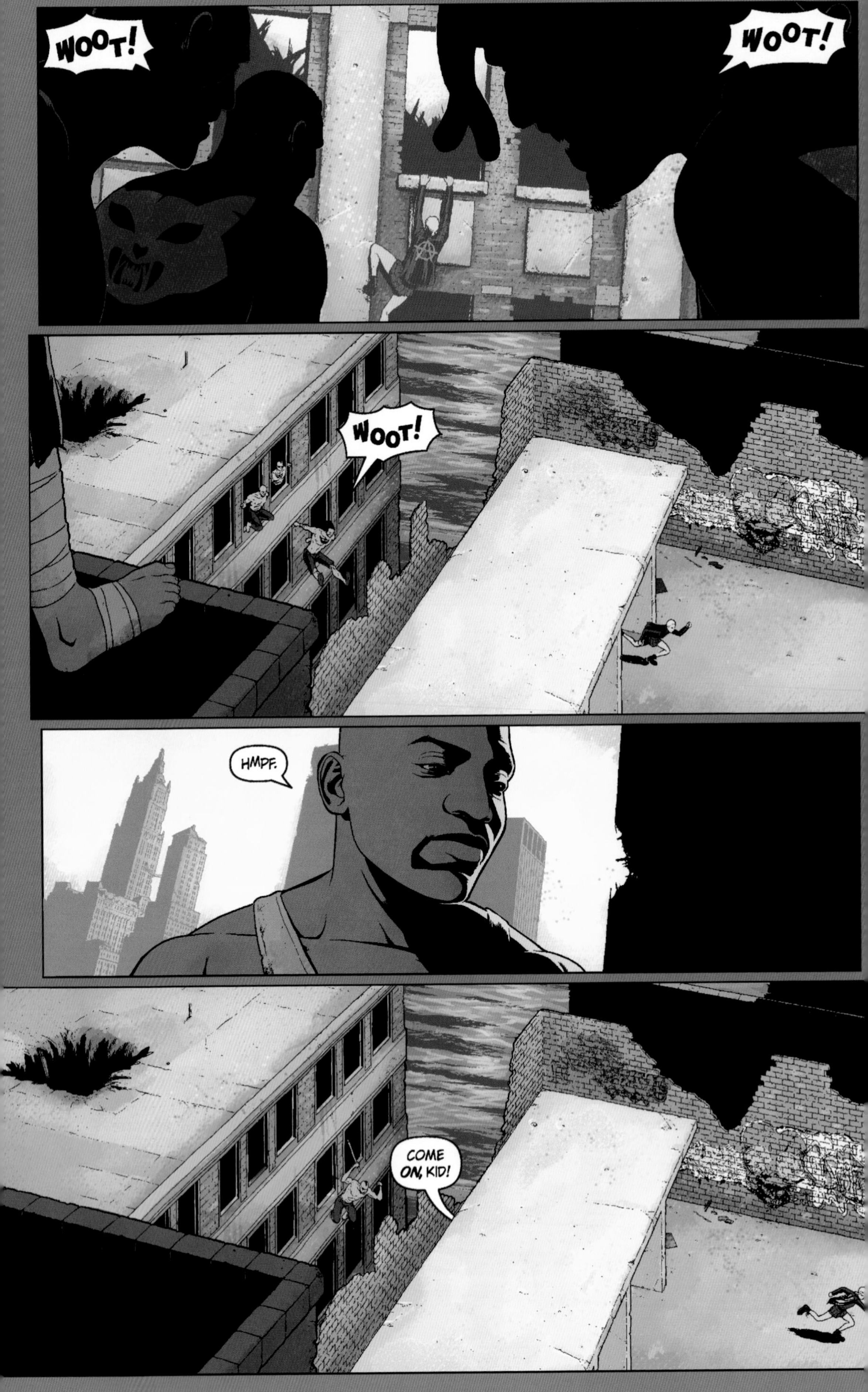
WOOT!
WOOT!
WOOT!
HMPF.
COME ON, KID!

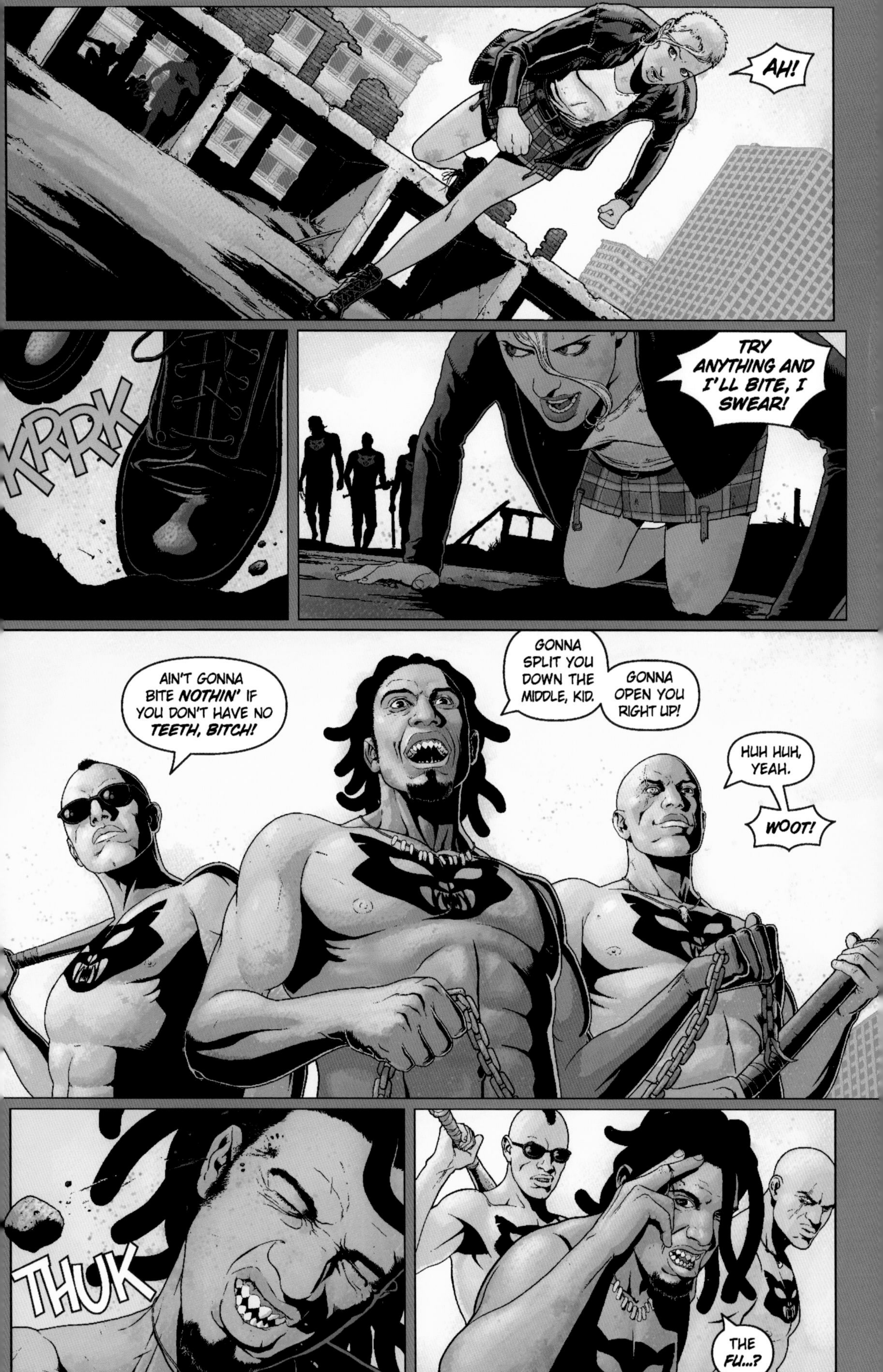
AH!
KRRK
TRY ANYTHING AND I'LL BITE, I SWEAR!
AIN'T GONNA BITE NOTHIN' IF YOU DON'T HAVE NO TEETH, BITCH!
GONNA SPLIT YOU DOWN THE MIDDLE, KID.
GONNA OPEN YOU RIGHT UP!
HUH HUH, YEAH.
WOOT!
THUK
THE FU...?

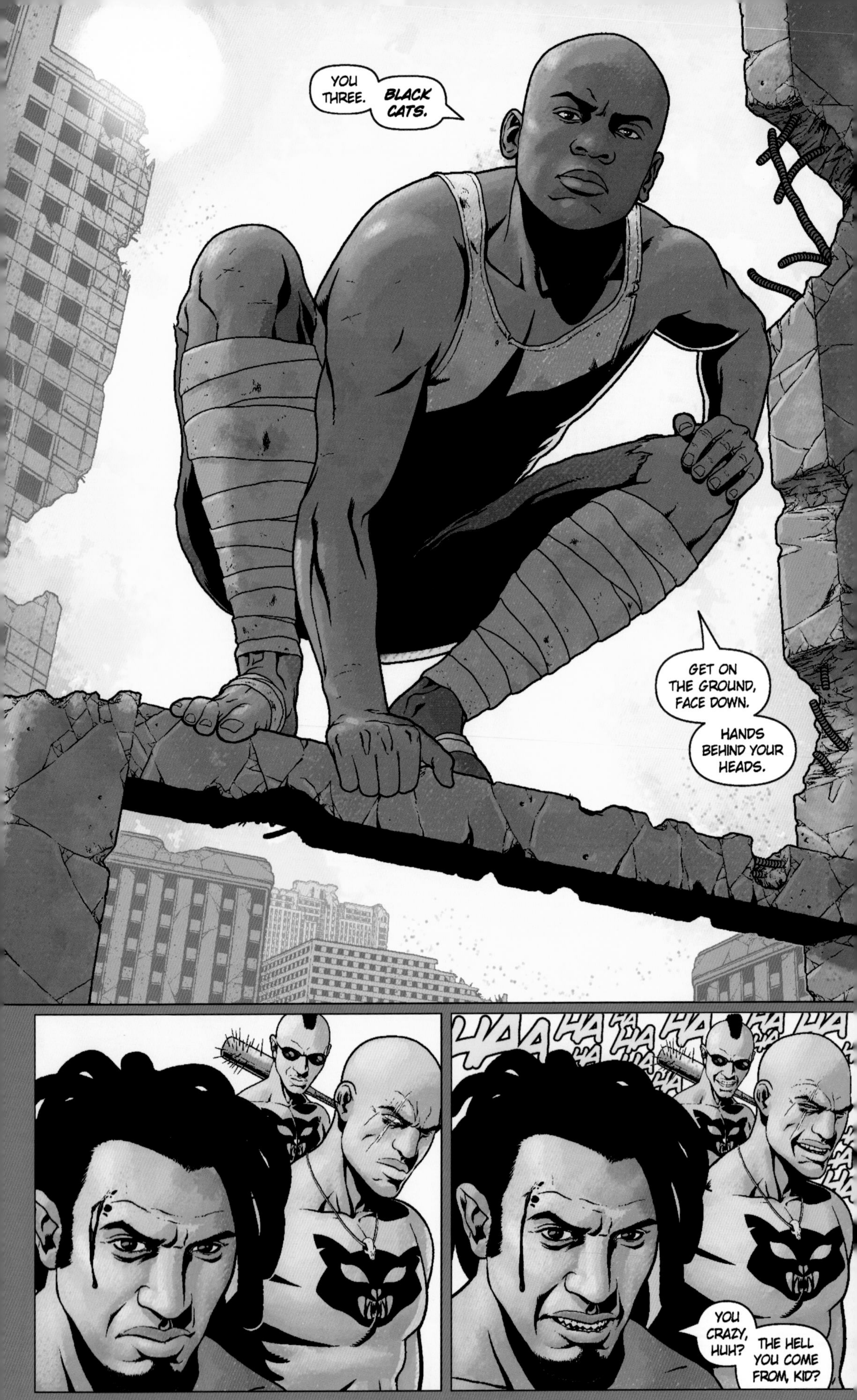
YOU THREE. *BLACK CATS.*
GET ON THE GROUND, FACE DOWN.
HANDS BEHIND YOUR HEADS.
YOU CRAZY, HUH?
THE HELL YOU COME FROM, KID?

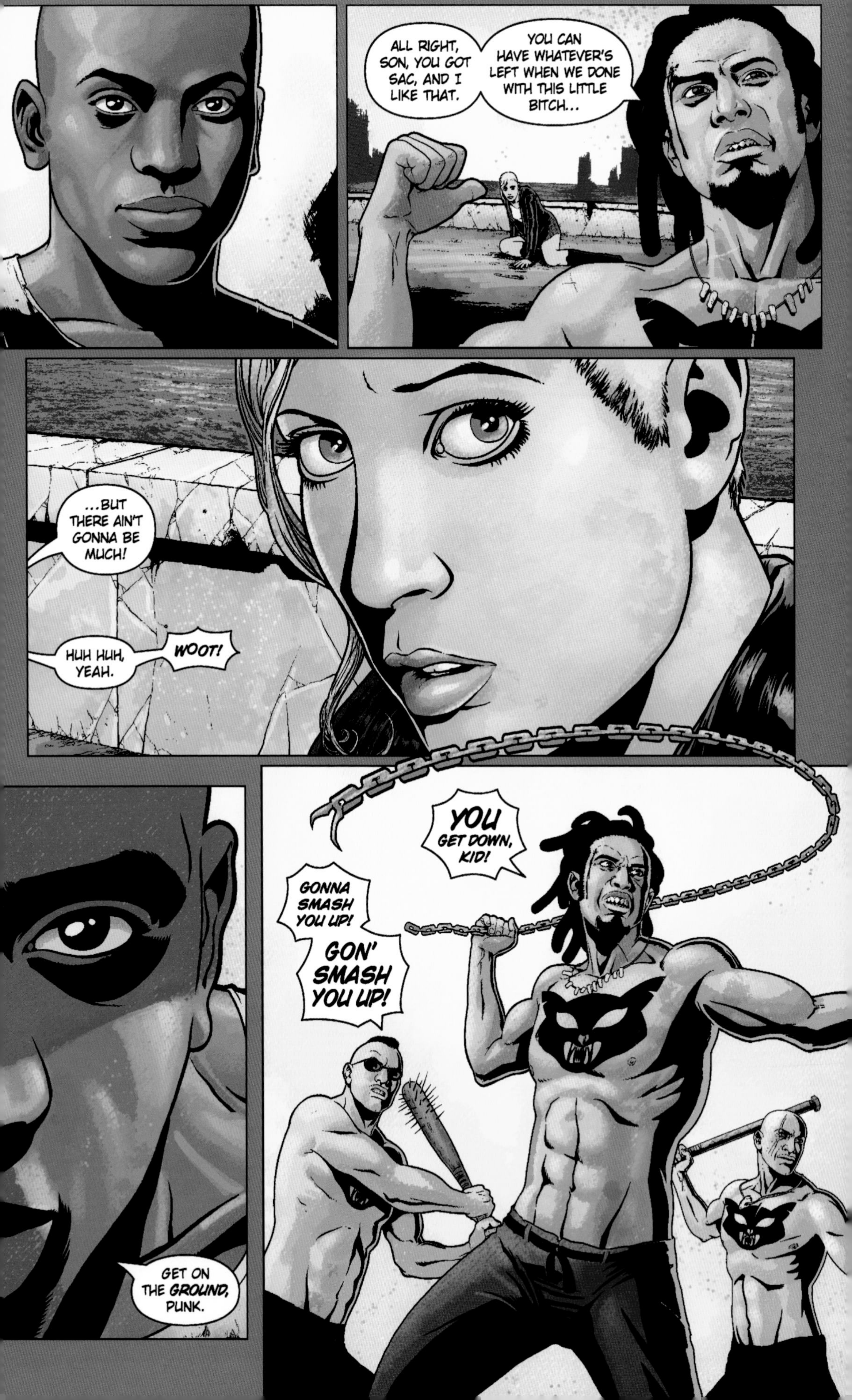
ALL RIGHT, SON, YOU GOT SAC, AND I LIKE THAT.
YOU CAN HAVE WHATEVER'S LEFT WHEN WE DONE WITH THIS LITTLE BITCH...
...BUT THERE AIN'T GONNA BE MUCH!
HUH HUH, YEAH.
WOOT!
GET ON THE GROUND, PUNK.
YOU GET DOWN, KID!
GONNA SMASH YOU UP!
GON' SMASH YOU UP!

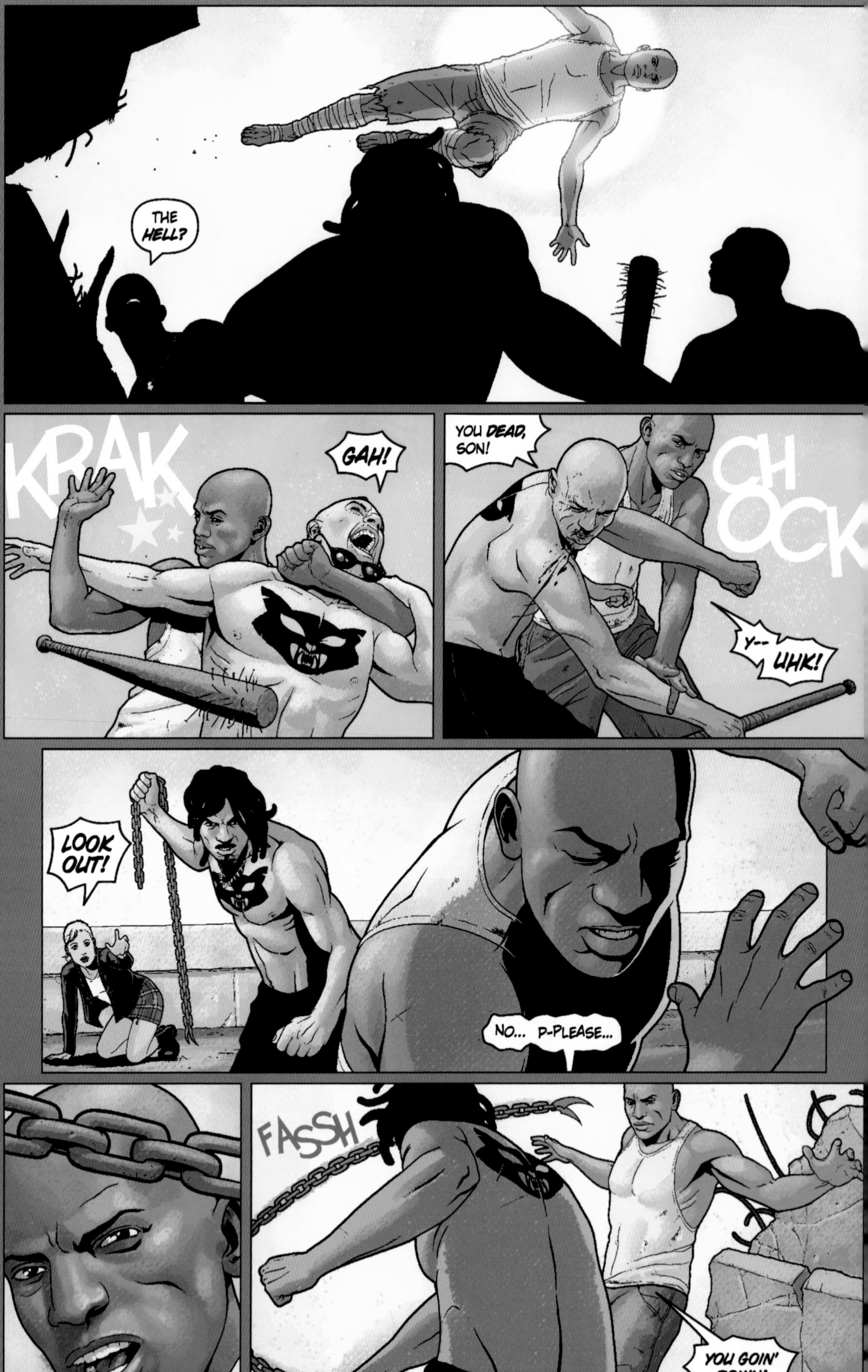
THE HELL?
KRAK
GAH!
YOU DEAD, SON!
CH OCK
Y-- UHK!
LOOK OUT!
NO... P-PLEASE...
FASSH
YOU GOIN' DOWN!

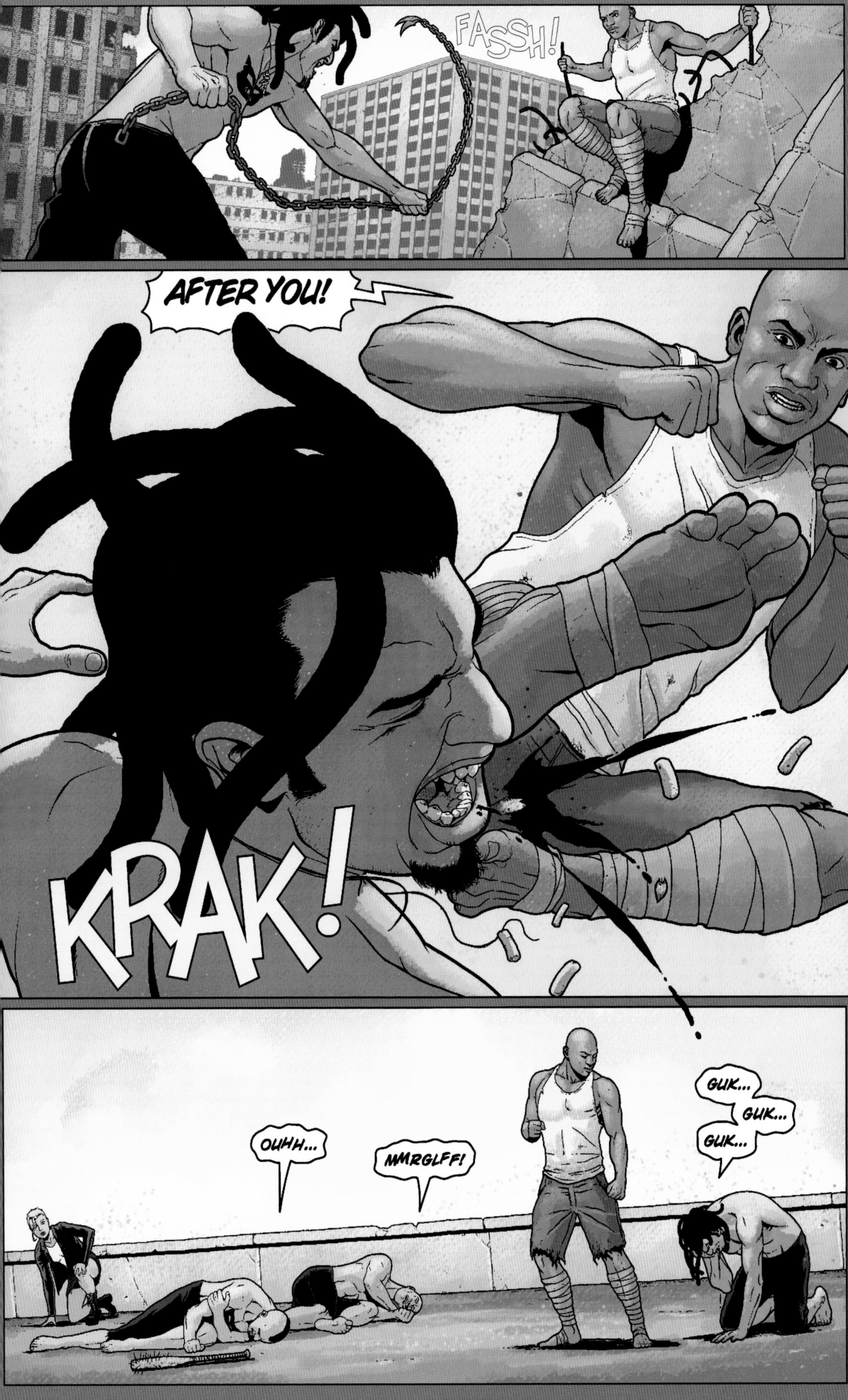
FASSH!
AFTER YOU!
KRAK!
OUHH...
MMRGLFF!
GUK...
GUK...
GUK...

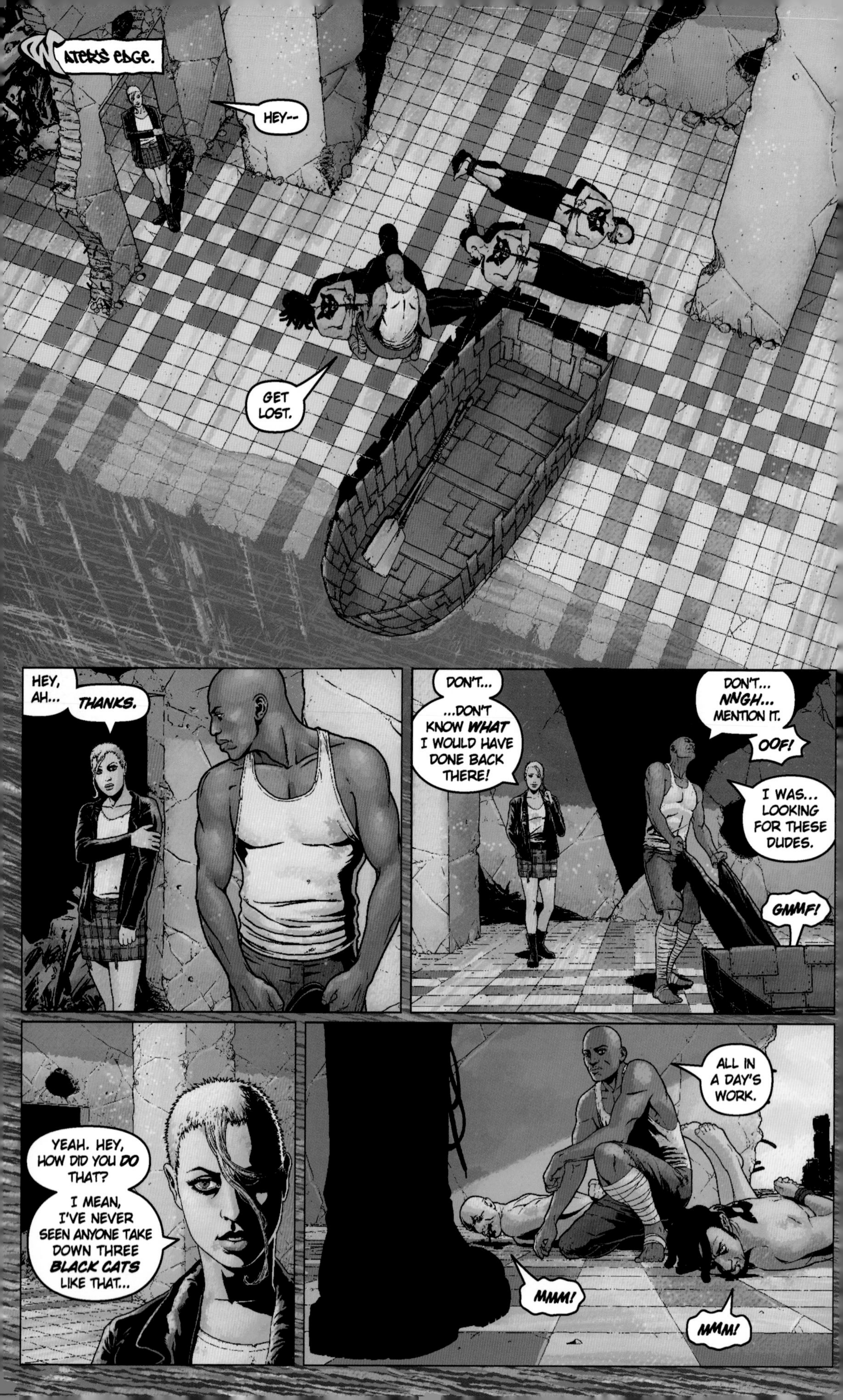
WATER'S EDGE.
HEY--
GET LOST.
HEY, AH... THANKS.
DON'T...
...DON'T KNOW WHAT I WOULD HAVE DONE BACK THERE!
DON'T... NNGH... MENTION IT.
OOF!
I WAS... LOOKING FOR THESE DUDES.
GMMF!
YEAH. HEY, HOW DID YOU DO THAT?
I MEAN, I'VE NEVER SEEN ANYONE TAKE DOWN THREE BLACK CATS LIKE THAT...
ALL IN A DAY'S WORK.
MMM!
MMM!

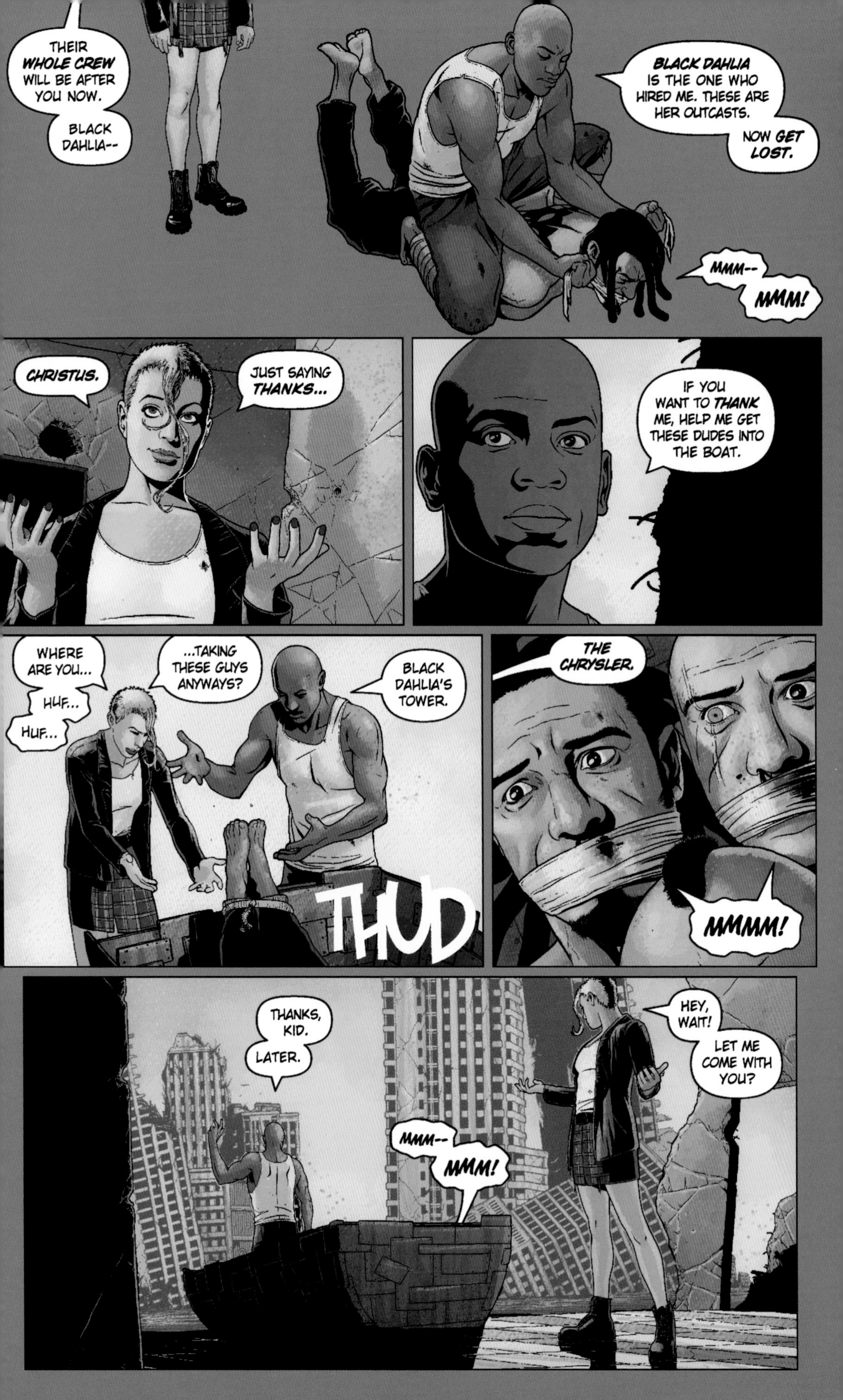
THEIR WHOLE CREW WILL BE AFTER YOU NOW.
BLACK DAHLIA--
BLACK DAHLIA IS THE ONE WHO HIRED ME. THESE ARE HER OUTCASTS.
NOW GET LOST.
MMM--
MMM!
CHRISTUS.
JUST SAYING THANKS...
IF YOU WANT TO THANK ME, HELP ME GET THESE DUDES INTO THE BOAT.
WHERE ARE YOU...
HUF...
HUF...
...TAKING THESE GUYS ANYWAYS?
BLACK DAHLIA'S TOWER.
THUD
THE CHRYSLER.
MMMM!
THANKS, KID.
LATER.
HEY, WAIT!
LET ME COME WITH YOU?
MMM--
MMM!

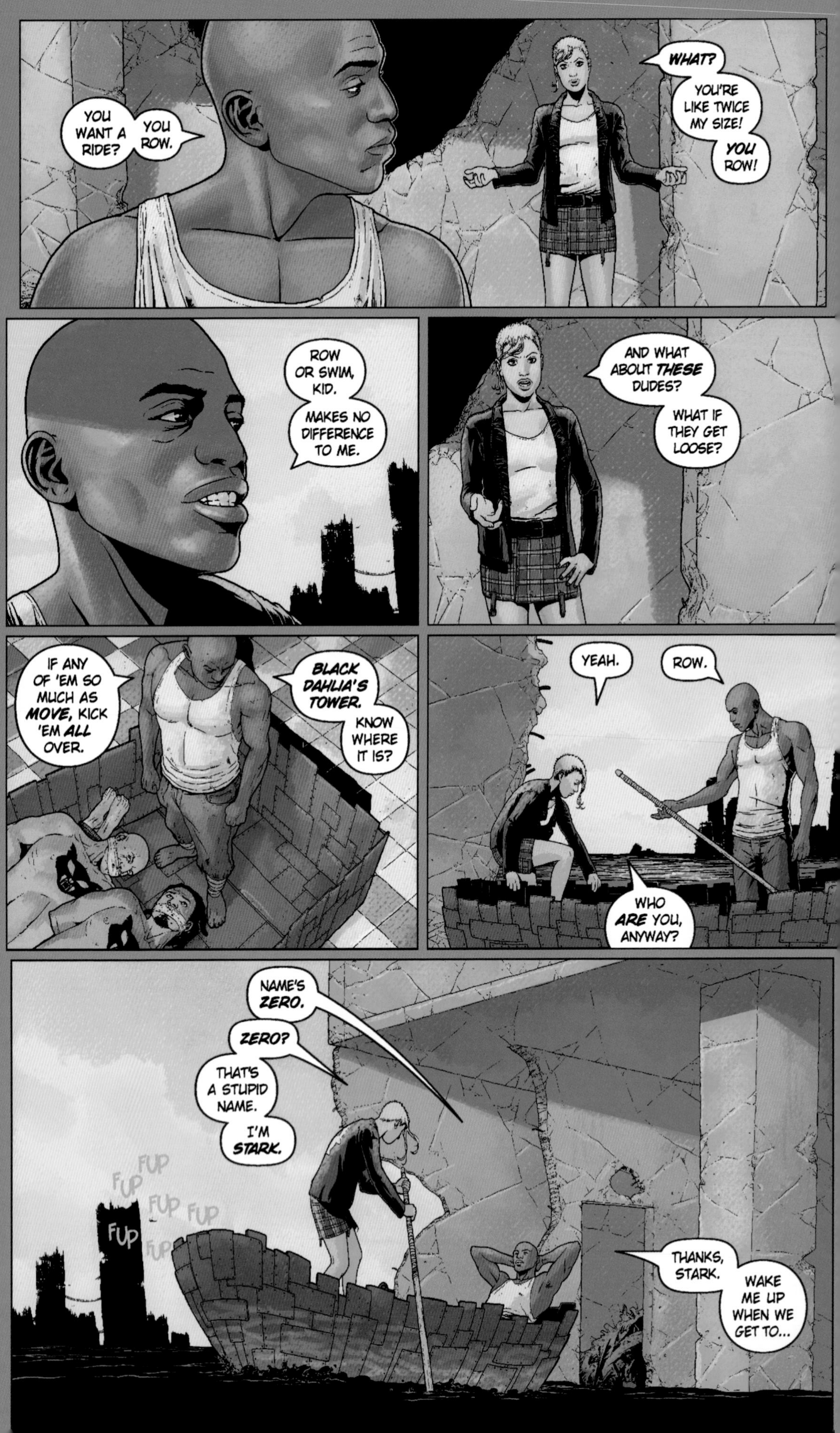
YOU WANT A RIDE?
YOU ROW.
WHAT?
YOU'RE LIKE TWICE MY SIZE!
YOU ROW!
ROW OR SWIM, KID.
MAKES NO DIFFERENCE TO ME.
AND WHAT ABOUT THESE DUDES?
WHAT IF THEY GET LOOSE?
IF ANY OF 'EM SO MUCH AS MOVE, KICK 'EM ALL OVER.
BLACK DAHLIA'S TOWER.
KNOW WHERE IT IS?
YEAH.
ROW.
WHO ARE YOU, ANYWAY?
NAME'S ZERO.
ZERO?
THAT'S A STUPID NAME.
I'M STARK.
FUP FUP FUP FUP FUP FUP
THANKS, STARK.
WAKE ME UP WHEN WE GET TO...

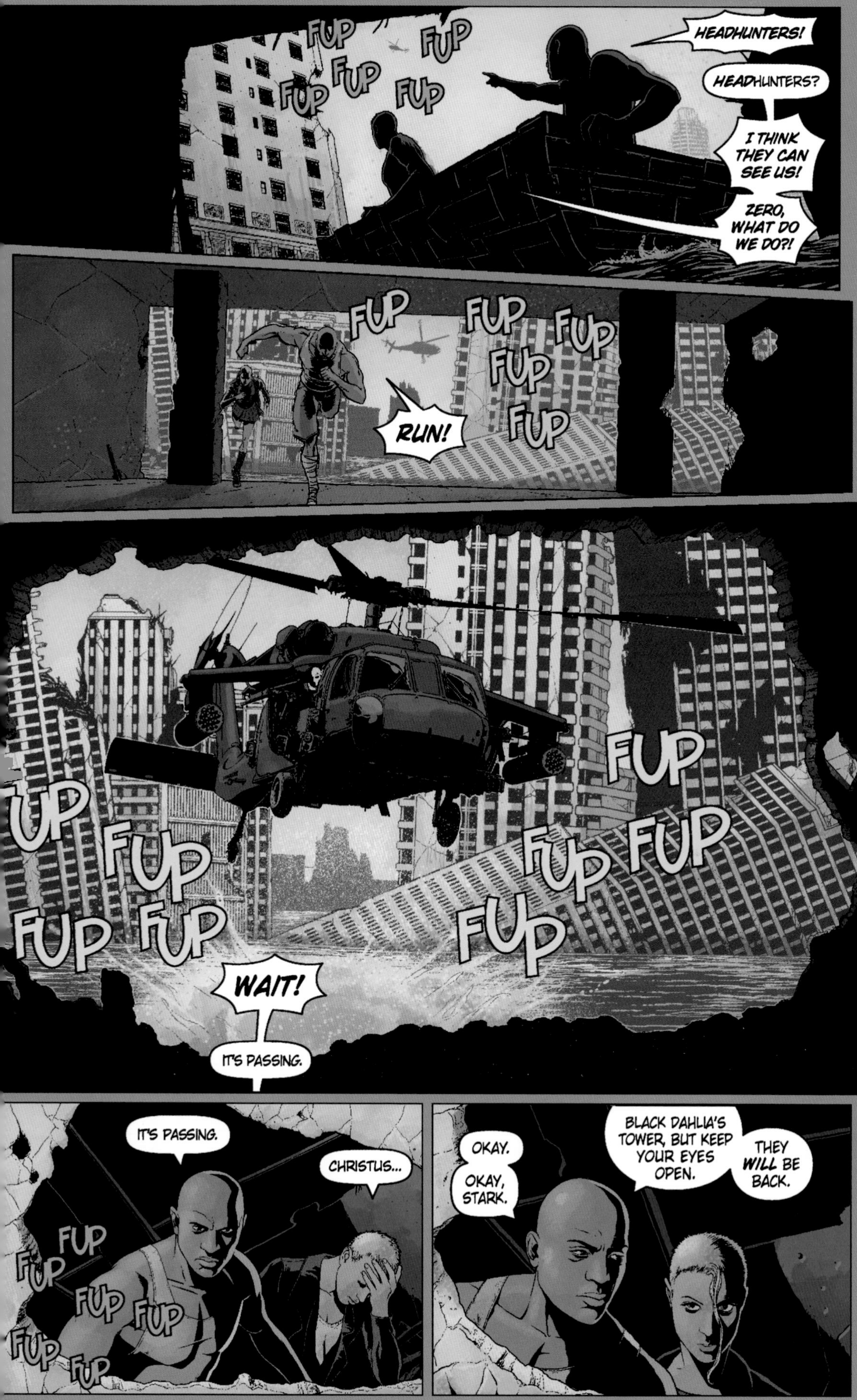
FUP
FUP
FUP
FUP
FUP
HEADHUNTERS!
HEADHUNTERS?
I THINK THEY CAN SEE US!
ZERO, WHAT DO WE DO?!
FUP
FUP
FUP
FUP
FUP
RUN!
UP
FUP
FUP
FUP
FUP
FUP
FUP
FUP
WAIT!
IT'S PASSING.
FUP
FUP
FUP
FUP
FUP
FUP
IT'S PASSING.
CHRISTUS...
OKAY.
OKAY, STARK.
BLACK DAHLIA'S TOWER, BUT KEEP YOUR EYES OPEN.
THEY WILL BE BACK.

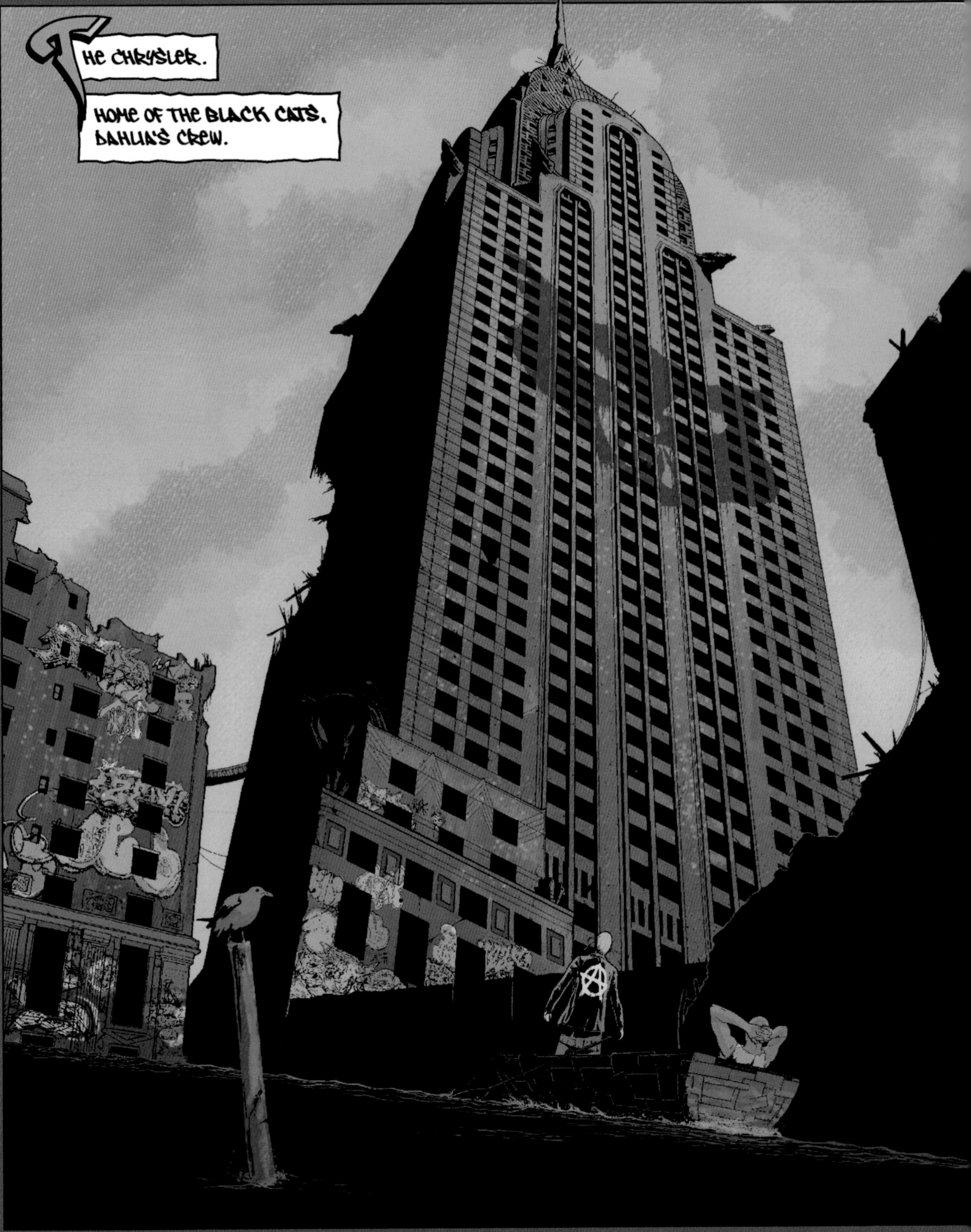
The Chrysler.
Home of the Black Cats. Dahlia's crew.

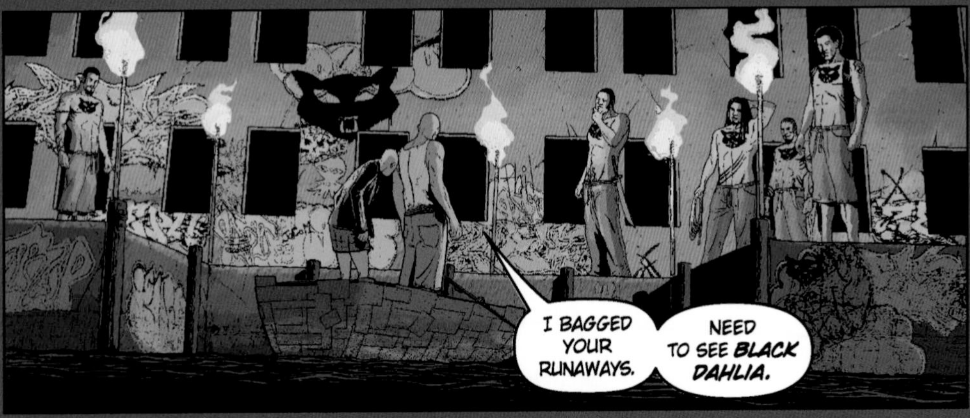
I bagged your runaways.
Need to see Black Dahlia.

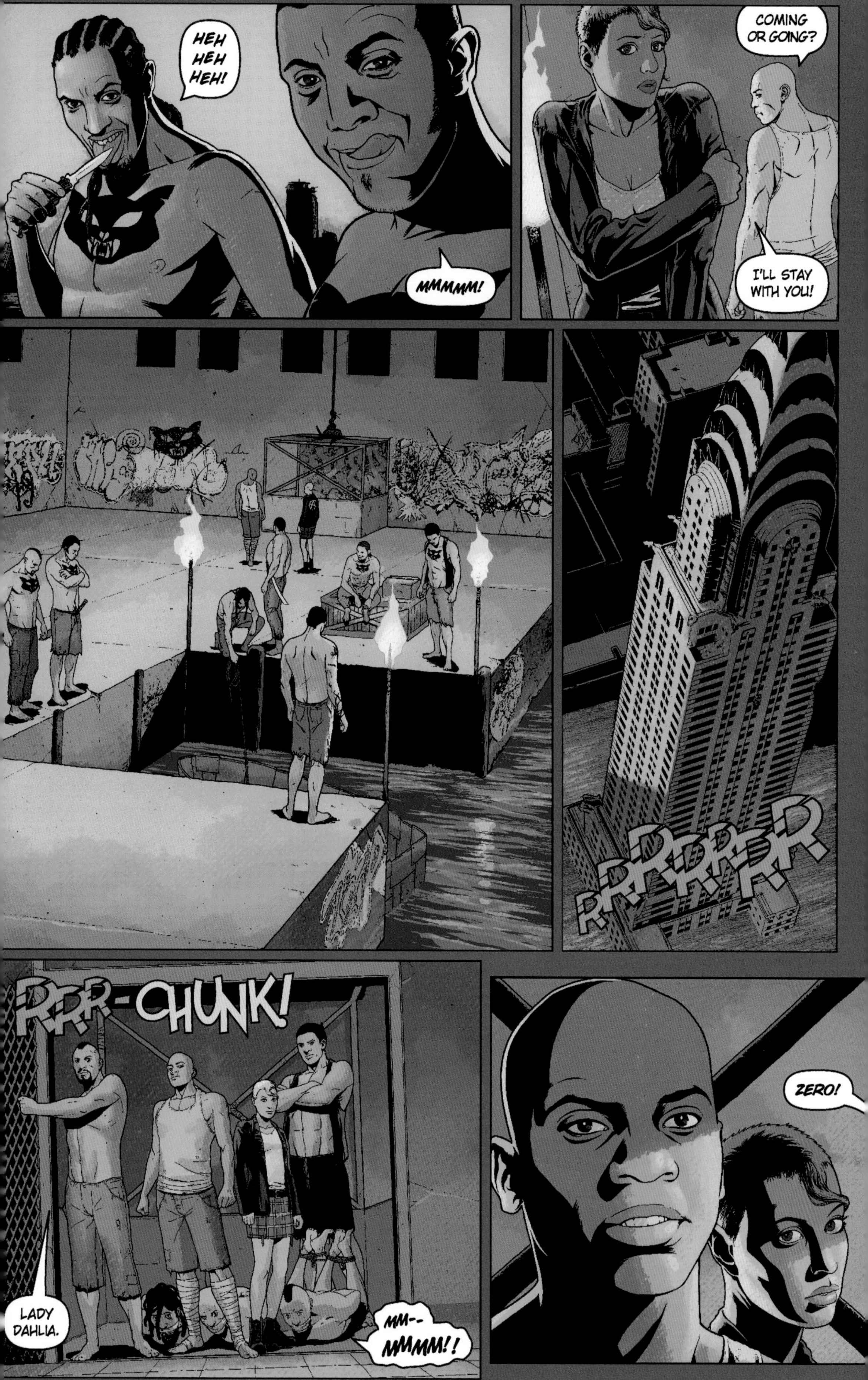
HEH HEH HEH!
MMMMM!
COMING OR GOING?
I'LL STAY WITH YOU!
RRRRRRRRR
RRR-CHUNK!
LADY DAHLIA.
MM-MMMM!!
ZERO!

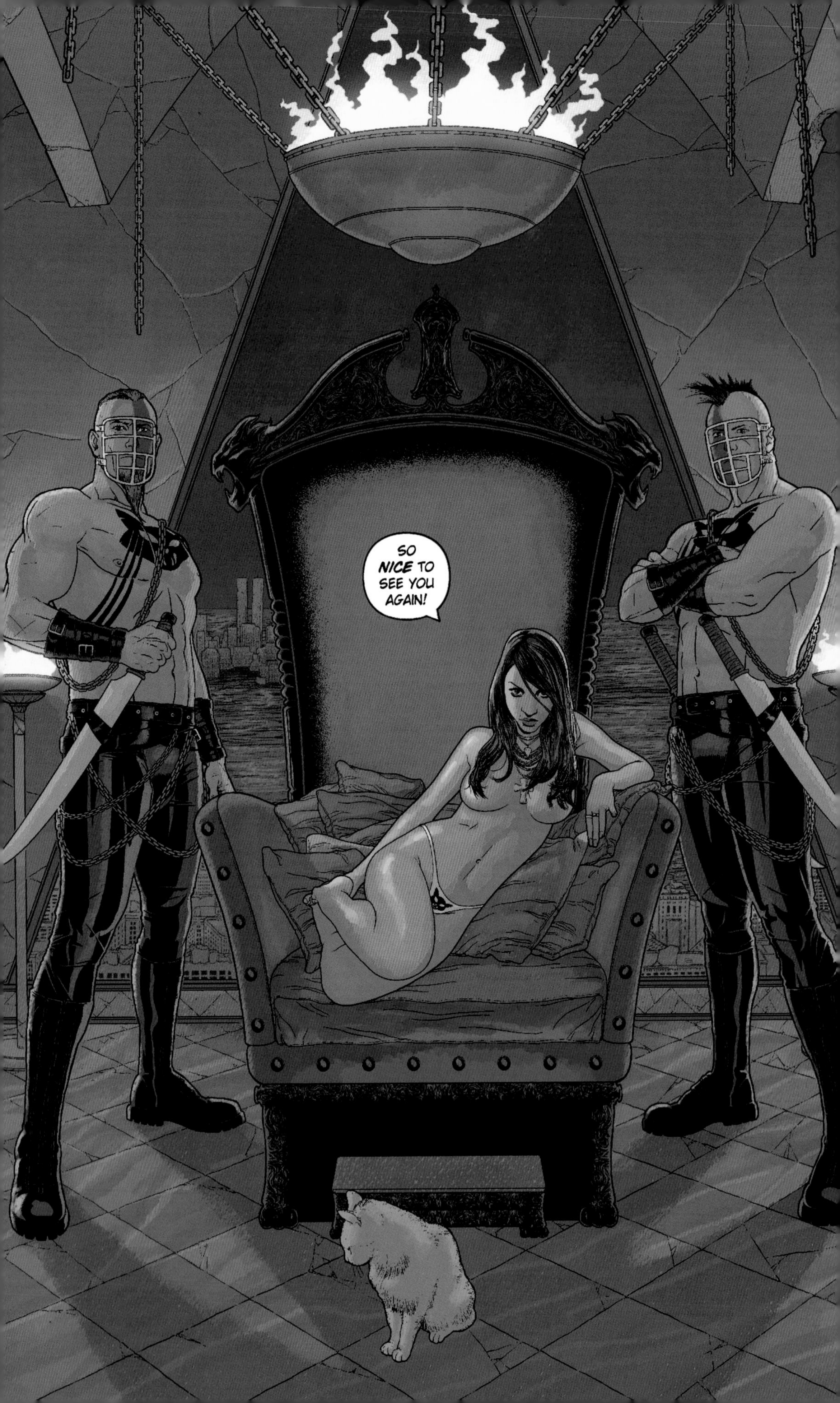
SO NICE TO SEE YOU AGAIN!

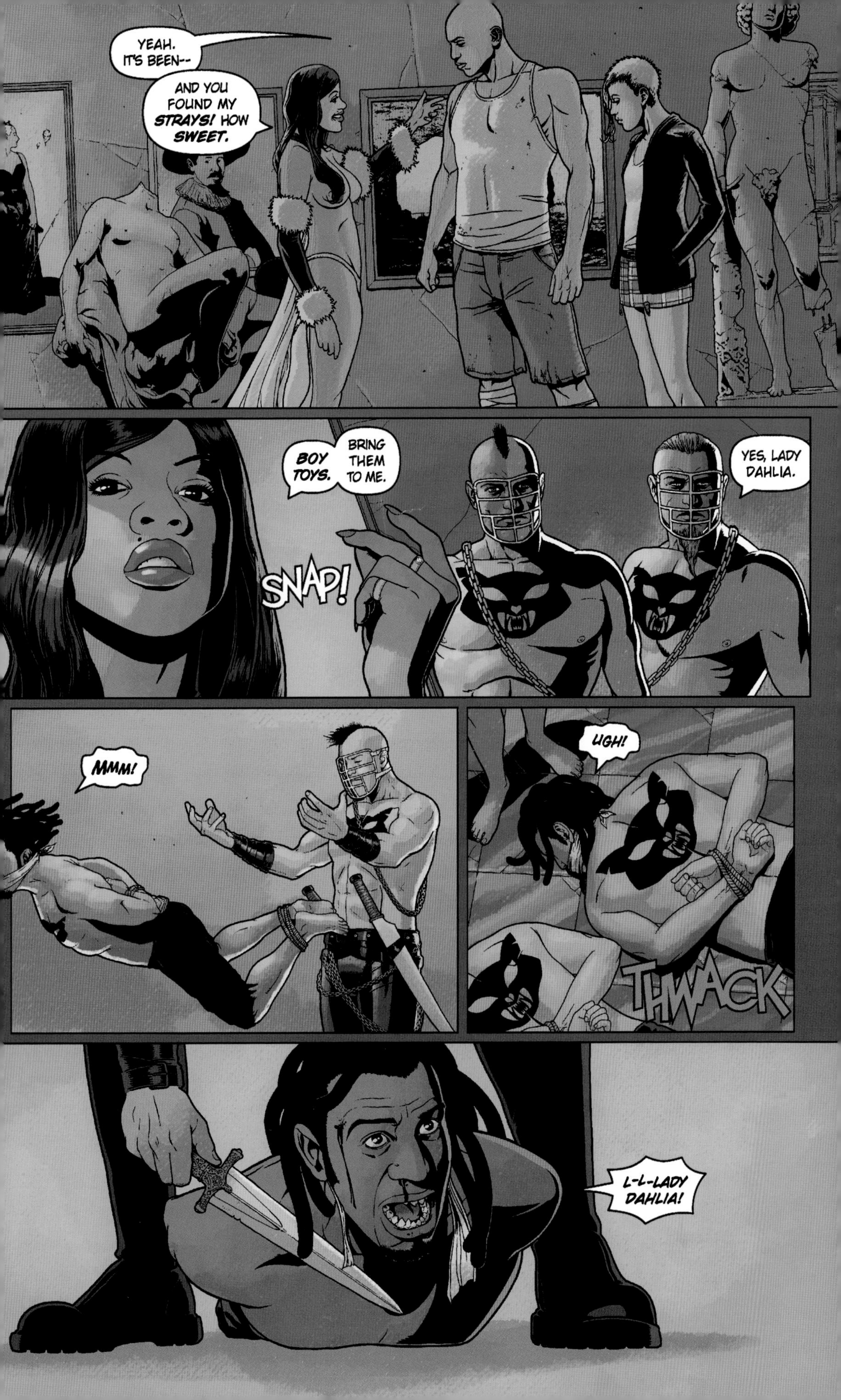
YEAH. IT'S BEEN--
AND YOU FOUND MY *STRAYS!* HOW *SWEET.*
BOY TOYS.
BRING THEM TO ME.
SNAP!
YES, LADY DAHLIA.
MMM!
UGH!
THWACK
L-L-LADY DAHLIA!

PLEASE, *PLEASE*, WE DIDN'T MEAN ANYTHING! WE WERE GONNA GIVE IT *ALL* BACK...

YOU *STOLE* MY DRUGS, AND *THEN* YOU *LEFT* MY TOWER WITHOUT PERMISSION!

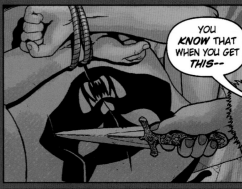

YOU *KNOW* THAT WHEN YOU GET *THIS--*

--YOU'RE MINE *FOREVER.*

MMM!

OH NO, OH *CHRISTUS* PLEASE NO--

ESUCHRISTUS CAN'T HEAR YOU. YOU'RE *MINE*, LITTLE STRAY.

MINE!

N-N-N-N--

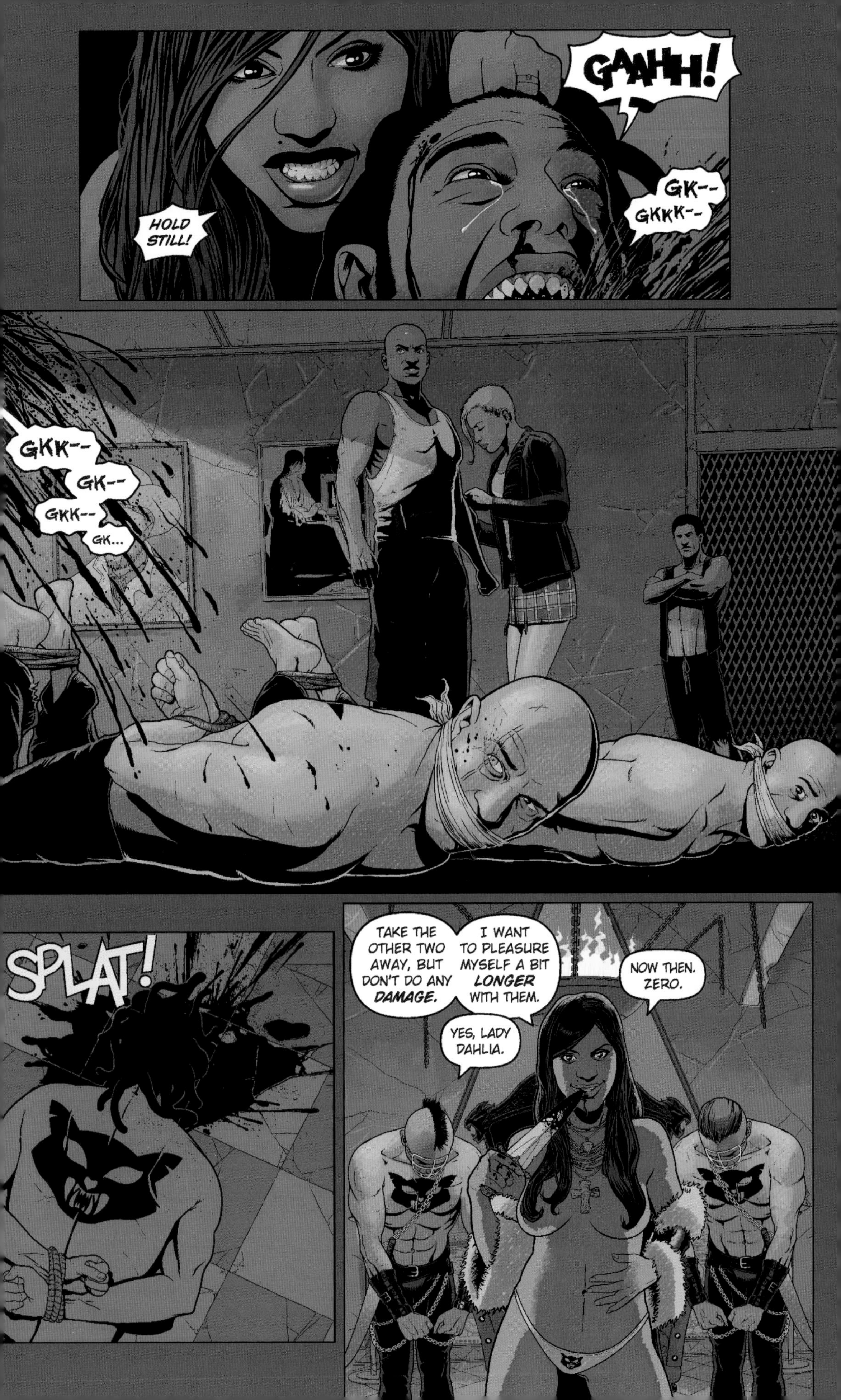
GAAHH!
HOLD STILL!
GK-- GKKK--
GKK--
GK--
GKK--
GK...
SPLAT!
TAKE THE OTHER TWO AWAY, BUT DON'T DO ANY DAMAGE.
I WANT TO PLEASURE MYSELF A BIT LONGER WITH THEM.
YES, LADY DAHLIA.
NOW THEN. ZERO.

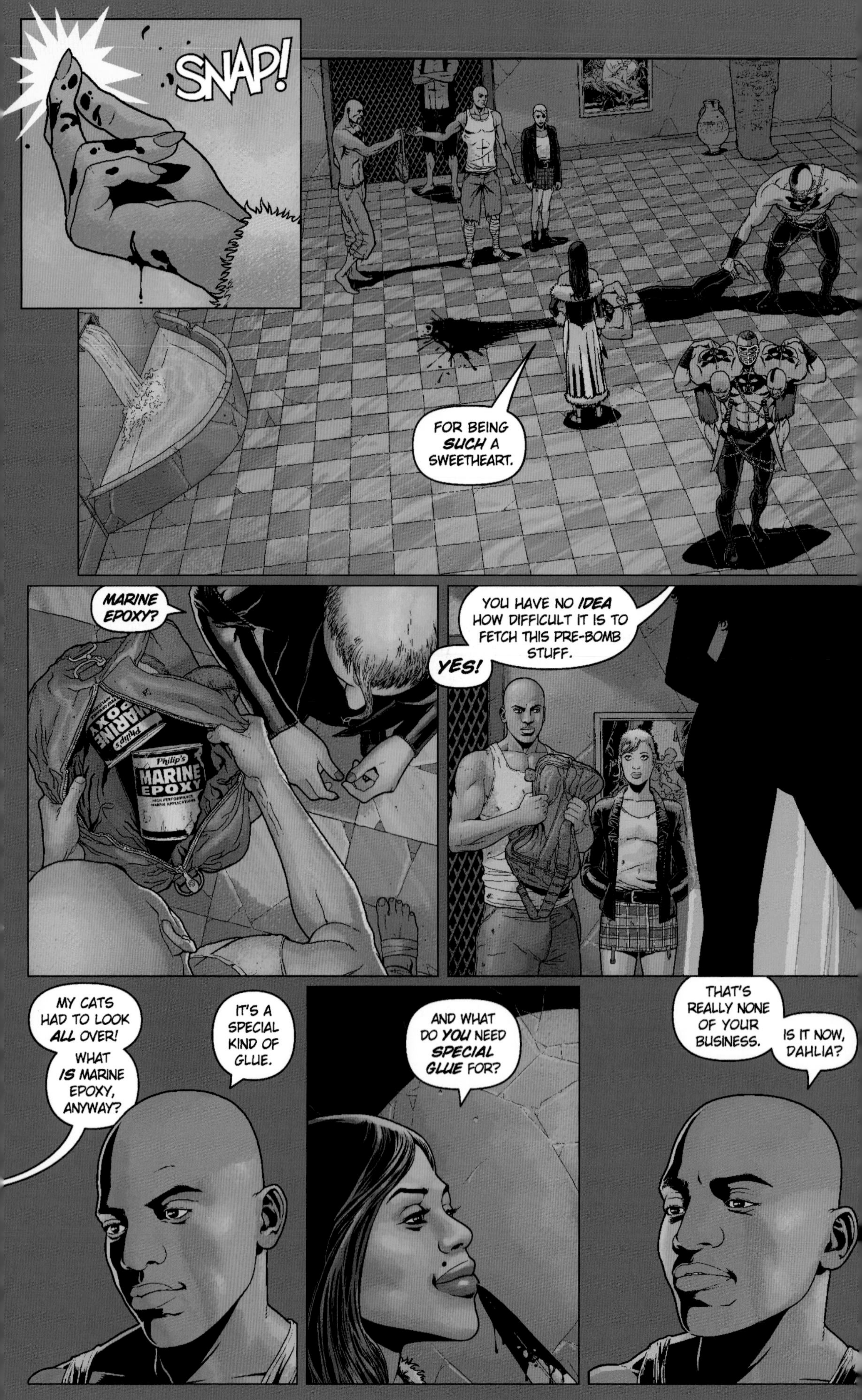
SNAP!
FOR BEING SUCH A SWEETHEART.
MARINE EPOXY?
Philip's MARINE EPOXY
YOU HAVE NO IDEA HOW DIFFICULT IT IS TO FETCH THIS PRE-BOMB STUFF.
YES!
MY CATS HAD TO LOOK ALL OVER! WHAT IS MARINE EPOXY, ANYWAY?
IT'S A SPECIAL KIND OF GLUE.
AND WHAT DO YOU NEED SPECIAL GLUE FOR?
THAT'S REALLY NONE OF YOUR BUSINESS.
IS IT NOW, DAHLIA?

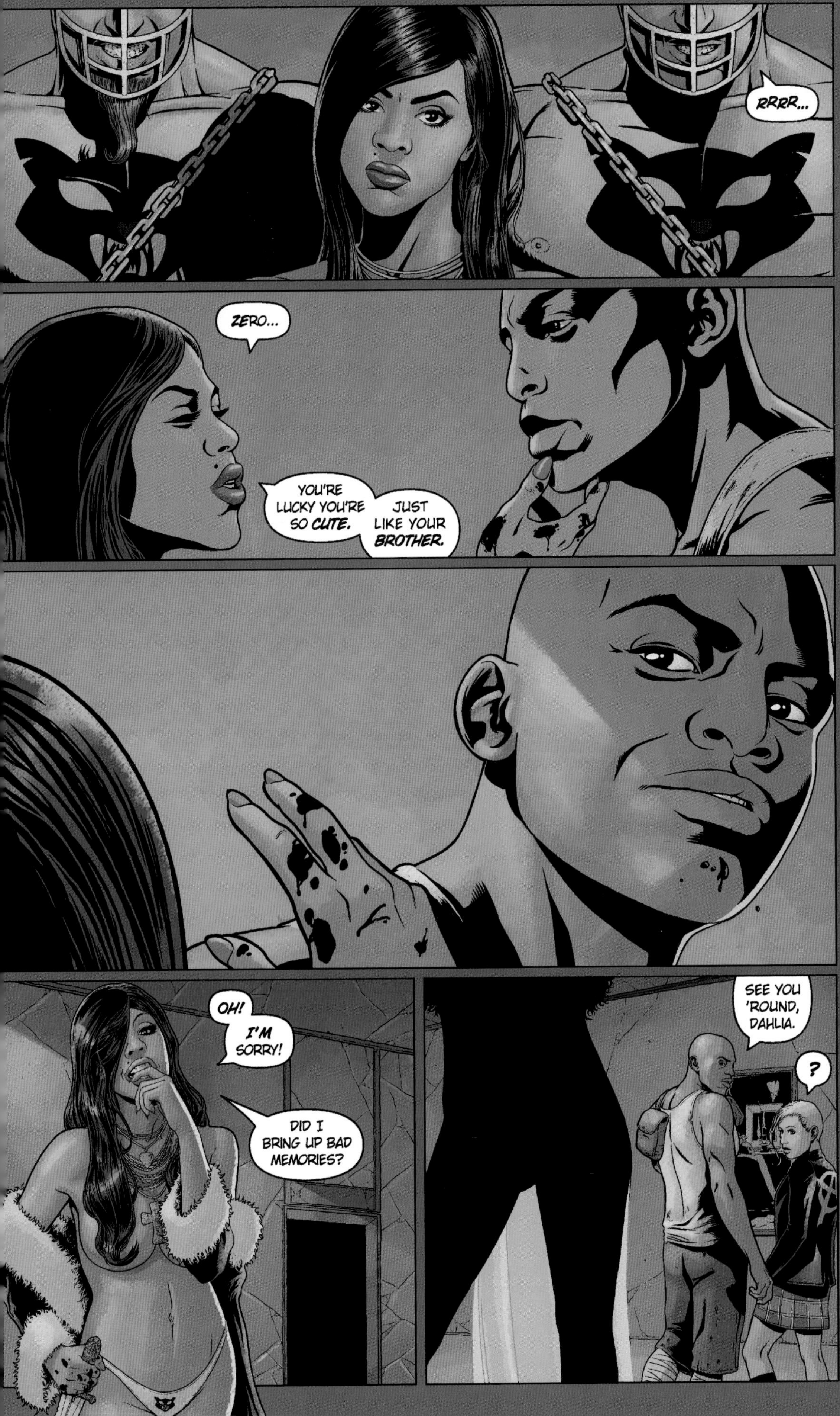
RRRR...
ZERO...
YOU'RE LUCKY YOU'RE SO CUTE.
JUST LIKE YOUR BROTHER.
OH!
I'M SORRY!
DID I BRING UP BAD MEMORIES?
SEE YOU 'ROUND, DAHLIA.
?

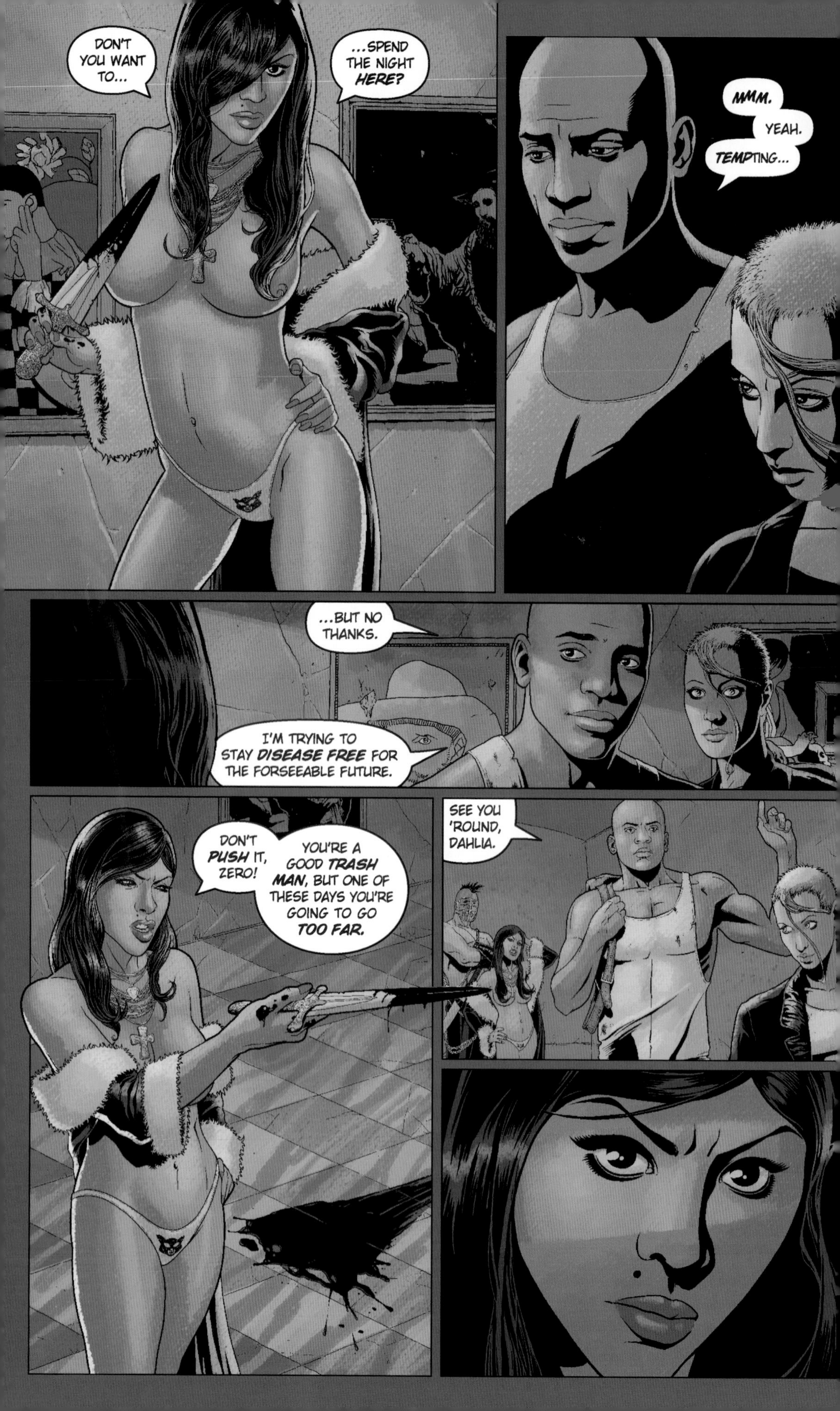
DON'T YOU WANT TO...
...SPEND THE NIGHT HERE?
MMM.
YEAH.
TEMPTING...
...BUT NO THANKS.
I'M TRYING TO STAY DISEASE FREE FOR THE FORSEEABLE FUTURE.
DON'T PUSH IT, ZERO!
YOU'RE A GOOD TRASH MAN, BUT ONE OF THESE DAYS YOU'RE GOING TO GO TOO FAR.
SEE YOU 'ROUND, DAHLIA.

The JOCOM Daily ✦ Serving Those Who Serve ✦ July 18, 2007 ✦ Vol. 66, No. 14

DAWN'S EARLY LIGHT

REMEMBER:

NEVER TALK TO THE TOWER INHABITANTS UNDER ANY CIRCUMSTANCES! LEAVE IT TO YOUR LIEUTENANT OR SERGEANT.

BACK PAGE: SARGE'S TIPS FOR TAKIN' ON THE TOWERS!

Report on Midtown Towers Finds Rise in Attacks

The attack came without warning.

Sgt. Thomas David and Spc. Enfield Palmer were returning from a routine harvesting mission with dozens of young human specimens for the Advanced Genetic Research Initiative. Then they discovered the bloody corpses of the pilot and copilot of their CH-47 Chinook helicopter. Spc. Palmer radioed back to base for support, but he was cut off mid-transmission.

A retrieval team rushed to the site only to find the bodies of Sgt. Palmer, and Spc. Enfield along with the pilot and co-pilot.

Sadly, all the human specimens escaped.

Such attacks are growing more common in the Midtown cluster of towers. The latest Intelligence Estimate (IE) puts the increase as high as 11 percent.

Lt. Col. William Elias, who is in charge of the new IE, described the trend as "disturbing." Until recently, the Midtown cluster was considered far more passive than the Downtown cluster, located further south.

"The Midtown towers are somewhat less concentrated than in Downtown," Elias said. "This means Midtown gangs aren't packed so tightly together, so naturally, they're less belligerent."

The cause of the surge in violence is not known, but the text of the report speculates that the tower dwellers are "adapting and organizing themselves against JOCOM incursions."

Neither the Joint Chiefs nor the office of the Director of the Reconstruction of the United States of America see the rise in violence forestalling long-term strategic goals.

"The new data in no way changes JOCOM's overwhelming advantage in technology and firepower," DRUSA said in a statement released yesterday to *Dawn's Early Light*. "JOCOM can meet any resistance from tower dwellers with overwhelming force."

Strategists in the Office of the Joint Chiefs of Staff (OJCS) calculate the Midtown cluster will continue to provide AGRI with human specimens for its ongoing and vital research into the reconstruction of the United States of America.

"Living human biological samples are absolutely vital to JOCOM's research goals, and the tower dwellers provide an almost limitless supply," Lt. Gen. Maxwell Carter, JOCOM-A chief of staff, said.

Still, the increased violence can leave JOCOM personnel feeling rattled and uneasy.

"I'm at the point where I'll just shoot the bastards on sight. I was stabbed in the leg last time I was out harvesting. Why take chances?" a trooper said. Planners in the OJCS are also adopting this point of view.

"Clearly the thing to do here is get tough," Lt. Col. Elias wrote in the Intelligence Estimate. "The tower dwellers only respect force. Our soldiers and marines will simply have to adopt more aggressive rules of engagement when carrying out harvesting missions.

"Our primary objective, at all times, is force protection." ✦

Points of Danger in the Midtown Cluster

Below are some of the major Midtown buildings and their associated gangs. The towers may look derelict, but they teem with vicious gangs–exercise extreme caution in and near these locations.

The **Black Cats** occupy the **Chrysler Building.**

The **Empire State Building** is controlled by the ruthless gang known as the **True Bloods.**

JOKERS

The **Pan Am Building** is controlled by the **Jokers.** While not numerous, they are one of the most dangerous and unpredictable gangs.

SARGE'S TIPS 'N' TACTICS

Stay alert ✦ Stay focused ✦ Stay alive

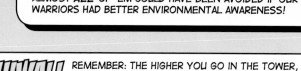
TAKIN' ON THE TOWERS!

LISTEN UP, *SOLDIER!* THERE HAVE BEEN A LOT OF MISSION CASUALTIES IN THE PAST FEW WEEKS. ALMOST *ALL* OF 'EM COULD HAVE BEEN AVOIDED IF OUR WARRIORS HAD BETTER ENVIRONMENTAL AWARENESS!

HIWALL REMEMBER: THE HIGHER YOU GO IN THE TOWER, THE MORE DANGEROUS THE NATIVES! THE HIGHEST SECTION IS KNOWN AS *HIWALL*. IT'S WHERE MOST OF THE *GANGSTERS* LIVE. THEY'RE THE ELITE OF TOWER SOCIETY, AND THEY LIVE IN RELATIVE LUXURY IN THE UPPER LEVELS. GANGSTERS ARE ALSO THE MOST VICIOUS TOWER INHABITANTS AND THE MOST BELLIGERENT. ANYONE OPERATING IN THE HIGHER LEVELS MUST BE ON THE LOOKOUT FOR AMBUSHES AT ALL TIMES!

THE EDGE RIGHT BELOW HIWALL, THIS IS WHERE THE PRODUCTIVE MEMBERS OF THE TOWER SOCIETY LIVE, THE WORKERS AND FOOD GATHERERS. BUT DON'T LET YOUR GUARD DOWN! YOUNGER GANGSTERS ALSO INHABIT THE EDGE. THESE TOUGHS HAVE YET TO PROVE THEMSELVES, AND ARE PRONE TO ATTACKING JOCOM PERSONNEL AS A MEANS OF "GRADUATING" TO FULL GANG MEMBERSHIP.

THE SINK THE TOWER DWELLERS ARE CRUDE BUT RESOURCEFUL MECHANICS AND ENGINEERS. *THE SINK* IS WHERE MOST OF THE FOOD PRODUCTION AND MECHANICAL INFRASTRUCTURE OF THE TOWERS ARE LOCATED. BUT THE JURY-RIGGED MACHINERY CAN ITSELF PROVE HAZARDOUS! MOREOVER, THE NOISE MAKES IT DIFFICULT TO DETECT THE APPROACH OF HOSTILE NATIVES. WHEN TRAVERSING *ANY* PORTION OF A TOWER, *KEEP SAFETIES OFF AND SHOOT TO KILL!*

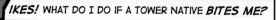
THE DUMP THE *OUTCASTS* LIVE IN THE LOWEST SECTION, CALLED *THE DUMP* BECAUSE ALL THE NASTINESS FROM THE SINK IS DEPOSITED HERE, MAKING IT VERY UNPLEASANT. ALSO, THE PROXIMITY TO THE WATER MAKES THIS SECTION VULNERABLE TO ATTACK BY GANGS FROM RIVAL TOWERS. DISEASE AND INFECTION ARE THE MAIN HAZARD HERE. REMEMBER, DUE TO THE HIGH INCIDENCE OF MUTATION AND RADIATION DISEASE, *DUMP RESIDENTS ARE NOT SUITABLE SPECIMENS FOR HARVESTING!*

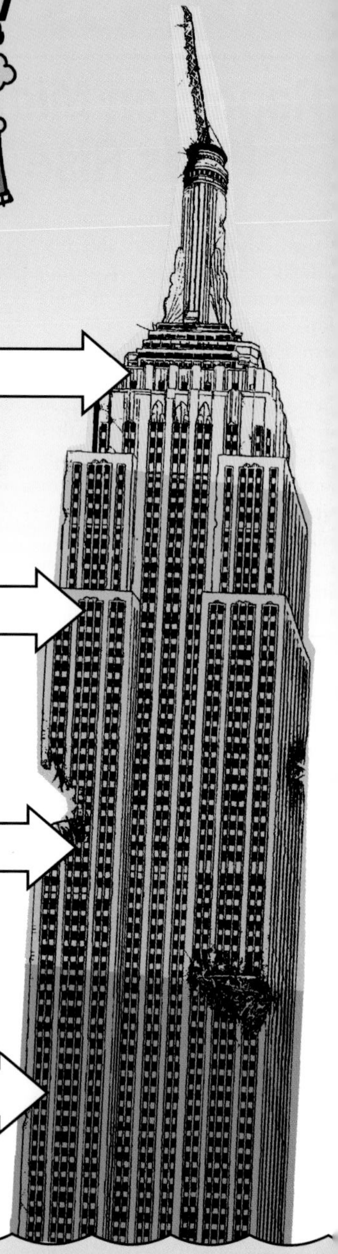

YIKES! WHAT DO I DO IF A TOWER NATIVE *BITES ME?*

THE MOST IMPORTANT THING IS TO *STAY CALM.* JOCOM HAS DEVELOPED A PROTOCOL FOR EXACTLY THIS SITUATION!

1.

IMMEDIATELY SHOOT AND KILL THE NATIVE. MAKE SURE HIS FRIENDS SEE YOU, OR THEY'LL TRY THE SAME THING!

2.

AS SOON AS YOU GET BACK TO BASE, HAVE THE MEDICAL CORPS LOOK AT THAT BITE! IT'S PROBABLY INFECTED.

3.

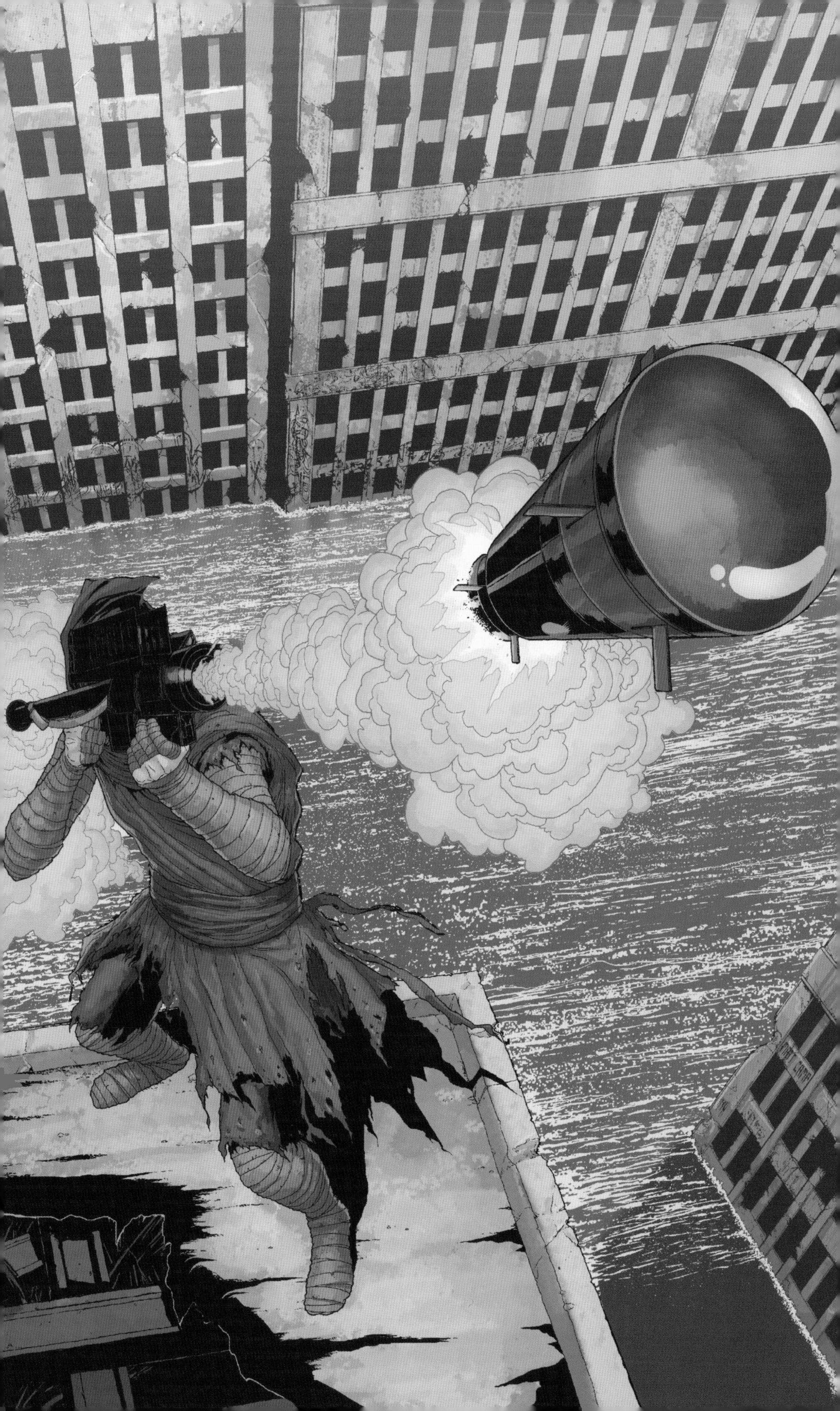

ZEROKILLER

CHAPTER 2

TWILIGHT'S LAST GLEAMING

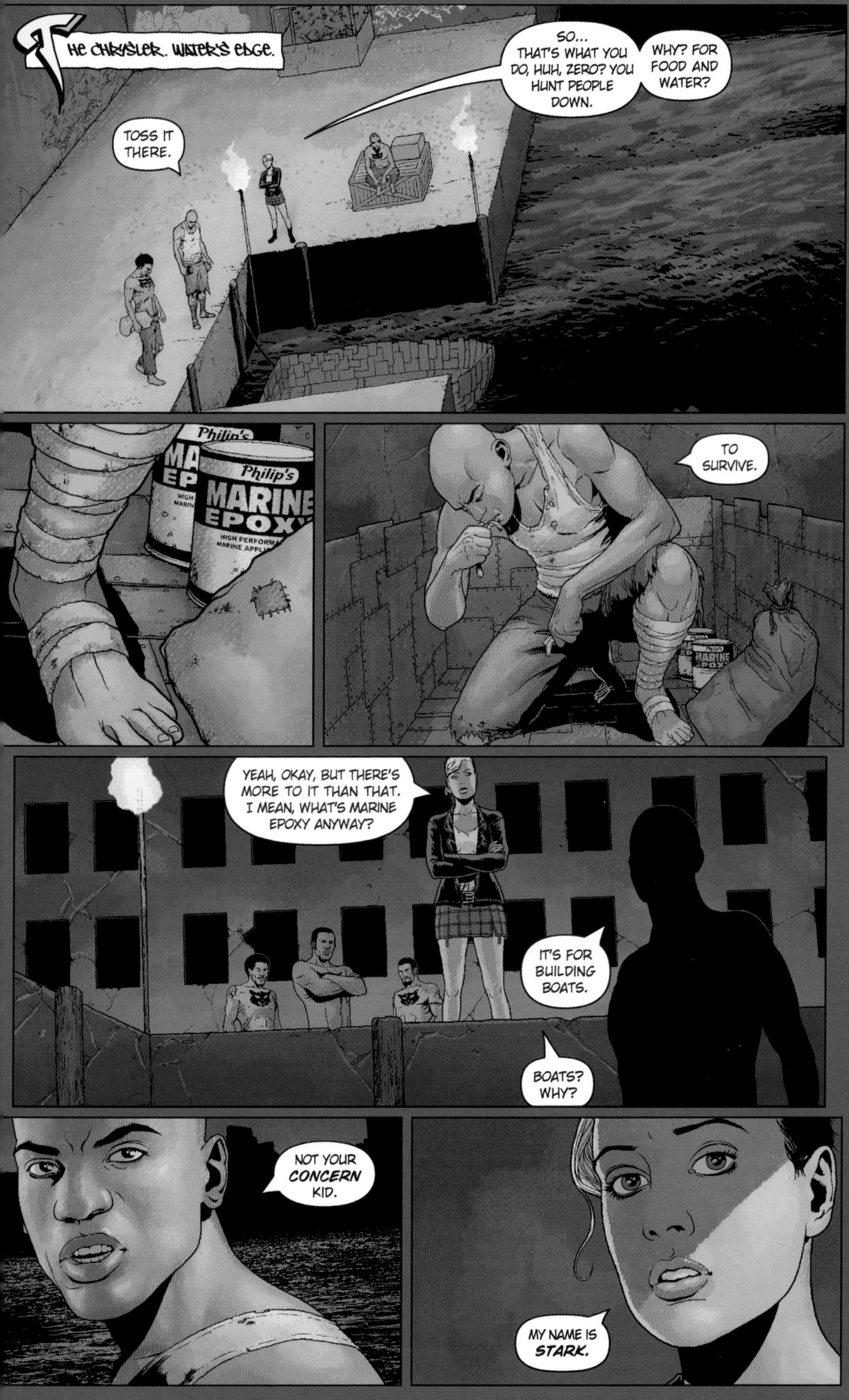
THE CHRYSLER. WATER'S EDGE.
SO... THAT'S WHAT YOU DO, HUH, ZERO? YOU HUNT PEOPLE DOWN.
WHY? FOR FOOD AND WATER?
TOSS IT THERE.
Philip's MARINE EPOXY HIGH PERFORMA MARINE APPLI
TO SURVIVE.
YEAH, OKAY, BUT THERE'S MORE TO IT THAN THAT. I MEAN, WHAT'S MARINE EPOXY ANYWAY?
IT'S FOR BUILDING BOATS.
BOATS? WHY?
NOT YOUR CONCERN KID.
MY NAME IS STARK.

BYE, *STARK.*

HEY!

LOOK-- LOOK, MAN. ZERO?

WHERE'RE YOU GOING?

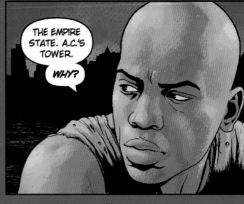

THE EMPIRE STATE. A.C.'S TOWER.

WHY?

CAN I... CAN I COME WITH YOU?

IT'S NOT SAFE.

I KNOW, BUT... I DON'T HAVE ANYPLACE TO GO...

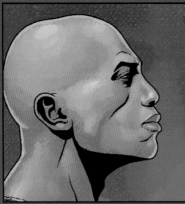

YOU WANT TO ROW?

FINE.

BUT I'M NOT TAKING *CARE* OF YOU, OKAY? WE GET TO THE EMPIRE, THAT'S *IT.*

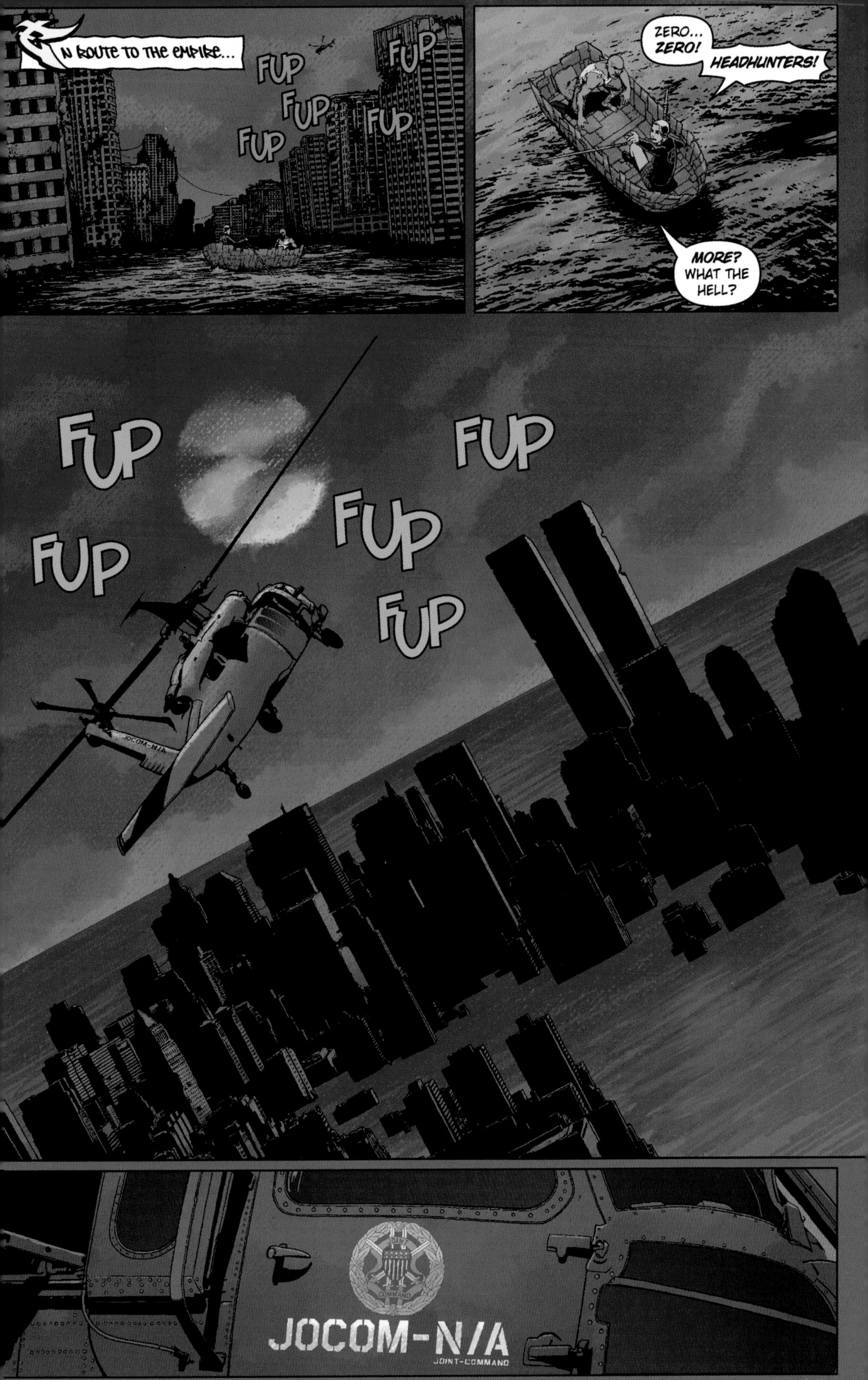

N ROUTE TO THE EMPIRE...
FUP
FUP
FUP
FUP
FUP
ZERO... ZERO!
HEADHUNTERS!
MORE? WHAT THE HELL?
FUP
FUP
FUP
FUP
FUP
JOCOM-N/A
JOCOM-N/A
JOINT-COMMAND

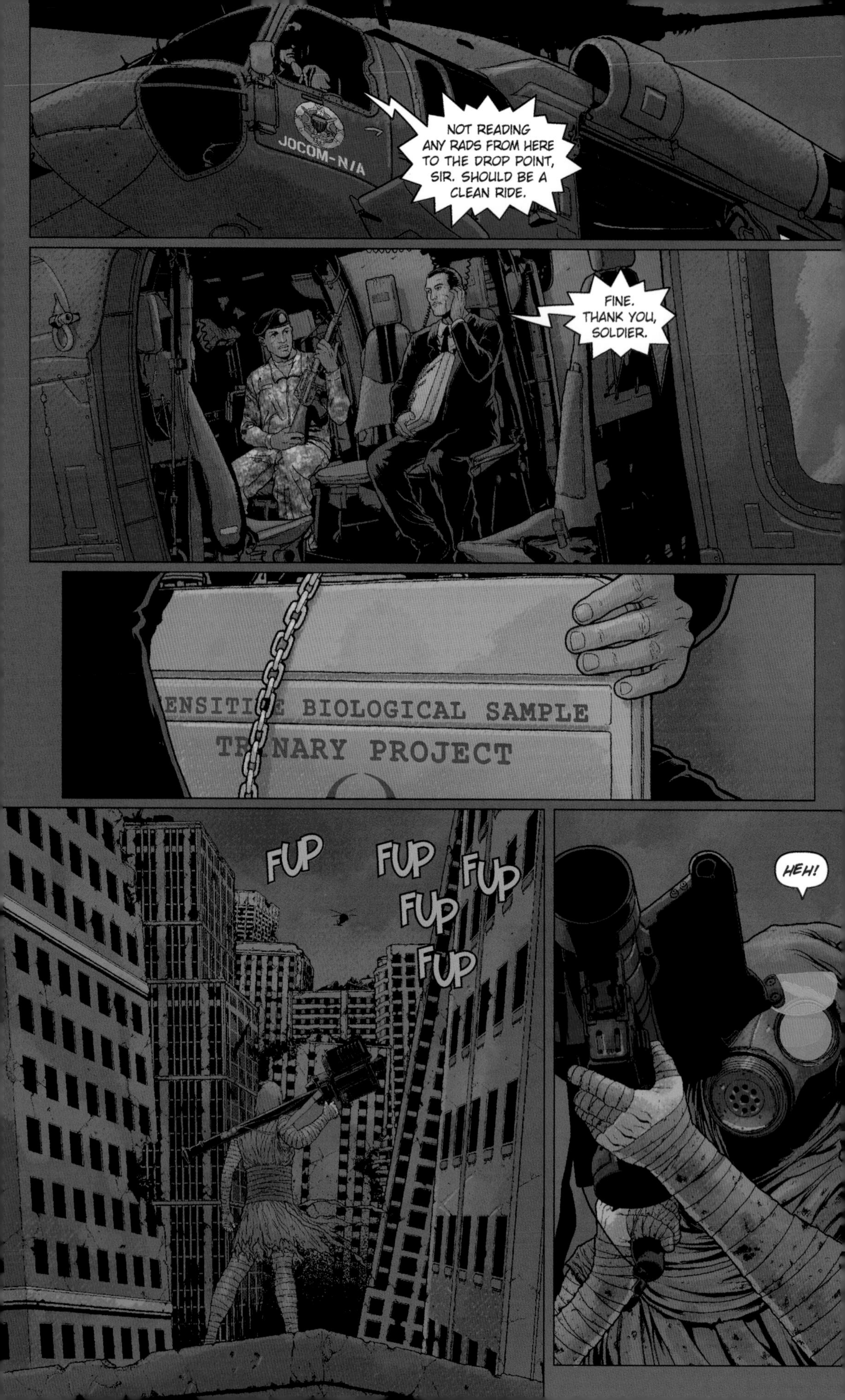
JOCOM-N/A
NOT READING ANY RADS FROM HERE TO THE DROP POINT, SIR. SHOULD BE A CLEAN RIDE.
FINE. THANK YOU, SOLDIER.
ENSITI E BIOLOGICAL SAMPLE
T NARY PROJECT
FUP
FUP
FUP
FUP
FUP
HEH!

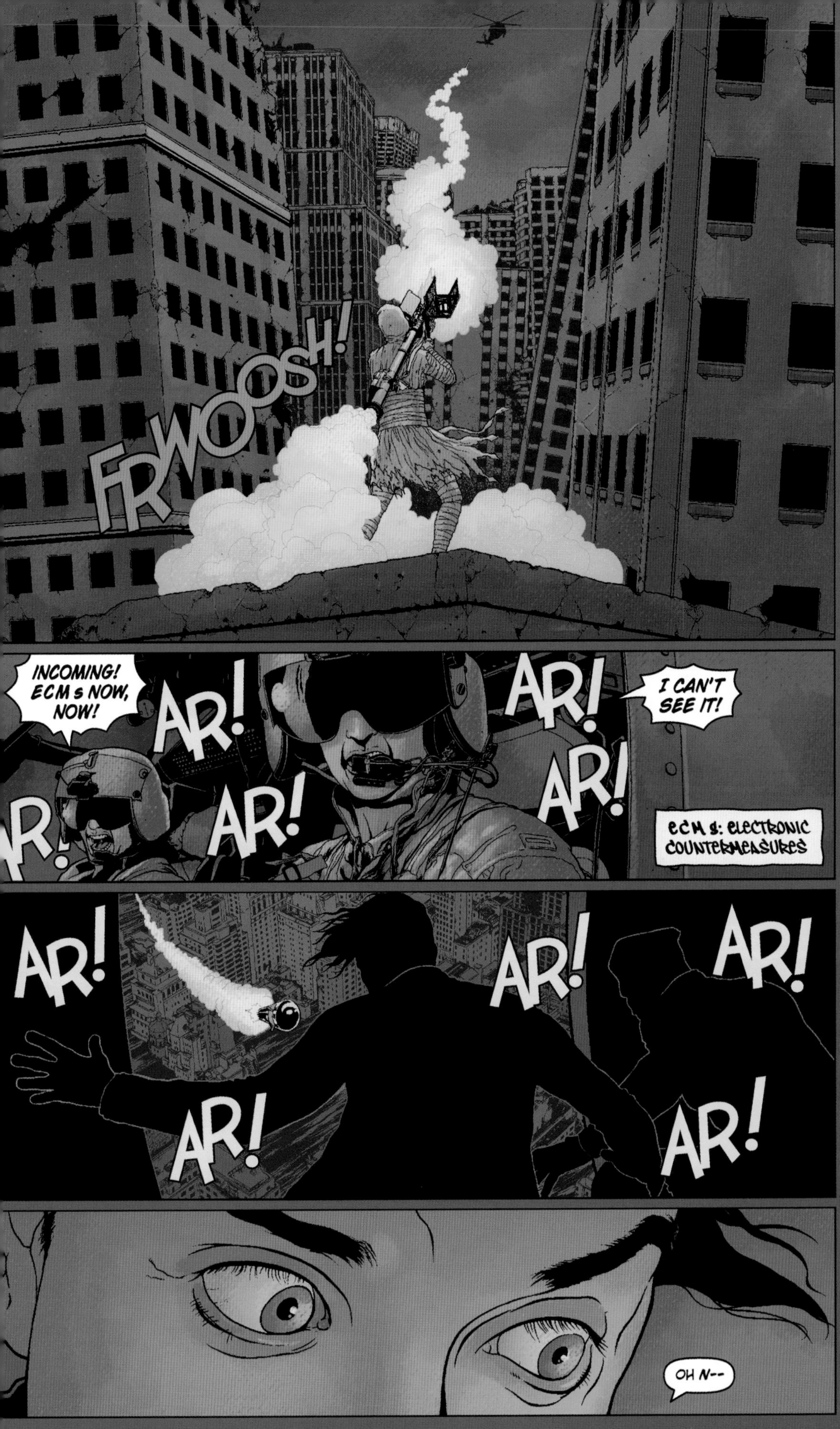
FRWOOSH!
INCOMING! ECMs NOW, NOW!
AR!
AR!
AR!
I CAN'T SEE IT!
AR!
AR!
ECMs: ELECTRONIC COUNTERMEASURES
AR!
AR!
AR!
AR!
AR!
OH N--

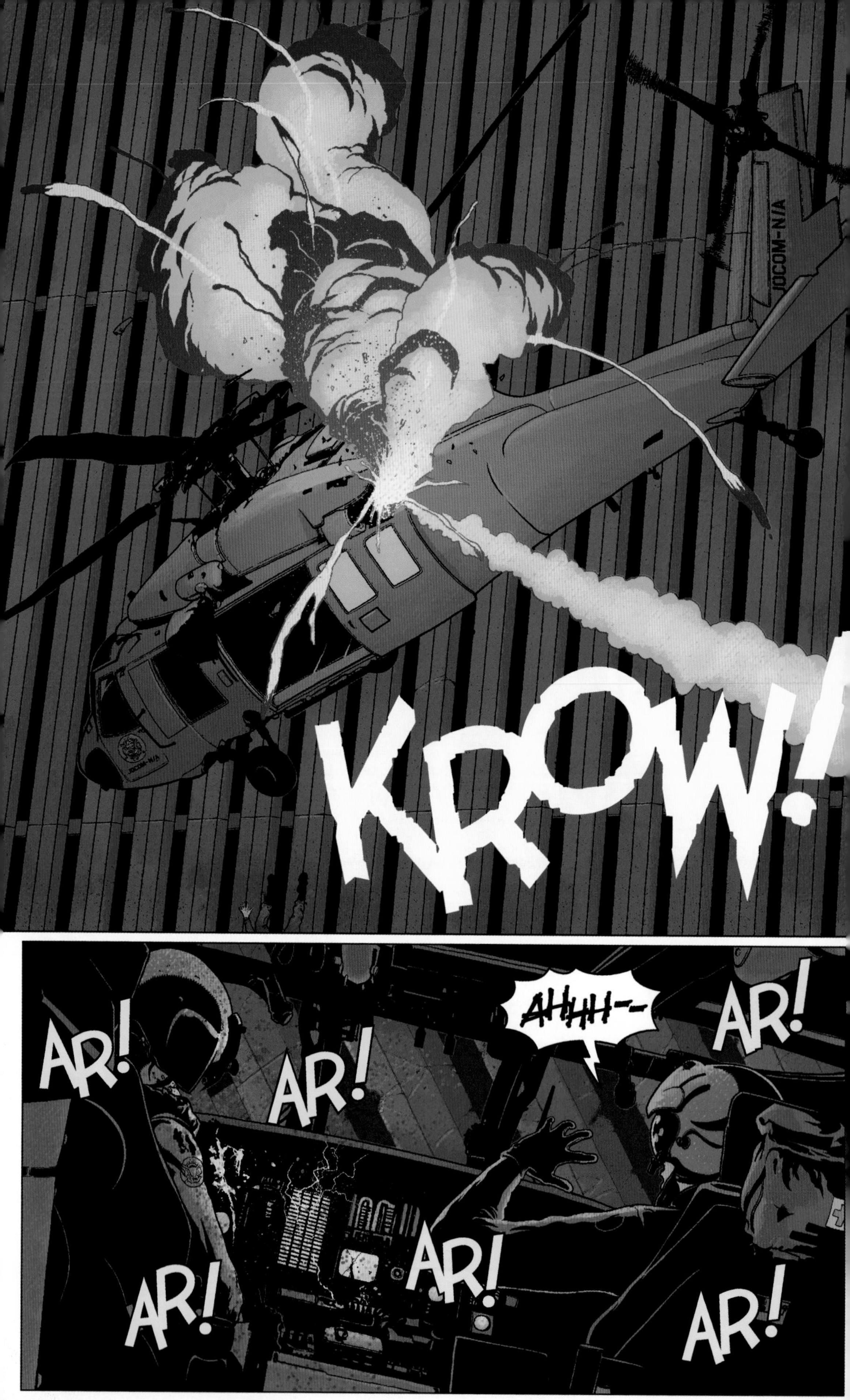
JOCOM-N/A
KROW!
AR!
AR!
AHHH--
AR!
AR!
AR!
AR!

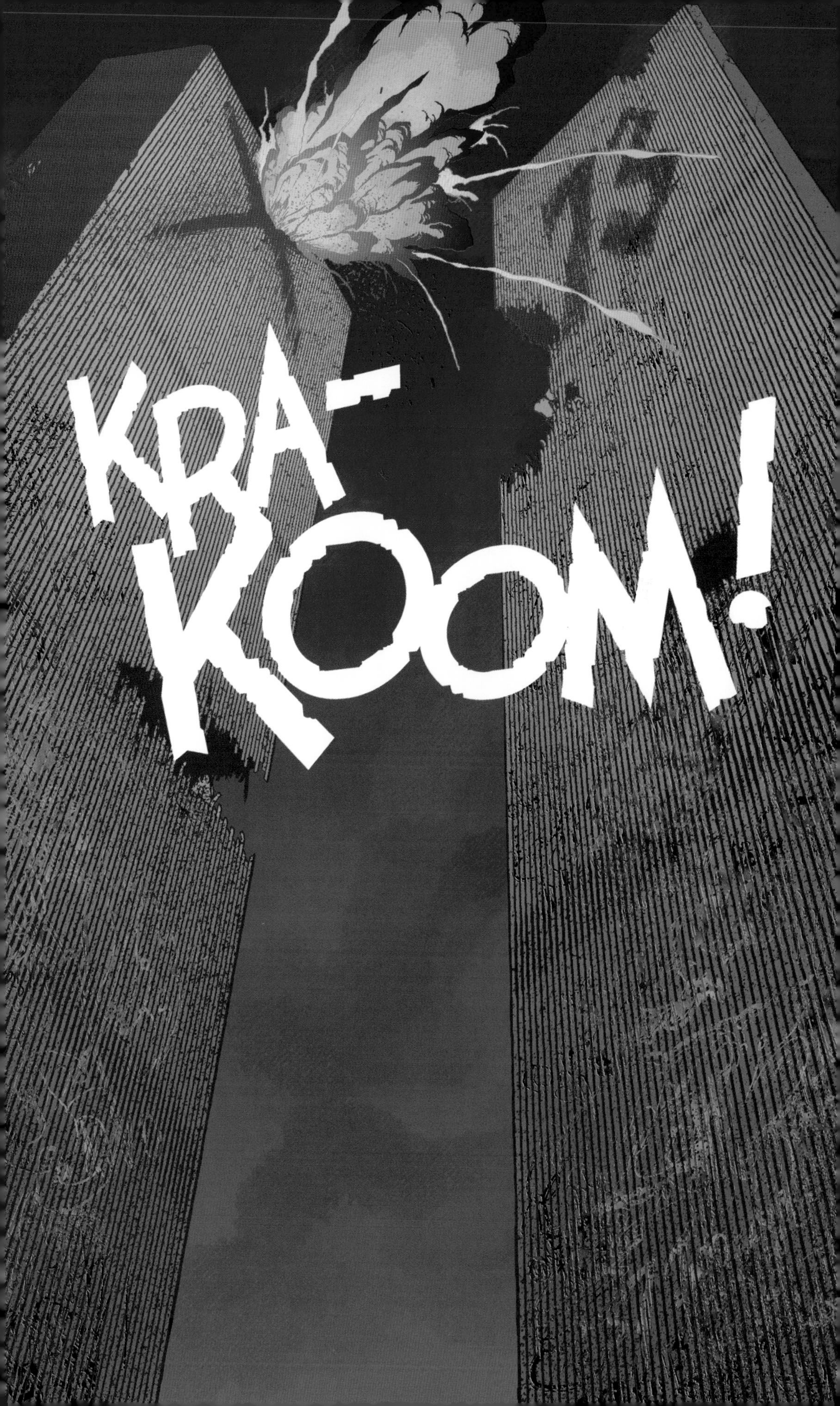
KRA-KOOM!

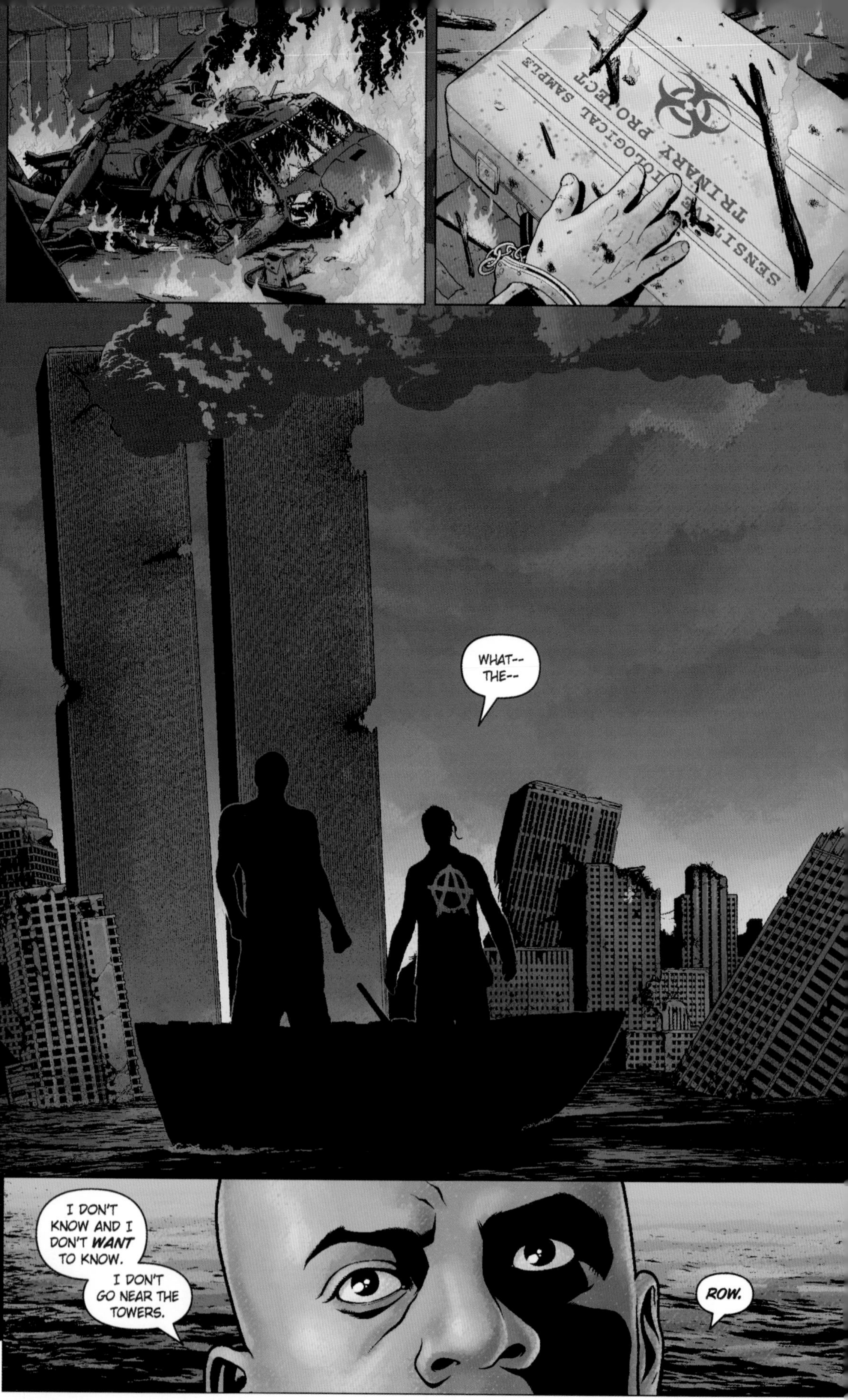

TRINARY PROJECT
SENSITIVE
WHAT-- THE--
I DON'T KNOW AND I DON'T *WANT* TO KNOW.
I DON'T GO NEAR THE TOWERS.
ROW.

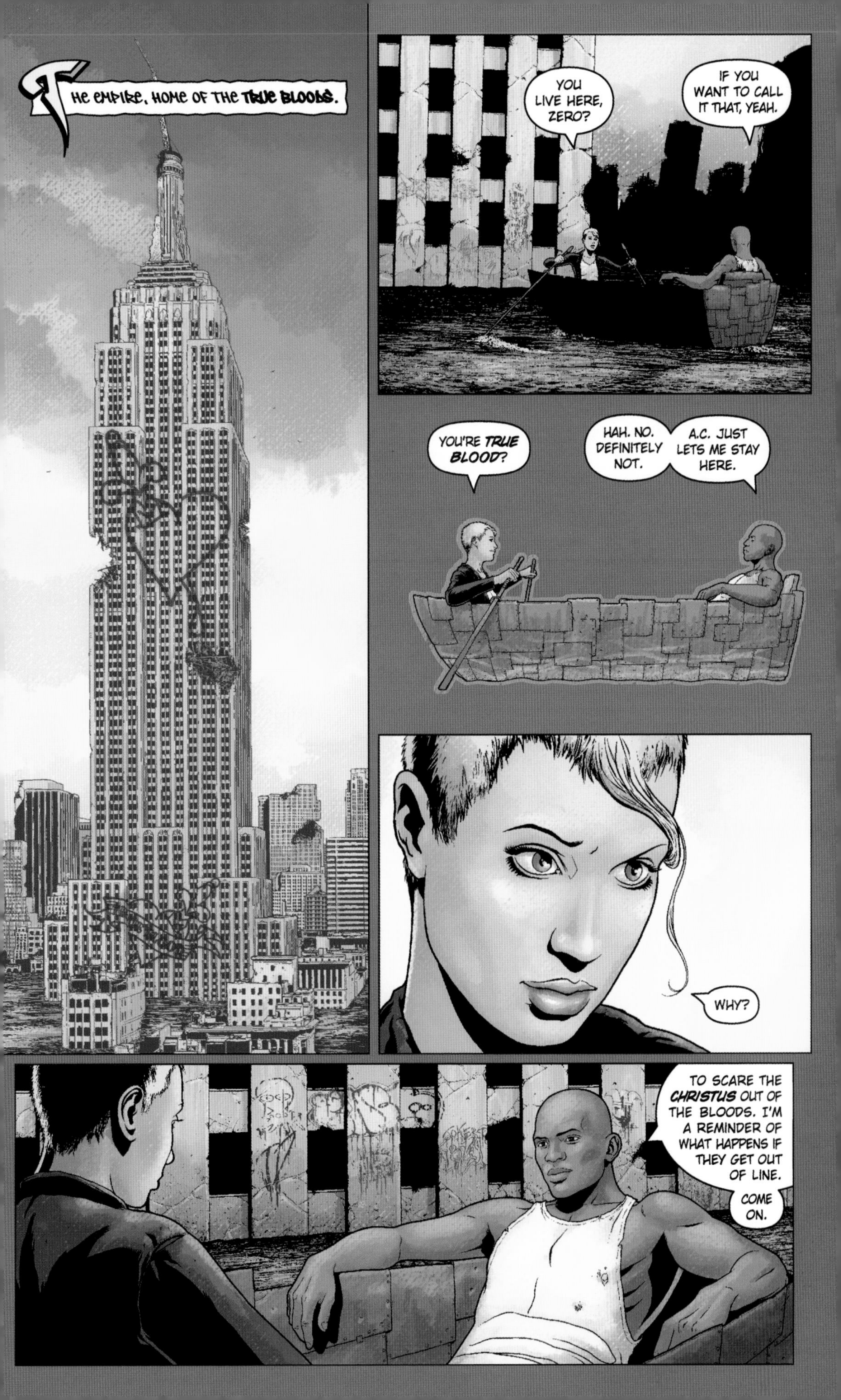
THE EMPIRE. HOME OF THE TRUE BLOODS.
YOU LIVE HERE, ZERO?
IF YOU WANT TO CALL IT THAT, YEAH.
YOU'RE TRUE BLOOD?
HAH. NO. DEFINITELY NOT.
A.C. JUST LETS ME STAY HERE.
WHY?
TO SCARE THE CHRISTUS OUT OF THE BLOODS. I'M A REMINDER OF WHAT HAPPENS IF THEY GET OUT OF LINE.
COME ON.

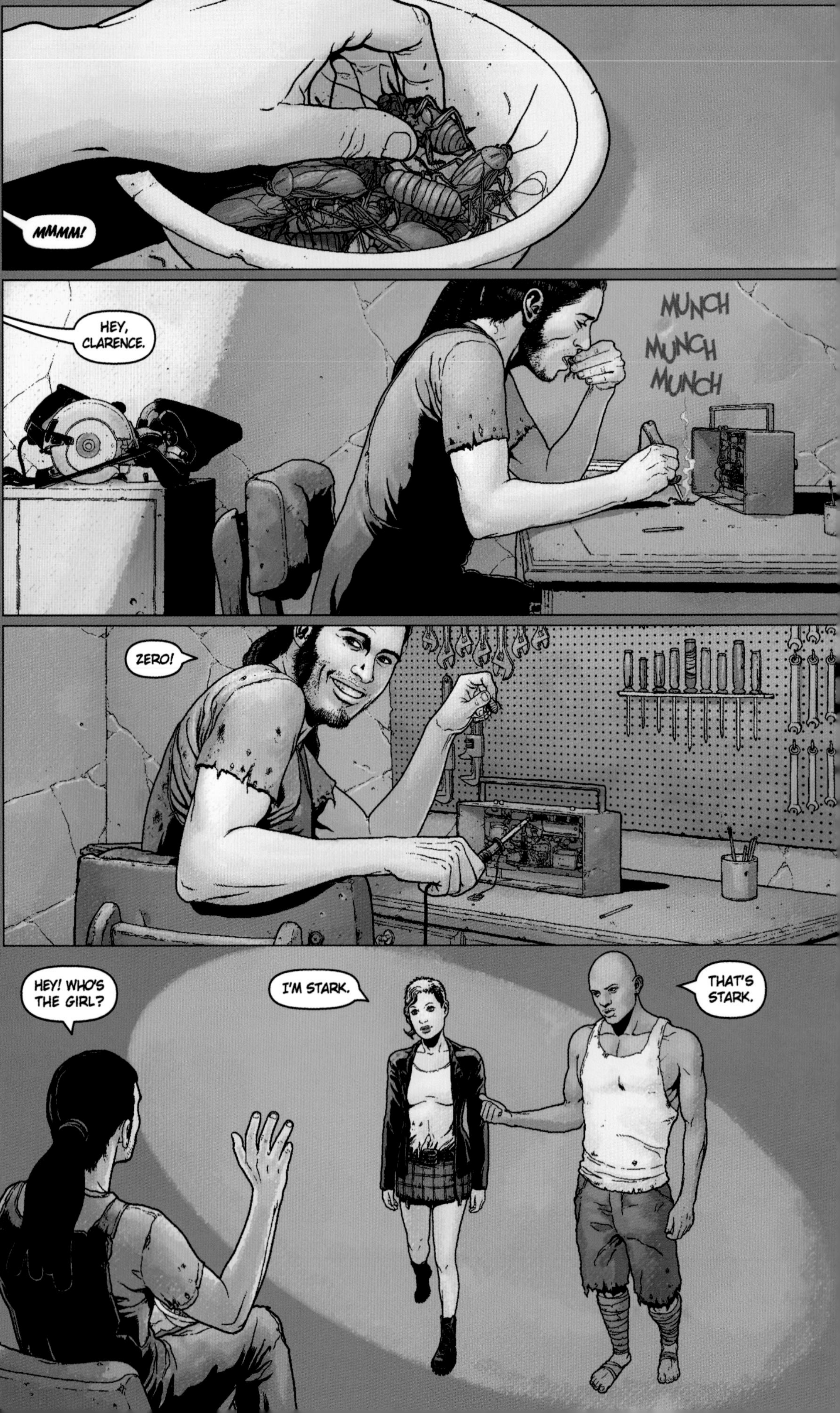
MMMM!
HEY, CLARENCE.
MUNCH
MUNCH
MUNCH
ZERO!
HEY! WHO'S THE GIRL?
I'M STARK.
THAT'S STARK.

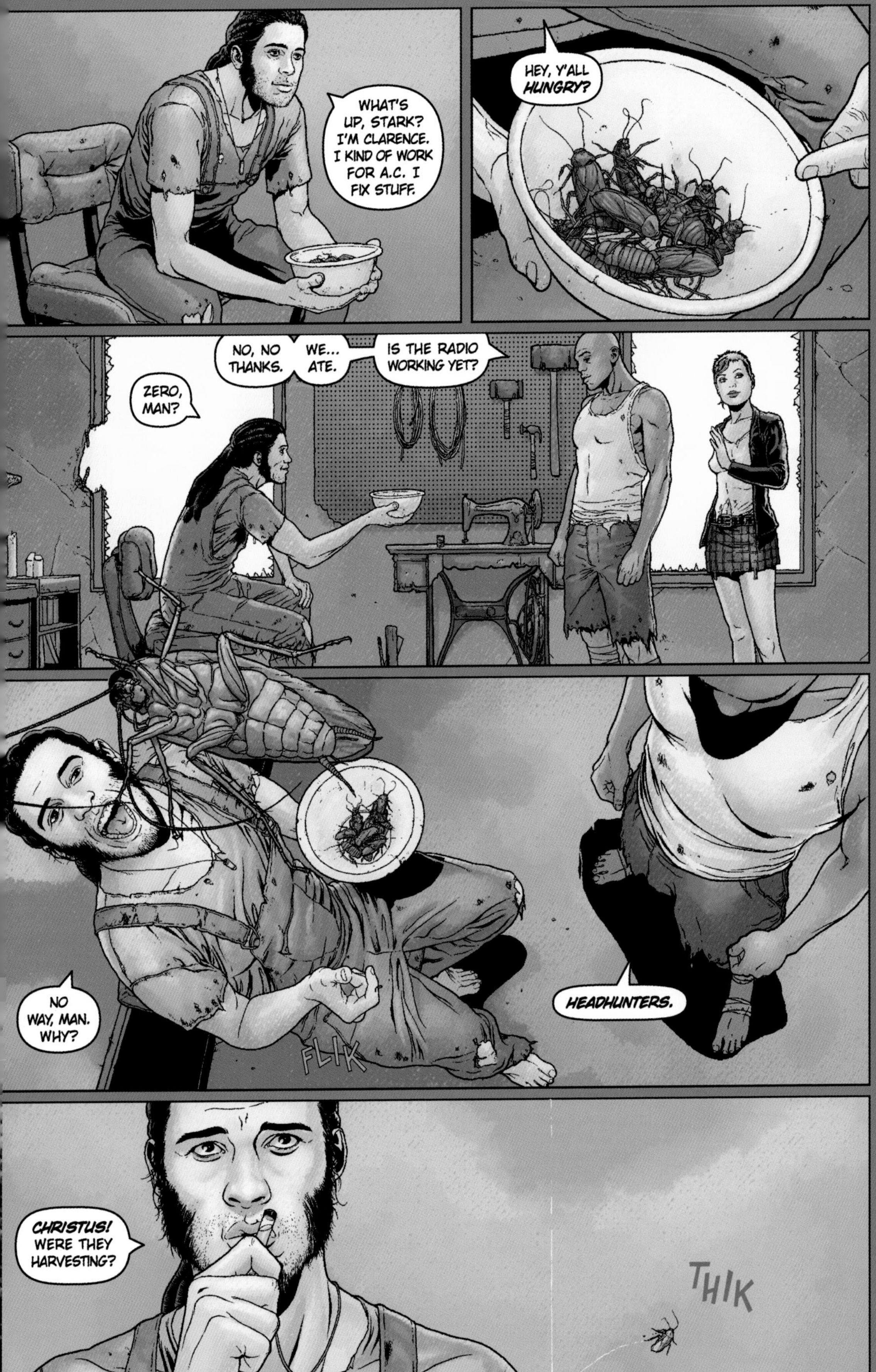
WHAT'S UP, STARK? I'M CLARENCE. I KIND OF WORK FOR A.C. I FIX STUFF.
HEY, Y'ALL *HUNGRY?*
ZERO, MAN?
NO, NO THANKS.
WE... ATE.
IS THE RADIO WORKING YET?
NO WAY, MAN. WHY?
FLIK
HEADHUNTERS.
CHRISTUS! WERE THEY HARVESTING?
THIK

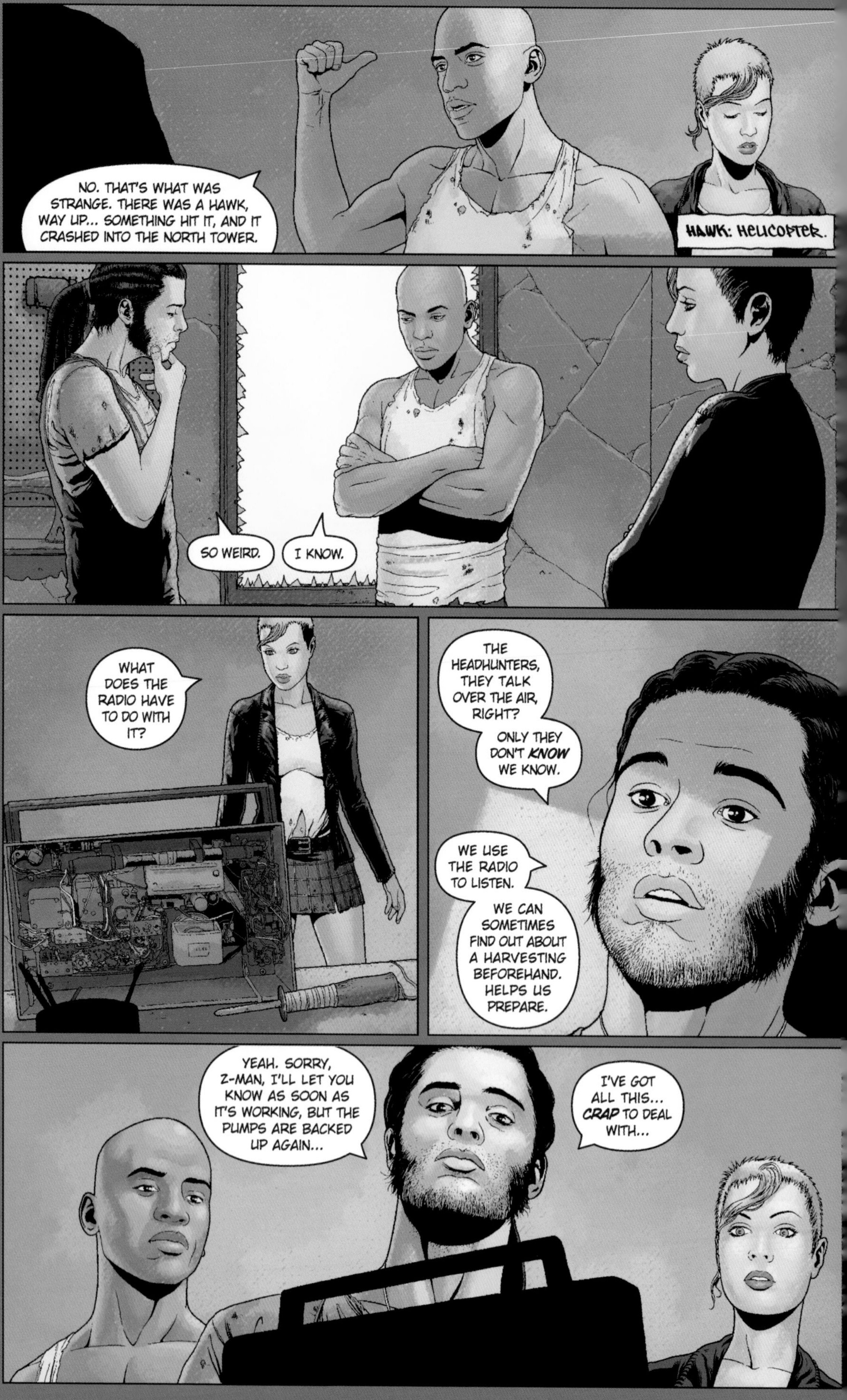
NO. THAT'S WHAT WAS STRANGE. THERE WAS A HAWK, WAY UP... SOMETHING HIT IT, AND IT CRASHED INTO THE NORTH TOWER.
HAWK: HELICOPTER.
SO WEIRD.
I KNOW.
WHAT DOES THE RADIO HAVE TO DO WITH IT?
THE HEADHUNTERS, THEY TALK OVER THE AIR, RIGHT?
ONLY THEY DON'T KNOW WE KNOW.
WE USE THE RADIO TO LISTEN.
WE CAN SOMETIMES FIND OUT ABOUT A HARVESTING BEFOREHAND. HELPS US PREPARE.
YEAH. SORRY, Z-MAN, I'LL LET YOU KNOW AS SOON AS IT'S WORKING, BUT THE PUMPS ARE BACKED UP AGAIN...
I'VE GOT ALL THIS... CRAP TO DEAL WITH...

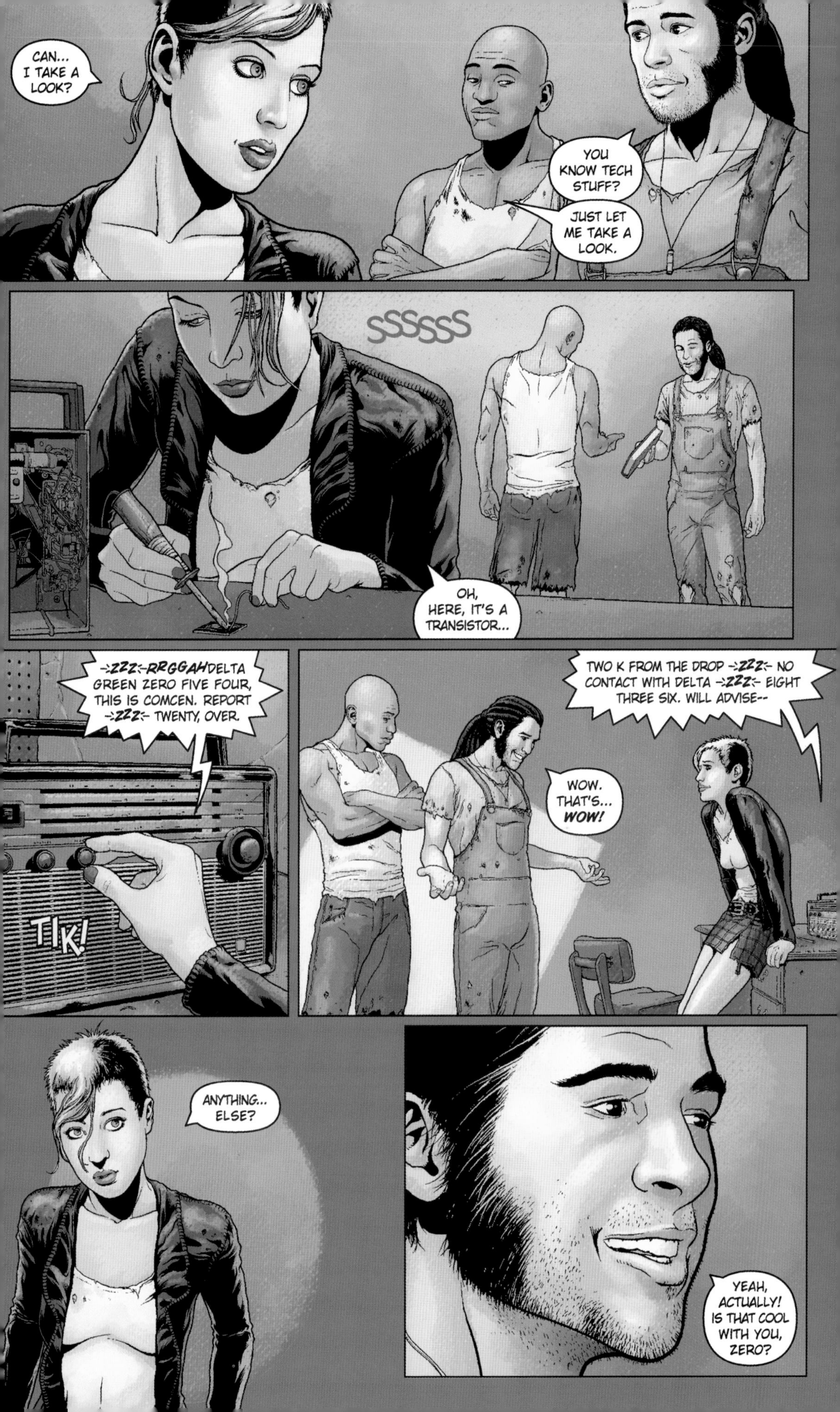

CAN... I TAKE A LOOK?
YOU KNOW TECH STUFF?
JUST LET ME TAKE A LOOK.
SSSSSS
OH, HERE, IT'S A TRANSISTOR...
-ZZZ- RRGGAH DELTA GREEN ZERO FIVE FOUR, THIS IS COMCEN. REPORT -ZZZ- TWENTY, OVER.
TIK!
TWO K FROM THE DROP -ZZZ- NO CONTACT WITH DELTA -ZZZ- EIGHT THREE SIX. WILL ADVISE--
WOW. THAT'S... WOW!
ANYTHING... ELSE?
YEAH, ACTUALLY! IS THAT COOL WITH YOU, ZERO?

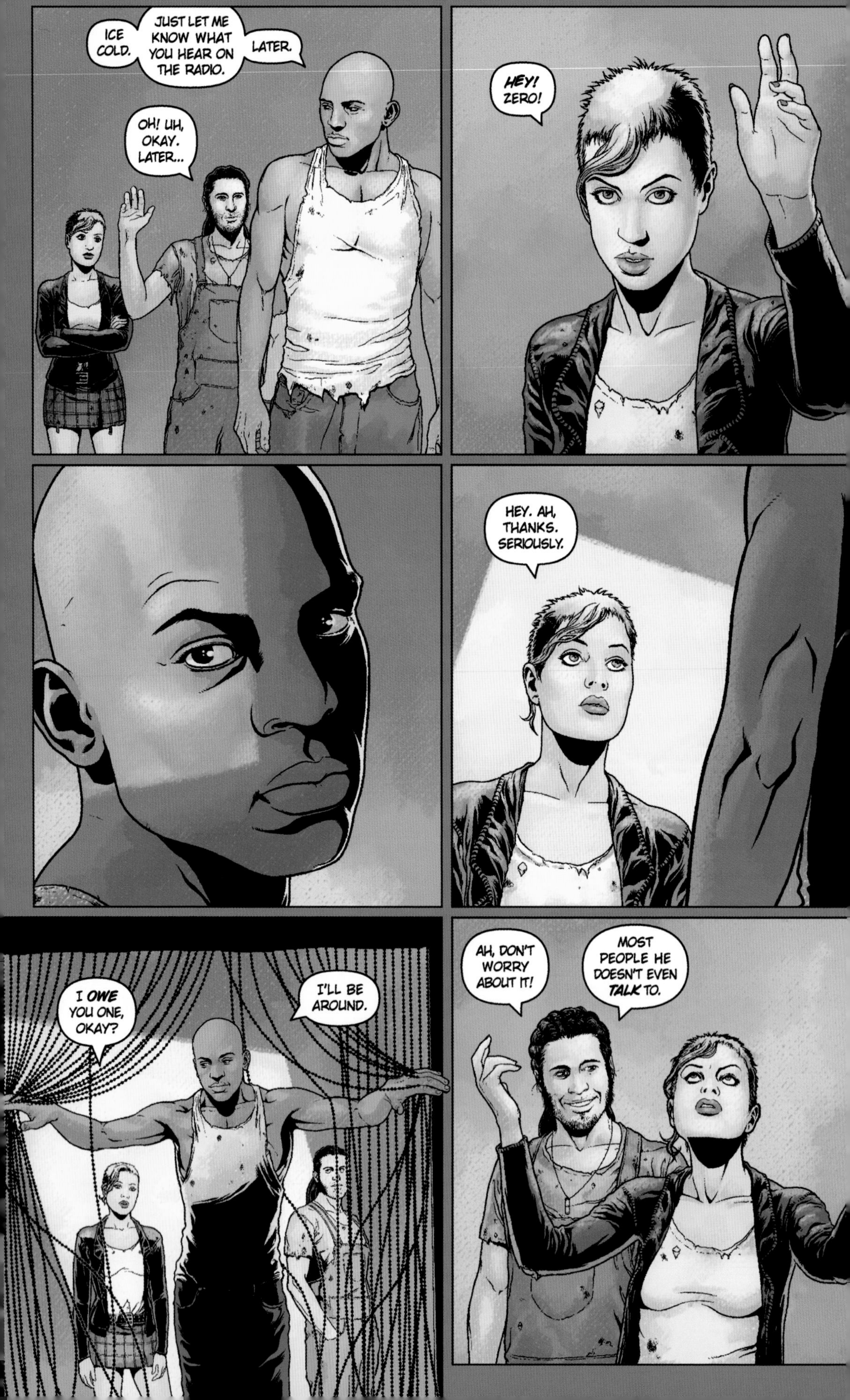
ICE COLD.
JUST LET ME KNOW WHAT YOU HEAR ON THE RADIO.
LATER.
OH! UH, OKAY. LATER...
HEY! ZERO!
HEY. AH, THANKS. SERIOUSLY.
I OWE YOU ONE, OKAY?
I'LL BE AROUND.
AH, DON'T WORRY ABOUT IT!
MOST PEOPLE HE DOESN'T EVEN TALK TO.

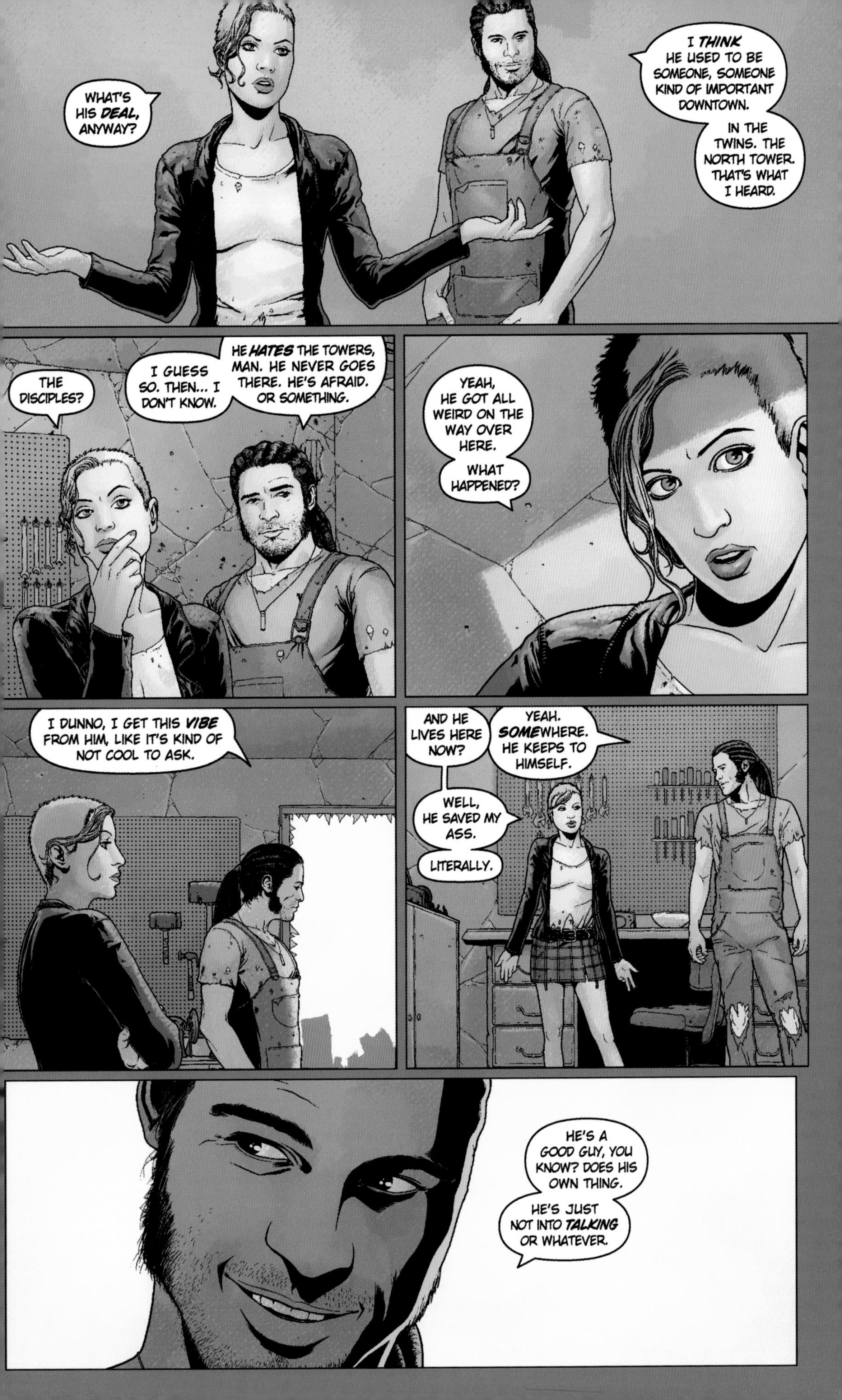
WHAT'S HIS DEAL, ANYWAY?
I THINK HE USED TO BE SOMEONE, SOMEONE KIND OF IMPORTANT DOWNTOWN.
IN THE TWINS. THE NORTH TOWER. THAT'S WHAT I HEARD.
THE DISCIPLES?
I GUESS SO. THEN... I DON'T KNOW.
HE HATES THE TOWERS, MAN. HE NEVER GOES THERE. HE'S AFRAID. OR SOMETHING.
YEAH, HE GOT ALL WEIRD ON THE WAY OVER HERE.
WHAT HAPPENED?
I DUNNO, I GET THIS VIBE FROM HIM, LIKE IT'S KIND OF NOT COOL TO ASK.
AND HE LIVES HERE NOW?
YEAH. SOMEWHERE. HE KEEPS TO HIMSELF.
WELL, HE SAVED MY ASS.
LITERALLY.
HE'S A GOOD GUY, YOU KNOW? DOES HIS OWN THING.
HE'S JUST NOT INTO TALKING OR WHATEVER.

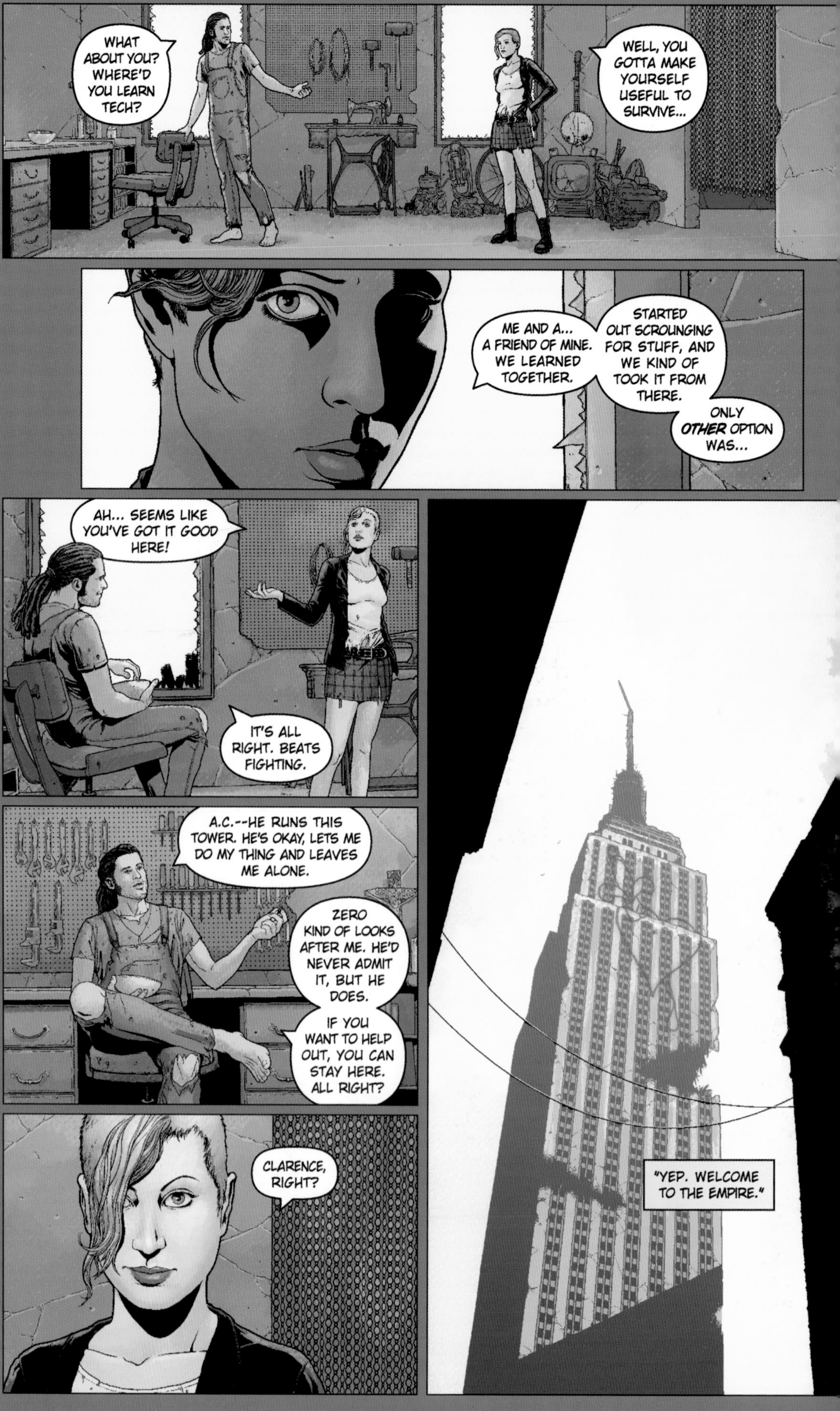
WHAT ABOUT YOU? WHERE'D YOU LEARN TECH?
WELL, YOU GOTTA MAKE YOURSELF USEFUL TO SURVIVE...
ME AND A... A FRIEND OF MINE. WE LEARNED TOGETHER.
STARTED OUT SCROUNGING FOR STUFF, AND WE KIND OF TOOK IT FROM THERE.
ONLY OTHER OPTION WAS...
AH... SEEMS LIKE YOU'VE GOT IT GOOD HERE!
IT'S ALL RIGHT. BEATS FIGHTING.
A.C.--HE RUNS THIS TOWER. HE'S OKAY, LETS ME DO MY THING AND LEAVES ME ALONE.
ZERO KIND OF LOOKS AFTER ME. HE'D NEVER ADMIT IT, BUT HE DOES.
IF YOU WANT TO HELP OUT, YOU CAN STAY HERE. ALL RIGHT?
CLARENCE, RIGHT?
"YEP. WELCOME TO THE EMPIRE."

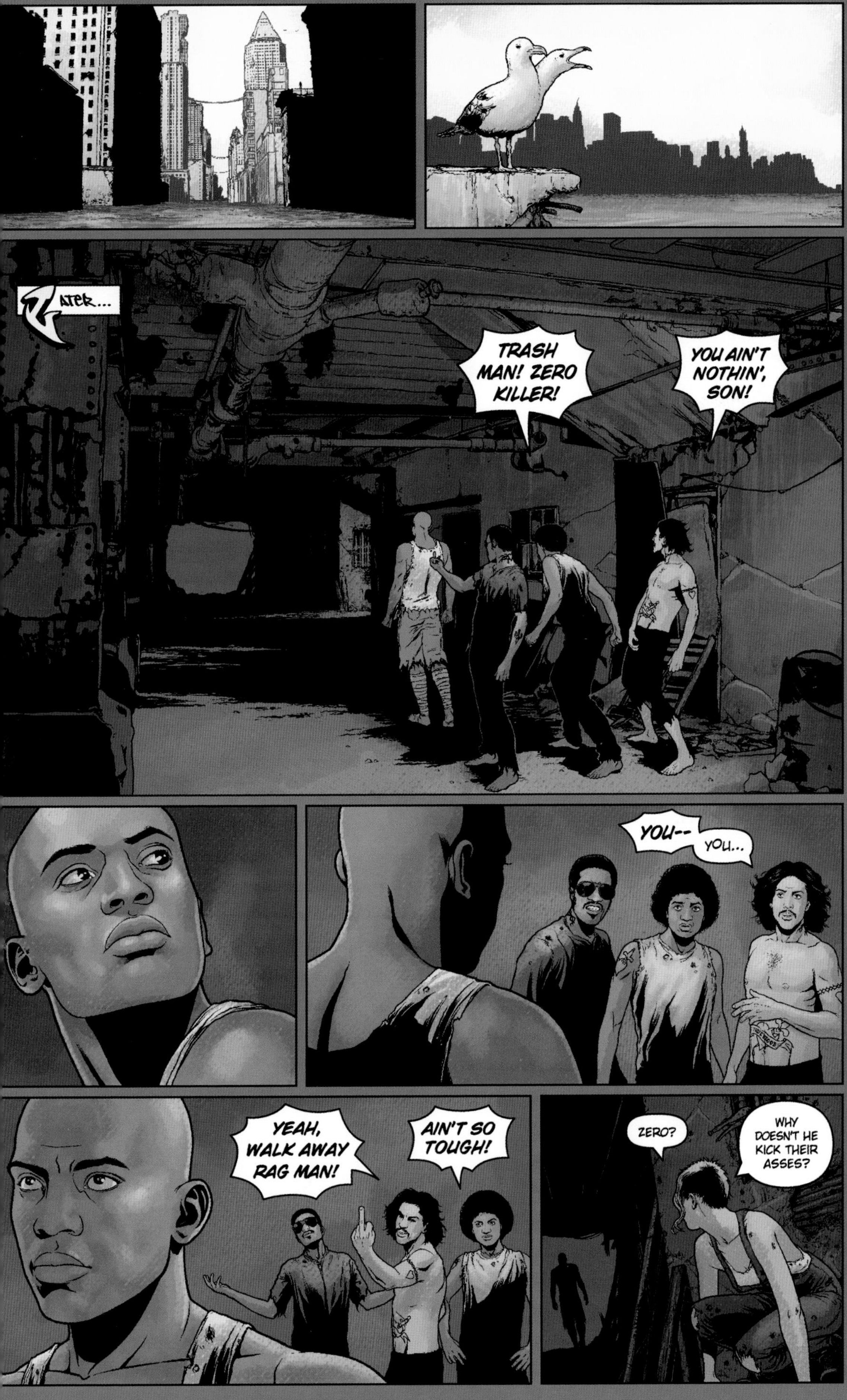
LATER...
TRASH MAN! ZERO KILLER!
YOU AIN'T NOTHIN', SON!
YOU--
YOU...
YEAH, WALK AWAY RAG MAN!
AIN'T SO TOUGH!
ZERO?
WHY DOESN'T HE KICK THEIR ASSES?

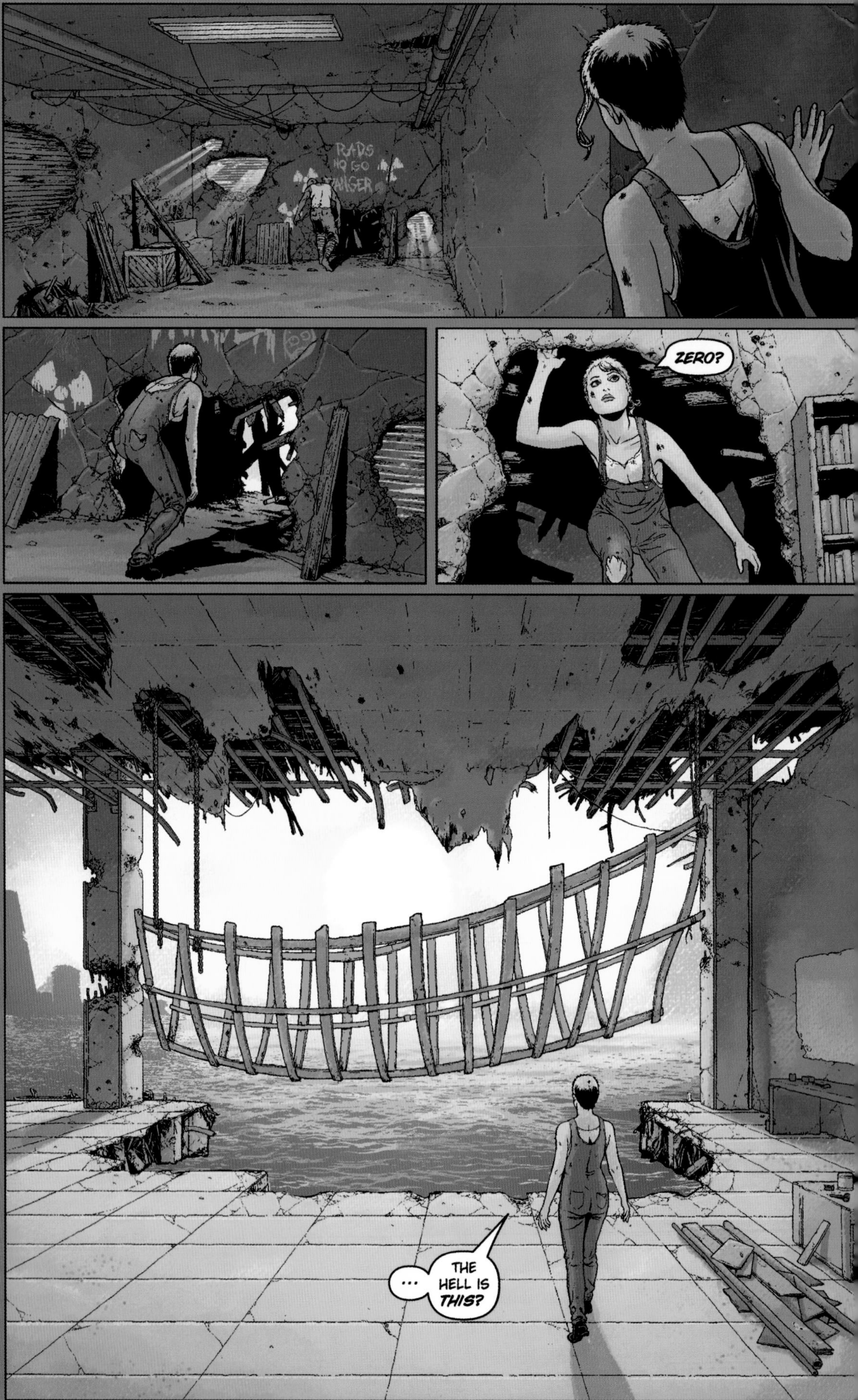
RADS
NO GO
DANGER
ZERO?
... THE HELL IS THIS?

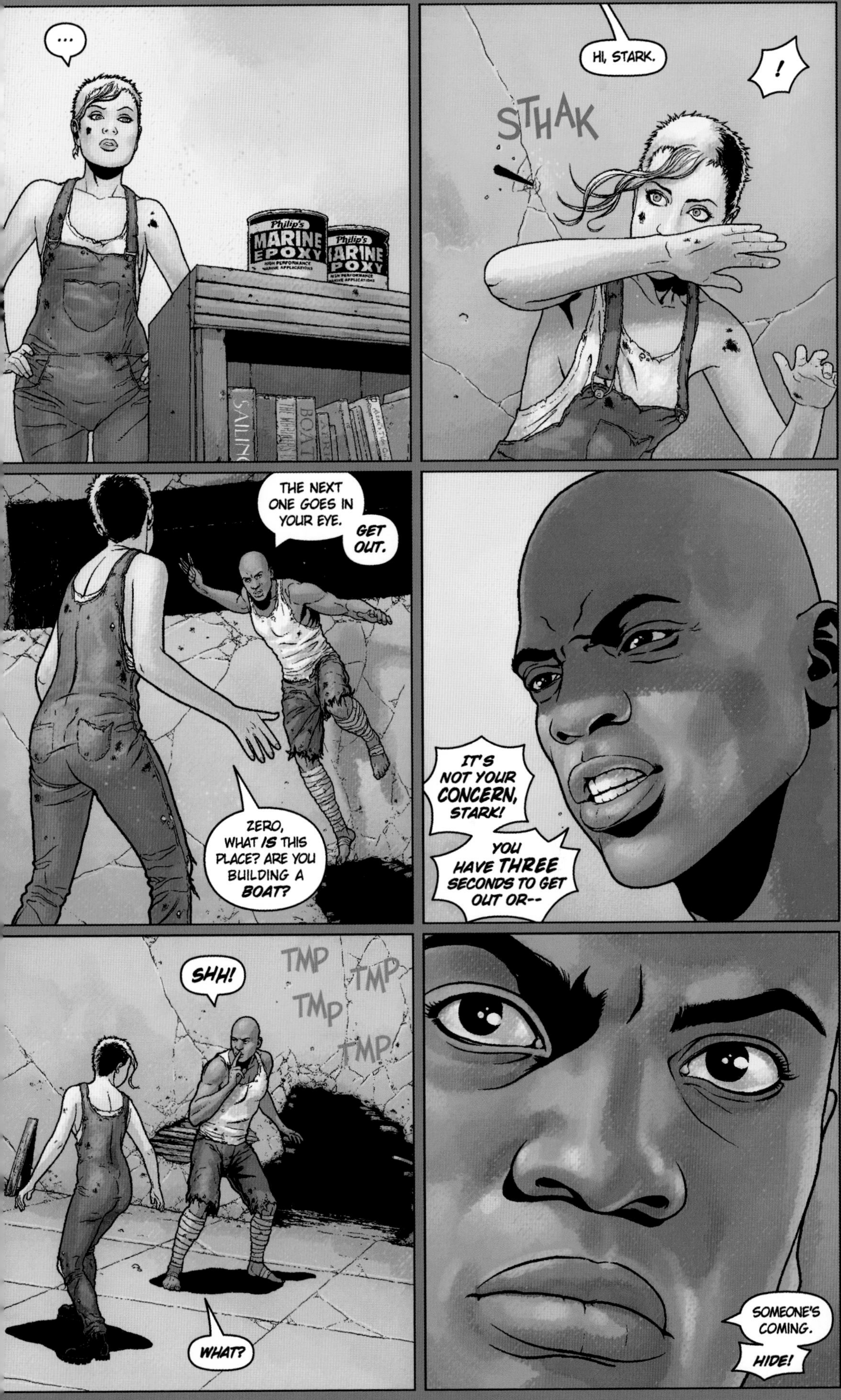
...
HI, STARK.
!
STHAK
THE NEXT ONE GOES IN YOUR EYE.
GET OUT.
ZERO, WHAT IS THIS PLACE? ARE YOU BUILDING A BOAT?
IT'S NOT YOUR CONCERN, STARK!
YOU HAVE THREE SECONDS TO GET OUT OR--
SHH!
TMP TMP TMP TMP
WHAT?
SOMEONE'S COMING.
HIDE!

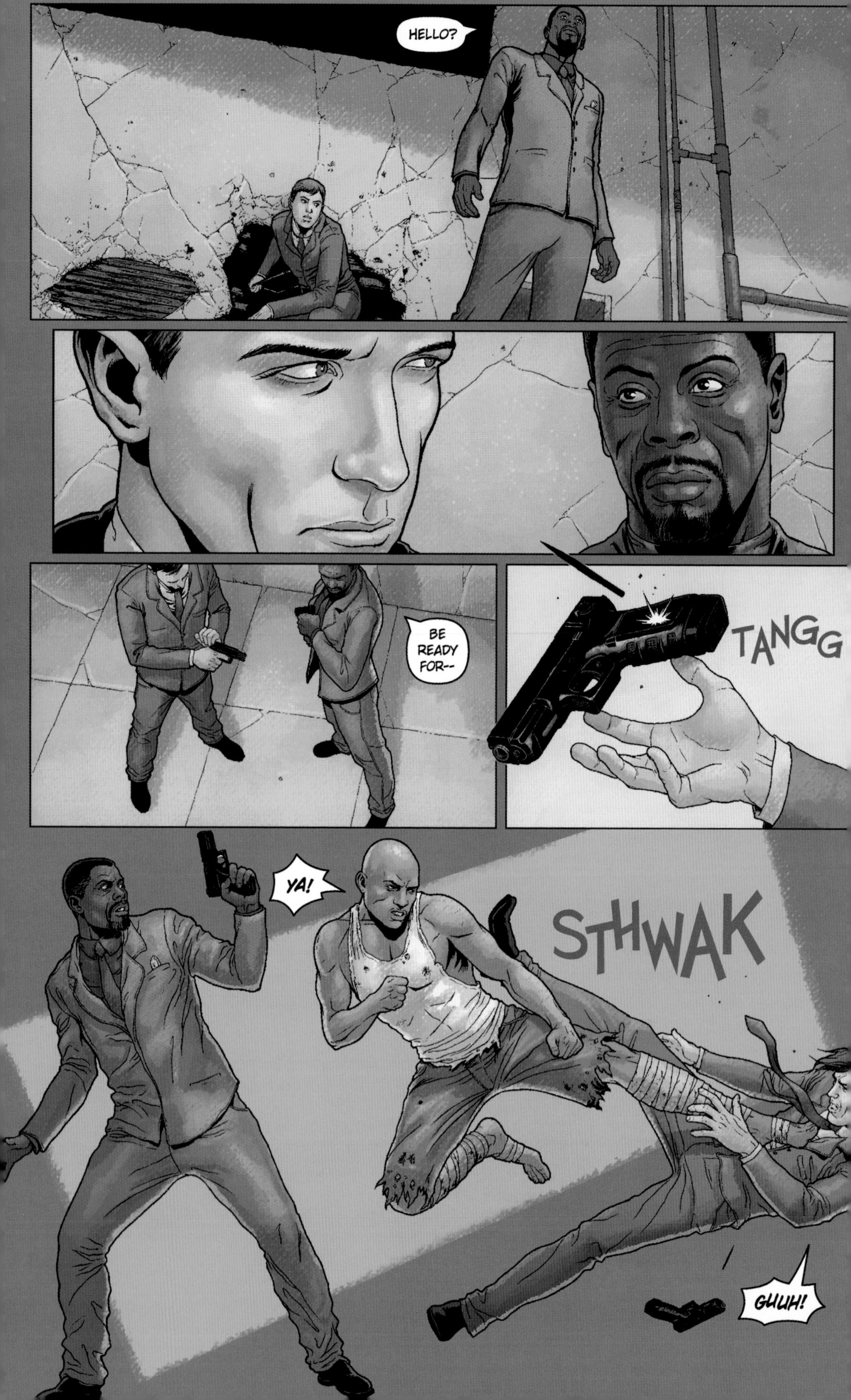
HELLO?
BE READY FOR--
TANGG
YA!
STHWAK
GUUH!

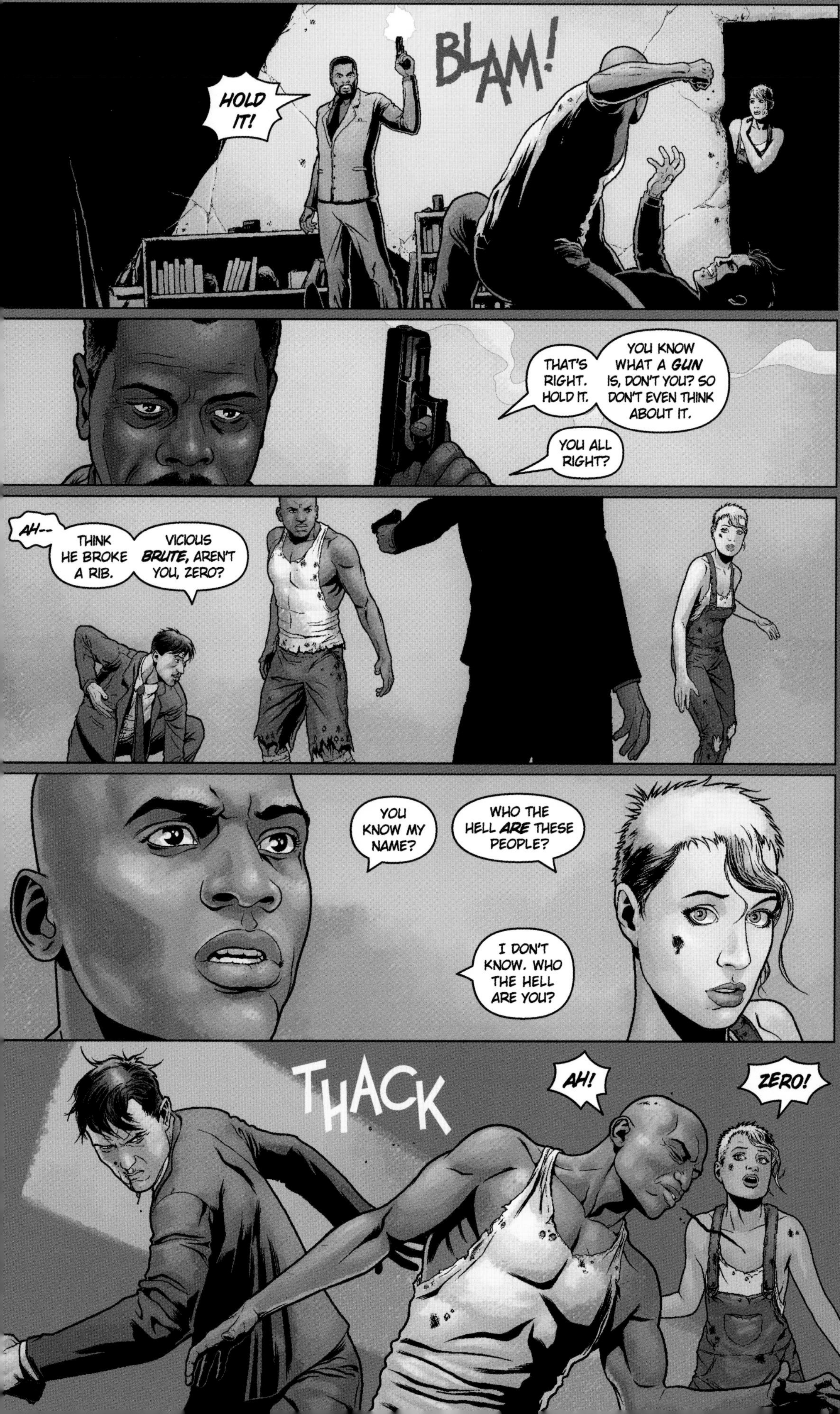
HOLD IT!
BLAM!
THAT'S RIGHT. HOLD IT.
YOU KNOW WHAT A GUN IS, DON'T YOU? SO DON'T EVEN THINK ABOUT IT.
YOU ALL RIGHT?
AH--
THINK HE BROKE A RIB.
VICIOUS BRUTE, AREN'T YOU, ZERO?
YOU KNOW MY NAME?
WHO THE HELL ARE THESE PEOPLE?
I DON'T KNOW. WHO THE HELL ARE YOU?
THACK
AH!
ZERO!

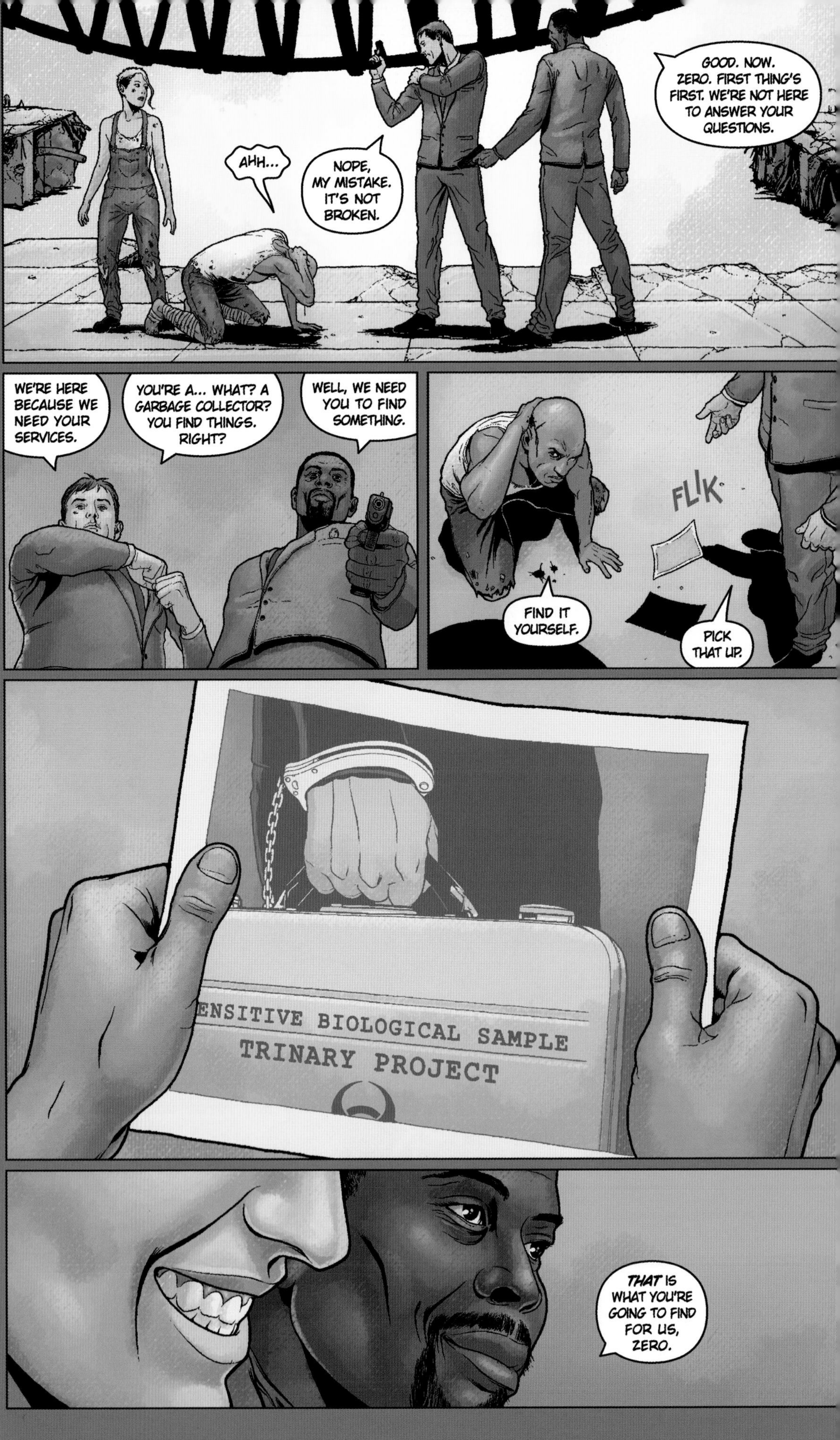

AHH...
NOPE, MY MISTAKE. IT'S NOT BROKEN.
GOOD. NOW. ZERO. FIRST THING'S FIRST. WE'RE NOT HERE TO ANSWER YOUR QUESTIONS.
WE'RE HERE BECAUSE WE NEED YOUR SERVICES.
YOU'RE A... WHAT? A GARBAGE COLLECTOR? YOU FIND THINGS. RIGHT?
WELL, WE NEED YOU TO FIND SOMETHING.
FLIK
FIND IT YOURSELF.
PICK THAT UP.
ENSITIVE BIOLOGICAL SAMPLE
TRINARY PROJECT
THAT IS WHAT YOU'RE GOING TO FIND FOR US, ZERO.

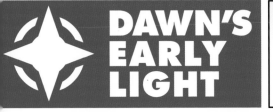

DAWN'S EARLY LIGHT

STAND PROUD!

IF YOU DON'T KNOW WHERE YOU'VE BEEN, YOU DON'T KNOW WHERE YOU'RE GOING. ON THE BACK PAGE, *CAPTAIN JOCOM* HIGHLIGHTS SOME OF THE EVENTS THAT SHAPED OUR COMMON DESTINY.

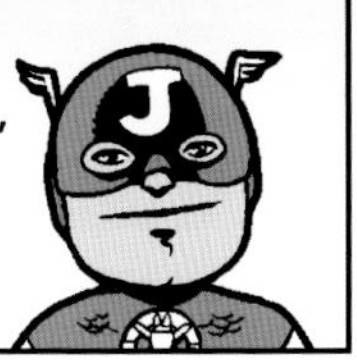

Black Hawk Down Over Twin Towers

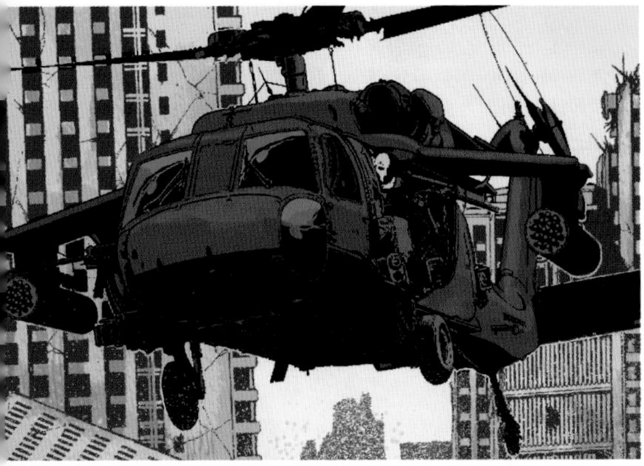

The UH-60 Black Hawk is manufactured in the Valley Forge Subterranean Industrial Complex by Sikorsky Aerospace, a corporate subsidiary of the Department of Acquisitions.

A Black Hawk helicopter on routine patrol was downed late yesterday afternoon. The personnel aboard the craft are missing and presumed dead.

According to preliminary information, the crash was not an accident, but the work of hostile tower dwellers. The attack may have even involved sophisticated surface-to-air missile technology.

At approximately 8:14 yesterday evening, Warrant Officer Steven Linski of Air Traffic Control received a distress signal from the doomed aircraft.

"They sounded like they were in a heap of trouble," he said. "And they definitely mentioned an incoming surface-to-air missile."

Special Investigations Command has not revealed the identities of the personnel involved in the crash.

Sources in the Defence Intelligence Agency (DIA) have not ruled out the possibility the Soviet Union supplied the assailants with the weapon systems needed to carry out such a strike.

"I think it's fairly safe to assume the Soviets have reconstituted themselves and are providing assistance to insurgent elements based in the towers of New York City," Defense Intelligence Secretary William Kristol said.

Special Investigations Command (SIC) has assigned a task force to investigate the crash.

"Unfortunately, the site of the crash is the North Tower of the Twin Towers. The gangs inhabiting the Twins are among the most dangerous," Lt. Bill Evers, an investigator with SIC, said.

"We're requesting an escort of [Special Task Force] troopers before we visit the crash site."

Attacks against JOCOM personnel operating in the ruins of New York City are becoming more and more frequent, but an assault against a helicopter in mid-flight is a relatively new development.

Kristol recommended "swift, harsh" retaliation for the attack.

"It seems the strike was staged somewhere in midtown," Kristol said. "I think it's perfectly justifiable for us to use tactical nuclear weapons on six or so buildings in the area, really clean them out, to teach the people living in them a lesson."

Richard Perle, National Security Advisor to the Director of the Reconstruction of the United States of America (DRUSA), called for a less severe response.

"I'm sure we could get the message across by destroying just one or two buildings," he said. ✦

THE JOCOM CREED

"With all my heart, my body, and my mind, I will serve JOCOM. I will not feel pity, remorse, or compassion for my enemies, the enemies of the reconstruction of the United States of America. My honor is loyalty, and I will obey the orders of my superiors at all times, without question. I will not allow weakness to deter me from completing my mission. Death holds no fear over me, and victory is my only joy."

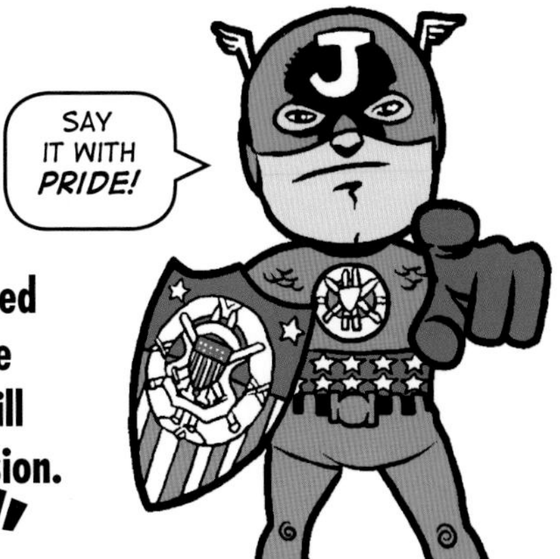
SAY IT WITH *PRIDE!*

WWW.ZEROKILLER.COM

Knowledge is the ultimate weapon!

WHERE EAGLES DARE

Words of wisdom from the Captain ✦ Honor, duty, loyalty, pride

KNOW WHAT YOU'RE FIGHTING FOR! JOCOM IS BUILDING A BRIGHT FUTURE OUT OF THE ASHES OF THE PAST, AND ALL OUR FIGHTING MEN ARE ADVISED TO LEARN ABOUT THE EVENTS THAT LED UP TO ***ZERO HOUR.***

STAY STRONG, STAY LOYAL! YOUR COUNTRY NEEDS ***YOU,*** SOLDIER!

1945: Rather than use atomic weapons directly on Japan, US President Harry Truman demonstrates their power on an uninhabited island. As a result, hard-liners in the Japanese military seize control of Japan and vow to fight the Allies regardless of their use of atomic weapons. The United States invades the island of Kyushu; the Soviet Union invades Hokkaido in the north.

1947: World War II ends. Three million Japanese dead, 300,000 Allied casualties. A Soviet Democratic Republic of Japan (DRJ) is formed in the north and a parliamentary South Japan, supported by the United States, is founded in the south.

1951: Following the communist unification of Korea, the Soviets and Chinese establish the Comprehensive Asian Mutual Assistance Treaty (CAMAT). Signatories include North Japan, Russia, China, and Korea.

1954: French expelled from Indochina; North Vietnam joins CAMAT.

The Chinese People's Liberation Army (PLA) invades Taiwan. Taipei falls in days. The battered and demoralized Taiwanese defenders retreat and launch guerrilla raids on the PLA. Eisenhower sends US troops to Taiwan without a congressional declaration of war.

1956: Suez Canal Crisis. Egypt, Syria, Iraq, Lebanon, and Iran develop Soviet ties and enact socialist economic reforms.

Taiwanese and U.S. forces expel the mainland Chinese People's Liberation Army from Taiwan after two years of brutal war.

1963: Iranian communists, armed with Soviet and Chinese weapons, seize power and depose the tottering shah of Iran. Soviet troops swiftly move into Tehran to bolster the fledgling communist government, over vigorous protests from the United States. Iran joins CAMAT.

1968: Afghanistan joins CAMAT, but the move triggers religious uprisings in Pakistan and Afghanistan. Communists are restored to power by a joint Chinese, Korean, and Soviet invasion, but insurgencies thrive in the countryside.

1971: Soviets land a man on the moon and return him safely to Earth, mere weeks ahead of the United States, in a nail-biting photo finish to the Space Race.

The DRJ invades South Japan, aided by China and Korea. Although the United States is faced with a deteriorating situation in Vietnam, Congress declares war on North Japan.

1973: The Yom Kippur war erupts when Egypt and Syria launch joint surprise attacks on Israel. Soviet/Iranian-backed guerrillas from Lebanon also take part. The war goes badly for Israel, and within weeks Syrian forces are at the gates of Tel Aviv. Israel launches nuclear strikes on Tehran and Damascus. It escalates into Zero Hour, a massive global exchange. Over 90 percent of the human population perishes in the span of twenty-four hours.

Nixon and Ford are removed from power in the chaos, along with most of the Senate and the House. United States Constitution suspended indefinitely. The Joint Military Command, JOCOM, is formed.

2007: THE FORCES OF ***JOCOM*** ARE MAKING THE WORLD SAFE AGAIN FOR DEMOCRACY, THIRTY-FOUR YEARS AFTER THE TRAGIC SOVIET PROVOCATION THAT BROUGHT ABOUT ***ZERO HOUR***. WE'RE WORKING ***HARD*** TO BRING THE UNITED STATES OF AMERICA BACK TO ITS FORMER GLORY, AND WE'RE NOT GOING TO LET ANYTHING--OR ANYONE!--STAND IN OUR WAY. THE SOVIET UNION IS OUT THERE, SO ***STAY FOCUSED!***

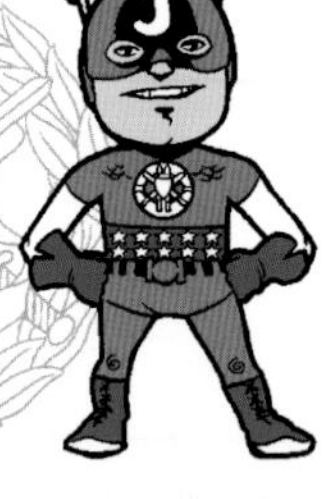

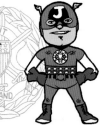

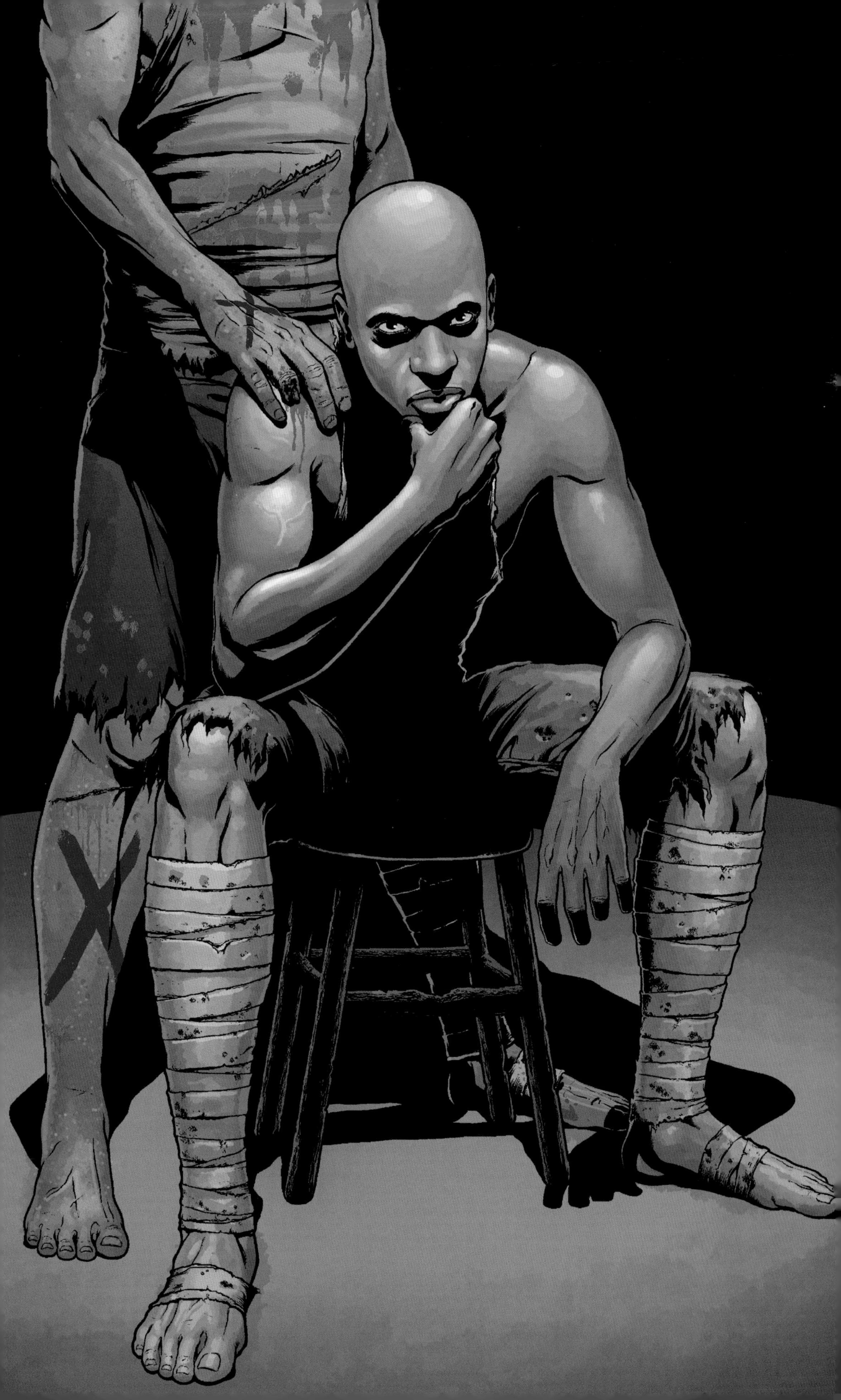

ZEROKILLER

CHAPTER 3
(I'D RATHER NOT GO) BACK TO THE OLD HOUSE

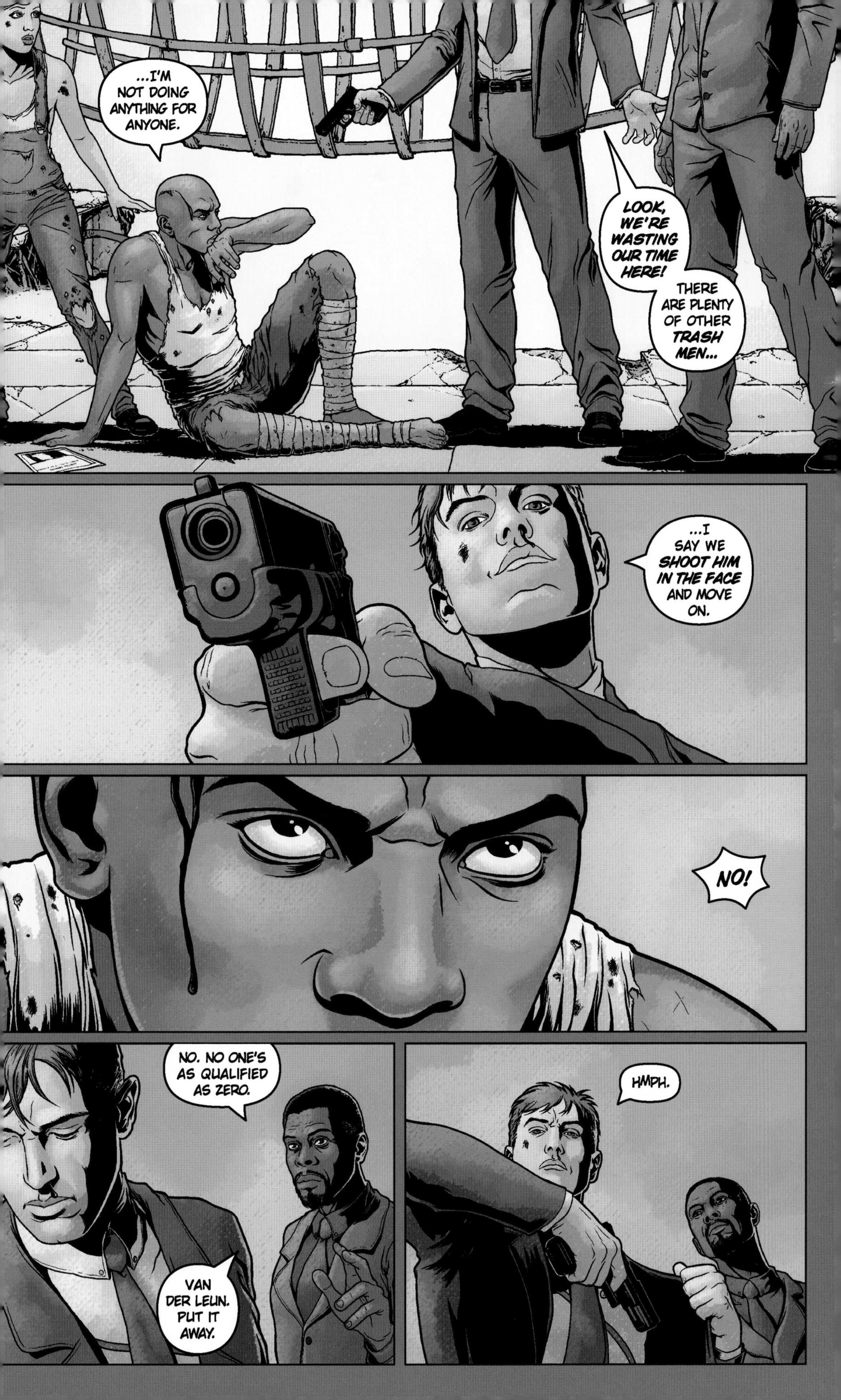

...I'M NOT DOING ANYTHING FOR ANYONE.
LOOK, WE'RE WASTING OUR TIME HERE!
THERE ARE PLENTY OF OTHER TRASH MEN...
...I SAY WE SHOOT HIM IN THE FACE AND MOVE ON.
NO!
NO. NO ONE'S AS QUALIFIED AS ZERO.
VAN DER LEUN. PUT IT AWAY.
HMPH.

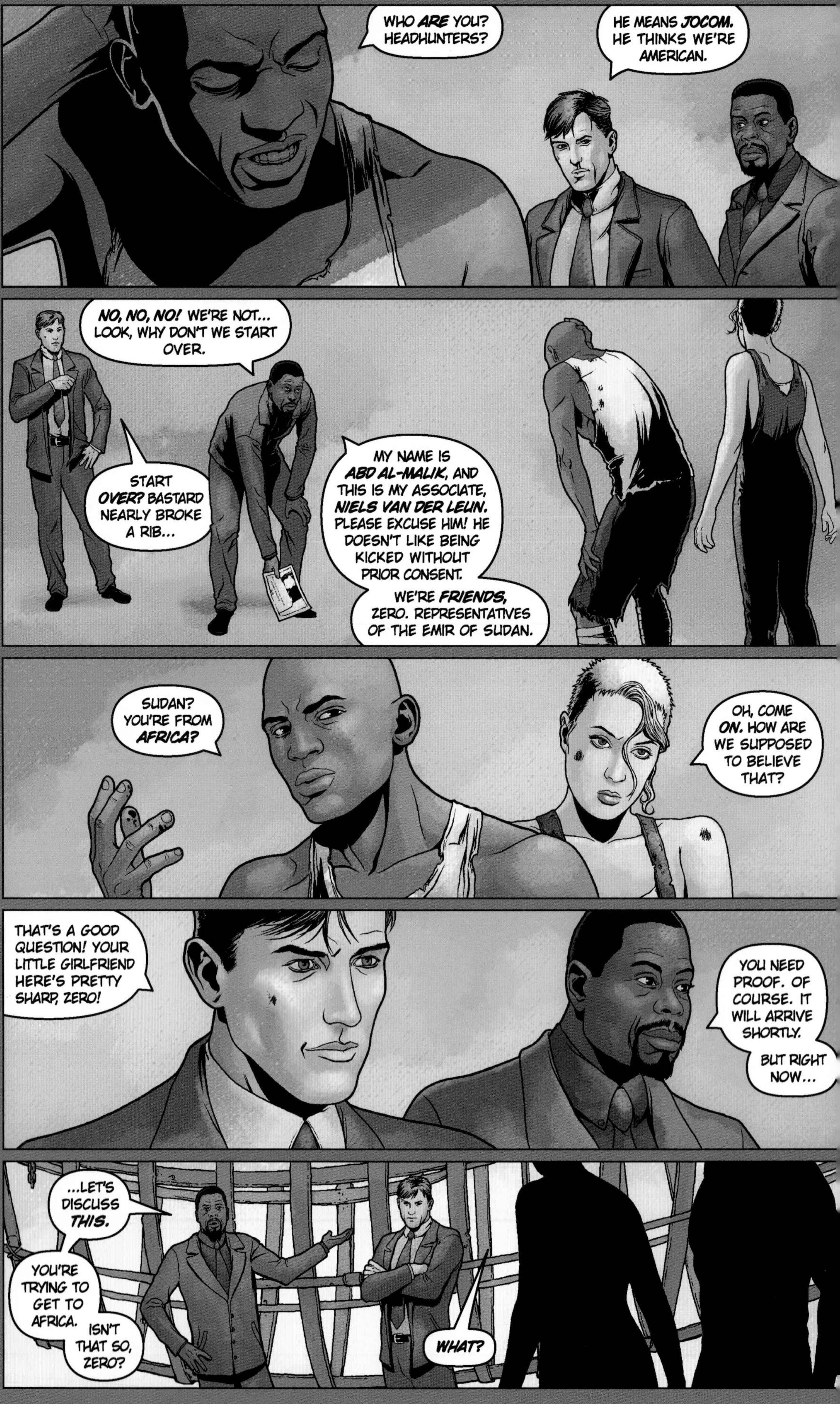
WHO ARE YOU? HEADHUNTERS?
HE MEANS JOCOM. HE THINKS WE'RE AMERICAN.
NO, NO, NO! WE'RE NOT... LOOK, WHY DON'T WE START OVER.
START OVER? BASTARD NEARLY BROKE A RIB...
MY NAME IS ABD AL-MALIK, AND THIS IS MY ASSOCIATE, NIELS VAN DER LEUN. PLEASE EXCUSE HIM! HE DOESN'T LIKE BEING KICKED WITHOUT PRIOR CONSENT.
WE'RE FRIENDS, ZERO. REPRESENTATIVES OF THE EMIR OF SUDAN.
SUDAN? YOU'RE FROM AFRICA?
OH, COME ON. HOW ARE WE SUPPOSED TO BELIEVE THAT?
THAT'S A GOOD QUESTION! YOUR LITTLE GIRLFRIEND HERE'S PRETTY SHARP, ZERO!
YOU NEED PROOF. OF COURSE. IT WILL ARRIVE SHORTLY.
BUT RIGHT NOW...
...LET'S DISCUSS THIS.
YOU'RE TRYING TO GET TO AFRICA.
ISN'T THAT SO, ZERO?
WHAT?

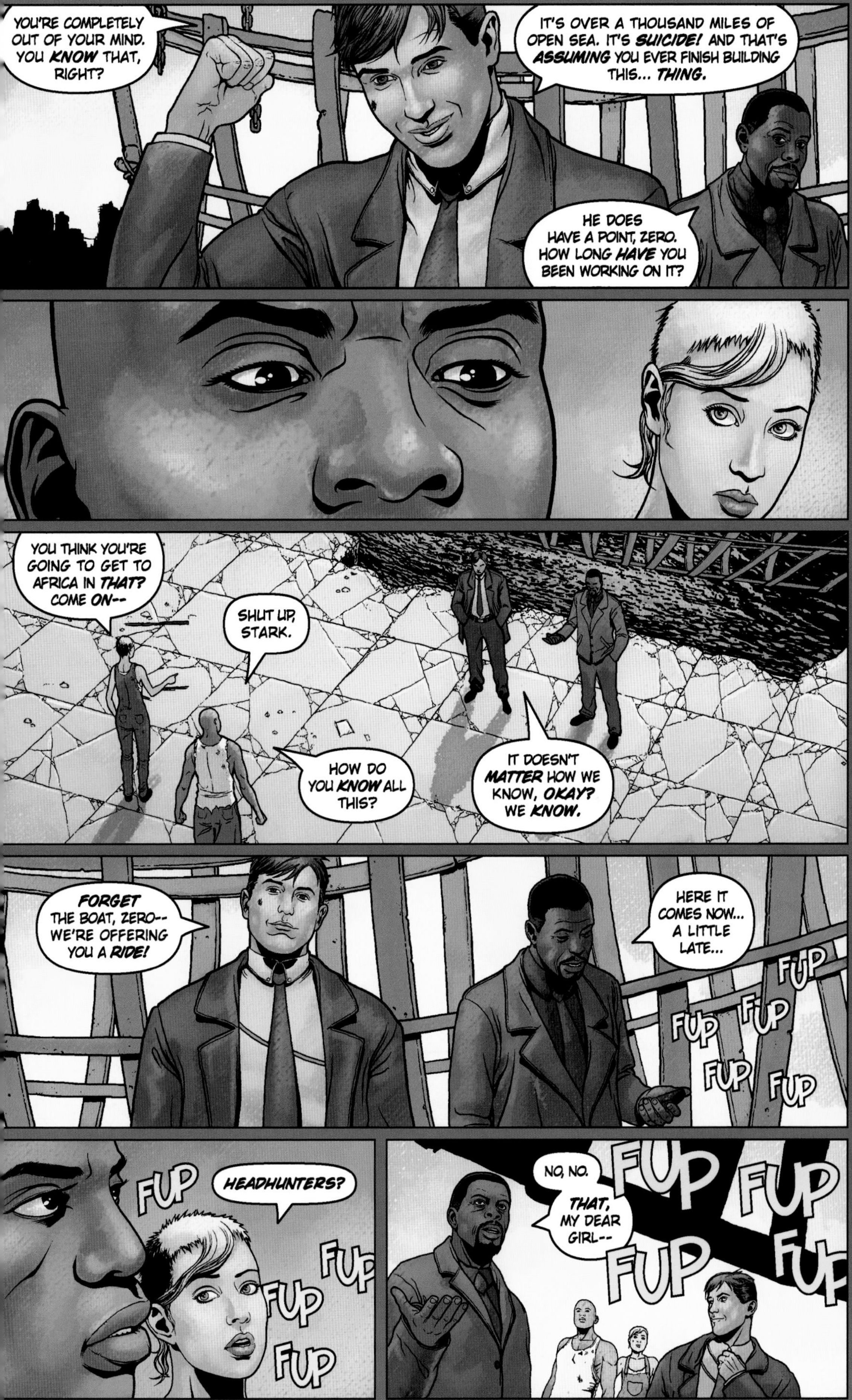
YOU'RE COMPLETELY OUT OF YOUR MIND. YOU KNOW THAT, RIGHT?
IT'S OVER A THOUSAND MILES OF OPEN SEA. IT'S SUICIDE! AND THAT'S ASSUMING YOU EVER FINISH BUILDING THIS... THING.
HE DOES HAVE A POINT, ZERO. HOW LONG HAVE YOU BEEN WORKING ON IT?
YOU THINK YOU'RE GOING TO GET TO AFRICA IN THAT? COME ON--
SHUT UP, STARK.
HOW DO YOU KNOW ALL THIS?
IT DOESN'T MATTER HOW WE KNOW, OKAY? WE KNOW.
FORGET THE BOAT, ZERO-- WE'RE OFFERING YOU A RIDE!
HERE IT COMES NOW... A LITTLE LATE...
FUP
FUP FUP
FUP FUP FUP
FUP
HEADHUNTERS?
FUP FUP FUP
NO, NO.
THAT, MY DEAR GIRL--
FUP FUP FUP FUP

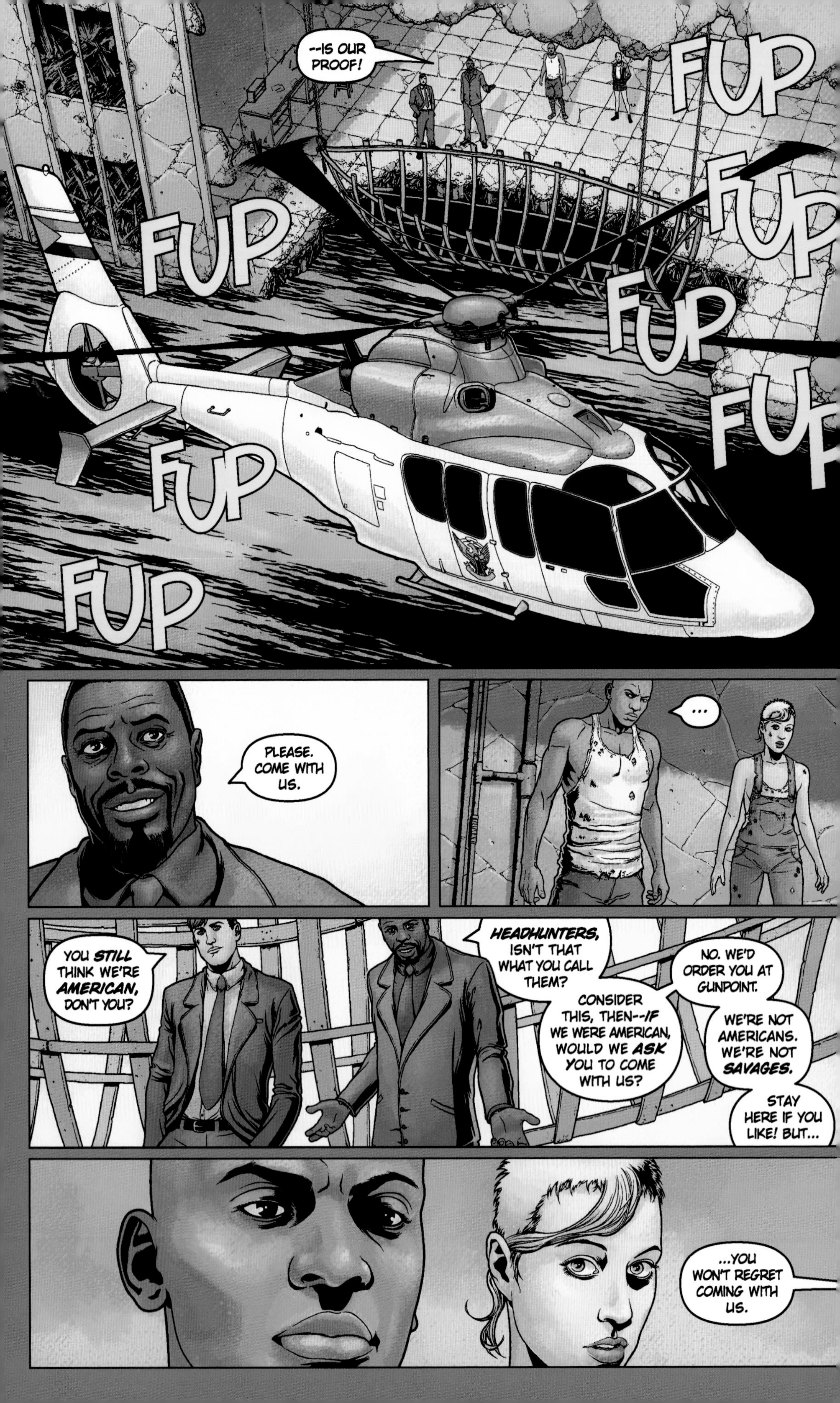
--IS OUR PROOF!
FUP
FUP
FUP
FUP
FUP
FUP
FUP
PLEASE. COME WITH US.
...
YOU STILL THINK WE'RE AMERICAN, DON'T YOU?
HEADHUNTERS, ISN'T THAT WHAT YOU CALL THEM?
CONSIDER THIS, THEN--IF WE WERE AMERICAN, WOULD WE ASK YOU TO COME WITH US?
NO. WE'D ORDER YOU AT GUNPOINT.
WE'RE NOT AMERICANS. WE'RE NOT SAVAGES.
STAY HERE IF YOU LIKE! BUT...
...YOU WON'T REGRET COMING WITH US.

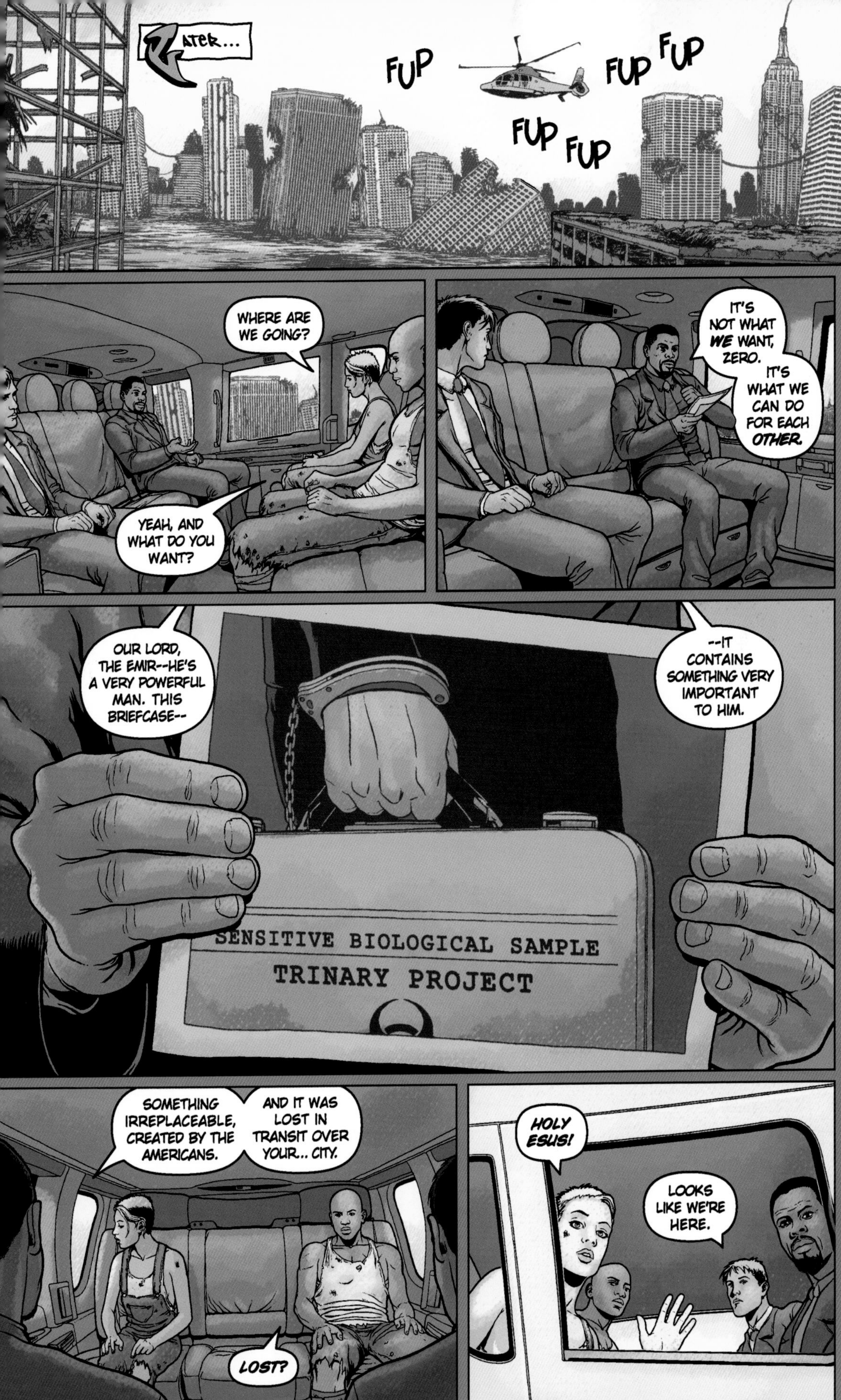
LATER...
FUP
FUP FUP
FUP FUP
WHERE ARE WE GOING?
YEAH, AND WHAT DO YOU WANT?
IT'S NOT WHAT WE WANT, ZERO.
IT'S WHAT WE CAN DO FOR EACH OTHER.
OUR LORD, THE EMIR--HE'S A VERY POWERFUL MAN. THIS BRIEFCASE--
--IT CONTAINS SOMETHING VERY IMPORTANT TO HIM.
SENSITIVE BIOLOGICAL SAMPLE
TRINARY PROJECT
SOMETHING IRREPLACEABLE, CREATED BY THE AMERICANS.
AND IT WAS LOST IN TRANSIT OVER YOUR... CITY.
LOST?
HOLY ESUS!
LOOKS LIKE WE'RE HERE.

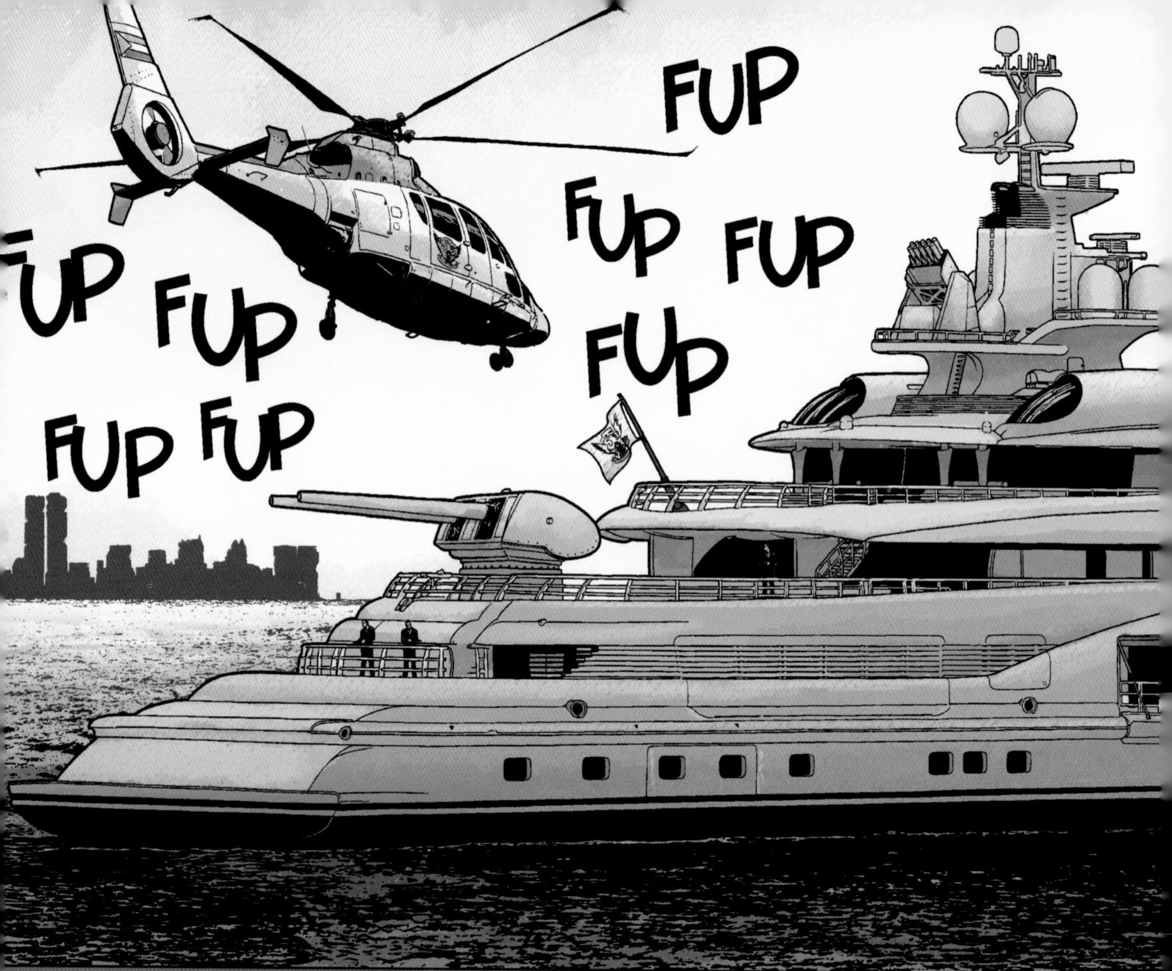
FUP
FUP FUP
FUP
FUP FUP
FUP FUP
FUP

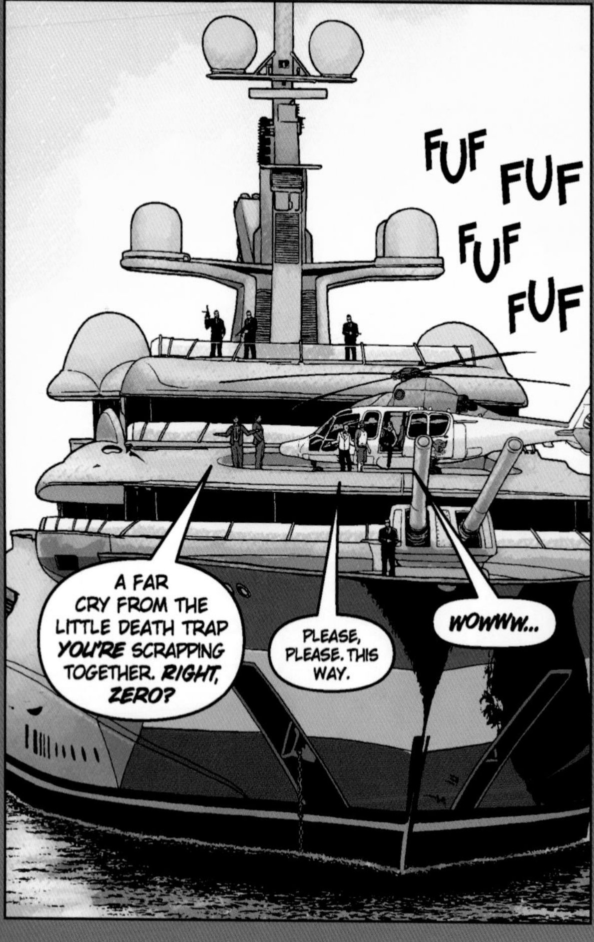
FUF FUF
FUF
FUF
A FAR CRY FROM THE LITTLE DEATH TRAP YOU'RE SCRAPPING TOGETHER. RIGHT, ZERO?
PLEASE, PLEASE. THIS WAY.
WOWWW...

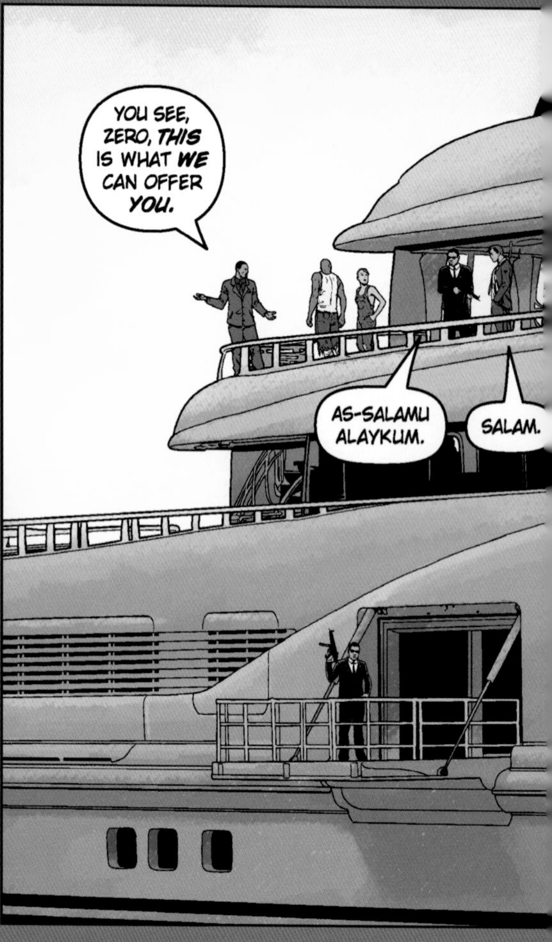
YOU SEE, ZERO, THIS IS WHAT WE CAN OFFER YOU.
AS-SALAMU ALAYKUM.
SALAM.

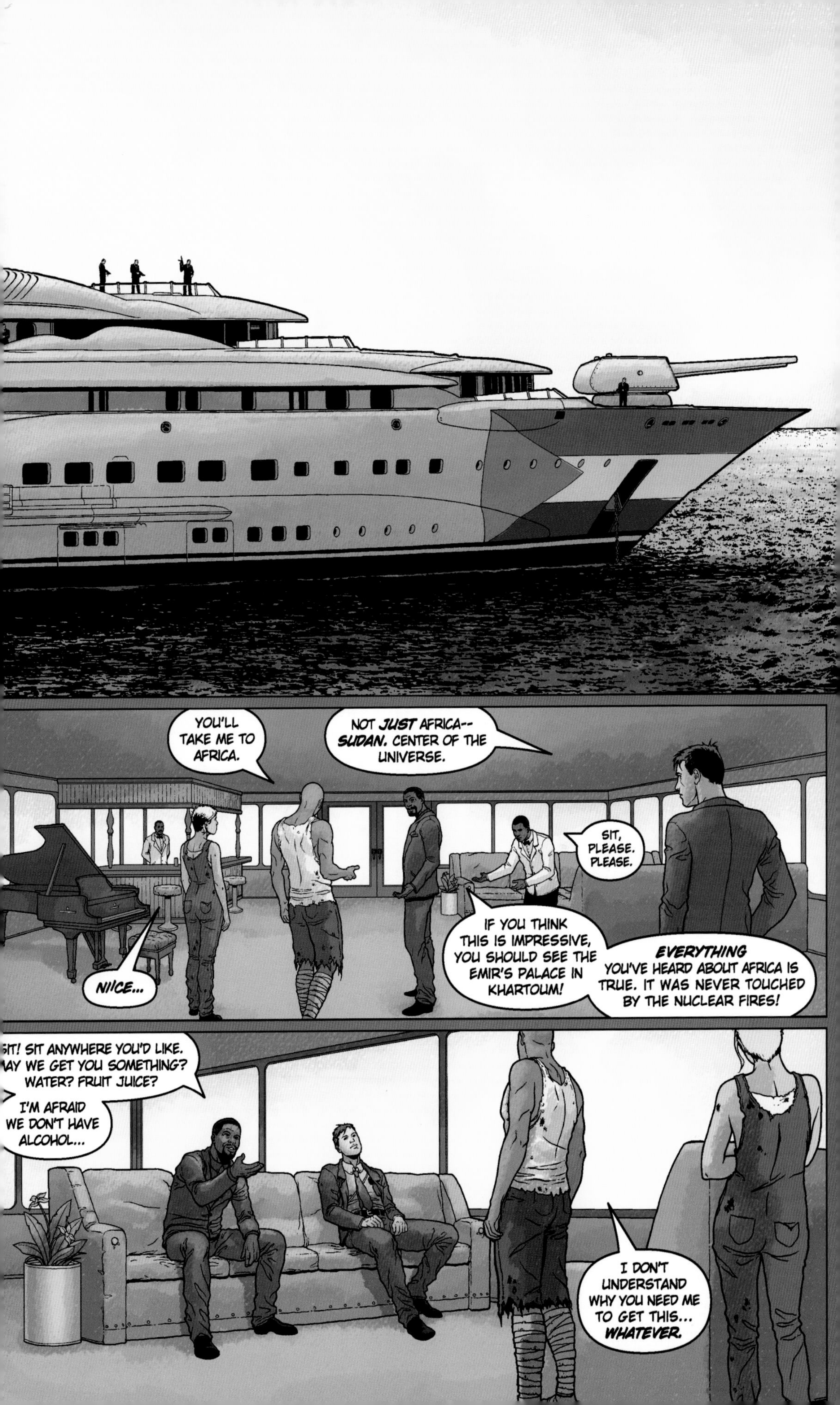

YOU'LL TAKE ME TO AFRICA.
NOT JUST AFRICA-- SUDAN. CENTER OF THE UNIVERSE.
SIT, PLEASE. PLEASE.
NIICE...
IF YOU THINK THIS IS IMPRESSIVE, YOU SHOULD SEE THE EMIR'S PALACE IN KHARTOUM!
EVERYTHING YOU'VE HEARD ABOUT AFRICA IS TRUE. IT WAS NEVER TOUCHED BY THE NUCLEAR FIRES!
SIT! SIT ANYWHERE YOU'D LIKE. MAY WE GET YOU SOMETHING? WATER? FRUIT JUICE?
I'M AFRAID WE DON'T HAVE ALCOHOL...
I DON'T UNDERSTAND WHY YOU NEED ME TO GET THIS... WHATEVER.

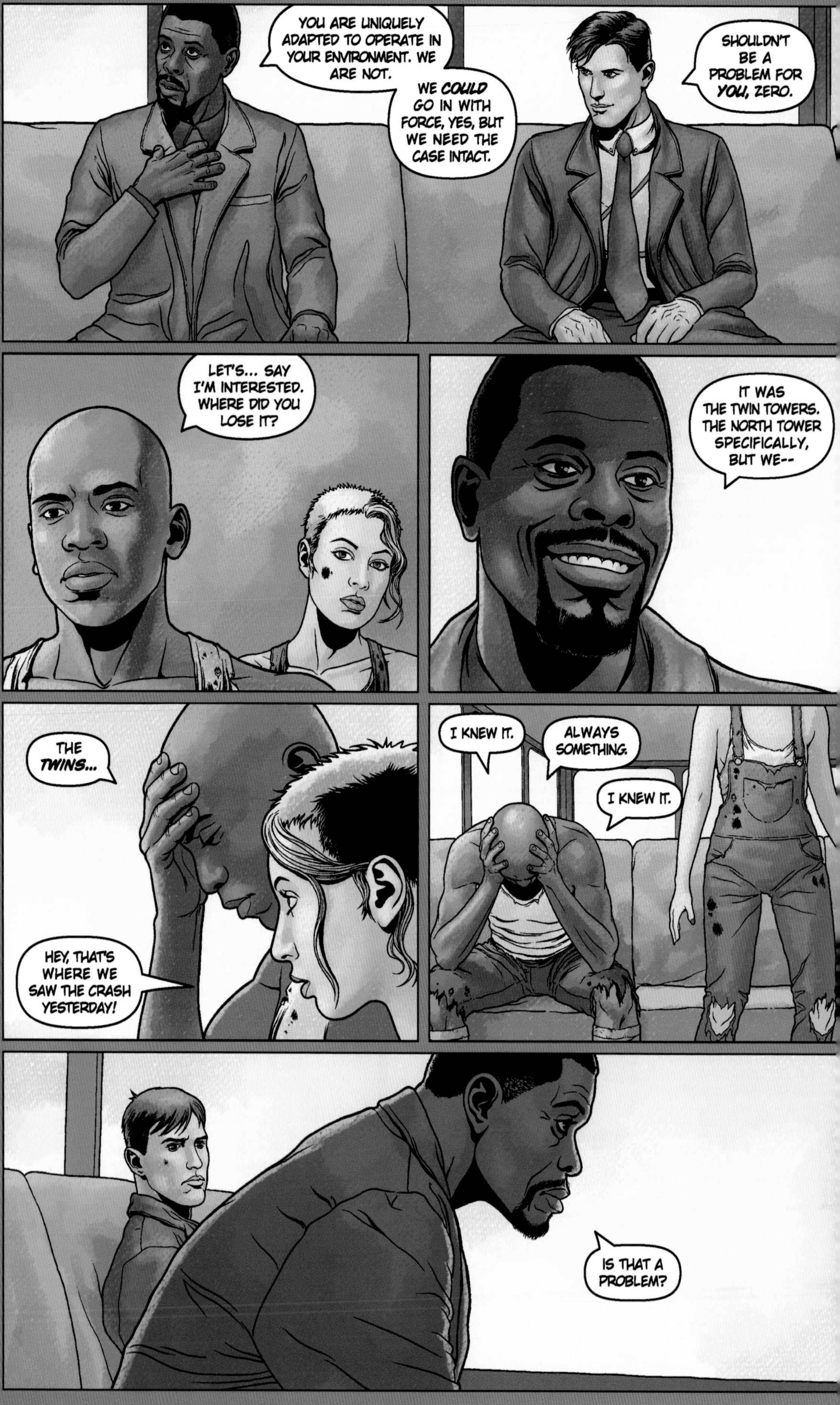
YOU ARE UNIQUELY ADAPTED TO OPERATE IN YOUR ENVIRONMENT. WE ARE NOT.
WE *COULD* GO IN WITH FORCE, YES, BUT WE NEED THE CASE INTACT.
SHOULDN'T BE A PROBLEM FOR *YOU,* ZERO.
LET'S... SAY I'M INTERESTED. WHERE DID YOU LOSE IT?
IT WAS THE TWIN TOWERS. THE NORTH TOWER SPECIFICALLY, BUT WE--
THE *TWINS...*
HEY, THAT'S WHERE WE SAW THE CRASH YESTERDAY!
I KNEW IT.
ALWAYS SOMETHING.
I KNEW IT.
IS THAT A PROBLEM?

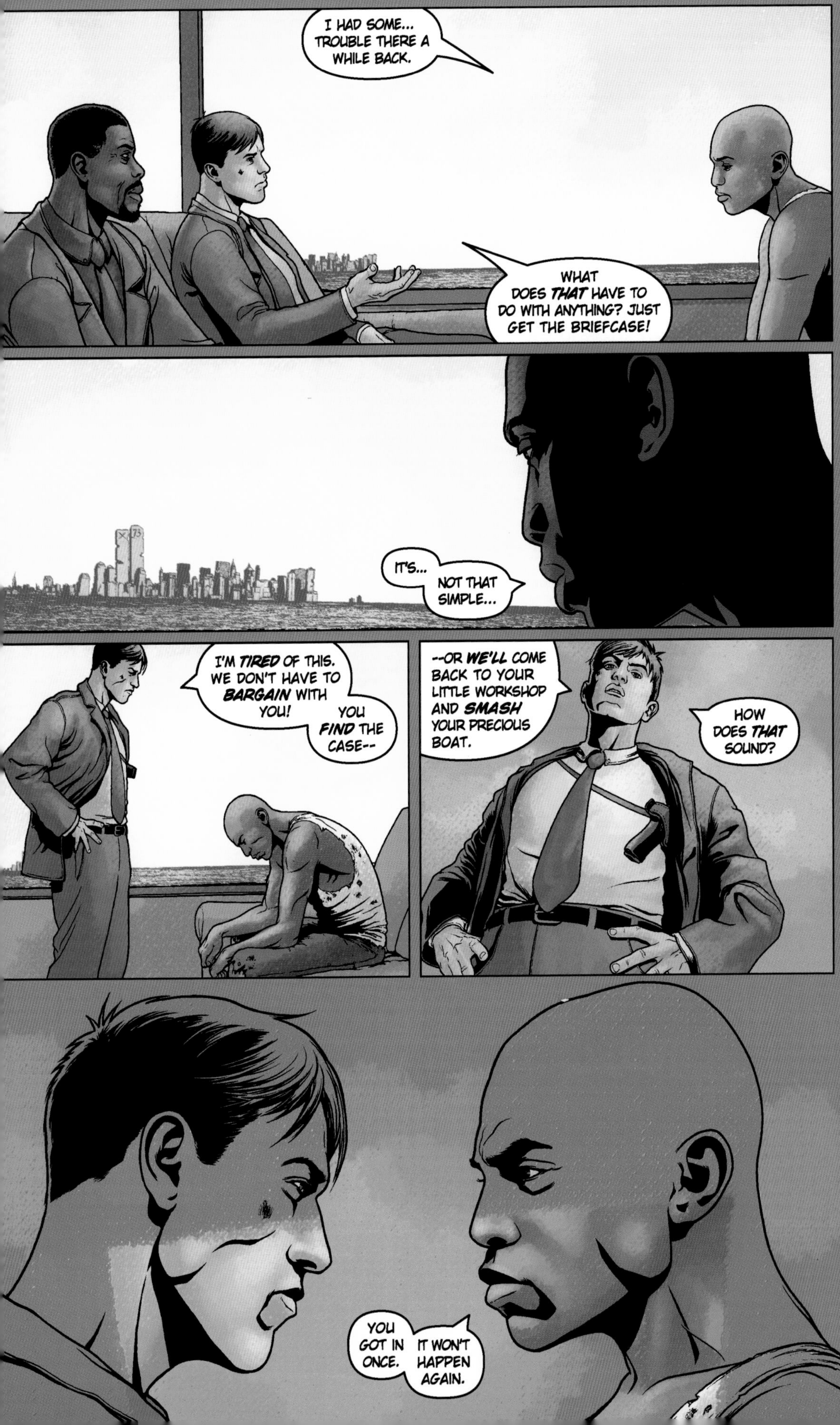
I HAD SOME... TROUBLE THERE A WHILE BACK.
WHAT DOES THAT HAVE TO DO WITH ANYTHING? JUST GET THE BRIEFCASE!
IT'S...
NOT THAT SIMPLE...
I'M TIRED OF THIS. WE DON'T HAVE TO BARGAIN WITH YOU!
YOU FIND THE CASE--
--OR WE'LL COME BACK TO YOUR LITTLE WORKSHOP AND SMASH YOUR PRECIOUS BOAT.
HOW DOES THAT SOUND?
YOU GOT IN ONCE.
IT WON'T HAPPEN AGAIN.

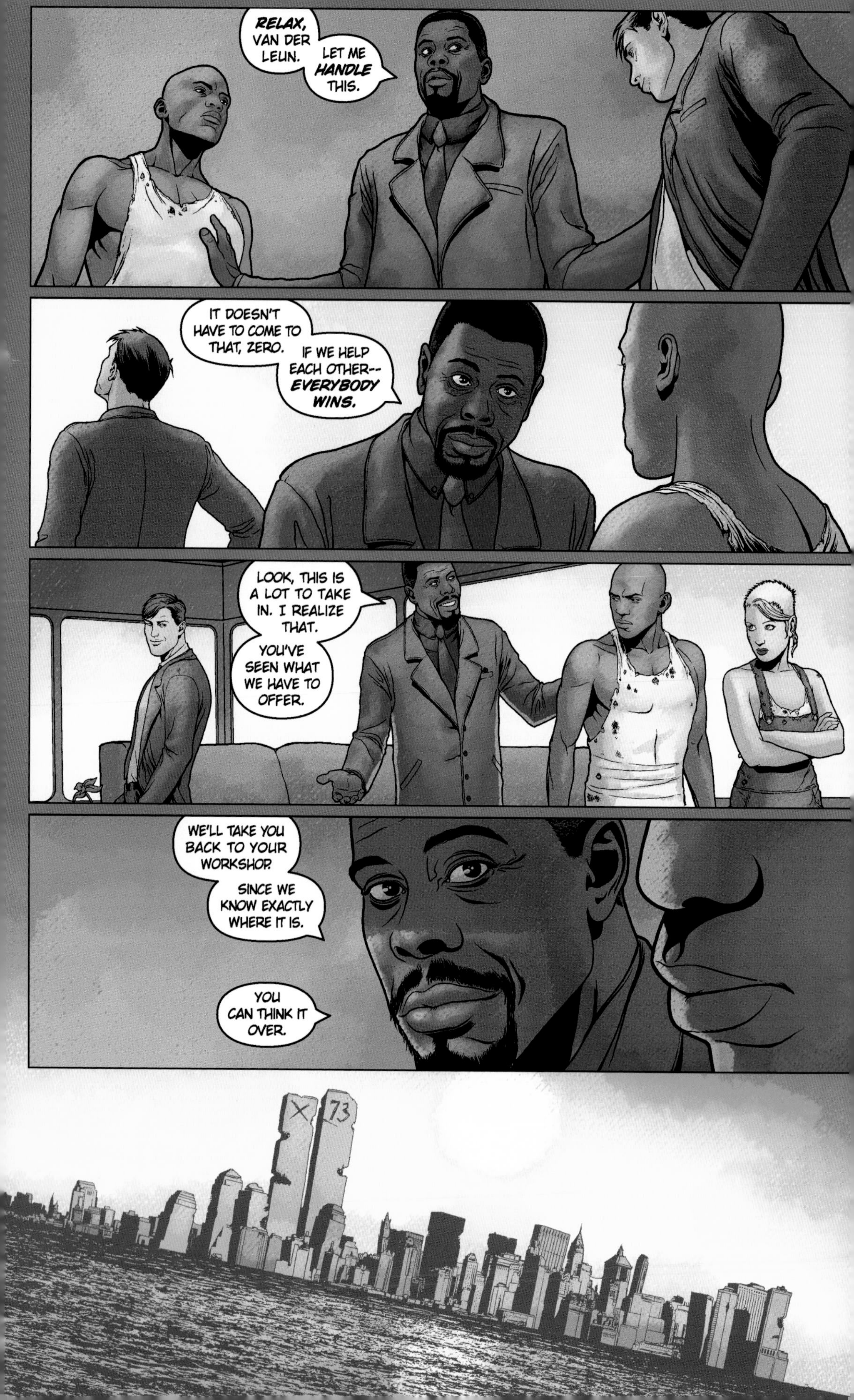

RELAX, VAN DER LEUN.
LET ME HANDLE THIS.
IT DOESN'T HAVE TO COME TO THAT, ZERO.
IF WE HELP EACH OTHER-- EVERYBODY WINS.
LOOK, THIS IS A LOT TO TAKE IN. I REALIZE THAT.
YOU'VE SEEN WHAT WE HAVE TO OFFER.
WE'LL TAKE YOU BACK TO YOUR WORKSHOP.
SINCE WE KNOW EXACTLY WHERE IT IS.
YOU CAN THINK IT OVER.
X
73

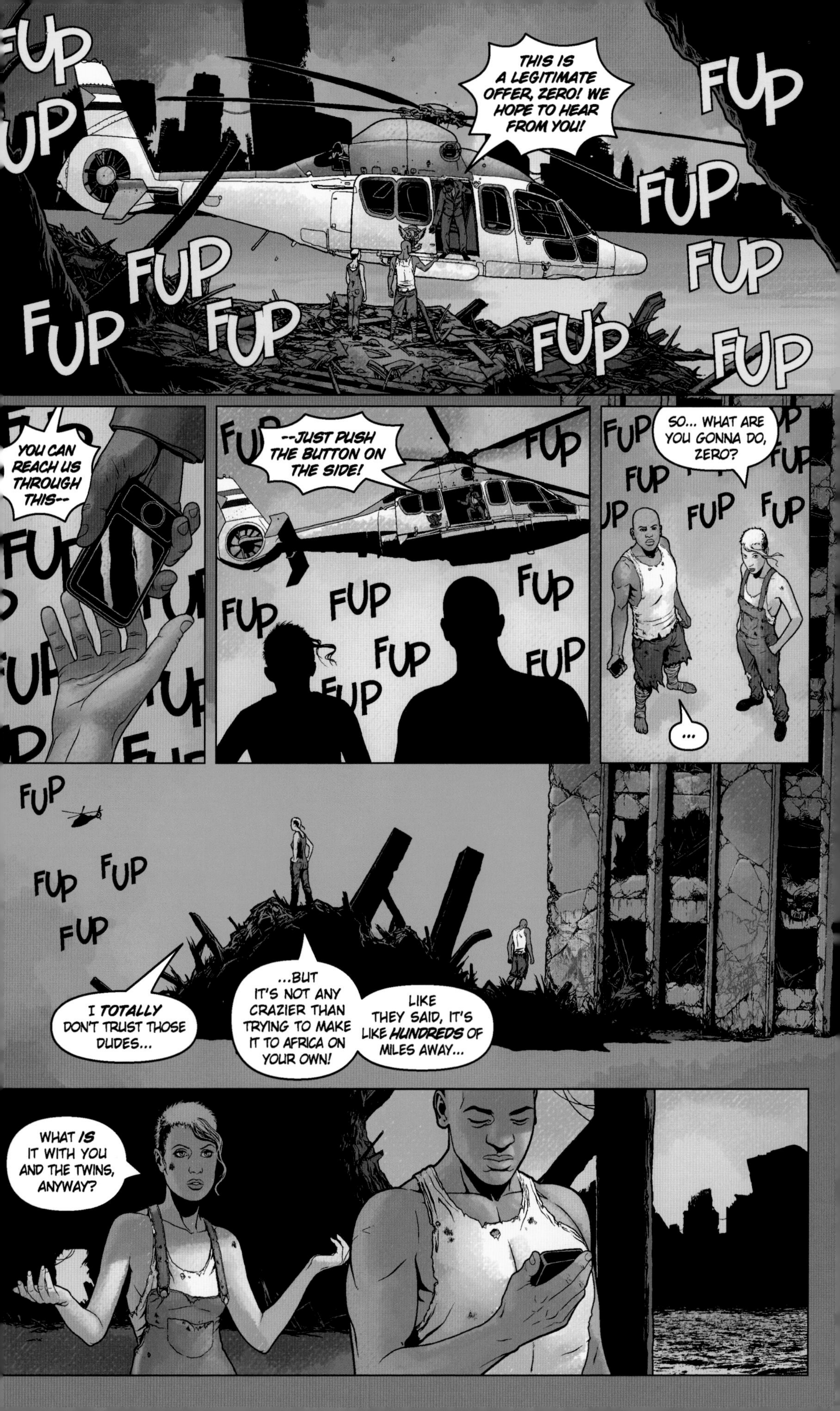
FUP
FUP
THIS IS A LEGITIMATE OFFER, ZERO! WE HOPE TO HEAR FROM YOU!
FUP
FUP
FUP
FUP
FUP
FUP
FUP
FUP
YOU CAN REACH US THROUGH THIS--
--JUST PUSH THE BUTTON ON THE SIDE!
FUP
FUP
FUP
FUP
FUP
FUP
SO... WHAT ARE YOU GONNA DO, ZERO?
FUP
FUP
FUP
...
FUP
FUP
FUP
FUP
I *TOTALLY* DON'T TRUST THOSE DUDES...
...BUT IT'S NOT ANY CRAZIER THAN TRYING TO MAKE IT TO AFRICA ON YOUR OWN!
LIKE THEY SAID, IT'S LIKE *HUNDREDS* OF MILES AWAY...
WHAT *IS* IT WITH YOU AND THE TWINS, ANYWAY?

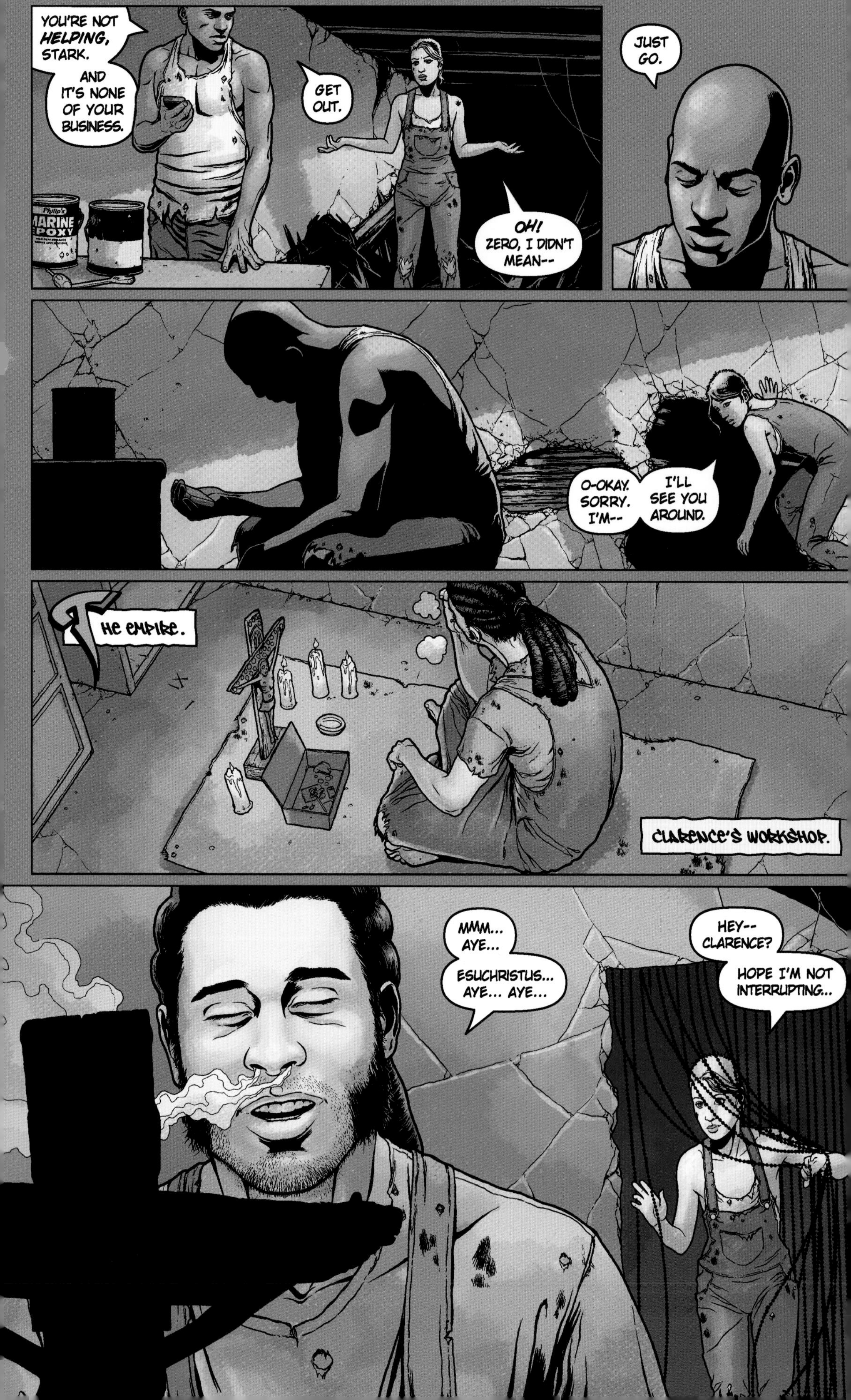

YOU'RE NOT HELPING, STARK.
AND IT'S NONE OF YOUR BUSINESS.
GET OUT.
OH! ZERO, I DIDN'T MEAN--
JUST GO.
Philip's MARINE EPOXY
O-OKAY. SORRY. I'M--
I'LL SEE YOU AROUND.
THE EMPIRE.
CLARENCE'S WORKSHOP.
MMM... AYE...
ESUCHRISTUS... AYE... AYE...
HEY-- CLARENCE?
HOPE I'M NOT INTERRUPTING...

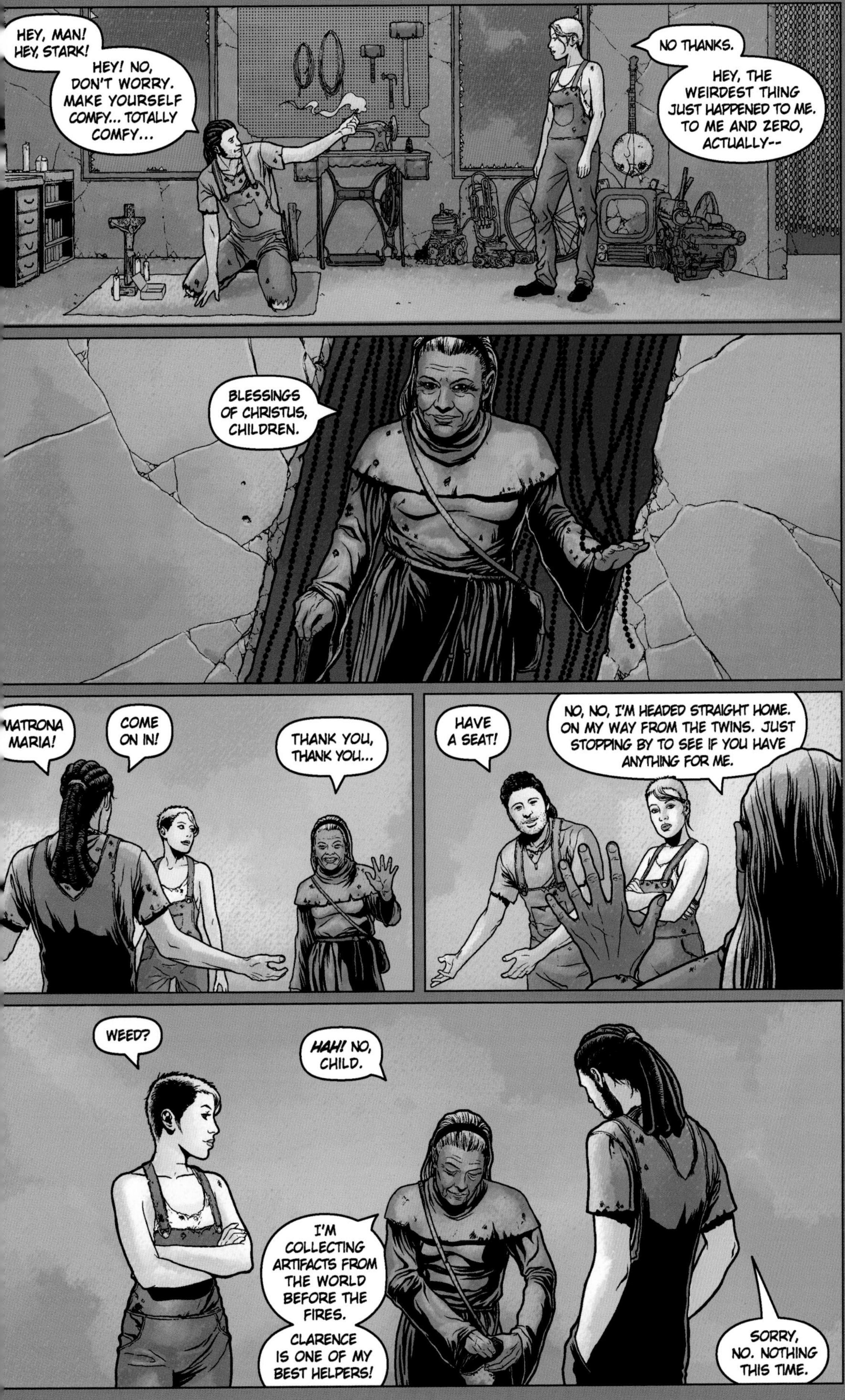
HEY, MAN! HEY, STARK!
HEY! NO, DON'T WORRY. MAKE YOURSELF COMFY... TOTALLY COMFY...
NO THANKS.
HEY, THE WEIRDEST THING JUST HAPPENED TO ME. TO ME AND ZERO, ACTUALLY--
BLESSINGS OF CHRISTUS, CHILDREN.
MATRONA MARIA!
COME ON IN!
THANK YOU, THANK YOU...
HAVE A SEAT!
NO, NO, I'M HEADED STRAIGHT HOME. ON MY WAY FROM THE TWINS. JUST STOPPING BY TO SEE IF YOU HAVE ANYTHING FOR ME.
WEED?
HAH! NO, CHILD.
I'M COLLECTING ARTIFACTS FROM THE WORLD BEFORE THE FIRES.
CLARENCE IS ONE OF MY BEST HELPERS!
SORRY, NO. NOTHING THIS TIME.

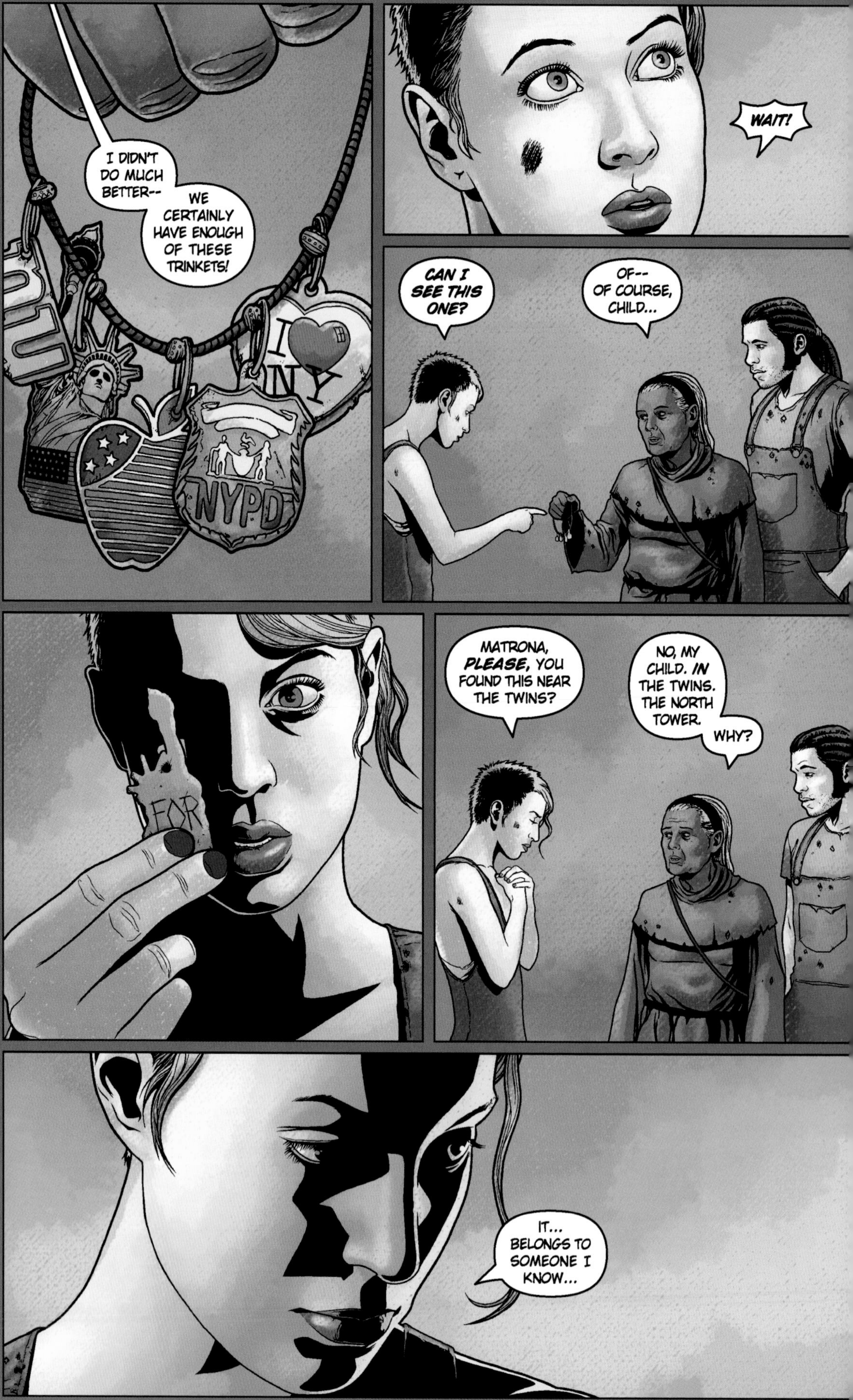
I DIDN'T DO MUCH BETTER--
WE CERTAINLY HAVE ENOUGH OF THESE TRINKETS!
I ♥ NY
NYPD
WAIT!
CAN I SEE THIS ONE?
OF-- OF COURSE, CHILD...
FOR
MATRONA, PLEASE, YOU FOUND THIS NEAR THE TWINS?
NO, MY CHILD. IN THE TWINS. THE NORTH TOWER.
WHY?
IT... BELONGS TO SOMEONE I KNOW...

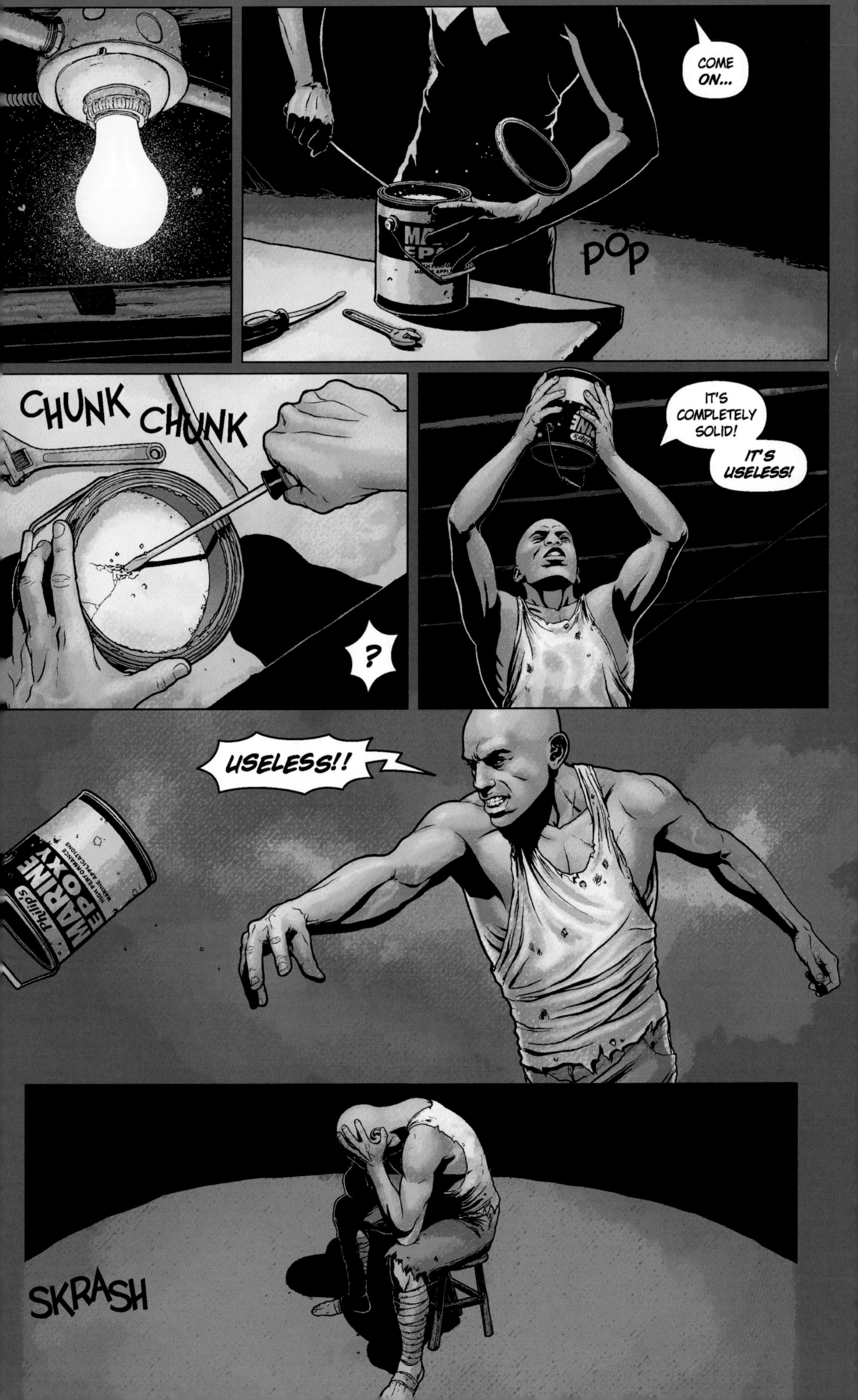

COME ON...
POP
CHUNK
CHUNK
?
IT'S COMPLETELY SOLID!
IT'S USELESS!
USELESS!!
Philip's MARINE EPOXY
HIGH PERFORMANCE
MARINE APPLICATIONS
SKRASH

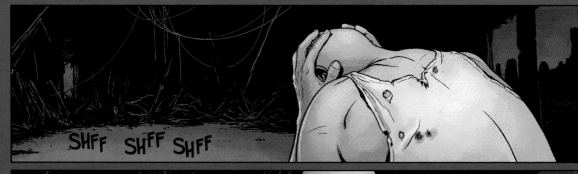

SHFF SHFF SHFF

SHFF SHFF SHFF

PLIp

SHFF SHFF SHFF

HEY, LITTLE BROTHER.

WHAT THE HELL DO I HAVE TO *DO?*

JUST GOT TO KEEP TRYING, THAT'S ALL.

BUT WE'VE *BEEN* TRYING!

I KNOW. I KNOW.

MAYBE THERE'S ANOTHER WAY.

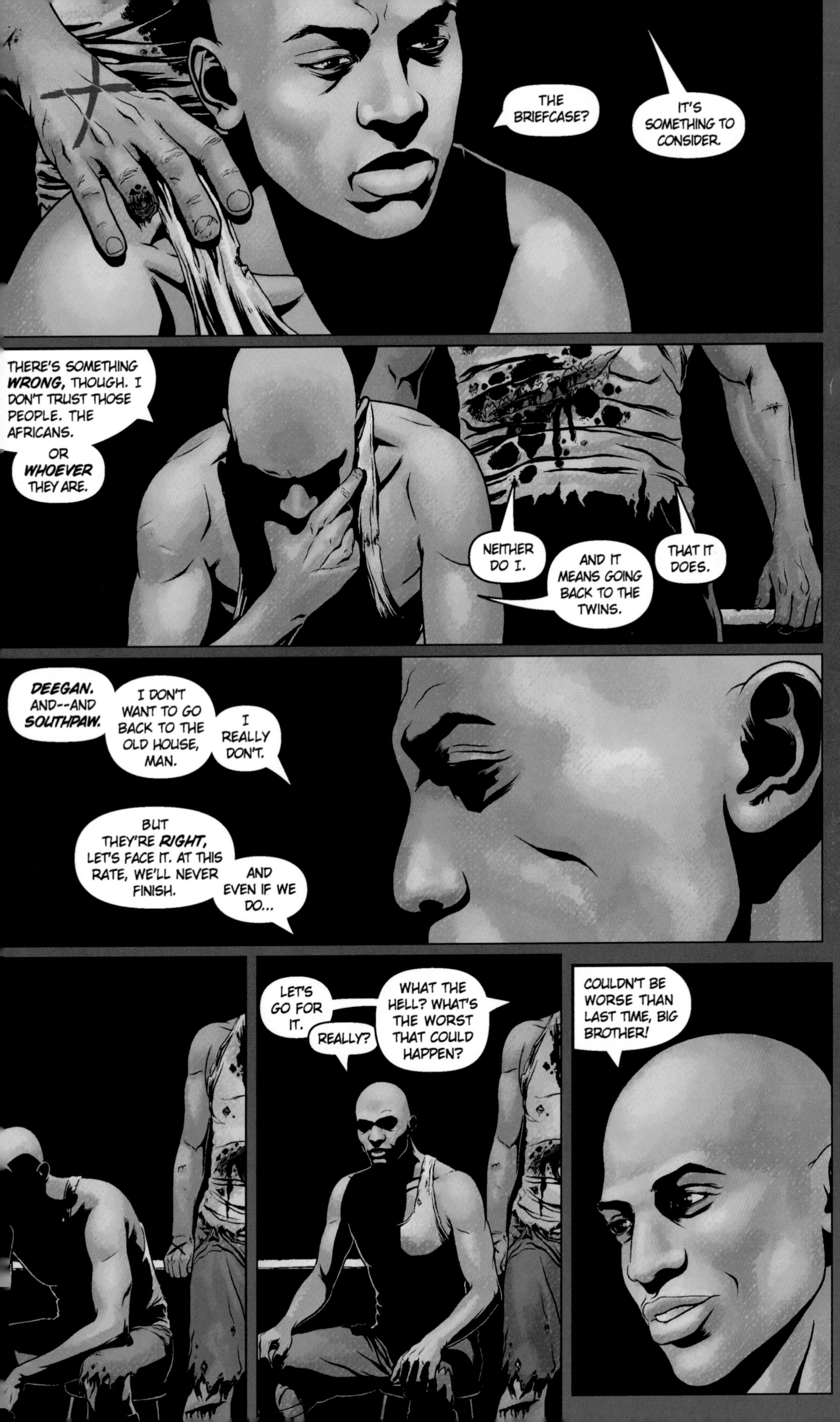
THE BRIEFCASE?
IT'S SOMETHING TO CONSIDER.
THERE'S SOMETHING WRONG, THOUGH. I DON'T TRUST THOSE PEOPLE. THE AFRICANS.
OR WHOEVER THEY ARE.
NEITHER DO I.
AND IT MEANS GOING BACK TO THE TWINS.
THAT IT DOES.
DEEGAN. AND--AND SOUTHPAW.
I DON'T WANT TO GO BACK TO THE OLD HOUSE, MAN.
I REALLY DON'T.
BUT THEY'RE RIGHT, LET'S FACE IT. AT THIS RATE, WE'LL NEVER FINISH.
AND EVEN IF WE DO...
LET'S GO FOR IT.
REALLY?
WHAT THE HELL? WHAT'S THE WORST THAT COULD HAPPEN?
COULDN'T BE WORSE THAN LAST TIME, BIG BROTHER!

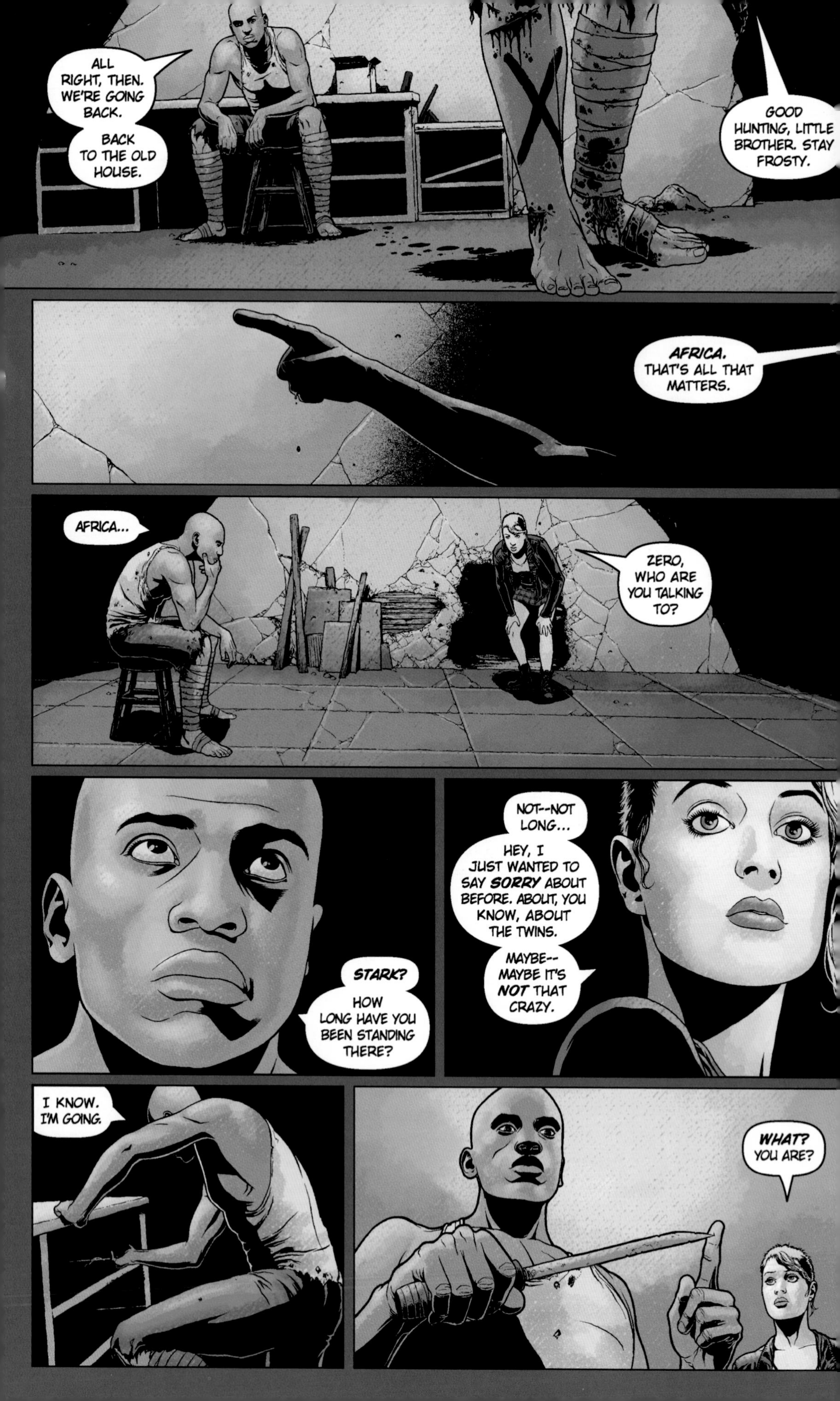
ALL RIGHT, THEN. WE'RE GOING BACK.
BACK TO THE OLD HOUSE.
GOOD HUNTING, LITTLE BROTHER. STAY FROSTY.
AFRICA. THAT'S ALL THAT MATTERS.
AFRICA...
ZERO, WHO ARE YOU TALKING TO?
STARK?
HOW LONG HAVE YOU BEEN STANDING THERE?
NOT--NOT LONG...
HEY, I JUST WANTED TO SAY SORRY ABOUT BEFORE. ABOUT, YOU KNOW, ABOUT THE TWINS.
MAYBE--MAYBE IT'S NOT THAT CRAZY.
I KNOW. I'M GOING.
WHAT? YOU ARE?

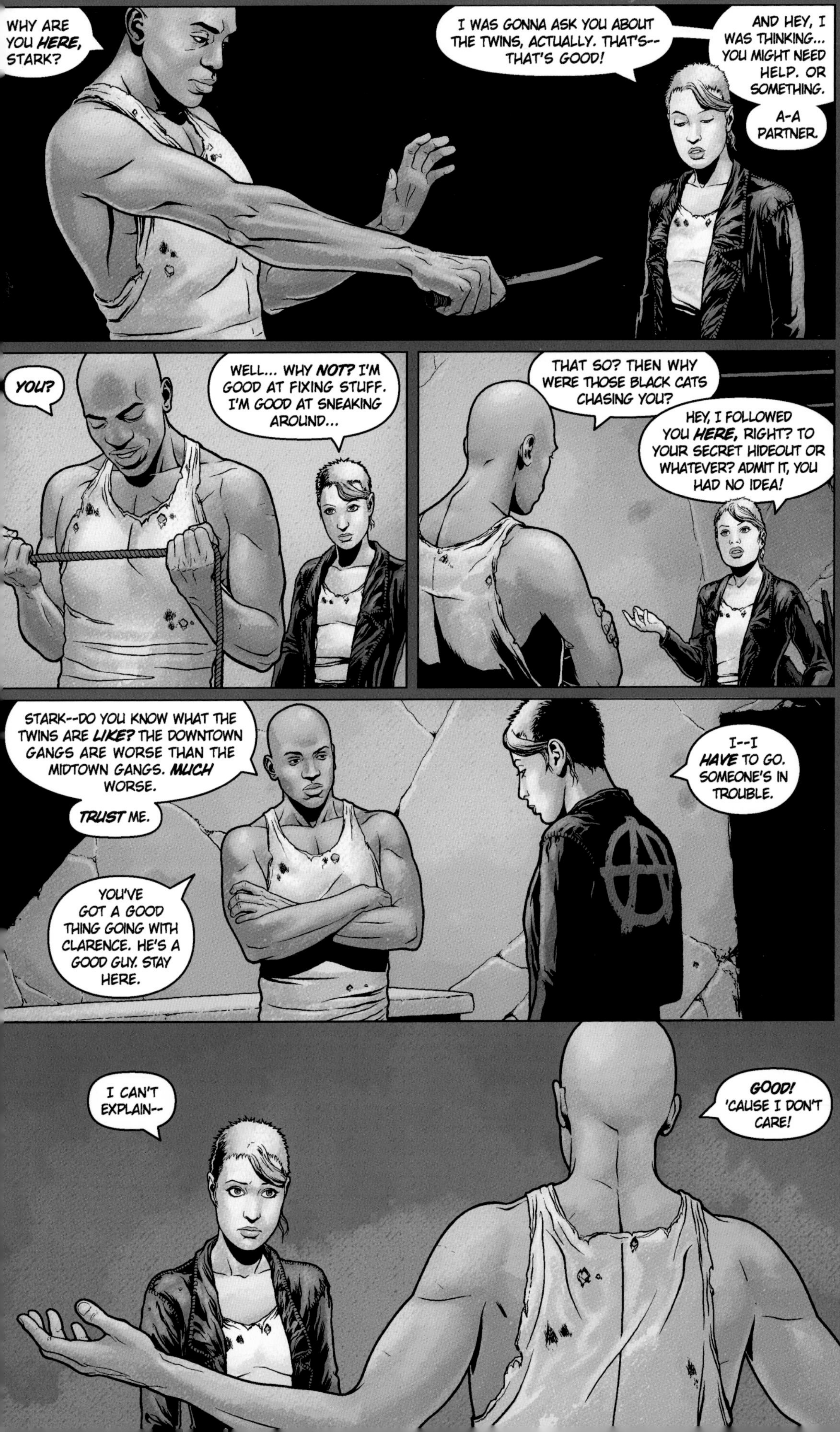
WHY ARE YOU *HERE*, STARK?
I WAS GONNA ASK YOU ABOUT THE TWINS, ACTUALLY. THAT'S-- THAT'S GOOD!
AND HEY, I WAS THINKING... YOU MIGHT NEED HELP. OR SOMETHING.
A-A PARTNER.
YOU?
WELL... WHY *NOT?* I'M GOOD AT FIXING STUFF. I'M GOOD AT SNEAKING AROUND...
THAT SO? THEN WHY WERE THOSE BLACK CATS CHASING YOU?
HEY, I FOLLOWED YOU *HERE*, RIGHT? TO YOUR SECRET HIDEOUT OR WHATEVER? ADMIT IT, YOU HAD NO IDEA!
STARK--DO YOU KNOW WHAT THE TWINS ARE *LIKE?* THE DOWNTOWN GANGS ARE WORSE THAN THE MIDTOWN GANGS. *MUCH* WORSE.
TRUST ME.
YOU'VE GOT A GOOD THING GOING WITH CLARENCE. HE'S A GOOD GUY. STAY HERE.
I--I *HAVE* TO GO. SOMEONE'S IN TROUBLE.
I CAN'T EXPLAIN--
GOOD! 'CAUSE I DON'T CARE!

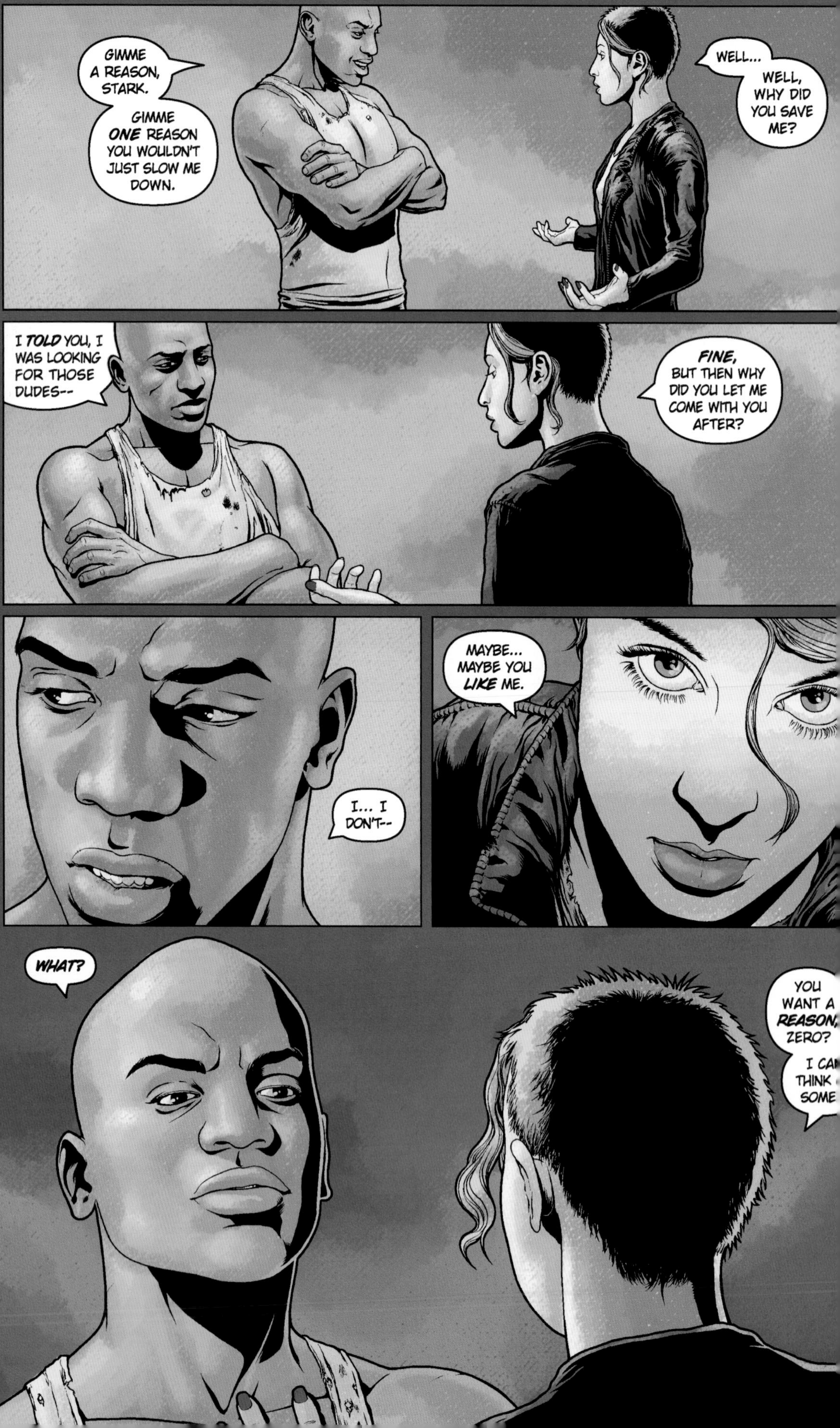
GIMME A REASON, STARK.
GIMME ONE REASON YOU WOULDN'T JUST SLOW ME DOWN.
WELL...
WELL, WHY DID YOU SAVE ME?
I TOLD YOU, I WAS LOOKING FOR THOSE DUDES--
FINE, BUT THEN WHY DID YOU LET ME COME WITH YOU AFTER?
I... I DON'T--
MAYBE... MAYBE YOU LIKE ME.
WHAT?
YOU WANT A REASON, ZERO?

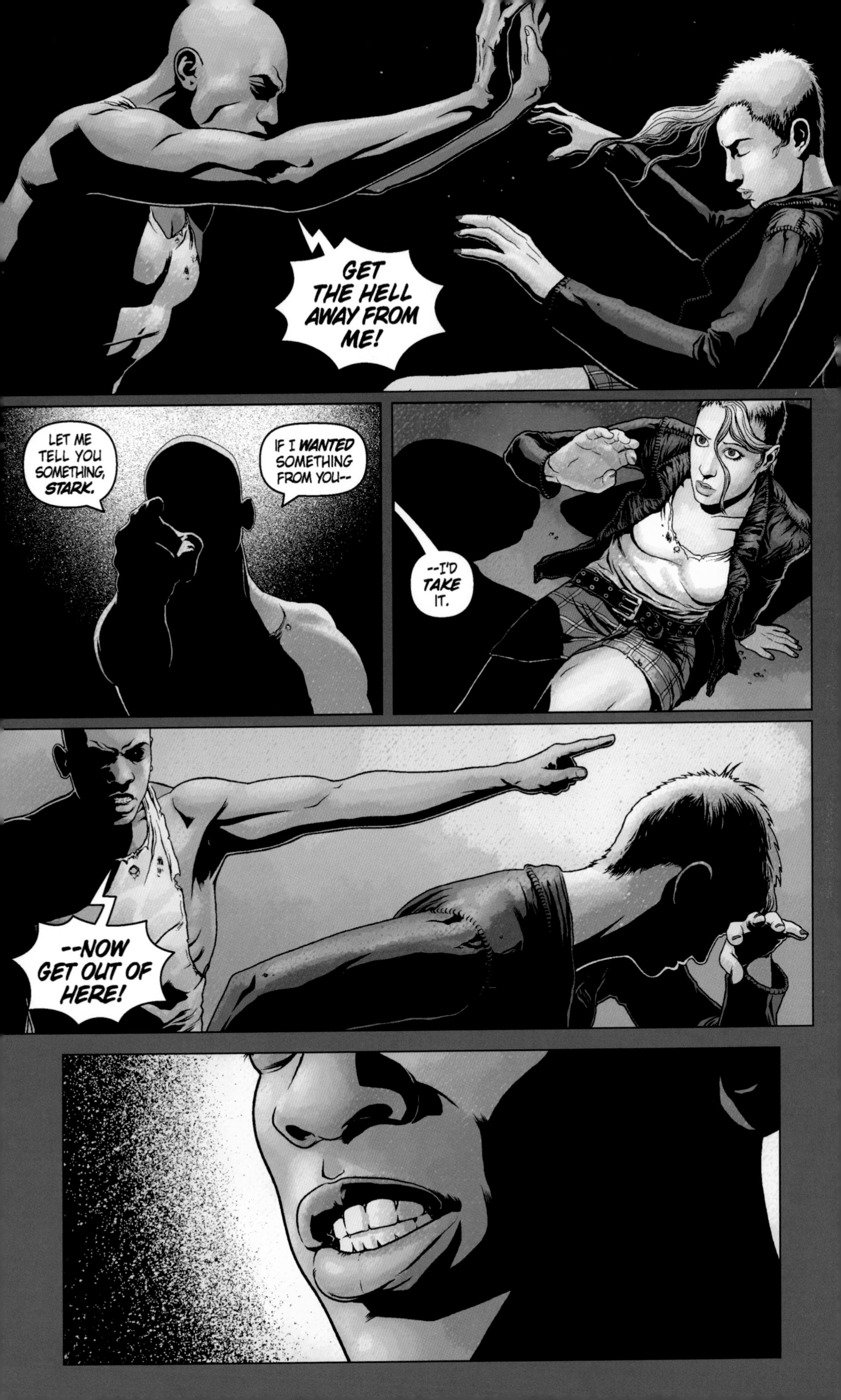
GET THE HELL AWAY FROM ME!
LET ME TELL YOU SOMETHING, STARK.
IF I WANTED SOMETHING FROM YOU--
--I'D TAKE IT.
--NOW GET OUT OF HERE!

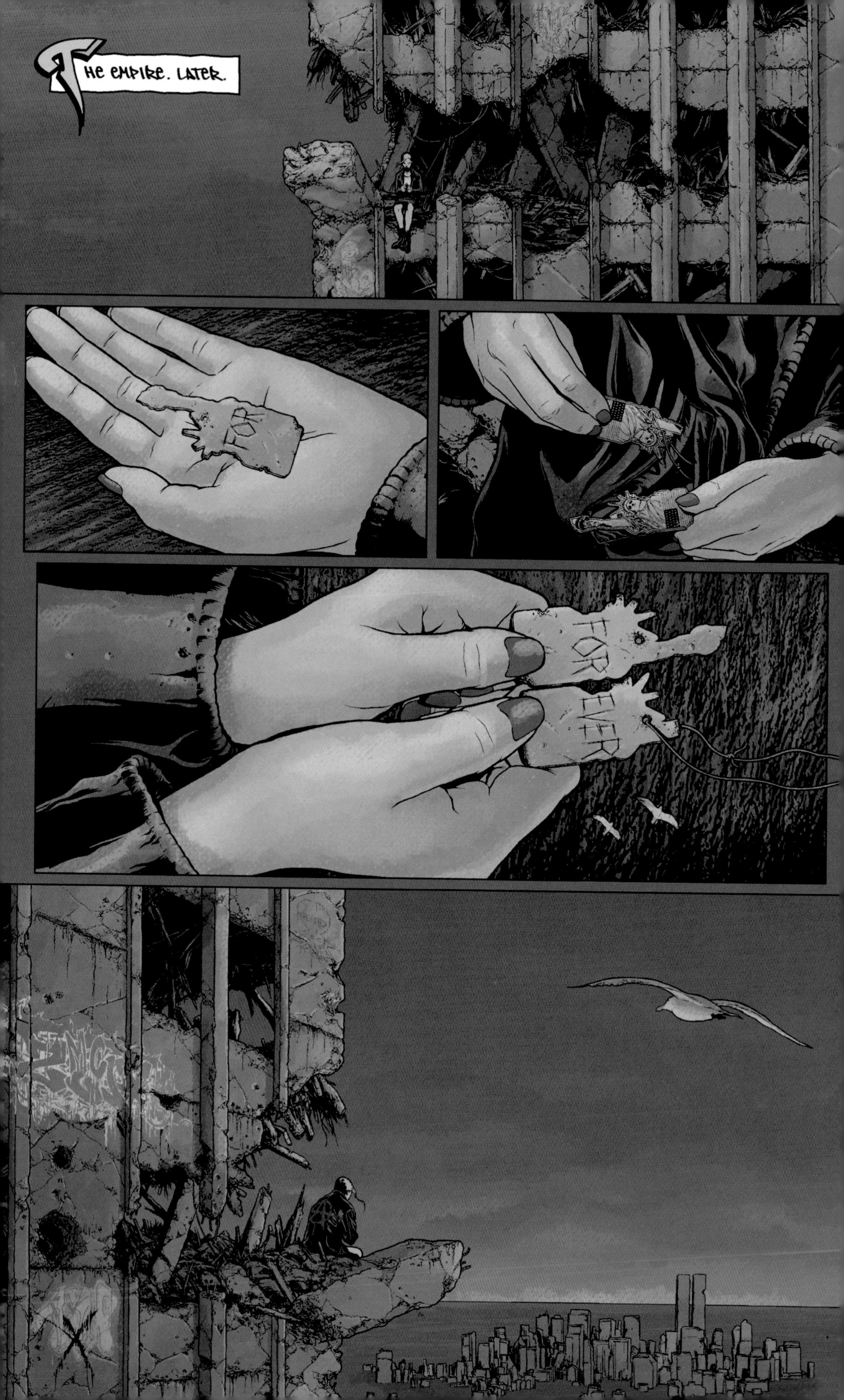
The empire. Later.
FOR
EVER

The JOCOM Daily ✦ Serving Those Who Serve ✦ July 20, 2007 ✦ Vol. 66, No. 16

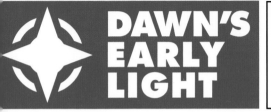

DAWN'S EARLY LIGHT

SARGE IS BACK!!

HE'LL ANSWER ***ALL*** THE TOUGHEST QUESTIONS FROM OUR BRAVE SOLDIERS IN A NEW EDITION OF HIS POPULAR "***LETTERS TO SARGE***" COLUMN!

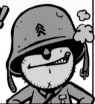

Sudanese Envoys to Meet Advanced Genetic Research Initiative Staff

. high-ranking delegation ·om the Emirate of Sudan meeting today with top of- cials from the Advanced ;enetic Research Initiative AGRI).

The substance of the talks ; a closely guarded secret, but ıvolves the "exchange of tech- ologies developed in AGRI .bs for access to raw materi- .s in Africa," Tony Snow, an .GRI spokesperson, said.

"This meeting is part of much broader strategic al- ance JOCOM is forging ʼith several African nations," now said.

Africa was spared the nu- lear holocaust that plunged ıe rest of the world in dark- ess in 1973.

"We had literally thou- ınds of contingency plans for nuclear exchange with the oviet Union. Turns out none f those plans included any :rikes on sub-Saharan Africa," John Bolton, a senior advisor to Joint Chiefs of Staff, said.

"Who could have guessed the Soviets forgot all about Africa, too?"

As a direct result, African nations, chief among them the Emirate of Sudan, have experienced an economic and cultural renaissance.

"It's hard to imagine, but before Zero Hour, Sudan was a total backwater, not the economic powerhouse it's poised to become," Douglas Feith, a military affairs coordinator for the Director of the Reconstruction of the United States of America (DRUSA), said.

"An unimpeded supply of oil is absolutely critical to all our goals, and there are huge reserves of the stuff in Sudan and off the coast of Nigeria," Bolton said.

The vast oil reserves in the Middle East were rendered useless in 1973 because of severe radioactive contamination. "Africa is the only game in town," Bolton said. "Fortunately, when 95 percent of the population of the United States was wiped out, so was 95 percent of our oil needs."

Richard Cheney, executive director of AGRI, denied rumors the meeting with the Sudanese envoy was convened in response to unforeseen complications arising from an earlier agreement.

"I consider rumor-mongering of this type to be treason of the highest order," he said.

"Our friends and allies in Africa desire access to the technological innovations we have pioneered in our underground research facilities," Cheney said. "We desire oil and raw materials with which to rebuild America. It's as simple as that." ✦

Cause of Downed Black Hawk Remains Mystery

No answers have surfaced in an investigation into a daring guerrilla attack that claimed a Black Hawk helicopter and the lives of its occupants yesterday.

A newly minted investigative task force has visited the crash site but uncovered few clues, according to Lt. Colonel Daniel Jackson, a spokesman for the Defense Intelligence agency.

"As with most forensic investigations in New York, what little physical evidence might have been present had been contaminated by the elements and by scavenger folk long before we arrived," Jackson said.

He declined to speculate as to whether the perpetrators of the attack had access to technologically sophisticated weaponry, or what their goal might have been.

In response to the attack, the Office of the Joint Chiefs of Staff ordered a more aggressive force posture for all future missions into New York.

"The tower dwellers are vicious and cunning," Gen. Tommy Franks, JOCOM-A Chief of Staff, said. "Until further notice, we have adopted a 'shoot on sight' policy to prevent any more losses of this kind."

Although rarely successful, attacks on helicopters patrolling the skies of New York are a common ordeal. ✦

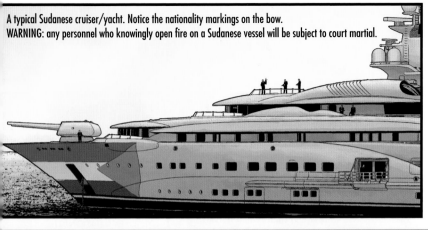

A typical Sudanese cruiser/yacht. Notice the nationality markings on the bow.
WARNING: any personnel who knowingly open fire on a Sudanese vessel will be subject to court martial.

Dear Sarge,

I received an order from a superior officer, but I'm having moral qualms about following it. What's the right course of action?

Sincerely,
Confused Specialist, JOCOM-A

KEEP THE FOLLOWING INTEL IN THE FRONT OF YOUR MIND AT ALL TIMES, **SPECIAL-IST!** SUPERIOR OFFICERS ARE AUTHORIZED TO **SHOOT** SUBORDINATES WHO REFUSE TO COMPLY WITH DIRECT ORDERS. THE FIGHTING MEN OF JOCOM **CANNOT AFFORD** THE LUXURY OF "MORAL QUALMS." SO NEVER QUESTION THE ORDERS OF A SUPERIOR OFFICER--**EVER!**

Dear Sarge,

I'm beginning to develop strange feelings for a particular female in the fertility crèches. She is very special to me, and I think I could share my life with her. Is this possible?

Sincerely,
Dreamy-Eyed Corporal, JOCOM-N/a

ABSOLUTELY NOT! THE FEELING YOU'RE DESCRIBING IS CALLED "LOVE," AND IT'S ANOTHER ONE OF THOSE LUX-URIES WE **JOCOM** WARRIORS CANNOT AFFORD. FORMING INTIMATE RELATIONSHIPS WITH YOUR FEMALE QUOTA IS **STRICTLY FORBIDDEN** AND COULD EARN YOU A COURT MARTIAL. IF YOU **MUST** HAVE COMPANIONSHIP, SEE YOUR BARRACKS QUARTERMASTER. HE MIGHT BE ABLE TO PROVIDE YOU WITH A DOG.

Dear Sarge,

I understand that, as the only hope for repopulating the Earth with a freedom-loving, democratic society, we have to take drastic measures when it comes to procreation. But I'm also troubled, because I try to lead a Christian life. So I have to ask: is our treatment of women in accordance with the Bible?

Sincerely,
Concerned 1st Lieutenant, JOCOM-F

OF COURSE IT IS! HOW MANY WIVES DID SOLOMON HAVE, AFTER ALL? AND WHAT ABOUT ABRAHAM AND LOT? IN DESPERATE TIMES, THE LORD UNDERSTANDS WE **MUST BEND THE RULES**, AND OUR SCIENTISTS FIGURE THE **FER-TILITY CRÈCHES** ARE THE BEST WAY TO MAINTAIN OUR GOALS FOR POPULATION GROWTH. REST ASSURED YOU ARE LIVING A LIFE WHOLLY COMPATIBLE WITH THE TEACHINGS OF THE BIBLE.

Dear Sarge,

What's the fastest way to earn a promotion?

Sincerely,
Ambitious Warrant Officer, JOCOM-N

REMEMBER ALL THE **TESTS** YOU TOOK RIGHT AFTER ENTER-ING SERVICE? THE PSYCH CORPS COOKED THOSE UP TO MEASURE EVERYTHING FROM INTELLIGENCE TO AGGRESSION TO SEXUAL POTENCY. YOUR SCORES ON THOSE TESTS, AND YOUR SERVICE RECORD, ARE THE MOST IMPORTANT THINGS WHEN DETERMINING ELIGIBIL-ITY FOR PROMOTION. YOU ARE **NOT** ALLOWED TO KNOW YOUR SCORES, BUT **DON'T WORRY!** THE TESTS ARE EXTREMELY ACCURATE.

Dear Sarge,

A few weeks ago, my best buddy died. We were squad mates, on a harvesting mission in the ruins of the Woolworth building, and we walked right into an ambush. One of the guys in the squad, Ramirez, died right there, he took an arrow or something right in the neck. He was lucky.

The tower people took all our weap-ons and tied us up. Then they dragged us really deep in the building, I don't know how many turns we made, whether we went up or down, because I took a hard knock on the head and was bleeding pretty bad.

Finally, we stopped in a room with all these knives and machetes on the wall. Just for fun, the tower people decided to torture us. My buddy got taken apart right before my eyes. They start-ed with his nose, then his crotch, then on to his arms, and then his legs. He was screaming goddawful the whole time until finally the noises just kind of died down and he had this faraway look in his eyes. I kept hearing some-one saying, "Hang in there, buddy, hang in there." After a while I realized it was me. Then I realized my buddy was dead.

I was about to get the same treatment but the backup squad arrived just in time. They killed the bastards tortur-ing us, except for one. They kept one alive so I could return the favor for what they did to my buddy. Believe me, by the time I was done he wished he'd never messed with JOCOM.

But now I'm having problems sleep-ing. Every time I close my eyes I see my buddy getting chopped up alive. I'm having weird thoughts, too, like sometimes I really want to hurt my-self—or someone else. I think I'm go-ing crazy living underground all the time. The fertility crèches don't help, either. I just want to kill everyone and everything, even the guys in my bat-talion. So far I haven't done anything but I'm getting scared because I don't know if I can fight it anymore. What do I do?

Sincerely,
Disturbed Private, JOCOM-A

SEE THE CARING STAFF IN THE MEDI-CAL CORPS FOR A COMPLETE PSYCH EVALUATION! THEY'LL GIVE YOU THE MEDS YOU NEED TO FEEL 100% AGAIN. YOU ARE **NOT** ALONE!

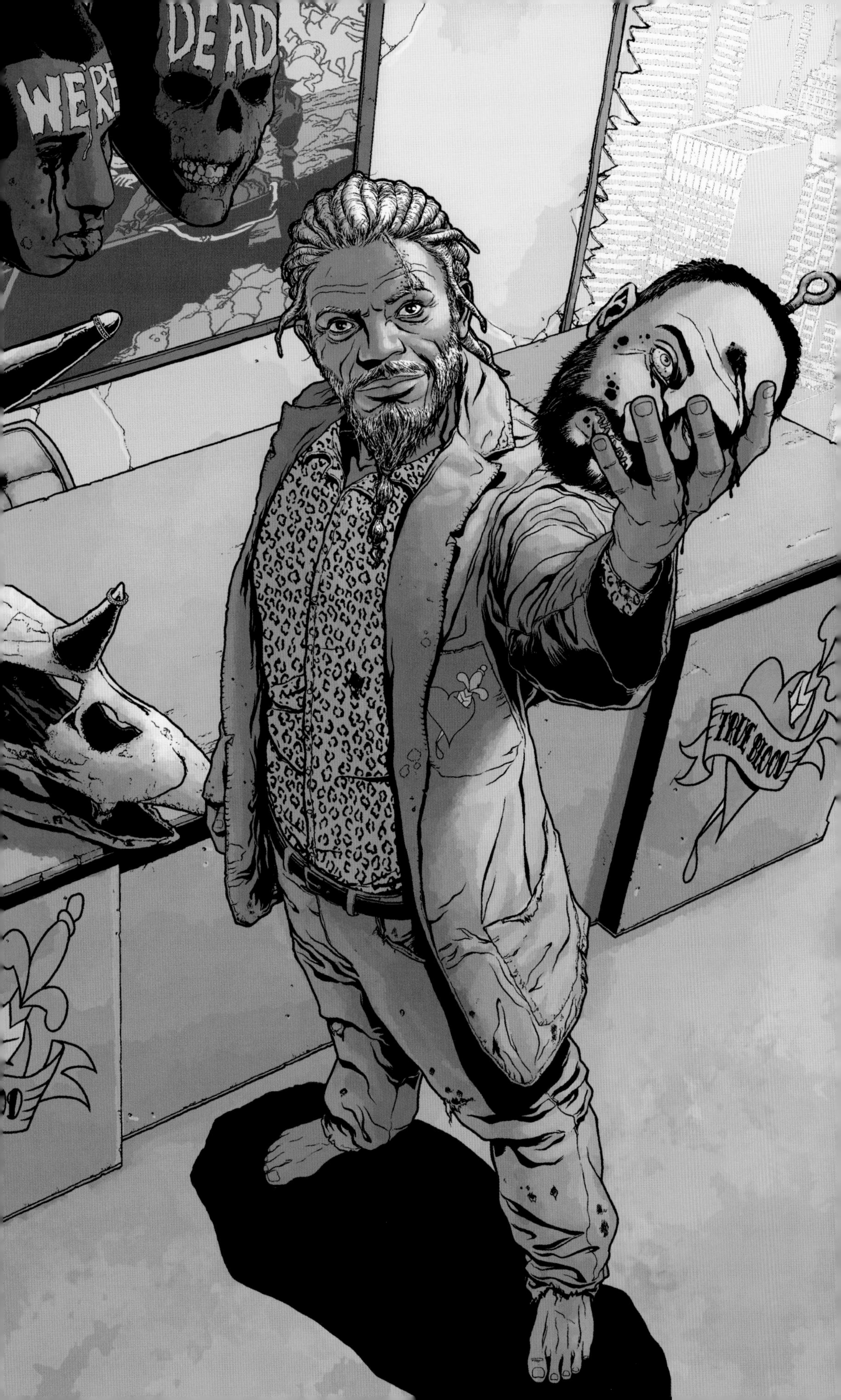

WE'RE
DEAD
TRUE BLOOD

ZEROKILLER

CHAPTER 4
LI'L RASCALS

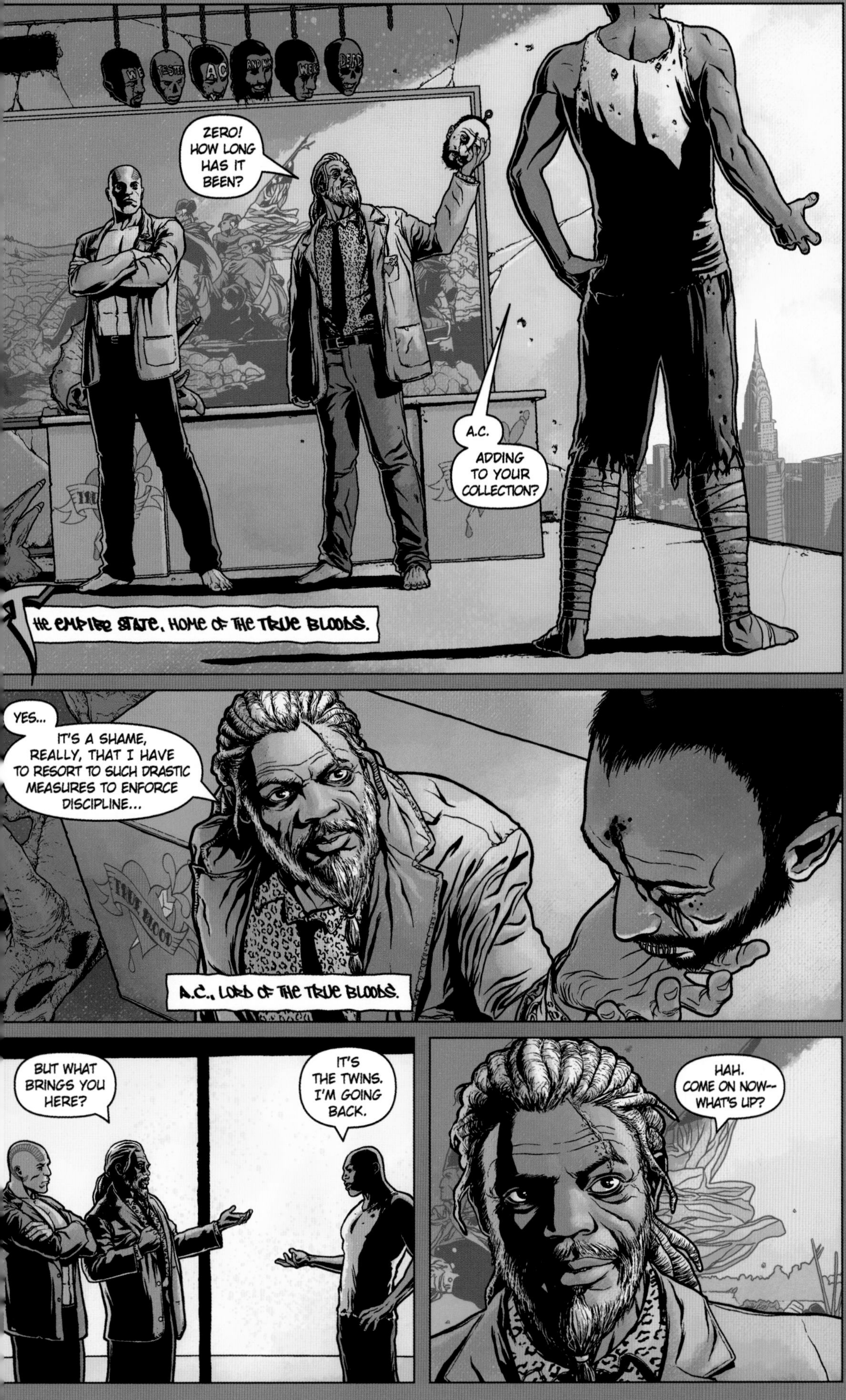
WE
AC
AND NOW
DEAD
ZERO! HOW LONG HAS IT BEEN?
A.C.
ADDING TO YOUR COLLECTION?
THE EMPIRE STATE. HOME OF THE TRUE BLOODS.
YES...
IT'S A SHAME, REALLY, THAT I HAVE TO RESORT TO SUCH DRASTIC MEASURES TO ENFORCE DISCIPLINE...
A.C., LORD OF THE TRUE BLOODS.
BUT WHAT BRINGS YOU HERE?
IT'S THE TWINS. I'M GOING BACK.
HAH. COME ON NOW-- WHAT'S UP?

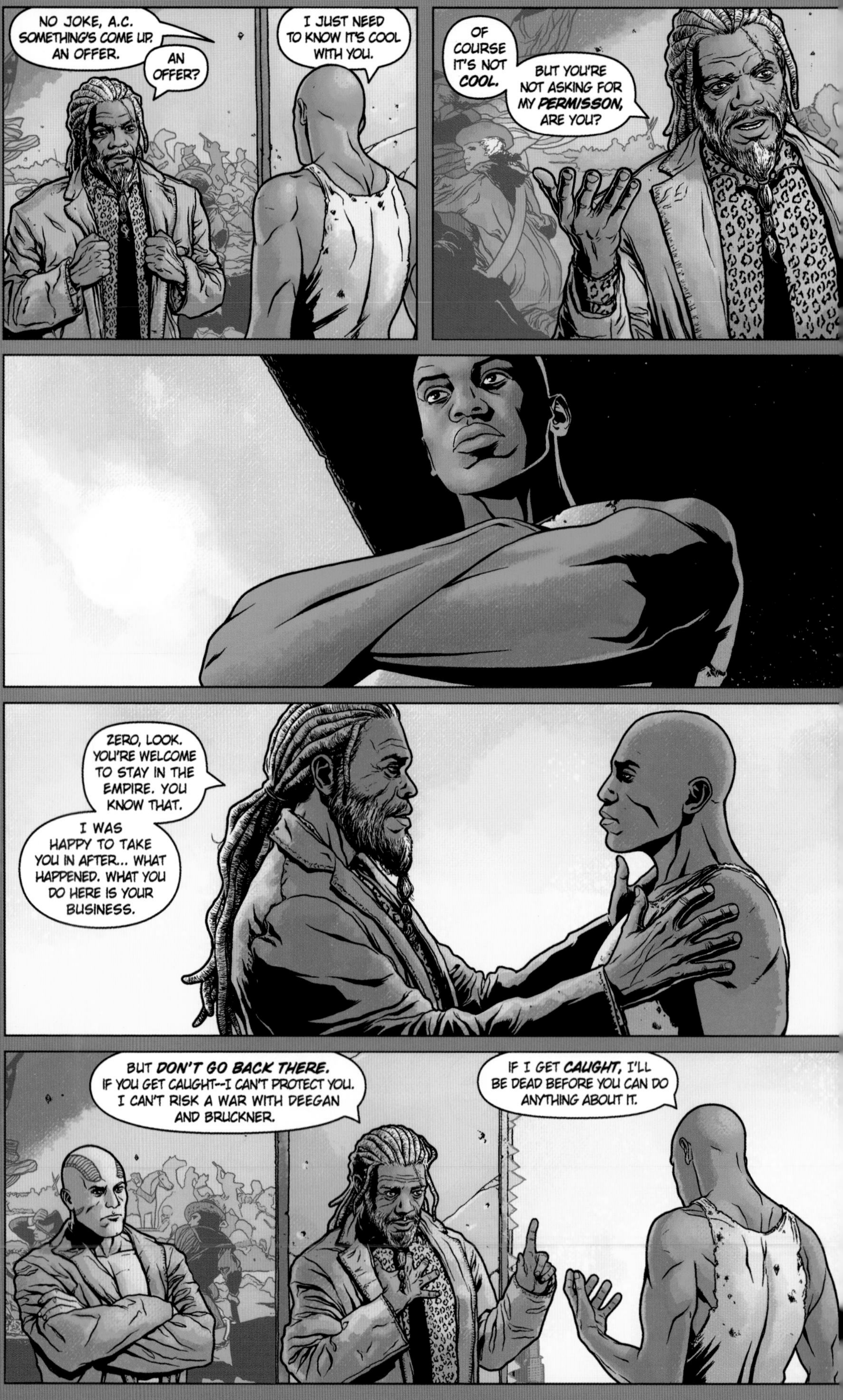
NO JOKE, A.C. SOMETHING'S COME UP. AN OFFER.
AN OFFER?
I JUST NEED TO KNOW IT'S COOL WITH YOU.
OF COURSE IT'S NOT COOL.
BUT YOU'RE NOT ASKING FOR MY PERMISSON, ARE YOU?
ZERO, LOOK. YOU'RE WELCOME TO STAY IN THE EMPIRE. YOU KNOW THAT.
I WAS HAPPY TO TAKE YOU IN AFTER... WHAT HAPPENED. WHAT YOU DO HERE IS YOUR BUSINESS.
BUT DON'T GO BACK THERE. IF YOU GET CAUGHT--I CAN'T PROTECT YOU. I CAN'T RISK A WAR WITH DEEGAN AND BRUCKNER.
IF I GET CAUGHT, I'LL BE DEAD BEFORE YOU CAN DO ANYTHING ABOUT IT.

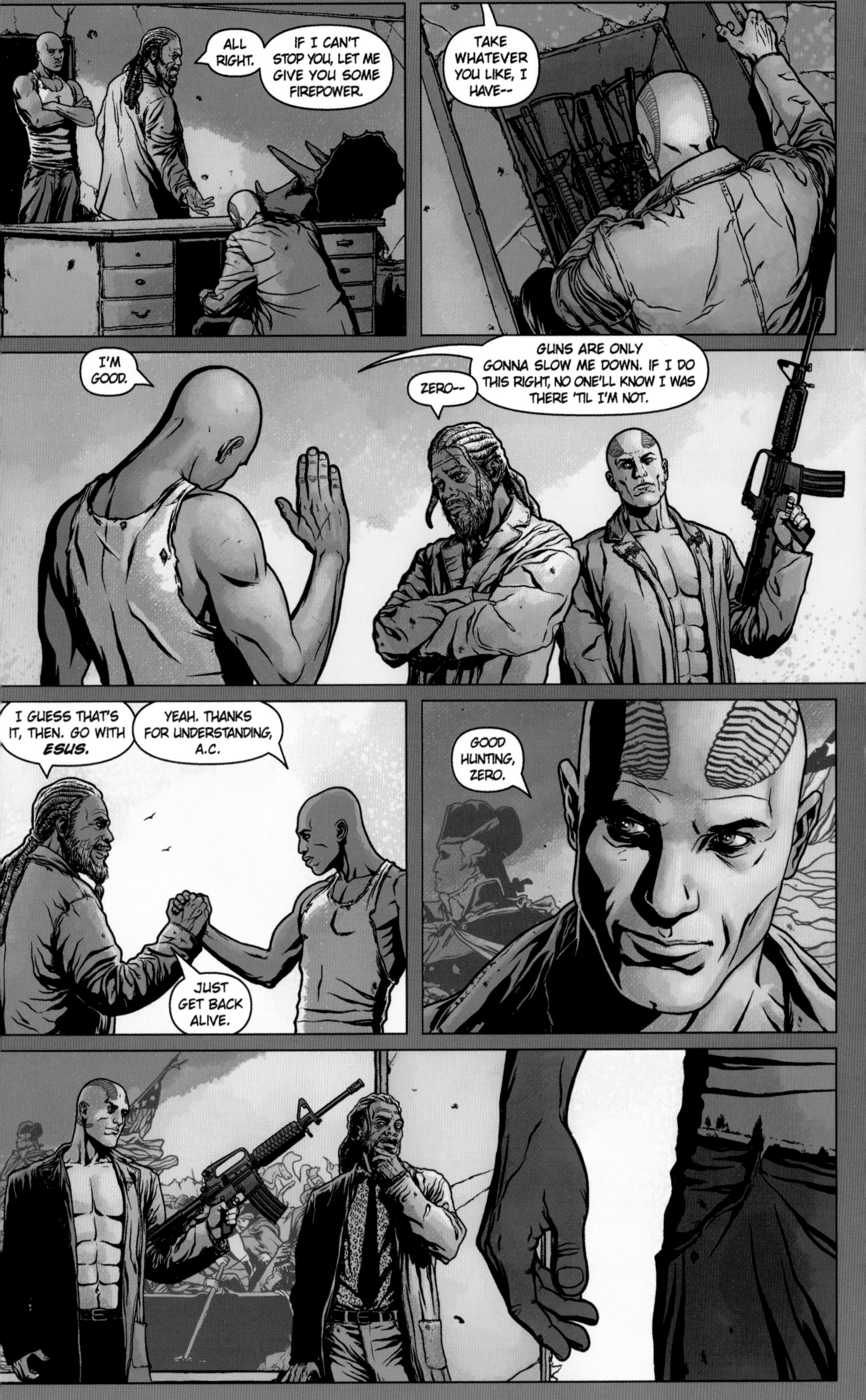

ALL RIGHT.
IF I CAN'T STOP YOU, LET ME GIVE YOU SOME FIREPOWER.
TAKE WHATEVER YOU LIKE, I HAVE--
I'M GOOD.
ZERO--
GUNS ARE ONLY GONNA SLOW ME DOWN. IF I DO THIS RIGHT, NO ONE'LL KNOW I WAS THERE 'TIL I'M NOT.
I GUESS THAT'S IT, THEN. GO WITH ESUS.
YEAH. THANKS FOR UNDERSTANDING, A.C.
JUST GET BACK ALIVE.
GOOD HUNTING, ZERO.

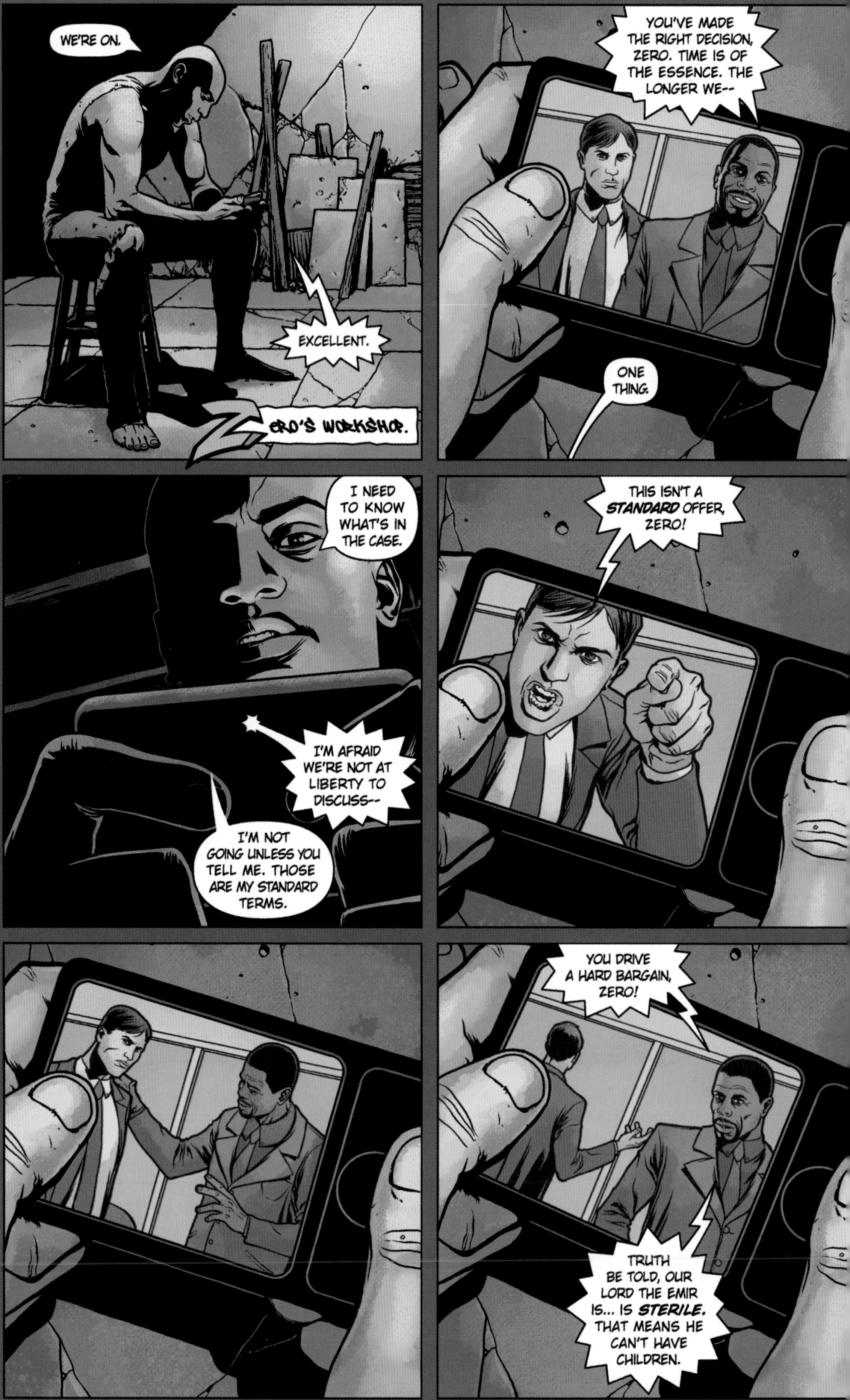
WE'RE ON.
EXCELLENT.
ZERO'S WORKSHOP.
YOU'VE MADE THE RIGHT DECISION, ZERO. TIME IS OF THE ESSENCE. THE LONGER WE--
ONE THING.
I NEED TO KNOW WHAT'S IN THE CASE.
I'M AFRAID WE'RE NOT AT LIBERTY TO DISCUSS--
I'M NOT GOING UNLESS YOU TELL ME. THOSE ARE MY STANDARD TERMS.
THIS ISN'T A STANDARD OFFER, ZERO!
YOU DRIVE A HARD BARGAIN, ZERO!
TRUTH BE TOLD, OUR LORD THE EMIR IS... IS STERILE. THAT MEANS HE CAN'T HAVE CHILDREN.

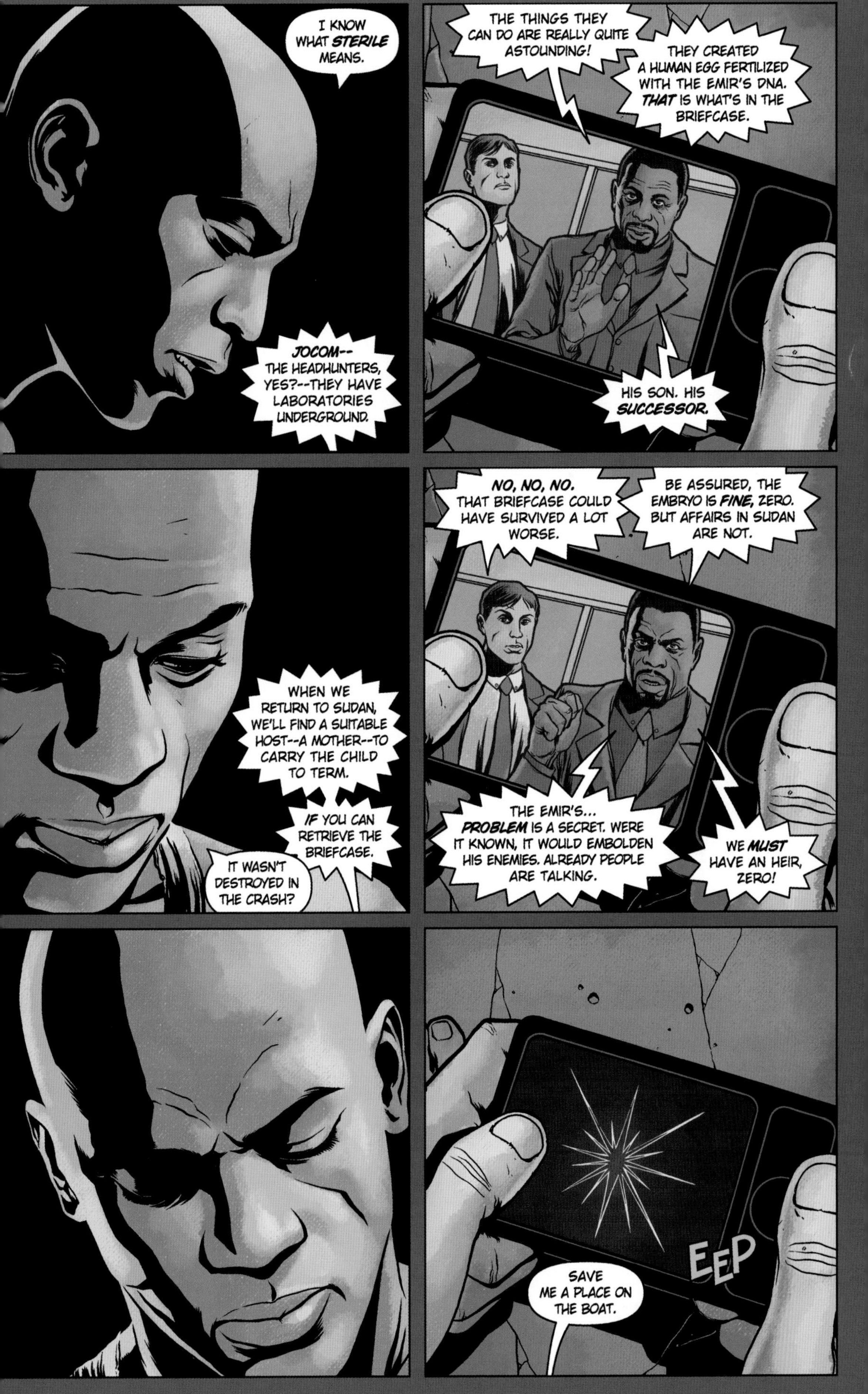

I KNOW WHAT **STERILE** MEANS.
THE THINGS THEY CAN DO ARE REALLY QUITE ASTOUNDING!
THEY CREATED A HUMAN EGG FERTILIZED WITH THE EMIR'S DNA. **THAT** IS WHAT'S IN THE BRIEFCASE.
JOCOM-- THE HEADHUNTERS, YES?--THEY HAVE LABORATORIES UNDERGROUND.
HIS SON. HIS **SUCCESSOR.**
WHEN WE RETURN TO SUDAN, WE'LL FIND A SUITABLE HOST--A MOTHER--TO CARRY THE CHILD TO TERM.
IF YOU CAN RETRIEVE THE BRIEFCASE.
IT WASN'T DESTROYED IN THE CRASH?
NO, NO, NO. THAT BRIEFCASE COULD HAVE SURVIVED A LOT WORSE.
BE ASSURED, THE EMBRYO IS **FINE,** ZERO. BUT AFFAIRS IN SUDAN ARE NOT.
THE EMIR'S... **PROBLEM** IS A SECRET. WERE IT KNOWN, IT WOULD EMBOLDEN HIS ENEMIES. ALREADY PEOPLE ARE TALKING.
WE **MUST** HAVE AN HEIR, ZERO!
EEP
SAVE ME A PLACE ON THE BOAT.

ZERO, IS THAT YOU?

MARIA? HANG ON...

IT *IS* YOU! BLESSINGS, ZERO.

I'M HEADING BACK TO THE CLOISTERS.

AND I HEARD ABOUT YOUR PLANS FROM THE GIRL--STARK. SHE WAS QUITE UPSET.

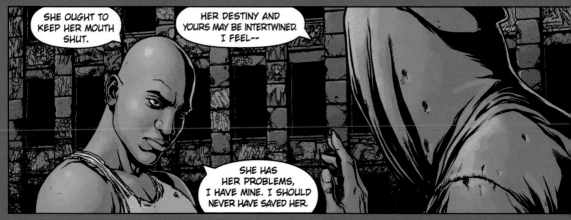

SHE OUGHT TO KEEP HER MOUTH SHUT.

HER DESTINY AND YOURS MAY BE INTERTWINED. I FEEL--

SHE HAS HER PROBLEMS, I HAVE MINE. I SHOULD NEVER HAVE SAVED HER.

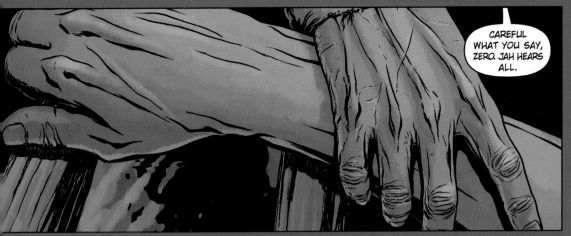

CAREFUL WHAT YOU SAY, ZERO. JAH HEARS ALL.

YEAH. I GUESS I'M GONNA NEED HIS HELP TONIGHT...

TAKE THIS.

AH, W-WHAT IS IT?

QUICKSILVER. IT WILL PROTECT YOU FROM *BARON SAMEDI.* *

*SATAN.

MAY THE LORD JAH BLESS YOU AND KEEP YOU. MAY ESUCHRISTUS DELIVER YOU FROM THE BARON.

...

I--UM. THANKS, MATRONA. I'LL SEE YOU AROUND, ALL RIGHT?

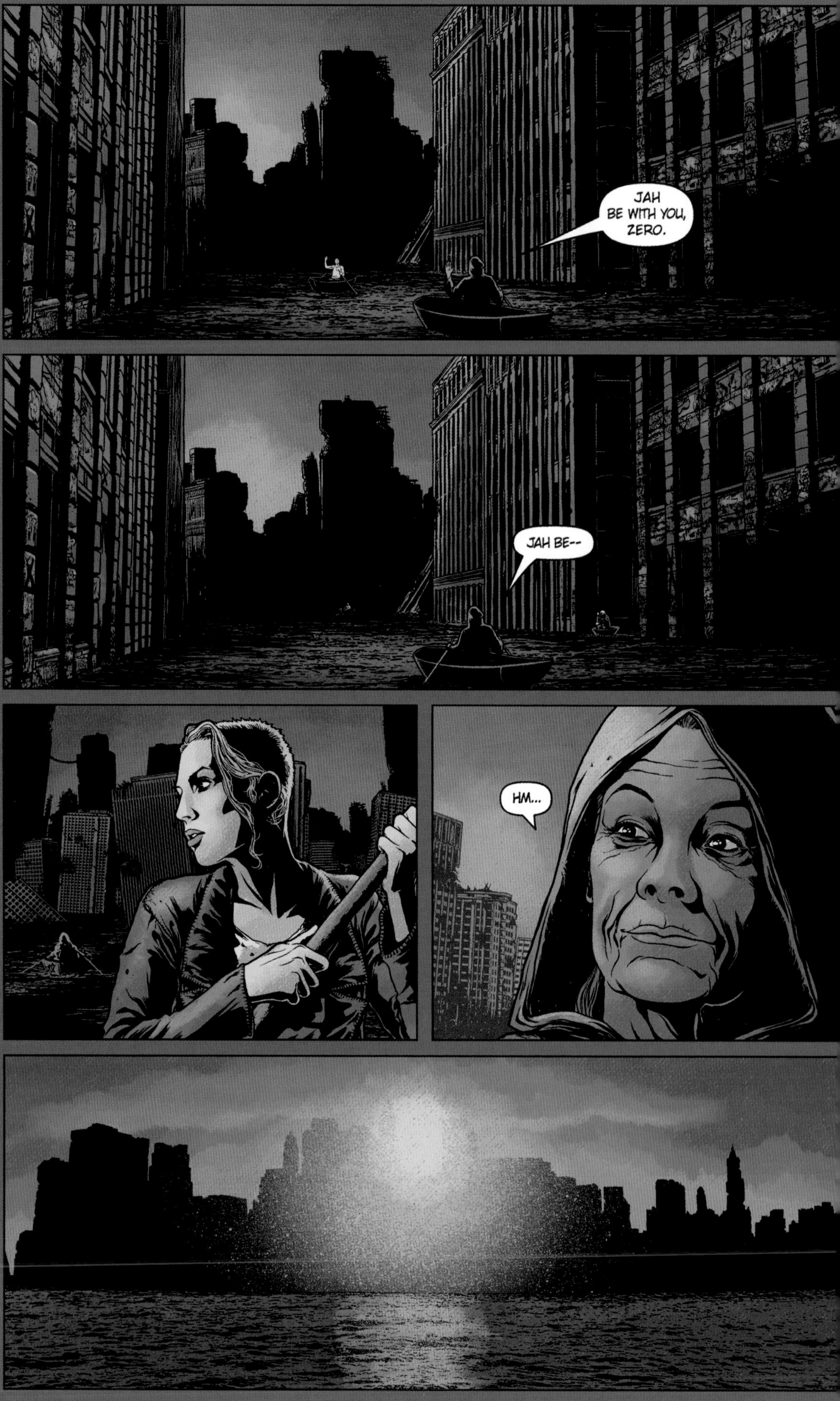
JAH BE WITH YOU, ZERO.
JAH BE--
HM...

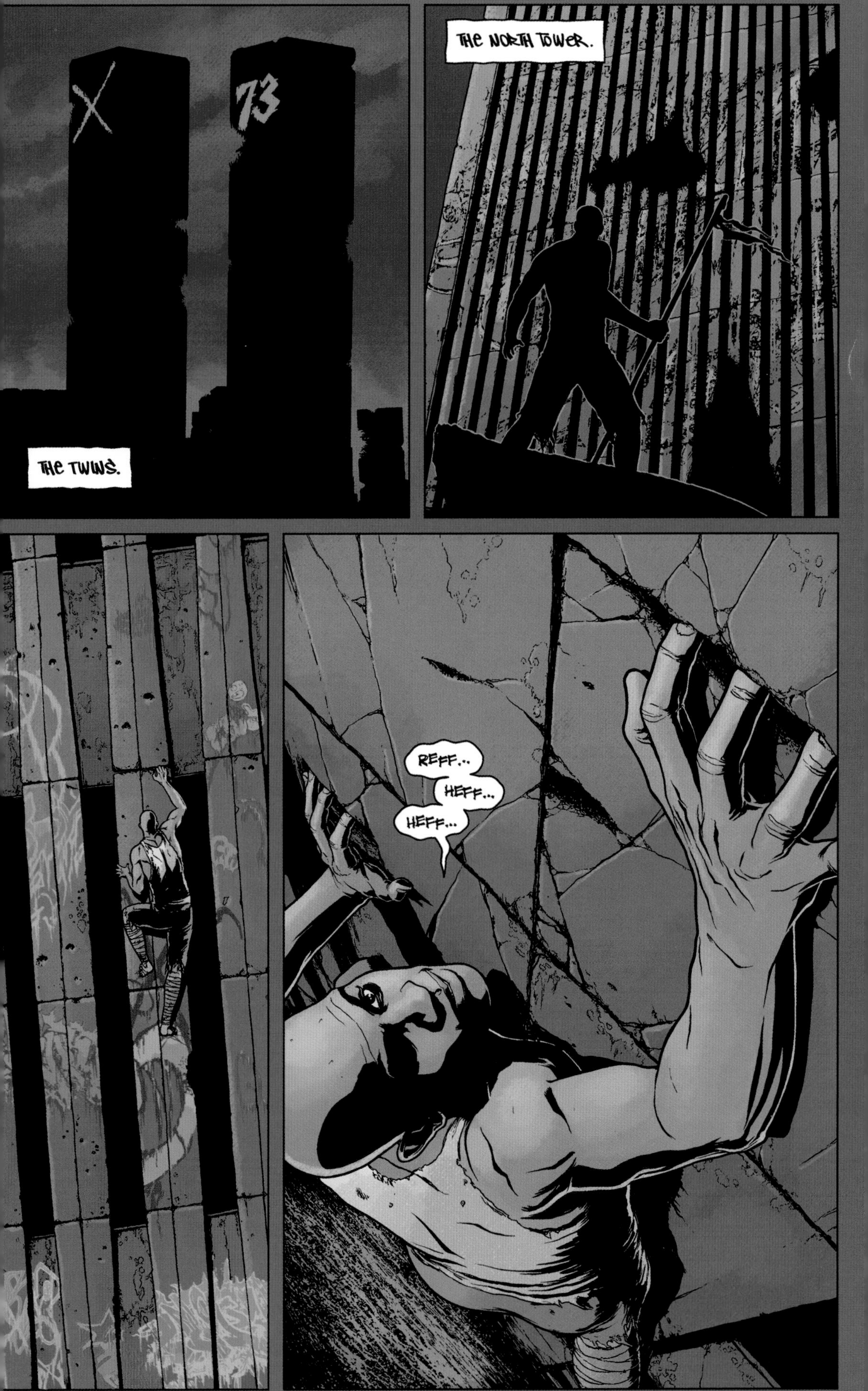
X
73
THE TWINS.
THE NORTH TOWER.
REFF...
HEFF...
HEFF...

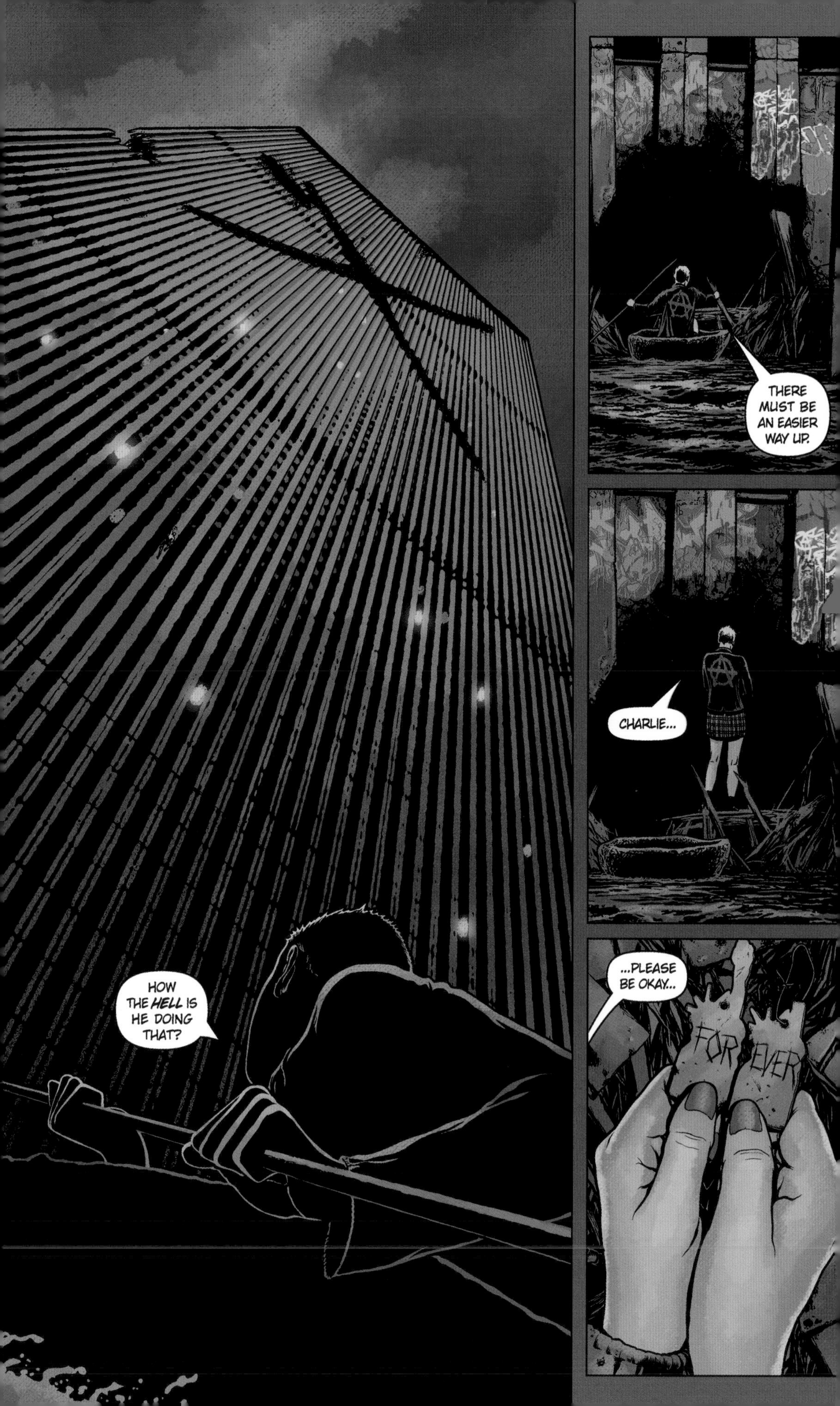
HOW THE *HELL* IS HE DOING THAT?
THERE MUST BE AN EASIER WAY UP.
CHARLIE...
...PLEASE BE OKAY...
FOR EVER

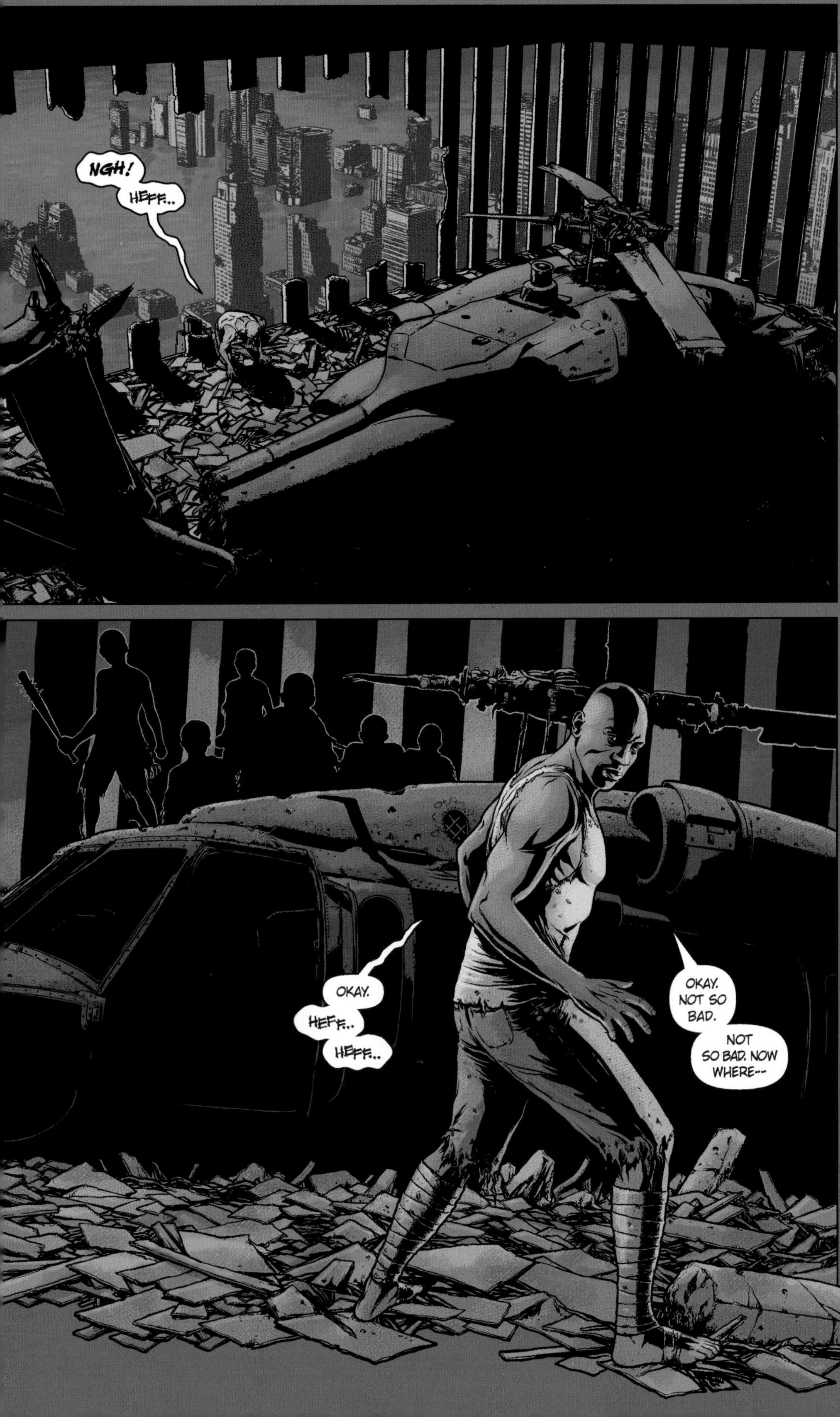
NGH!
HEFF...
OKAY.
HEFF...
HEFF...
OKAY. NOT SO BAD.
NOT SO BAD. NOW WHERE--

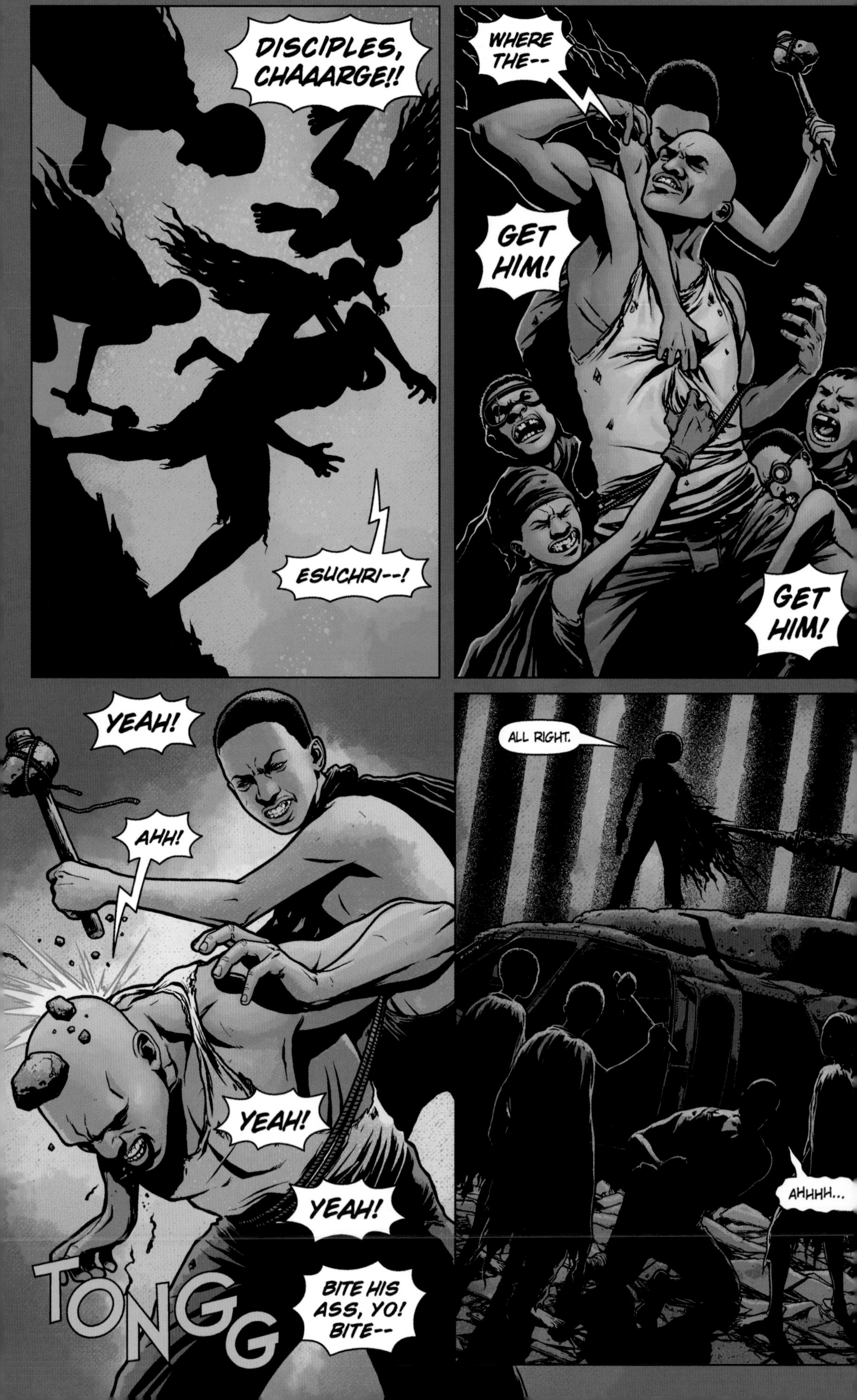
DISCIPLES, CHAAARGE!!
ESUCHRI--!
WHERE THE--
GET HIM!
GET HIM!
YEAH!
AHH!
YEAH!
YEAH!
TONGG
BITE HIS ASS, YO! BITE--
ALL RIGHT.
AHHHH...

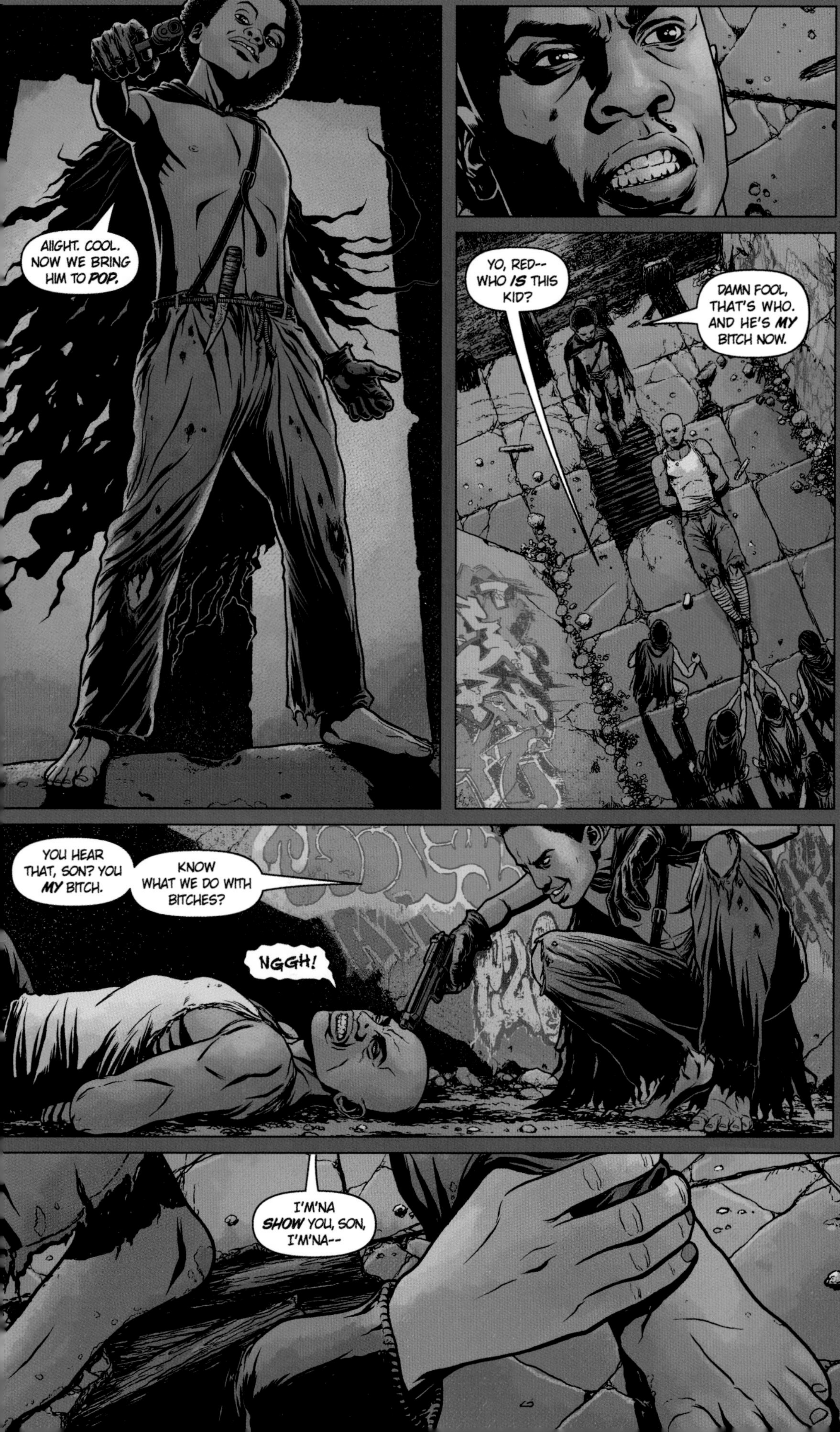
AIIGHT. COOL. NOW WE BRING HIM TO POP.
YO, RED-- WHO IS THIS KID?
DAMN FOOL, THAT'S WHO. AND HE'S MY BITCH NOW.
YOU HEAR THAT, SON? YOU MY BITCH.
KNOW WHAT WE DO WITH BITCHES?
NGGH!
I'M'NA SHOW YOU, SON, I'M'NA--

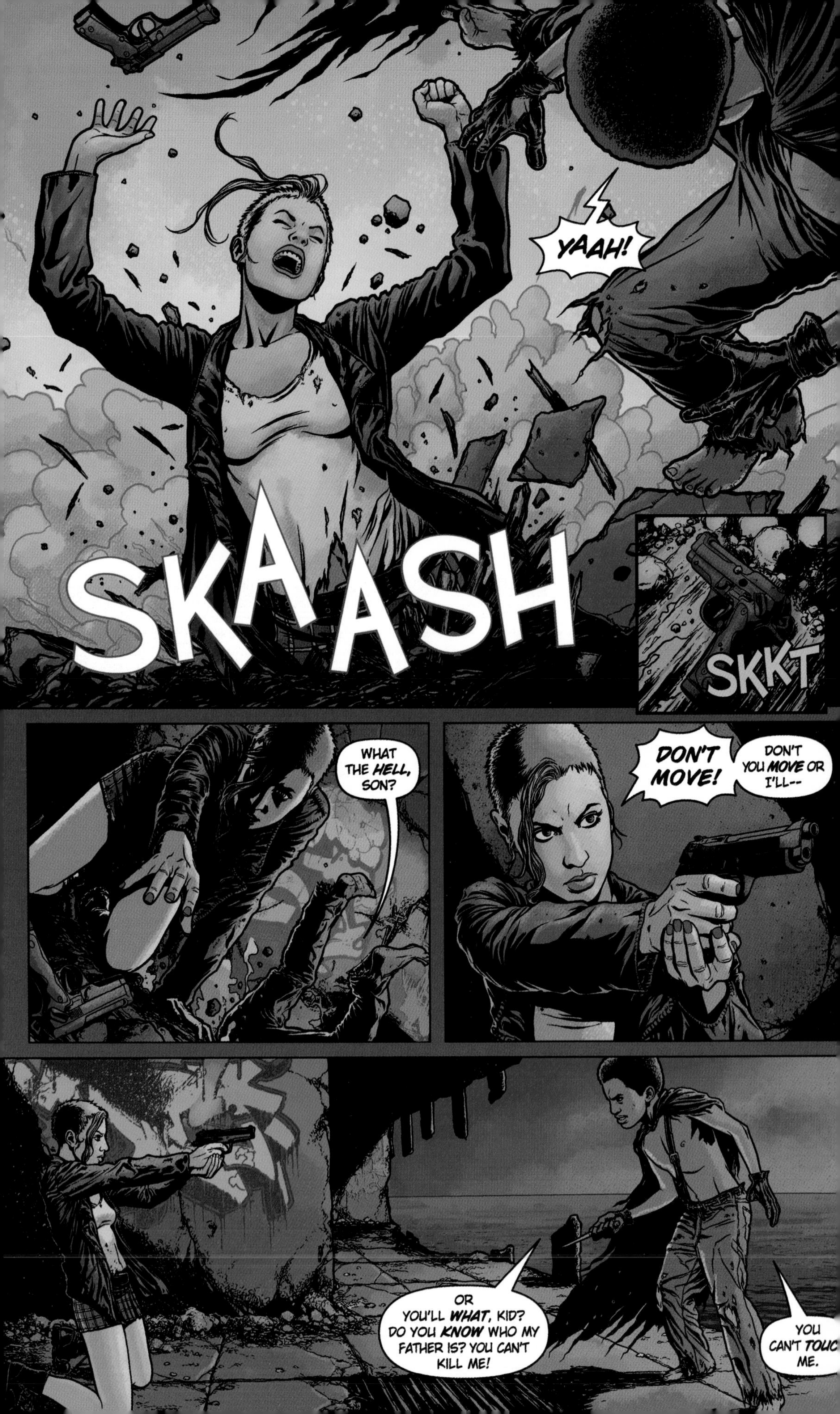
YAAH!
SKAASH
SKKT
WHAT THE HELL, SON?
DON'T MOVE!
DON'T YOU MOVE OR I'LL--
OR YOU'LL WHAT, KID? DO YOU KNOW WHO MY FATHER IS? YOU CAN'T KILL ME!
YOU CAN'T TOUC ME.

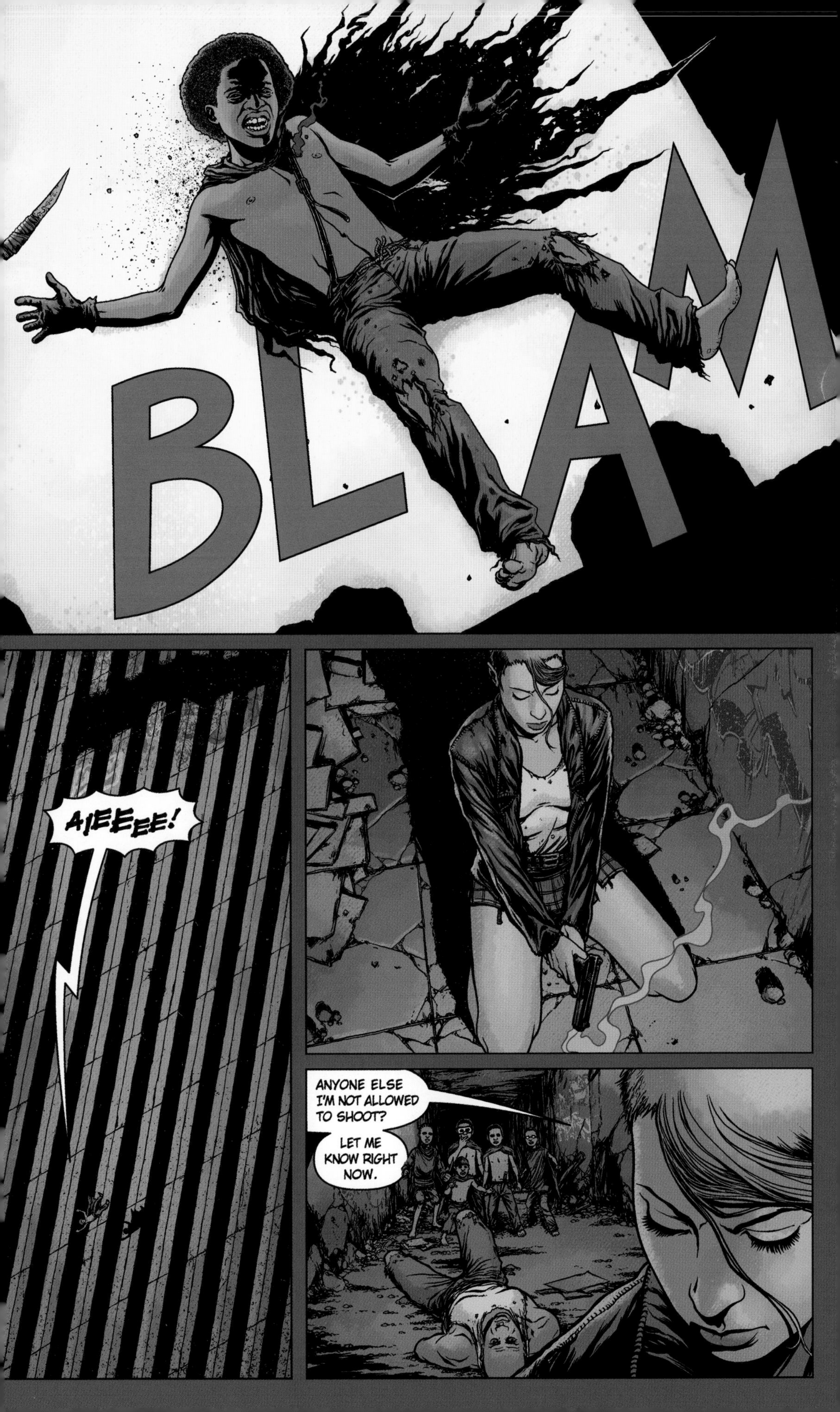
BLAM
AIEEEEE!
ANYONE ELSE I'M NOT ALLOWED TO SHOOT?
LET ME KNOW RIGHT NOW.

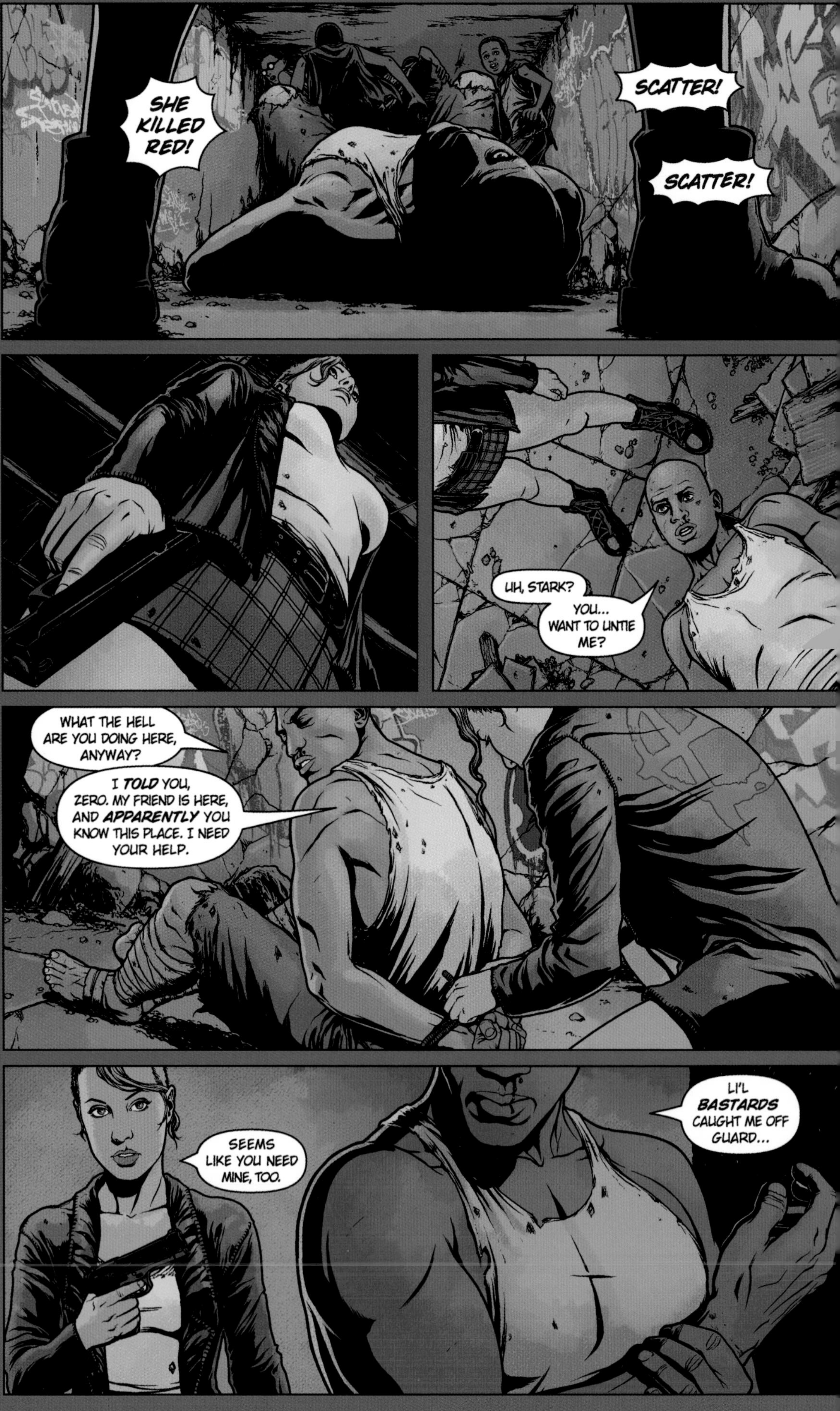
SHE KILLED RED!
SCATTER!
SCATTER!
UH, STARK? YOU... WANT TO UNTIE ME?
WHAT THE HELL ARE YOU DOING HERE, ANYWAY?
I *TOLD* YOU, ZERO. MY FRIEND IS HERE, AND *APPARENTLY* YOU KNOW THIS PLACE. I NEED YOUR HELP.
SEEMS LIKE YOU NEED MINE, TOO.
LI'L *BASTARDS* CAUGHT ME OFF GUARD...

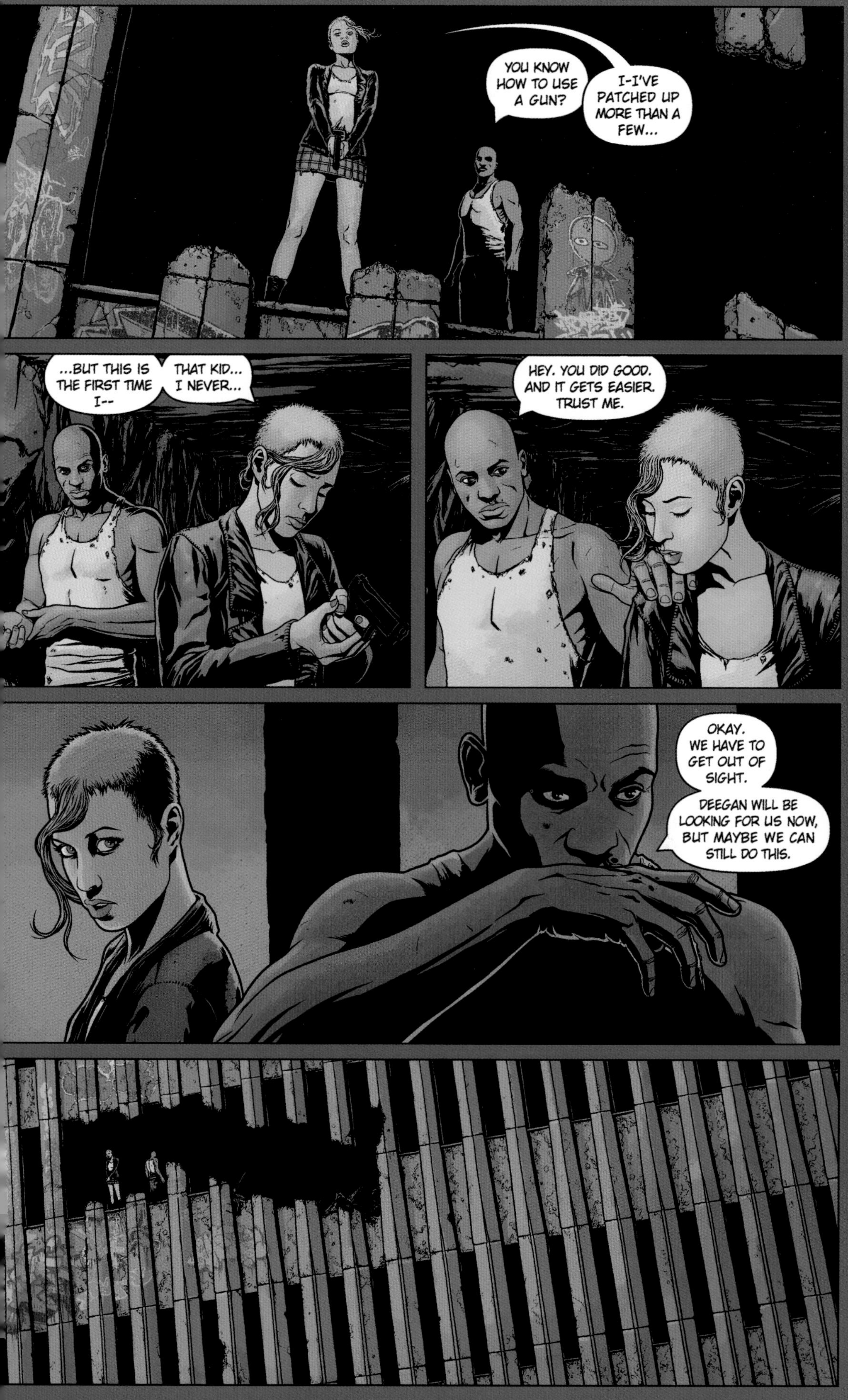
YOU KNOW HOW TO USE A GUN?
I-I'VE PATCHED UP MORE THAN A FEW...
...BUT THIS IS THE FIRST TIME I--
THAT KID... I NEVER...
HEY. YOU DID GOOD. AND IT GETS EASIER. TRUST ME.
OKAY. WE HAVE TO GET OUT OF SIGHT.
DEEGAN WILL BE LOOKING FOR US NOW, BUT MAYBE WE CAN STILL DO THIS.

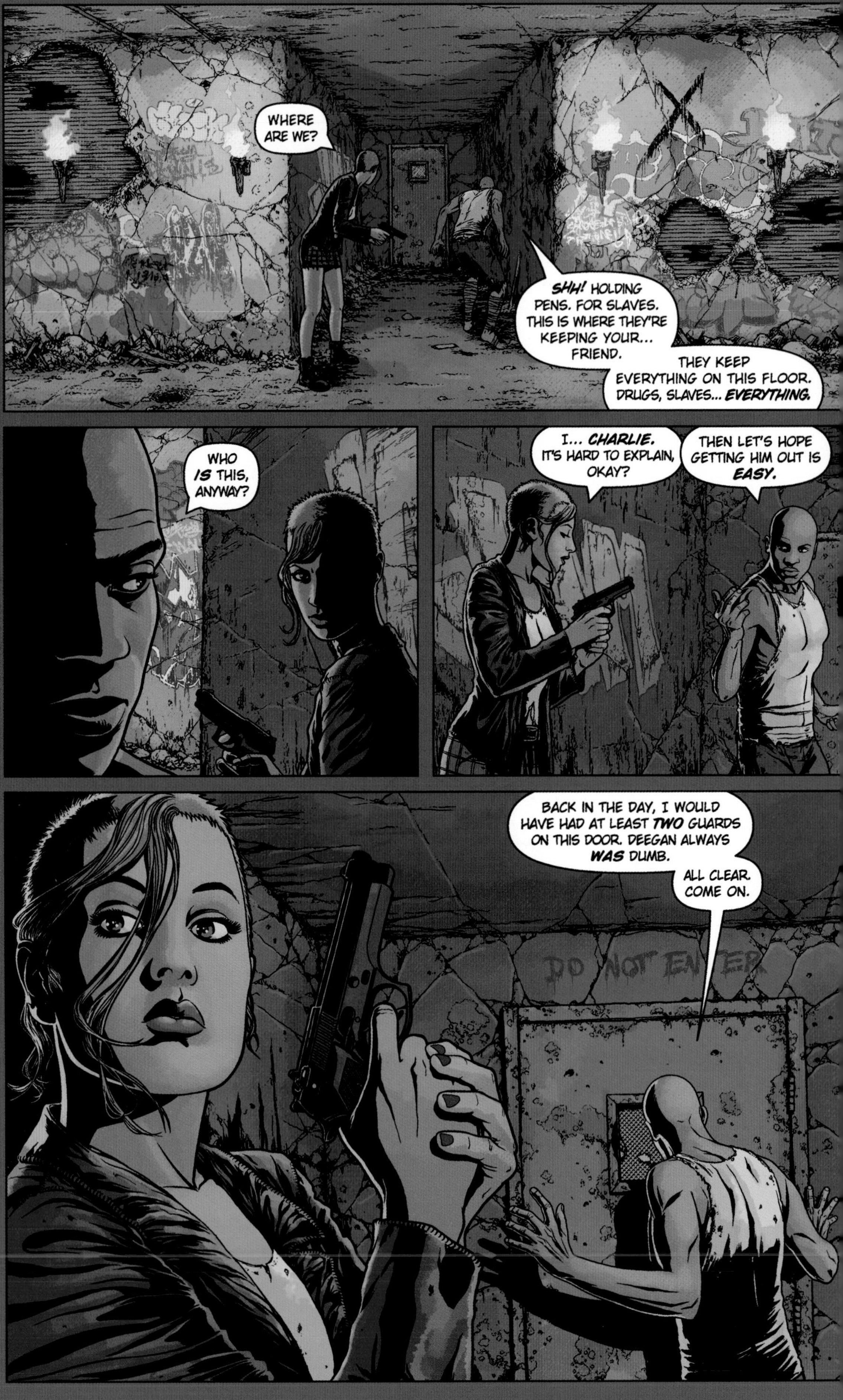
WHERE ARE WE?
SHH! HOLDING PENS. FOR SLAVES. THIS IS WHERE THEY'RE KEEPING YOUR... FRIEND.
THEY KEEP EVERYTHING ON THIS FLOOR. DRUGS, SLAVES... EVERYTHING.
WHO IS THIS, ANYWAY?
I... CHARLIE. IT'S HARD TO EXPLAIN, OKAY?
THEN LET'S HOPE GETTING HIM OUT IS EASY.
BACK IN THE DAY, I WOULD HAVE HAD AT LEAST TWO GUARDS ON THIS DOOR. DEEGAN ALWAYS WAS DUMB.
ALL CLEAR. COME ON.
DO NOT ENTER

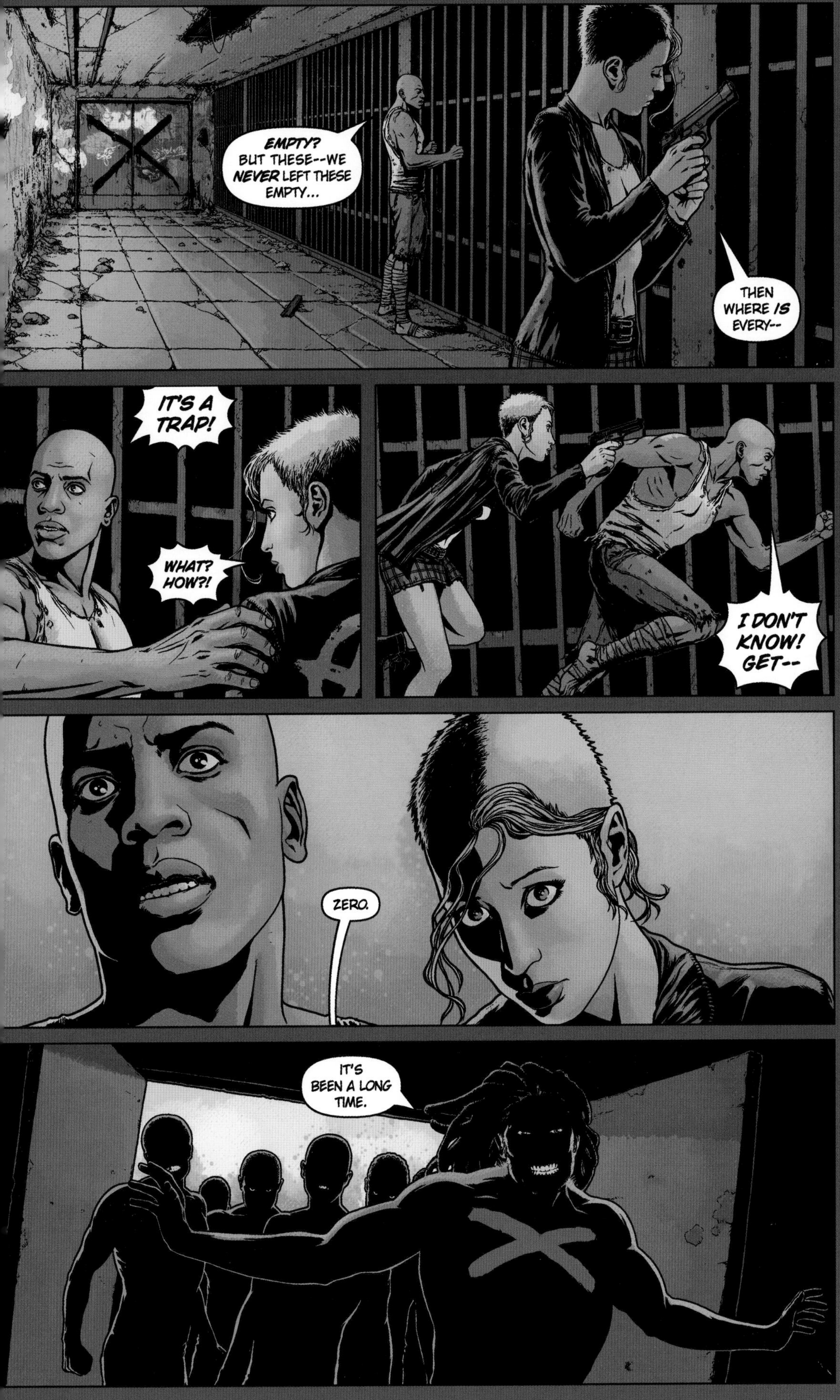
EMPTY? BUT THESE--WE NEVER LEFT THESE EMPTY...
THEN WHERE IS EVERY--
IT'S A TRAP!
WHAT? HOW?!
I DON'T KNOW! GET--
ZERO.
IT'S BEEN A LONG TIME.

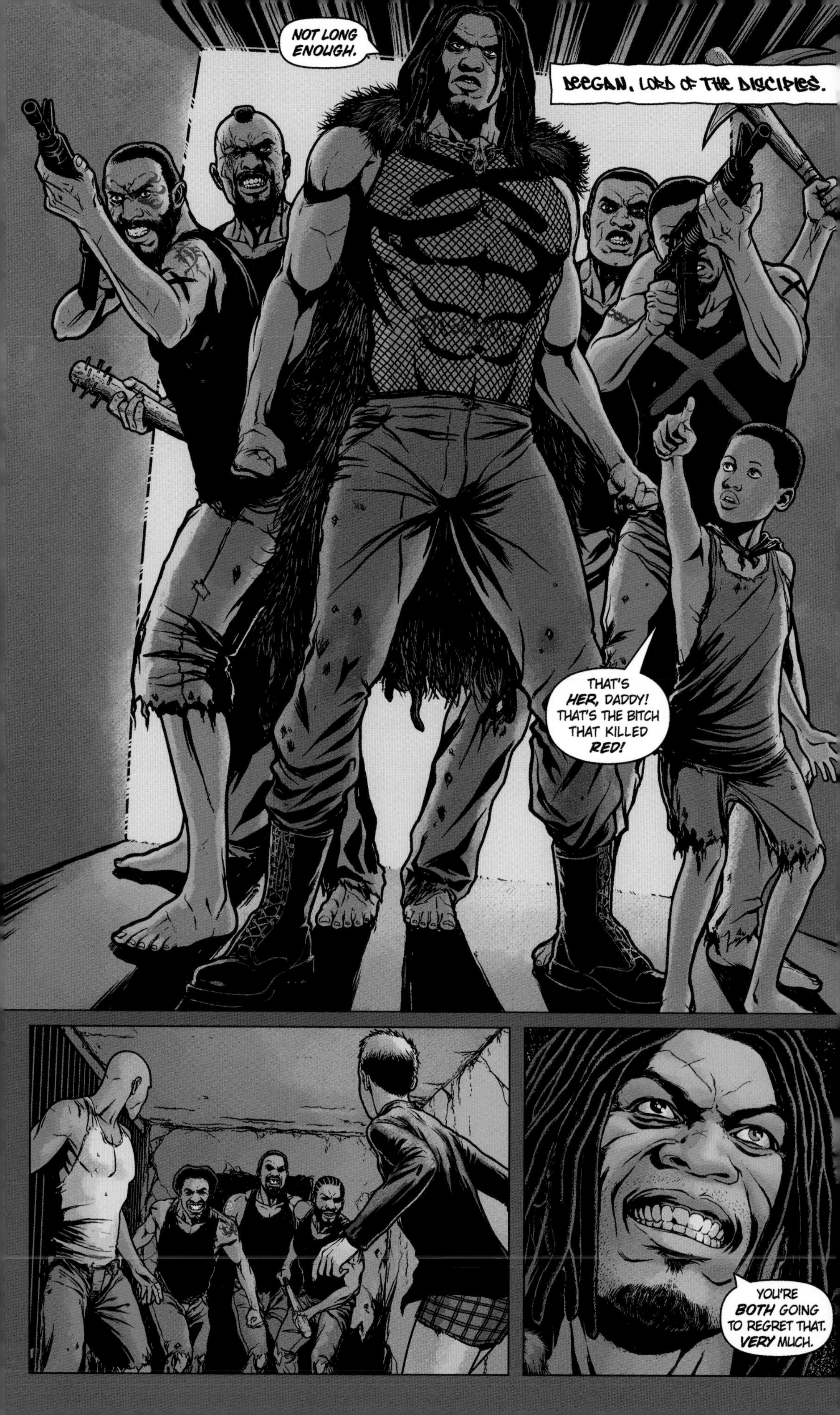
NOT LONG ENOUGH.
DEEGAN, LORD OF THE DISCIPLES.
THAT'S HER, DADDY! THAT'S THE BITCH THAT KILLED RED!
YOU'RE BOTH GOING TO REGRET THAT. VERY MUCH.

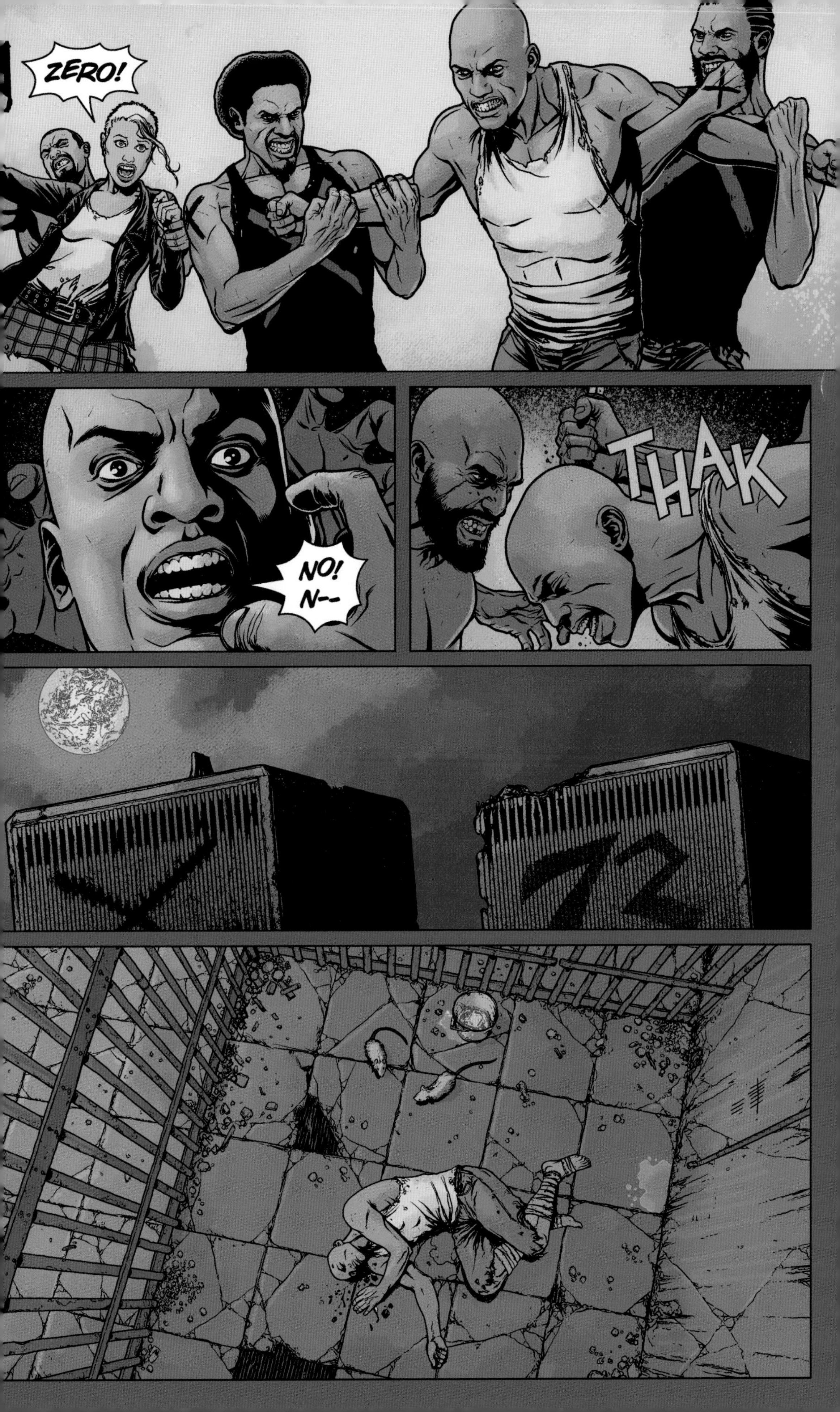
ZERO!
NO! N--
THAK

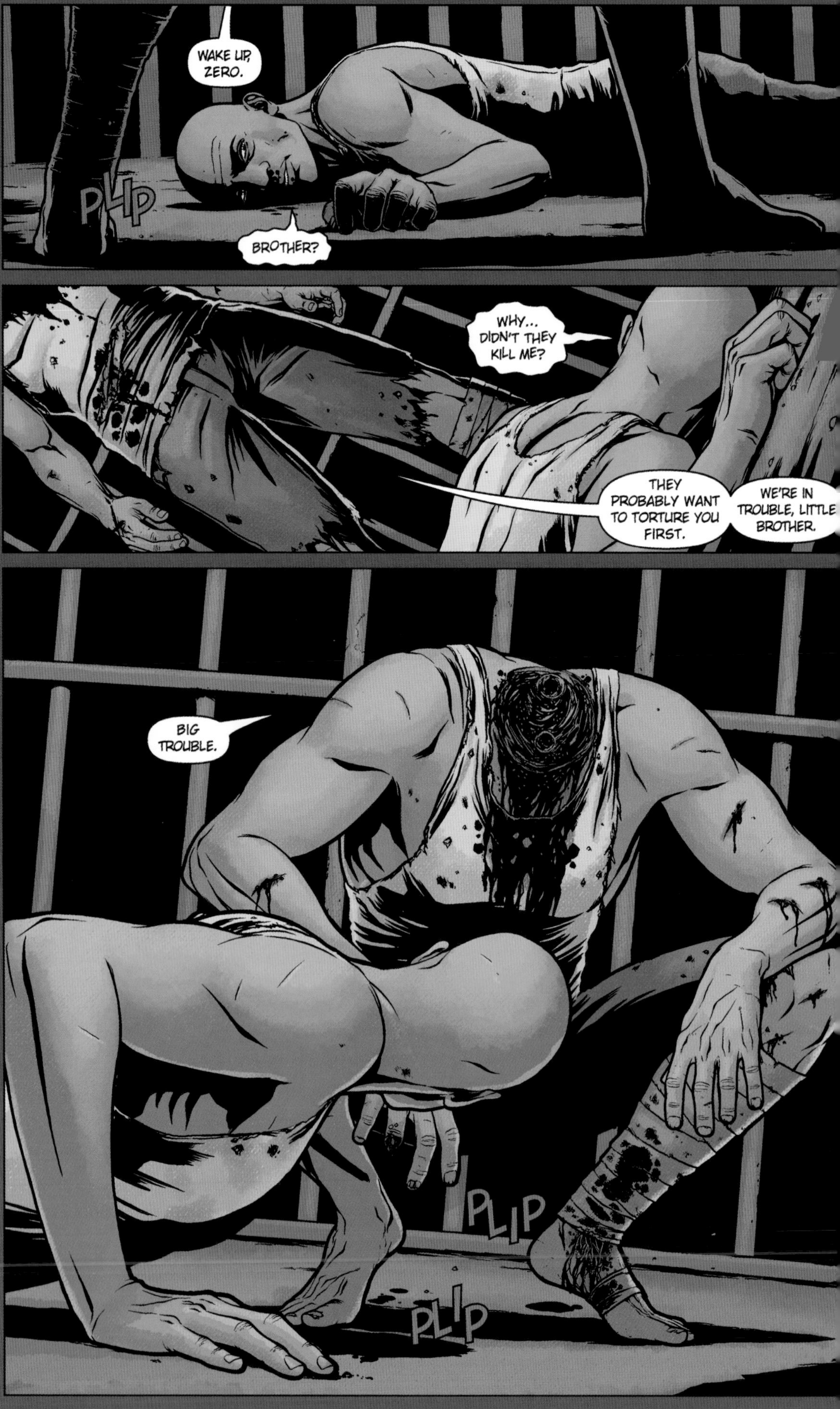
WAKE UP, ZERO.
PLIP
BROTHER?
WHY... DIDN'T THEY KILL ME?
THEY PROBABLY WANT TO TORTURE YOU FIRST.
WE'RE IN TROUBLE, LITTLE BROTHER.
BIG TROUBLE.
PLIP
PLIP

The JOCOM Daily ✦ Serving Those Who Serve ✦ July 21, 2007 ✦ Vol. 66, No. 17

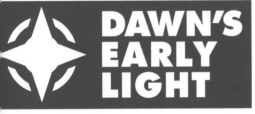

DAWN'S EARLY LIGHT

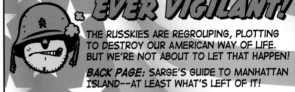

EVER VIGILANT!

THE RUSSKIES ARE REGROUPING, PLOTTING TO DESTROY OUR AMERICAN WAY OF LIFE. BUT WE'RE NOT ABOUT TO LET THAT HAPPEN!

BACK PAGE: SARGE'S GUIDE TO MANHATTAN ISLAND--AT LEAST WHAT'S LEFT OF IT!

›eadly Fertility ;rèche Violence

female revolt in the Nevada- ›rktown Complex fertility èche has left nine dead and ›zens wounded in one of the ost serious habitation security eaches in recent memory.

The women appear to have en led by a female working as reproductive adjutant. The ri- ers used stolen firearms to take veral enlisted men hostage. ›ey claimed to be protest- g "degrading and inhumane eatment."

"This female used her access ivileges to obtain the weapons ed in the assault. And this was ›e we trusted. It makes you onder when the next terrorist tack is coming," Major Stanley atts, who is in charge of crèche curity, said.

A Special Task Force (STF) sault squad stormed the èche, killing all the women sponsible. Tragically, all the ›stages were killed as well.

"In a situation like this, ›u just can't negotiate. We ›n't negotiate with terrorists," ichard Perle, national security ›visor, said.

He said reprisals against the st of the Yorktown female ›pulation are "imminent."

"This is actually an op- ›rtunity to try out our new ›rtical-stapling technology," ›rle said. "There won't be any ore female insurrections for a ›ry long time."

The names of the slain men e being withheld until their ›uad mates have been informed ‹ their deaths. ✦

Eurasian Recon Team MIA

Feared Dead, Soviets Likely Responsible

Three months have passed since the Defense Intelligence Agency (DIA) launched a Special Task Force (STF) operation to the Eurasian landmass, and there's no sign of the men who risked their lives to gather intelligence on Soviet activities.

The STF rangers are now officially missing in action.

"Sadly, I think we must conclude they met their fate at the hands of Soviet operatives," Paul Wolfowitz, Future War Planning Secretary, said.

In recent years, the DIA has sent out dozens of reconnaissance missions to Europe and Asia, to ascertain the strength of the Soviet threat in the post–Zero Hour operational environment. An "alarming" number, over 50 percent, have not returned.

Those that have returned brought back strong circumstantial evidence pointing to a vast network of functioning, even thriving, Soviet bases.

"In a lot of ways, it's the very absence of any conclusive evidence that is the most convincing proof," Wolfowitz said.

"We know they're out there, and we know they're concealing their activities, waiting for when we let down our guard," JOCOM-A Chief of Staff Tommy Franks said.

"It's only a matter of time before we find out what the Soviets are up to," Douglas Feith, DRUSA military affairs coordinator, said. "I'll stake my reputation on it."

The rangers returning from the Eurasian missions often have severe radiation-related health problems, but Feith ruled out the possibility radiation or other mishaps are the reason for the high loss rate.

"Look at those people inhabiting the ruins of New York. They survive, and without protective gear. There's absolutely no question. The Cold War never ended. It's just entered into a new phase," Feith said.

"It's mighty quiet over there," Captain Richard Sharpe, who has been on three Eurasian recon missions, said. "The NATO signatories — the Russians got them pretty good. We returned the favor

continued on page A4

Photograph of a Ukrainian village, from a recent recon operation. Soviet military complexes are undoubtedly buried beneath the seemingly abandoned structures.

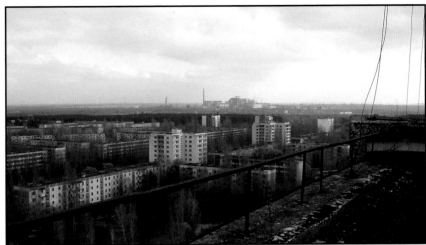

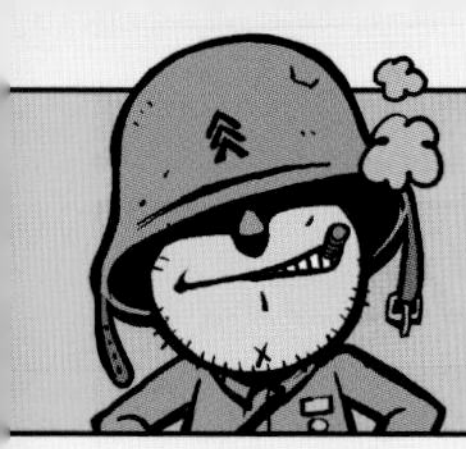

SARGE'S TIPS 'N' TACTICS

Stay alert ✦ Stay focused ✦ Stay alive

MANHATTAN: *HOT SPOTS IN THE OLD TOWN!*

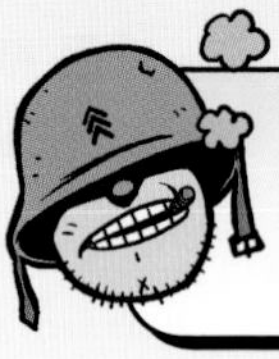

THE NUKES IN '73 CAUSED MANHATTAN TO SINK ABOUT 100 FEET INTO NEW YORK HARBOR. AND NOW THE RUINS ARE A VERY DANGEROUS PLACE, FELLA! USE THIS MAP TO AVOID RADIATION, GANGSTERS, AND OTHER ***"HOT SPOTS."***

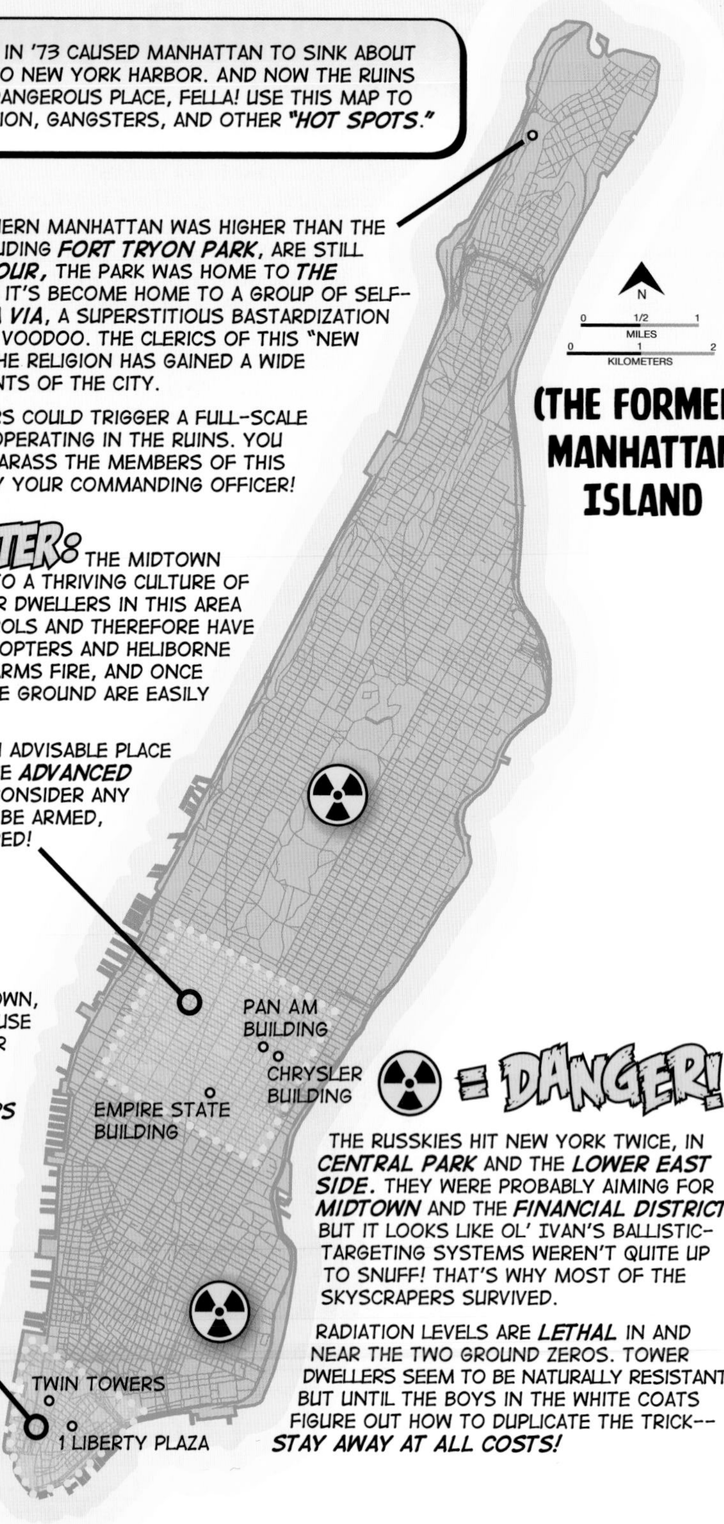

N
0 1/2 1
MILES
0 1 2
KILOMETERS
(THE FORMER) MANHATTAN ISLAND
PAN AM BUILDING
CHRYSLER BUILDING
EMPIRE STATE BUILDING
TWIN TOWERS
1 LIBERTY PLAZA
= DANGER!

THE CLOISTERS: NORTHERN MANHATTAN WAS HIGHER THAN THE REST OF THE CITY, AND PARTS, INCLUDING ***FORT TRYON PARK***, ARE STILL ABOVE THE WATER. BEFORE ***ZERO HOUR***, THE PARK WAS HOME TO ***THE CLOISTERS***, AN ART MUSEUM. NOW IT'S BECOME HOME TO A GROUP OF SELF-STYLED PROPHETS WHO PRACTICE ***LA VIA***, A SUPERSTITIOUS BASTARDIZATION OF CHRISTIANITY, BLACK MAGIC, AND VOODOO. THE CLERICS OF THIS "NEW FAITH" SEEM MOSTLY DOCILE, BUT THE RELIGION HAS GAINED A WIDE FOLLOWING AMONGST THE INHABITANTS OF THE CITY.

ANY ATTACKS AGAINST THE CLOISTERS COULD TRIGGER A FULL-SCALE INSURGENCY AGAINST OUR FORCES OPERATING IN THE RUINS. YOU ARE THEREFORE ORDERED ***NOT*** TO HARASS THE MEMBERS OF THIS COMMUNITY UNLESS ORDERED TO BY YOUR COMMANDING OFFICER!

MIDTOWN CLUSTER: THE MIDTOWN SKYSCRAPERS HAVE BECOME HOME TO A THRIVING CULTURE OF SAVAGE CRIMINAL GANGS. THE TOWER DWELLERS IN THIS AREA HAVE BEEN KNOWN TO AMBUSH PATROLS AND THEREFORE HAVE ACCESS TO STOLEN FIREARMS. HELICOPTERS AND HELIBORNE CREWS ARE VULNERABLE TO SMALL-ARMS FIRE, AND ONCE CHOPPERS ARE DOWN, TEAMS ON THE GROUND ARE EASILY ISOLATED AND OVERWHELMED.

THE ***MIDTOWN CLUSTER*** IS NOT AN ADVISABLE PLACE TO HARVEST LIVE SPECIMENS FOR THE ***ADVANCED GENETIC RESEARCH INITIATIVE***. CONSIDER ANY NATIVES YOU MEET IN THIS AREA TO BE ARMED, DANGEROUS, AND ***VERY*** BAD TEMPERED!

DOWNTOWN CLUSTER: ALTHOUGH GEOGRAPHICALLY SMALLER THAN MIDTOWN, THE GANGS IN THIS AREA, MAYBE BECAUSE OF THE CLOSE PROXIMITY AND GREATER AVERAGE HEIGHT OF THE BUILDINGS, ARE EVEN ***MORE*** SAVAGE THAN THEIR MIDTOWN COUSINS. THE ***TWIN TOWERS*** GANGS, WHICH IS CONTROLLED BY VICIOUS FRATERNAL TWINS, ***DEEGAN*** AND ***BRUCKNER***, DOMINATE THE DOWNTOWNAREA.

STRANDED JOCOM PATROLS LAST AN AVERAGE OF 47 SECONDS IN THE DOWNTOWN AREA BEFORE DISAPPEARING. TO DATE, NOT A SINGLE MIA PATROLMAN HAS BEEN RECOVERED, ALIVE OR DEAD.

THERE ARE REPORTS GANGSTERS IN THIS AREA PRACTICE TORTURE AS A SPECTATOR SPORT AND EVEN ***CANNIBALISM***. SO UNLESS YOU WANT TO END UP SOMEONE ELSE'S DINNER--***AVOID DOWNTOWN!***

THE RUSSKIES HIT NEW YORK TWICE, IN ***CENTRAL PARK*** AND THE ***LOWER EAST SIDE***. THEY WERE PROBABLY AIMING FOR ***MIDTOWN*** AND THE ***FINANCIAL DISTRICT***, BUT IT LOOKS LIKE OL' IVAN'S BALLISTIC-TARGETING SYSTEMS WEREN'T QUITE UP TO SNUFF! THAT'S WHY MOST OF THE SKYSCRAPERS SURVIVED.

RADIATION LEVELS ARE ***LETHAL*** IN AND NEAR THE TWO GROUND ZEROS. TOWER DWELLERS SEEM TO BE NATURALLY RESISTANT, BUT UNTIL THE BOYS IN THE WHITE COATS FIGURE OUT HOW TO DUPLICATE THE TRICK-- ***STAY AWAY AT ALL COSTS!***

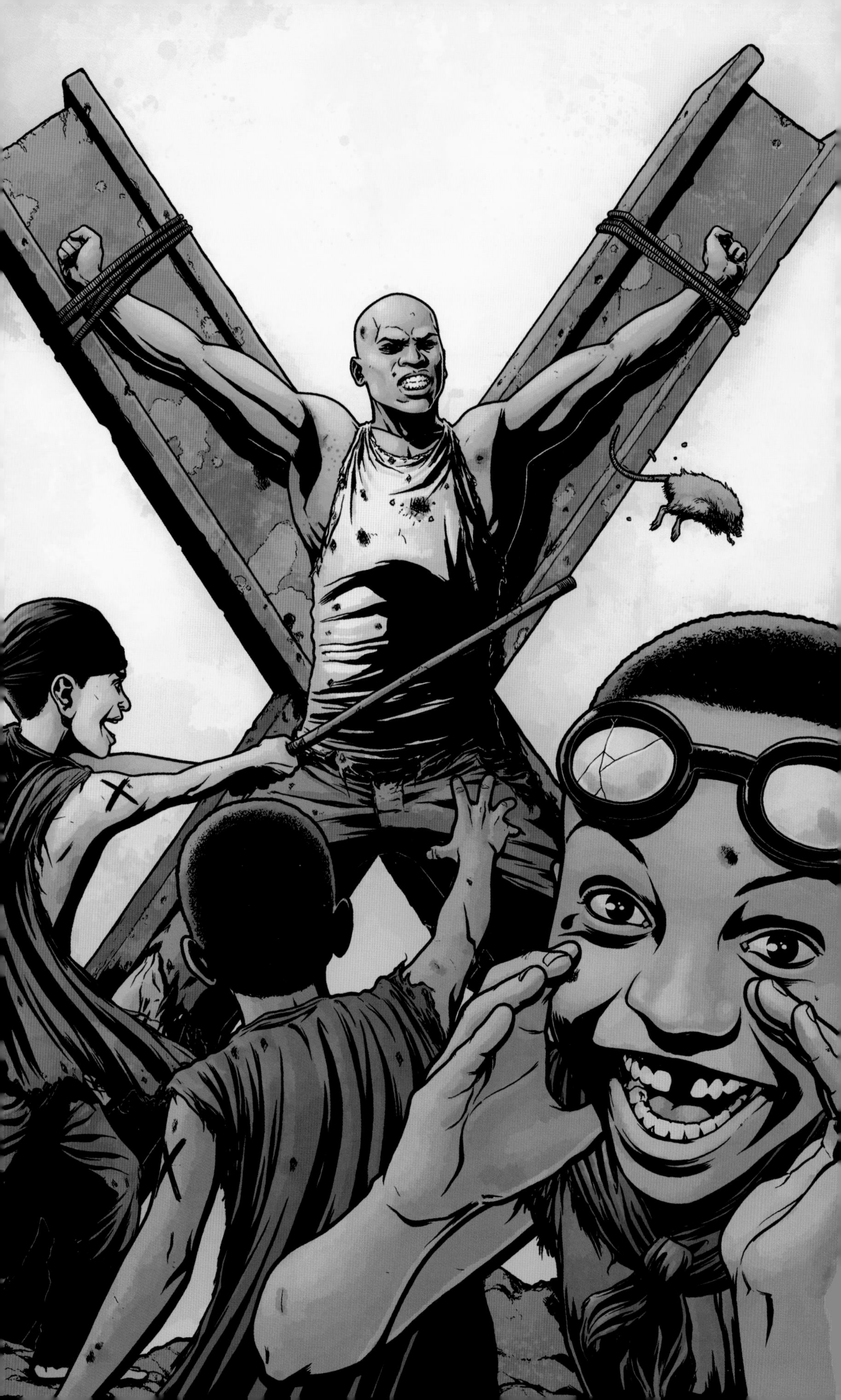

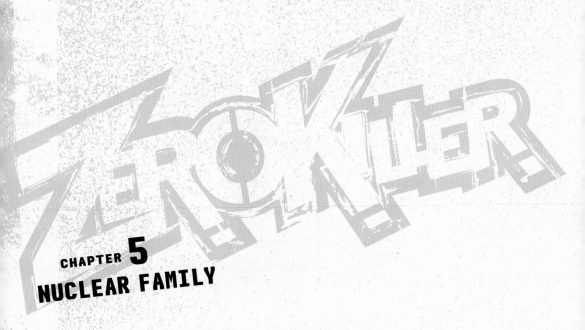

CHAPTER 5
NUCLEAR FAMILY

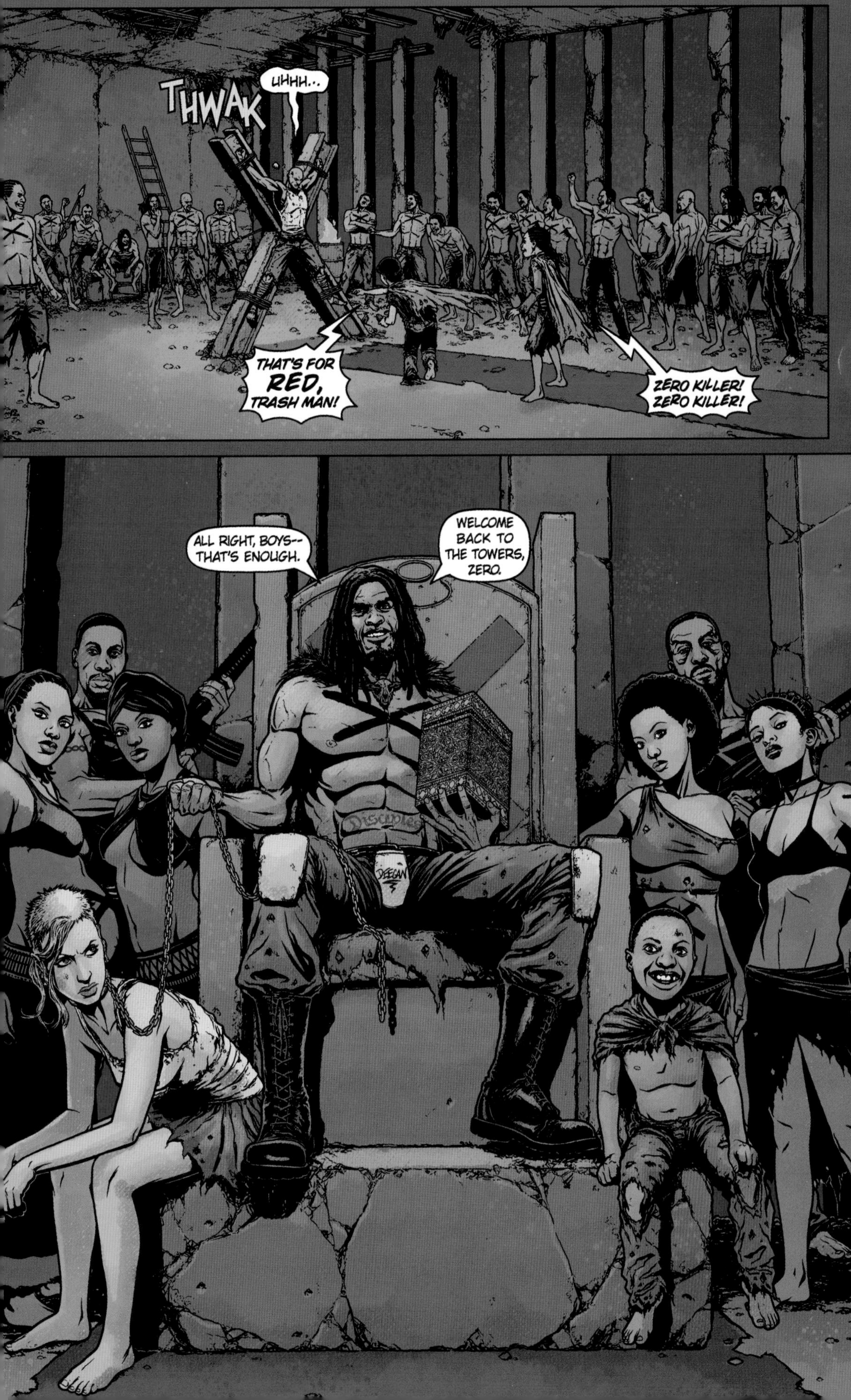
THWAK
UHHH...
THAT'S FOR RED, TRASH MAN!
ZERO KILLER! ZERO KILLER!
ALL RIGHT, BOYS-- THAT'S ENOUGH.
WELCOME BACK TO THE TOWERS, ZERO.
DISCIPLES
DEEGAN

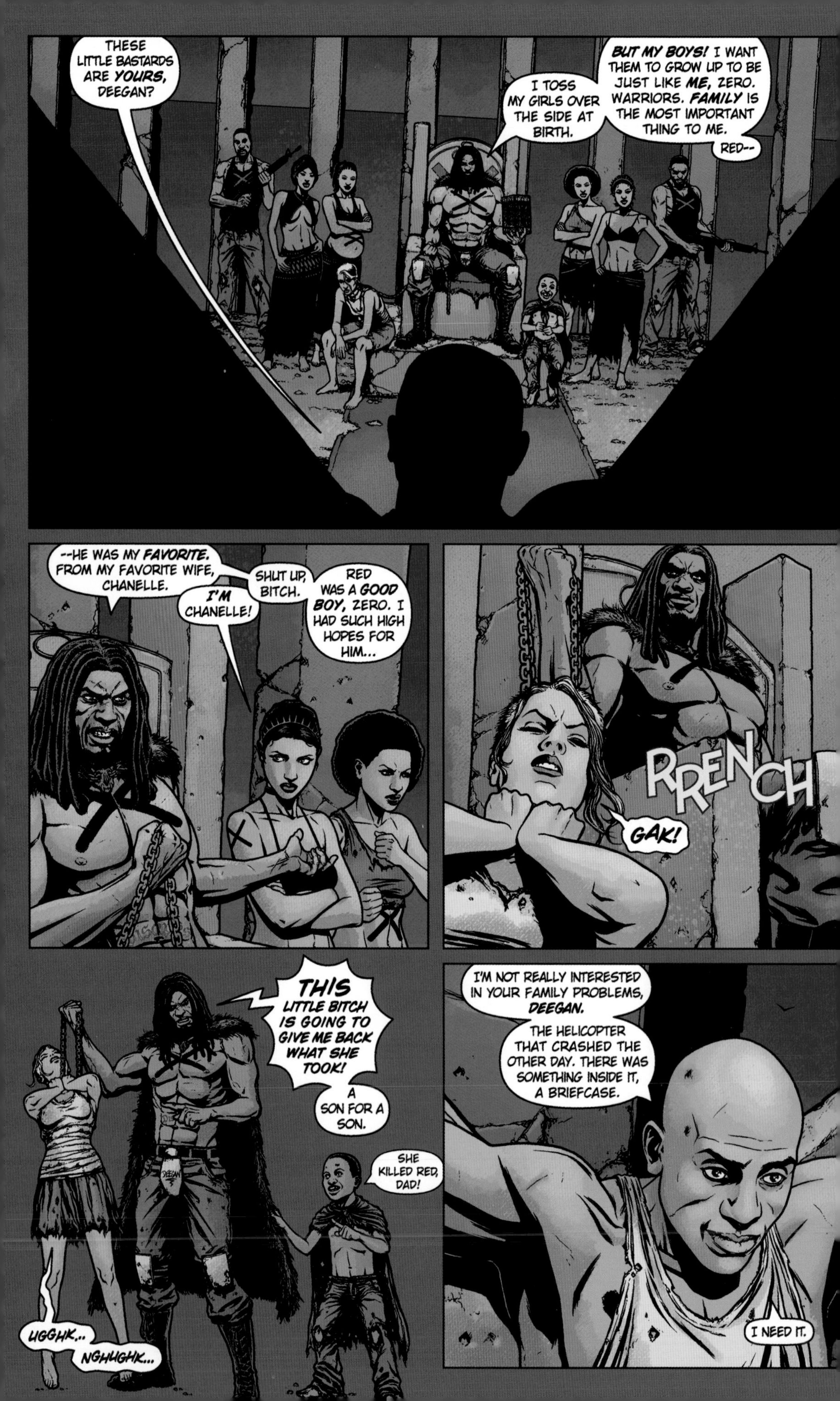
THESE LITTLE BASTARDS ARE *YOURS,* DEEGAN?
I TOSS MY GIRLS OVER THE SIDE AT BIRTH.
BUT MY BOYS! I WANT THEM TO GROW UP TO BE JUST LIKE *ME,* ZERO. WARRIORS. *FAMILY* IS THE MOST IMPORTANT THING TO ME.
RED--
--HE WAS MY *FAVORITE.* FROM MY FAVORITE WIFE, CHANELLE.
I'M CHANELLE!
SHUT UP, BITCH.
RED WAS A *GOOD BOY,* ZERO. I HAD SUCH HIGH HOPES FOR HIM...
RRENCH
GAK!
THIS LITTLE BITCH IS GOING TO GIVE ME BACK WHAT SHE TOOK!
A SON FOR A SON.
SHE KILLED RED, DAD!
UGGHK... NGHUGHK...
I'M NOT REALLY INTERESTED IN YOUR FAMILY PROBLEMS, *DEEGAN.*
THE HELICOPTER THAT CRASHED THE OTHER DAY. THERE WAS SOMETHING INSIDE IT, A BRIEFCASE.
I NEED IT.

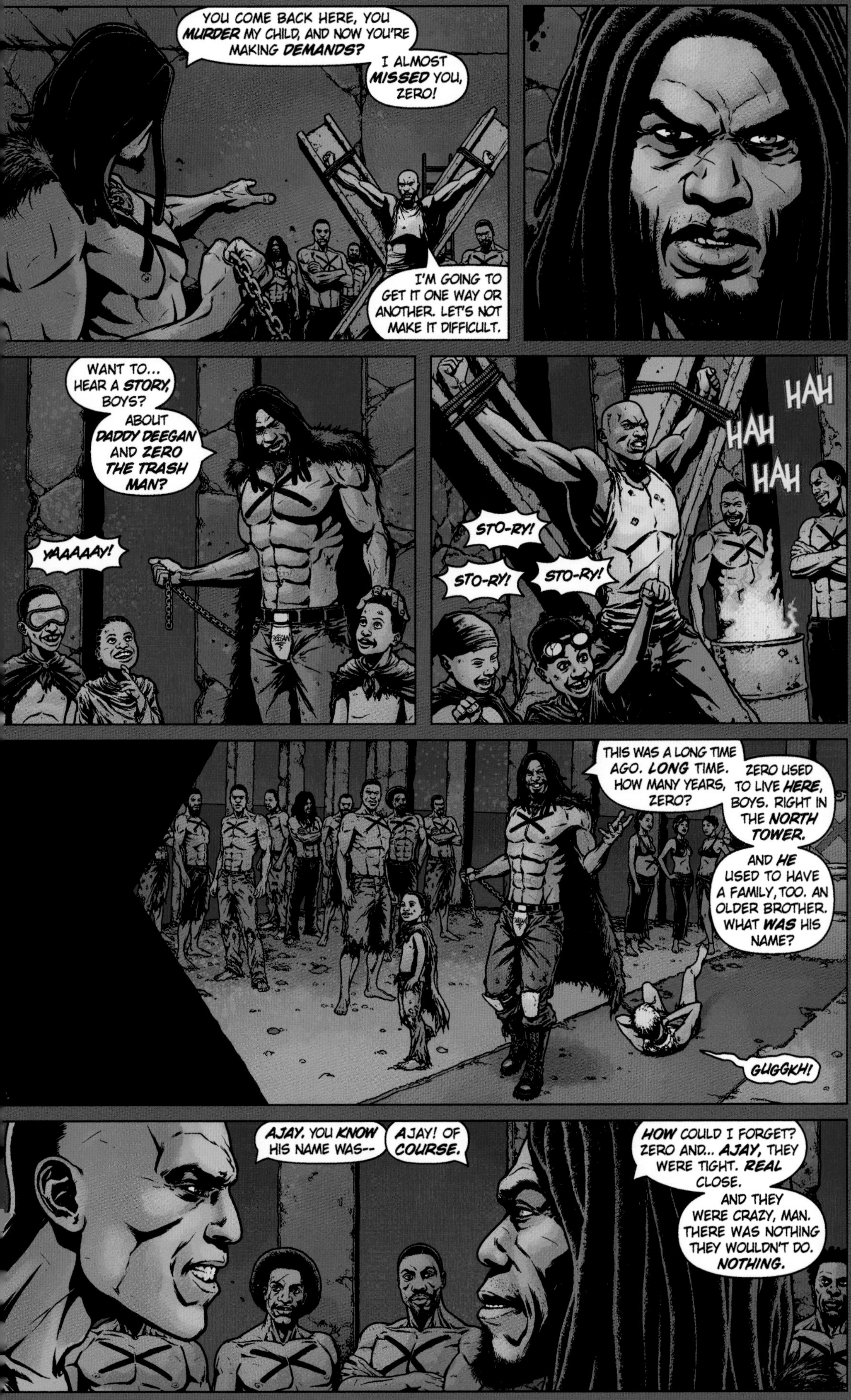
YOU COME BACK HERE, YOU MURDER MY CHILD, AND NOW YOU'RE MAKING DEMANDS?
I ALMOST MISSED YOU, ZERO!
I'M GOING TO GET IT ONE WAY OR ANOTHER. LET'S NOT MAKE IT DIFFICULT.
WANT TO... HEAR A STORY, BOYS? ABOUT DADDY DEEGAN AND ZERO THE TRASH MAN?
YAAAAAY!
HAH HAH HAH
STO-RY!
STO-RY!
STO-RY!
THIS WAS A LONG TIME AGO. LONG TIME. HOW MANY YEARS, ZERO?
ZERO USED TO LIVE HERE, BOYS. RIGHT IN THE NORTH TOWER.
AND HE USED TO HAVE A FAMILY, TOO. AN OLDER BROTHER. WHAT WAS HIS NAME?
GUGGKH!
AJAY. YOU KNOW HIS NAME WAS--
AJAY! OF COURSE.
HOW COULD I FORGET? ZERO AND... AJAY, THEY WERE TIGHT. REAL CLOSE.
AND THEY WERE CRAZY, MAN. THERE WAS NOTHING THEY WOULDN'T DO. NOTHING.

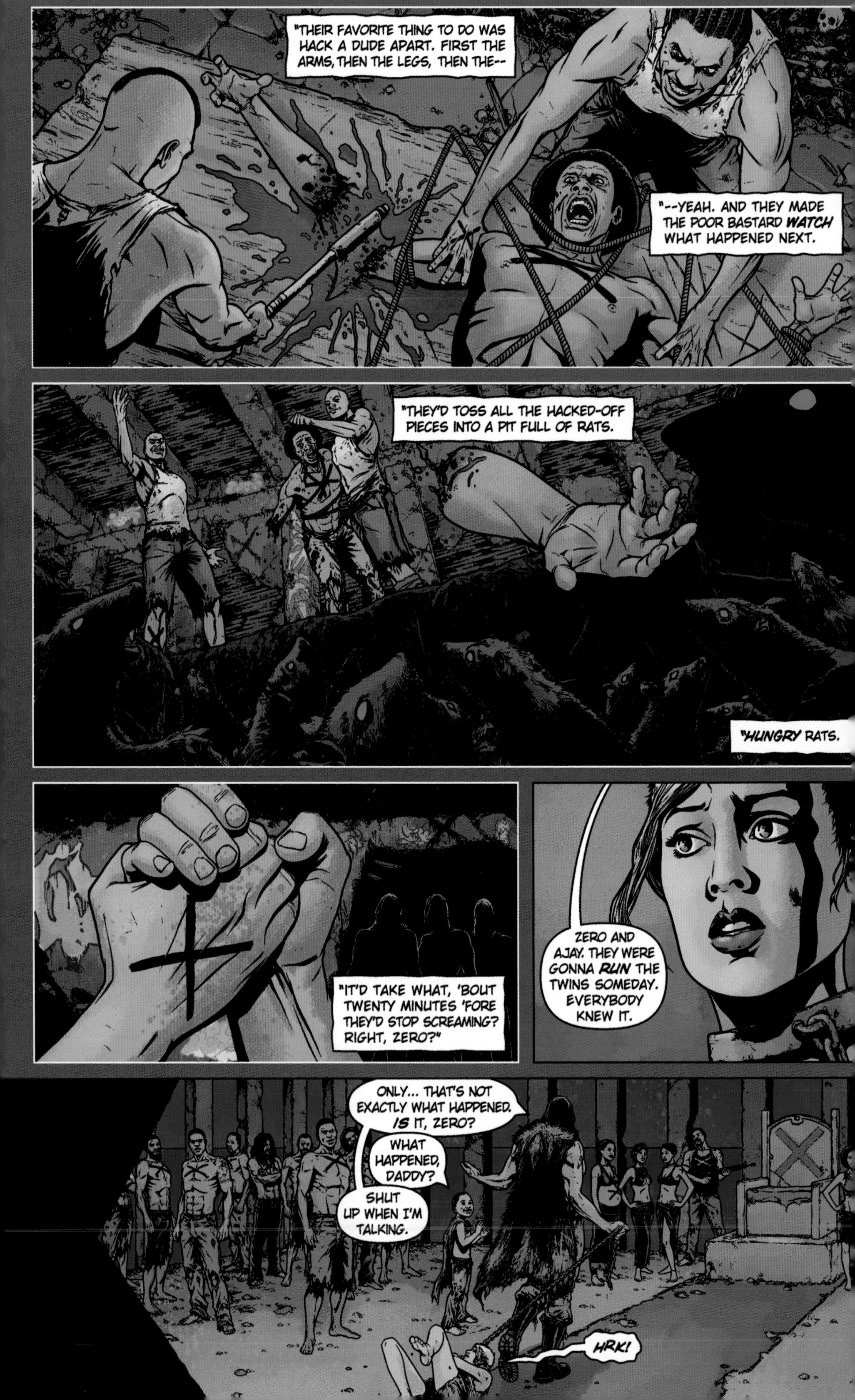
"THEIR FAVORITE THING TO DO WAS HACK A DUDE APART. FIRST THE ARMS, THEN THE LEGS, THEN THE--
"--YEAH. AND THEY MADE THE POOR BASTARD WATCH WHAT HAPPENED NEXT.
"THEY'D TOSS ALL THE HACKED-OFF PIECES INTO A PIT FULL OF RATS.
"HUNGRY RATS.
"IT'D TAKE WHAT, 'BOUT TWENTY MINUTES 'FORE THEY'D STOP SCREAMING? RIGHT, ZERO?"
ZERO AND AJAY. THEY WERE GONNA RUN THE TWINS SOMEDAY. EVERYBODY KNEW IT.
ONLY... THAT'S NOT EXACTLY WHAT HAPPENED. IS IT, ZERO?
WHAT HAPPENED, DADDY?
SHUT UP WHEN I'M TALKING.
HRK!

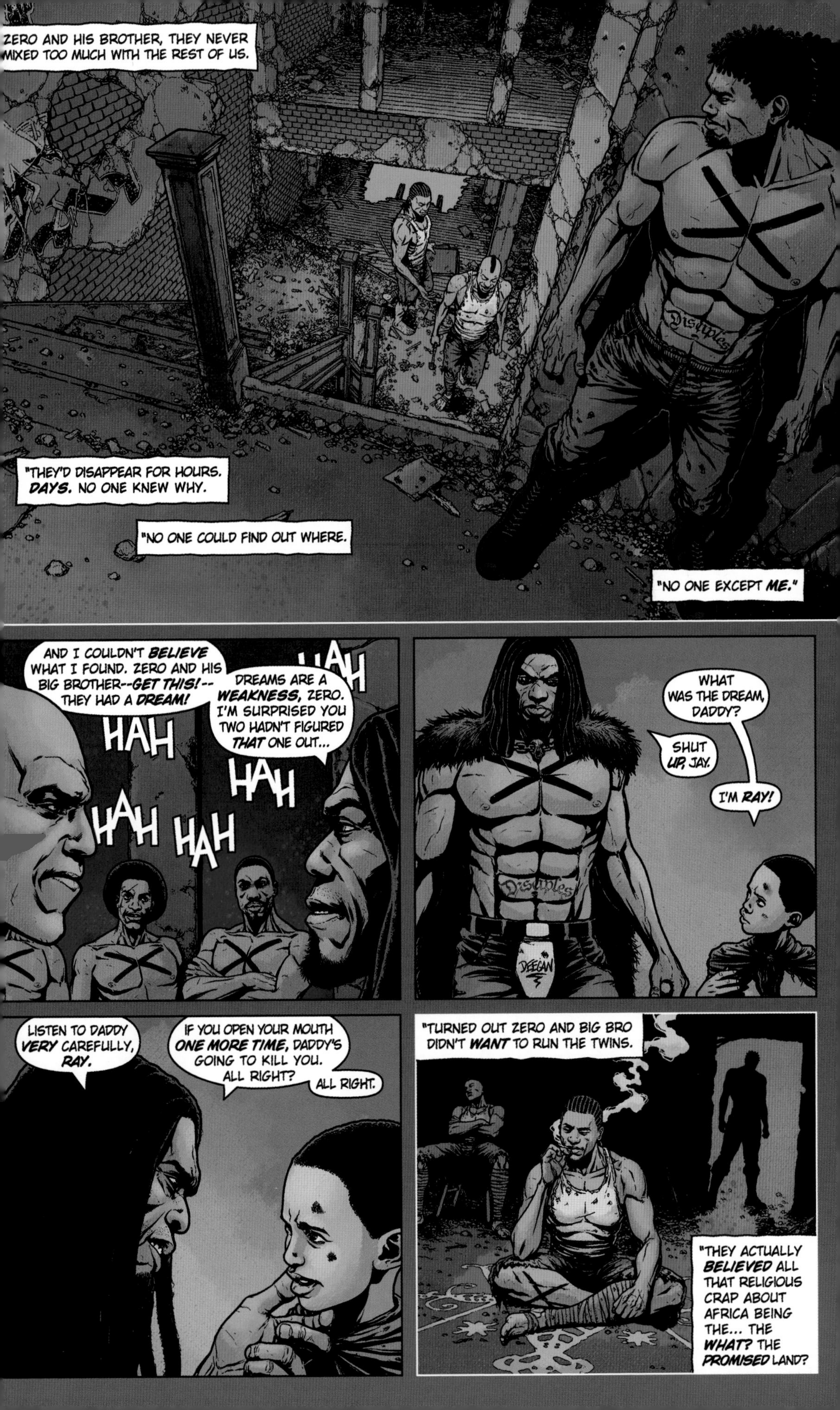
ZERO AND HIS BROTHER, THEY NEVER MIXED TOO MUCH WITH THE REST OF US.
"THEY'D DISAPPEAR FOR HOURS. DAYS. NO ONE KNEW WHY.
"NO ONE COULD FIND OUT WHERE.
"NO ONE EXCEPT ME."
AND I COULDN'T BELIEVE WHAT I FOUND. ZERO AND HIS BIG BROTHER--GET THIS!--THEY HAD A DREAM!
HAH
HAH
HAH
HAH
HAH
DREAMS ARE A WEAKNESS, ZERO. I'M SURPRISED YOU TWO HADN'T FIGURED THAT ONE OUT...
WHAT WAS THE DREAM, DADDY?
SHUT UP, JAY.
I'M RAY!
LISTEN TO DADDY VERY CAREFULLY, RAY.
IF YOU OPEN YOUR MOUTH ONE MORE TIME, DADDY'S GOING TO KILL YOU. ALL RIGHT?
ALL RIGHT.
"TURNED OUT ZERO AND BIG BRO DIDN'T WANT TO RUN THE TWINS.
"THEY ACTUALLY BELIEVED ALL THAT RELIGIOUS CRAP ABOUT AFRICA BEING THE... THE WHAT? THE PROMISED LAND?

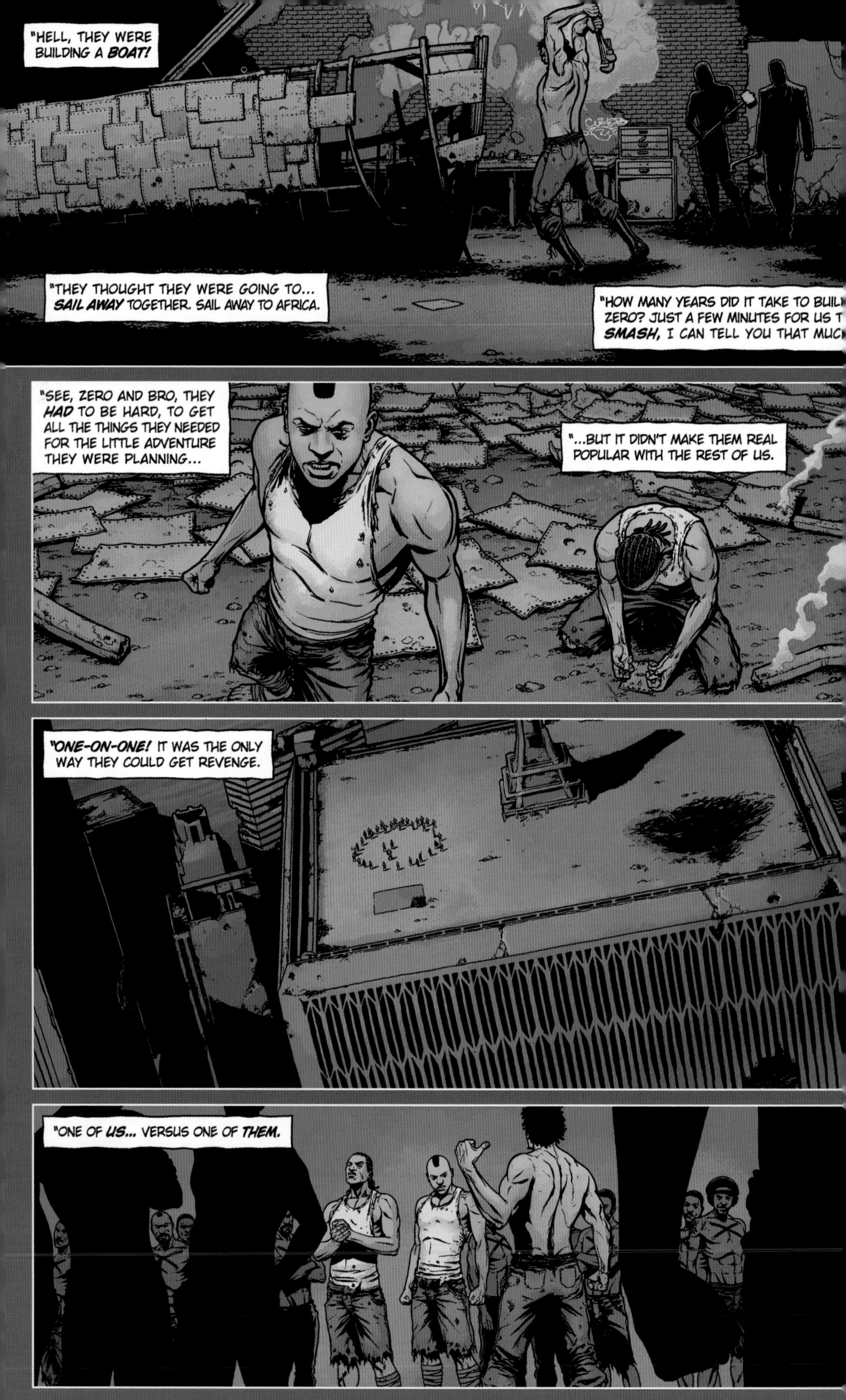
"HELL, THEY WERE BUILDING A BOAT!
"THEY THOUGHT THEY WERE GOING TO... SAIL AWAY TOGETHER. SAIL AWAY TO AFRICA.
"HOW MANY YEARS DID IT TAKE TO BUIL ZERO? JUST A FEW MINUTES FOR US T SMASH, I CAN TELL YOU THAT MUC
"SEE, ZERO AND BRO, THEY HAD TO BE HARD, TO GET ALL THE THINGS THEY NEEDED FOR THE LITTLE ADVENTURE THEY WERE PLANNING...
"...BUT IT DIDN'T MAKE THEM REAL POPULAR WITH THE REST OF US.
"ONE-ON-ONE! IT WAS THE ONLY WAY THEY COULD GET REVENGE.
"ONE OF US... VERSUS ONE OF THEM.

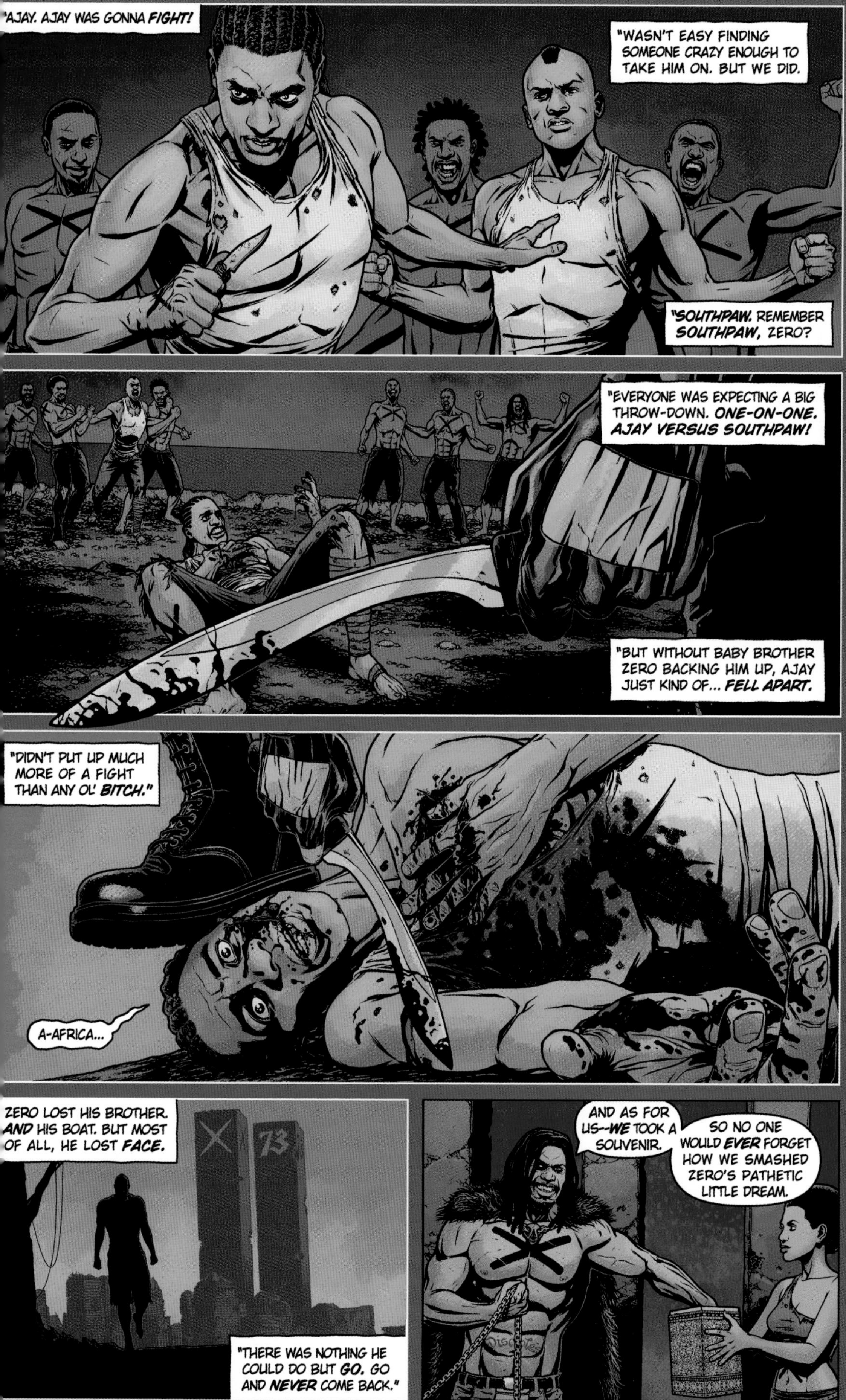
"AJAY. AJAY WAS GONNA *FIGHT!*
"WASN'T EASY FINDING SOMEONE CRAZY ENOUGH TO TAKE HIM ON. BUT WE DID.
"*SOUTHPAW.* REMEMBER *SOUTHPAW,* ZERO?
"EVERYONE WAS EXPECTING A BIG THROW-DOWN. *ONE-ON-ONE. AJAY VERSUS SOUTHPAW!*
"BUT WITHOUT BABY BROTHER ZERO BACKING HIM UP, AJAY JUST KIND OF... *FELL APART.*
"DIDN'T PUT UP MUCH MORE OF A FIGHT THAN ANY OL' *BITCH.*"
A-AFRICA...
ZERO LOST HIS BROTHER. *AND* HIS BOAT. BUT MOST OF ALL, HE LOST *FACE.*
73
"THERE WAS NOTHING HE COULD DO BUT *GO.* GO AND *NEVER* COME BACK."
AND AS FOR US--*WE* TOOK A SOUVENIR.
SO NO ONE WOULD *EVER* FORGET HOW WE SMASHED ZERO'S PATHETIC LITTLE DREAM.

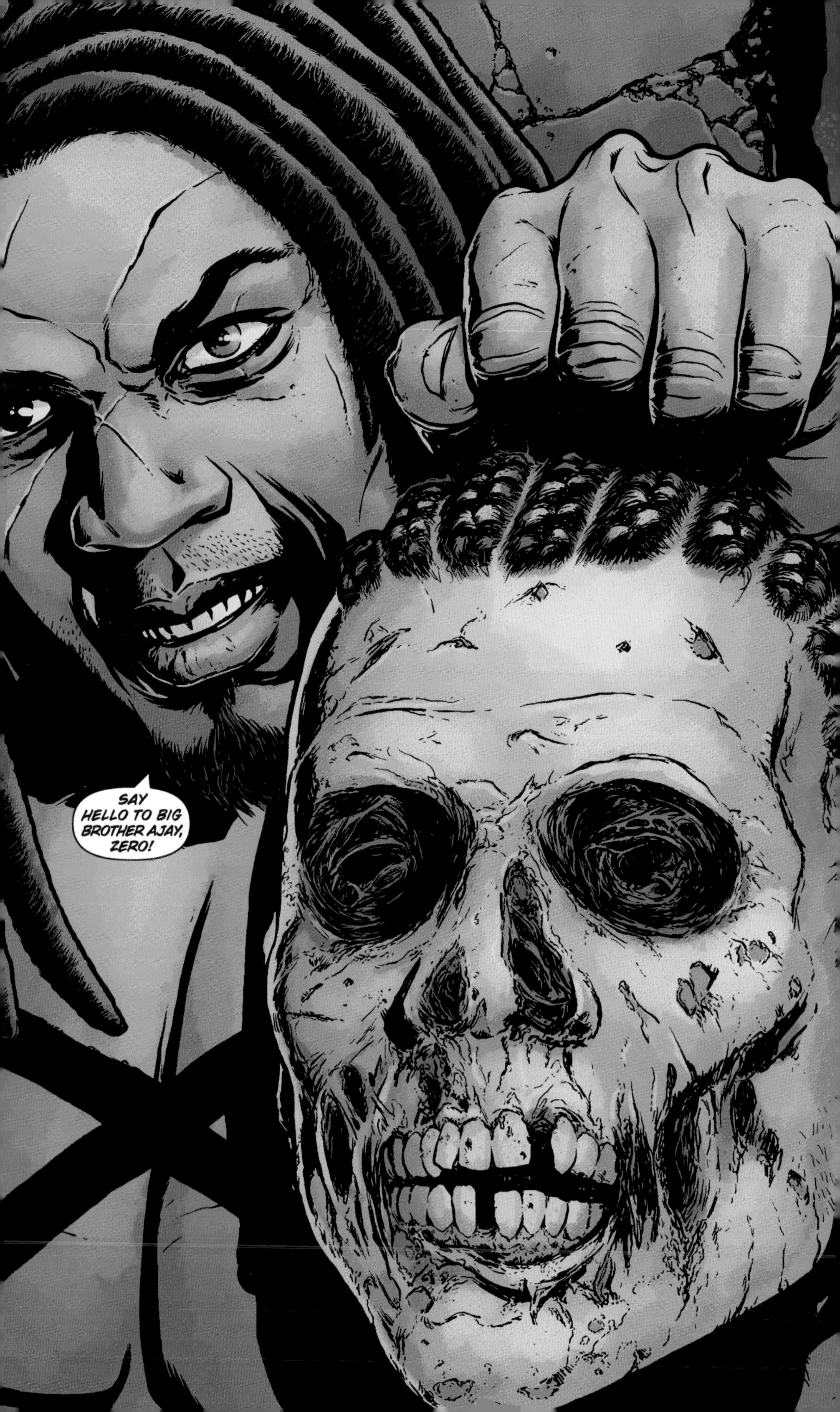
SAY HELLO TO BIG BROTHER AJAY, ZERO!

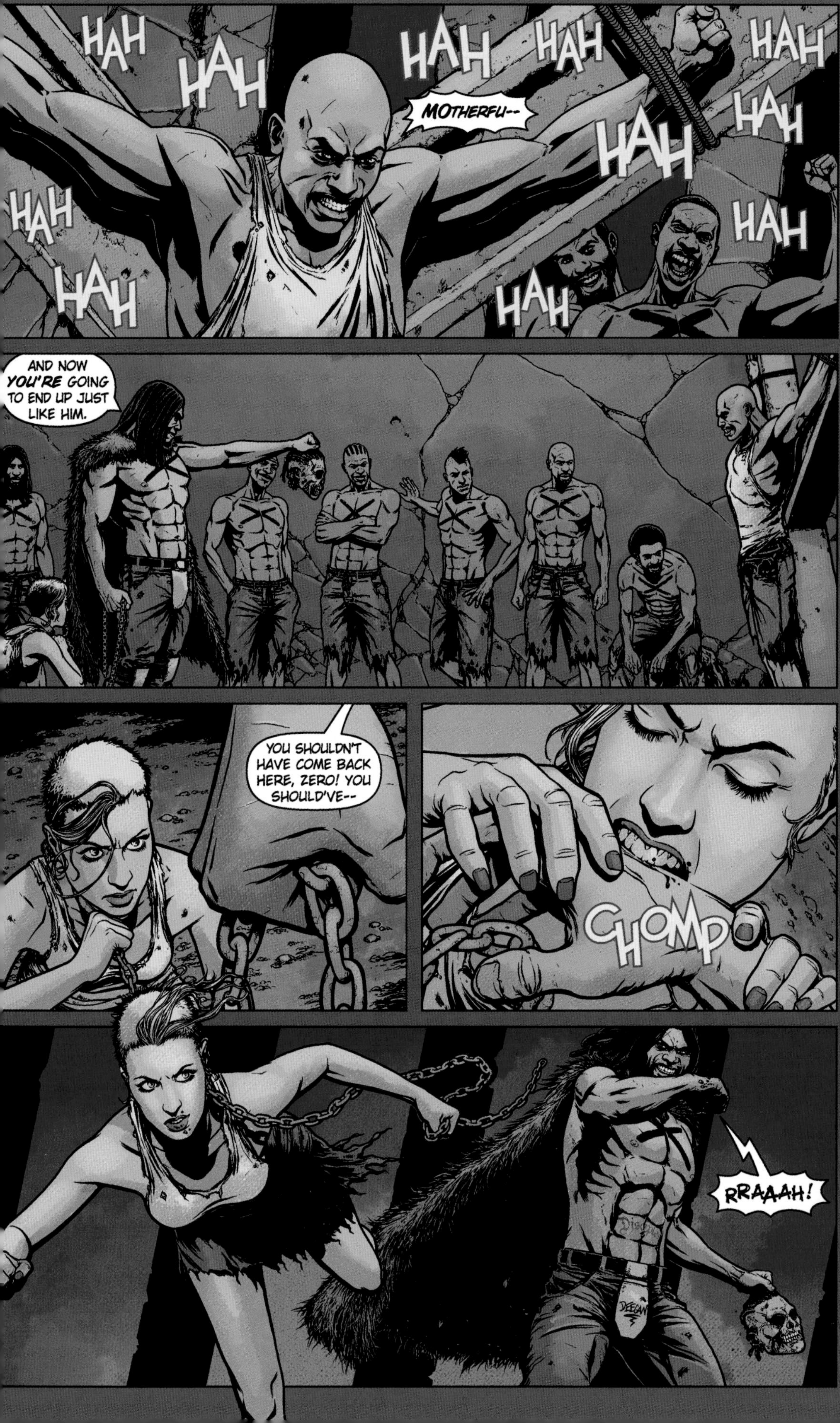
HAH HAH HAH HAH HAH
MOTHERFU--
HAH HAH HAH HAH HAH HAH
AND NOW YOU'RE GOING TO END UP JUST LIKE HIM.
YOU SHOULDN'T HAVE COME BACK HERE, ZERO! YOU SHOULD'VE--
CHOMP
RRAAAH!

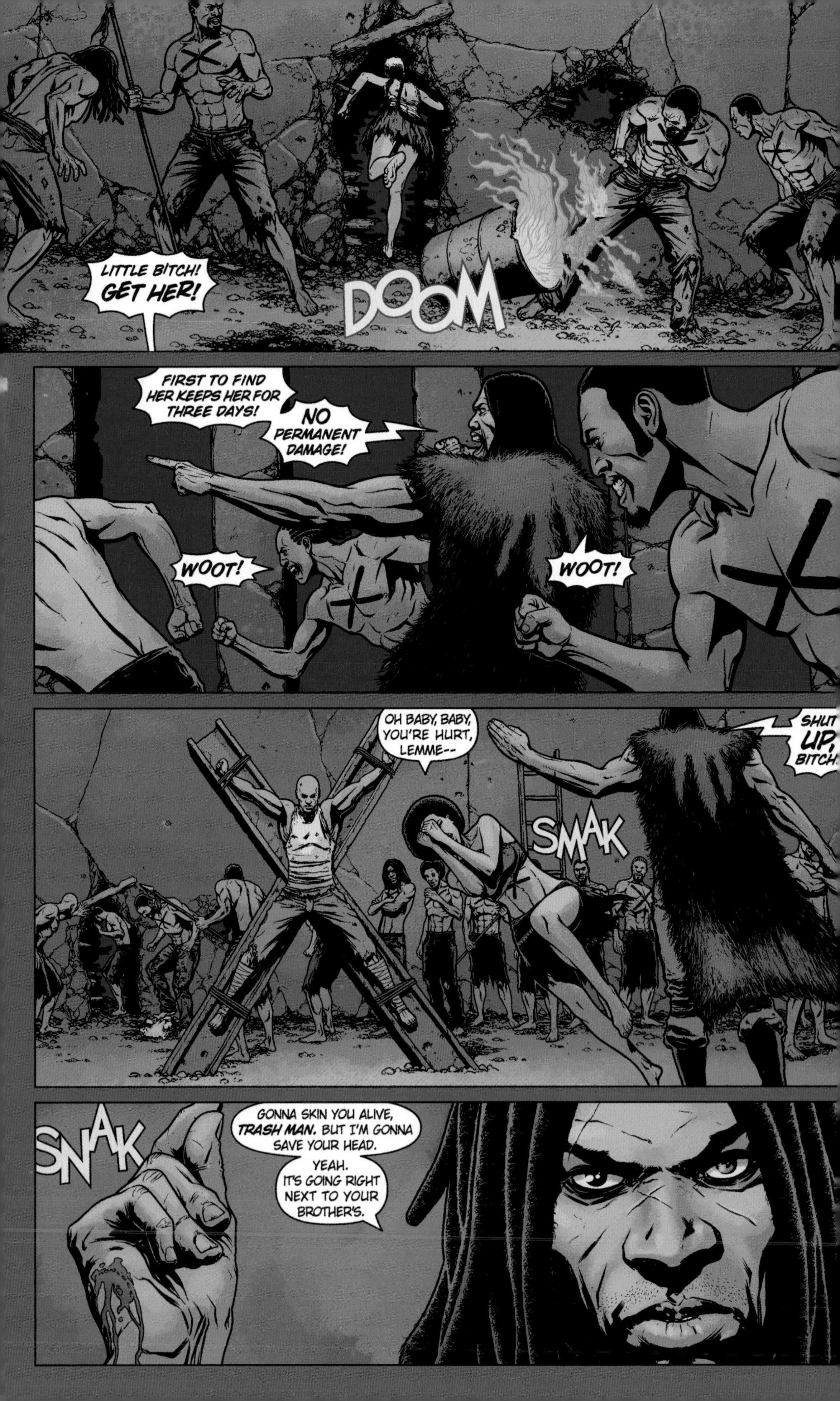
LITTLE BITCH! GET HER!
DOOM
FIRST TO FIND HER KEEPS HER FOR THREE DAYS!
NO PERMANENT DAMAGE!
WOOT!
WOOT!
OH BABY, BABY, YOU'RE HURT, LEMME--
SHUT UP, BITCH.
SMAK
SNAK
GONNA SKIN YOU ALIVE, TRASH MAN. BUT I'M GONNA SAVE YOUR HEAD.
YEAH. IT'S GOING RIGHT NEXT TO YOUR BROTHER'S.

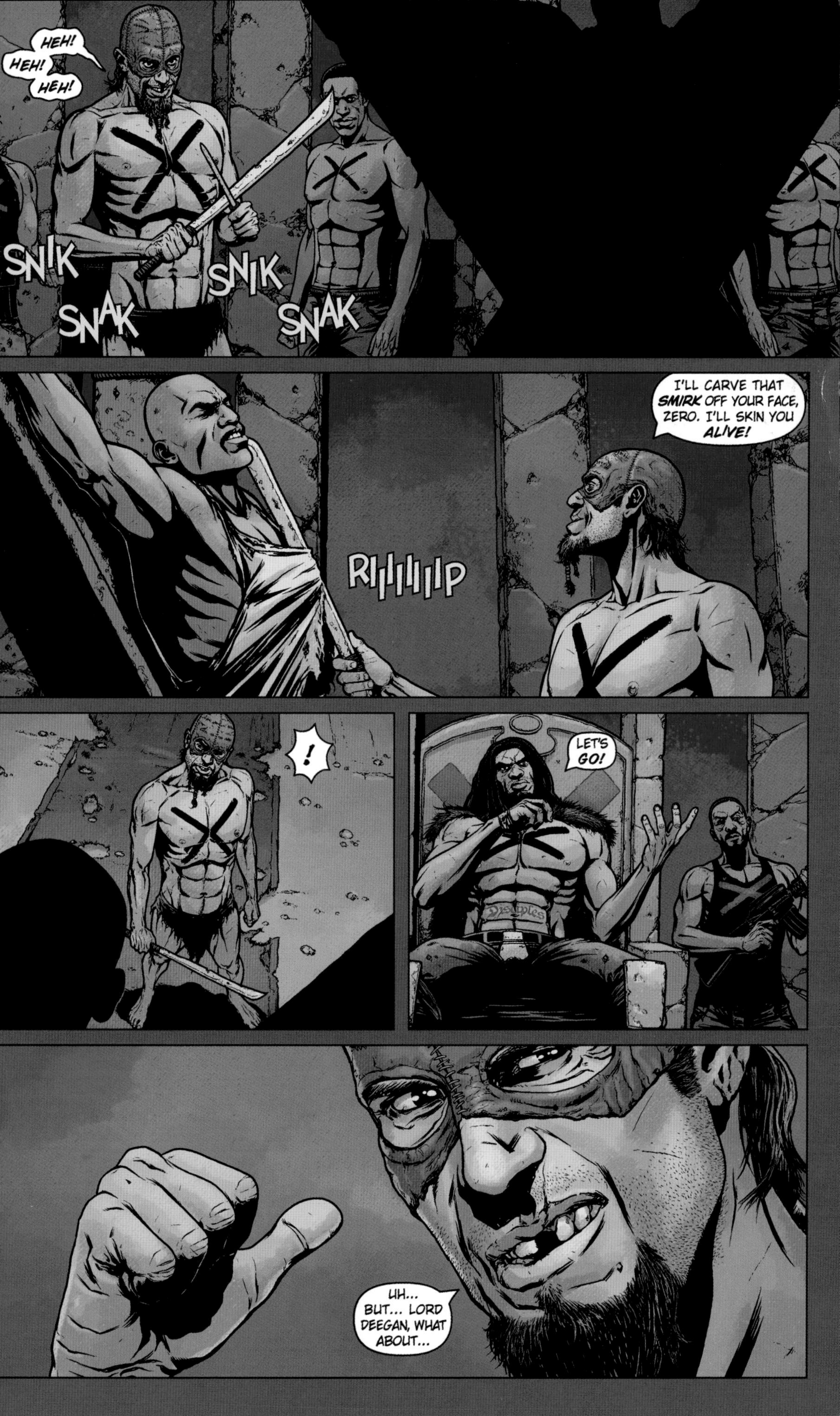
HEH!
HEH!
HEH!
SNIK
SNAK
SNIK
SNAK
I'LL CARVE THAT SMIRK OFF YOUR FACE, ZERO. I'LL SKIN YOU ALIVE!
RIIIIIIP
!
LET'S GO!
UH... BUT... LORD DEEGAN, WHAT ABOUT...

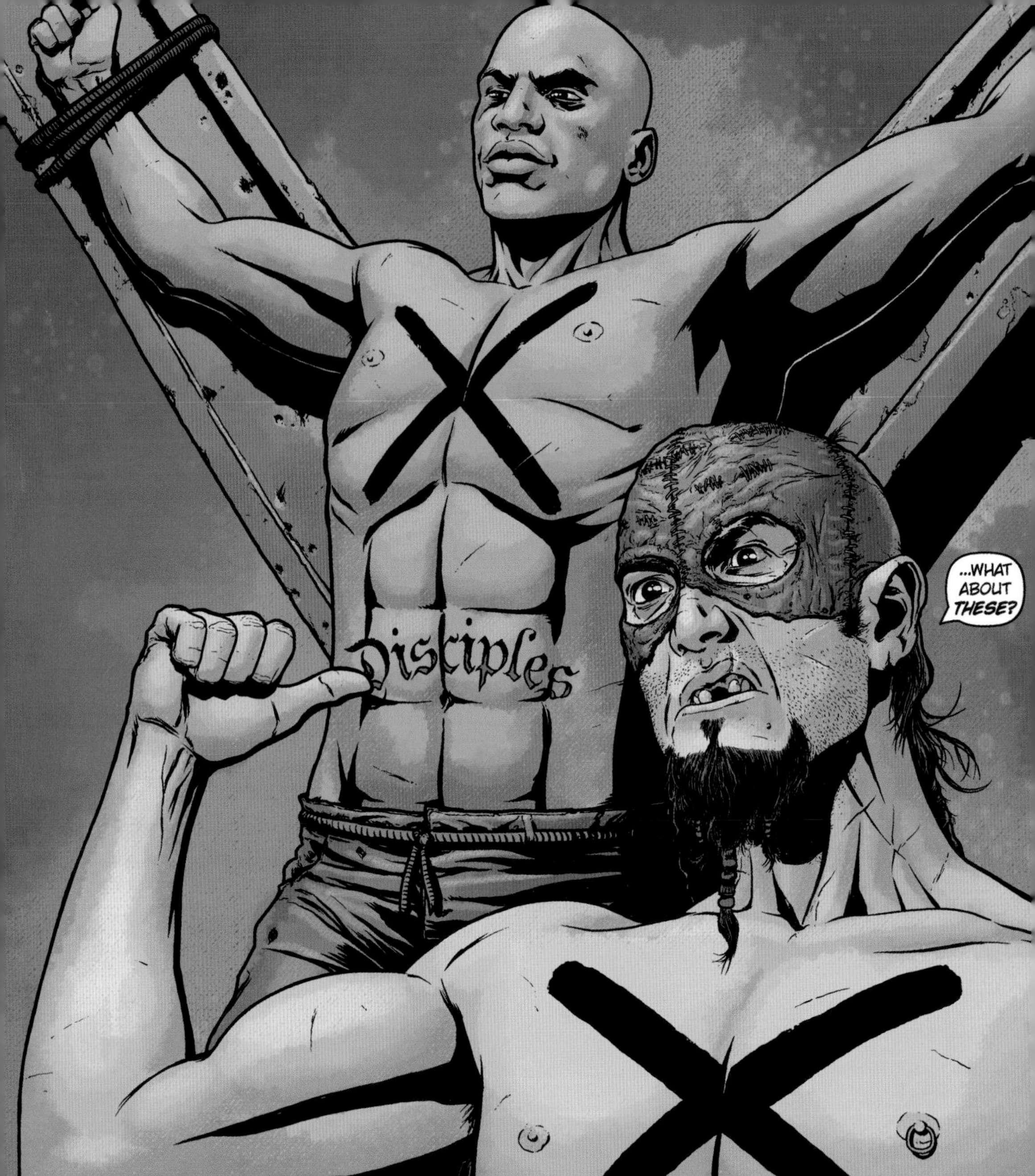
Disciples
...WHAT ABOUT THESE?

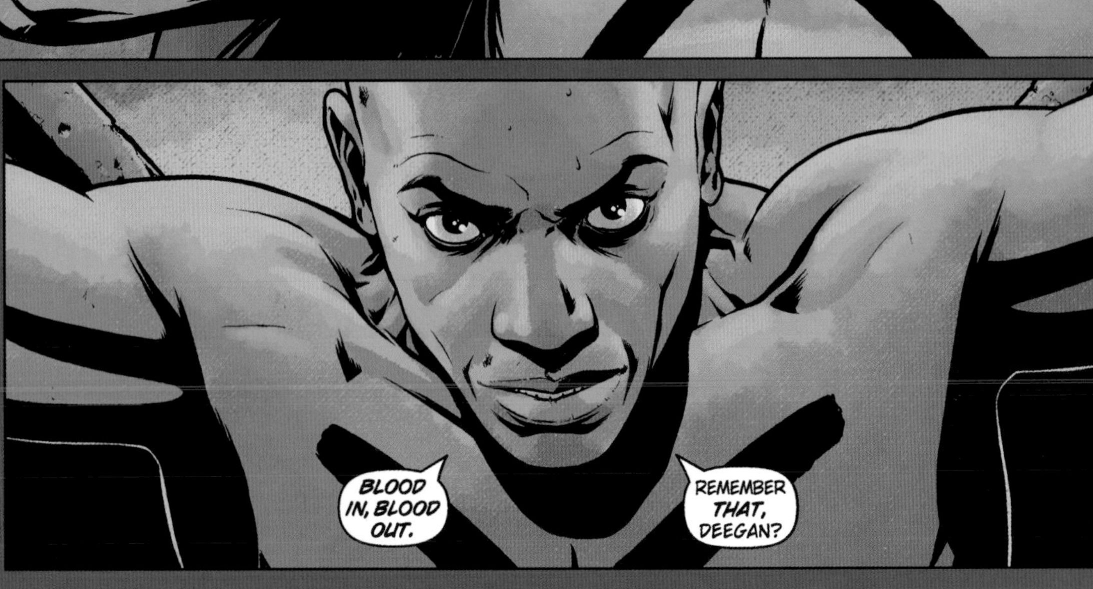
BLOOD IN, BLOOD OUT.
REMEMBER THAT, DEEGAN?

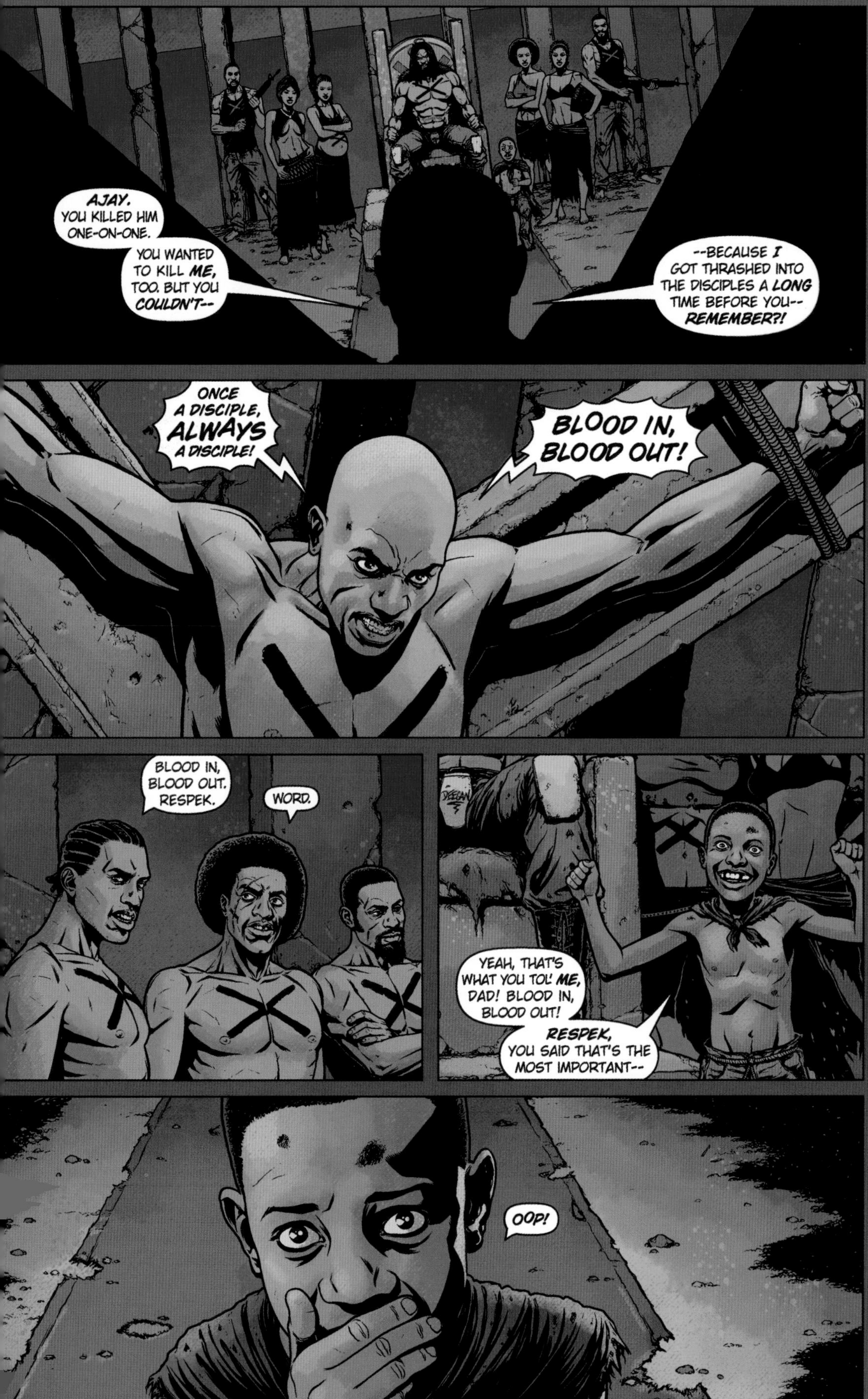
AJAY. YOU KILLED HIM ONE-ON-ONE.
YOU WANTED TO KILL ME, TOO. BUT YOU COULDN'T--
--BECAUSE I GOT THRASHED INTO THE DISCIPLES A LONG TIME BEFORE YOU-- REMEMBER?!
ONCE A DISCIPLE, ALWAYS A DISCIPLE!
BLOOD IN, BLOOD OUT!
BLOOD IN, BLOOD OUT. RESPEK.
WORD.
YEAH, THAT'S WHAT YOU TOL' ME, DAD! BLOOD IN, BLOOD OUT!
RESPEK, YOU SAID THAT'S THE MOST IMPORTANT--
OOP!

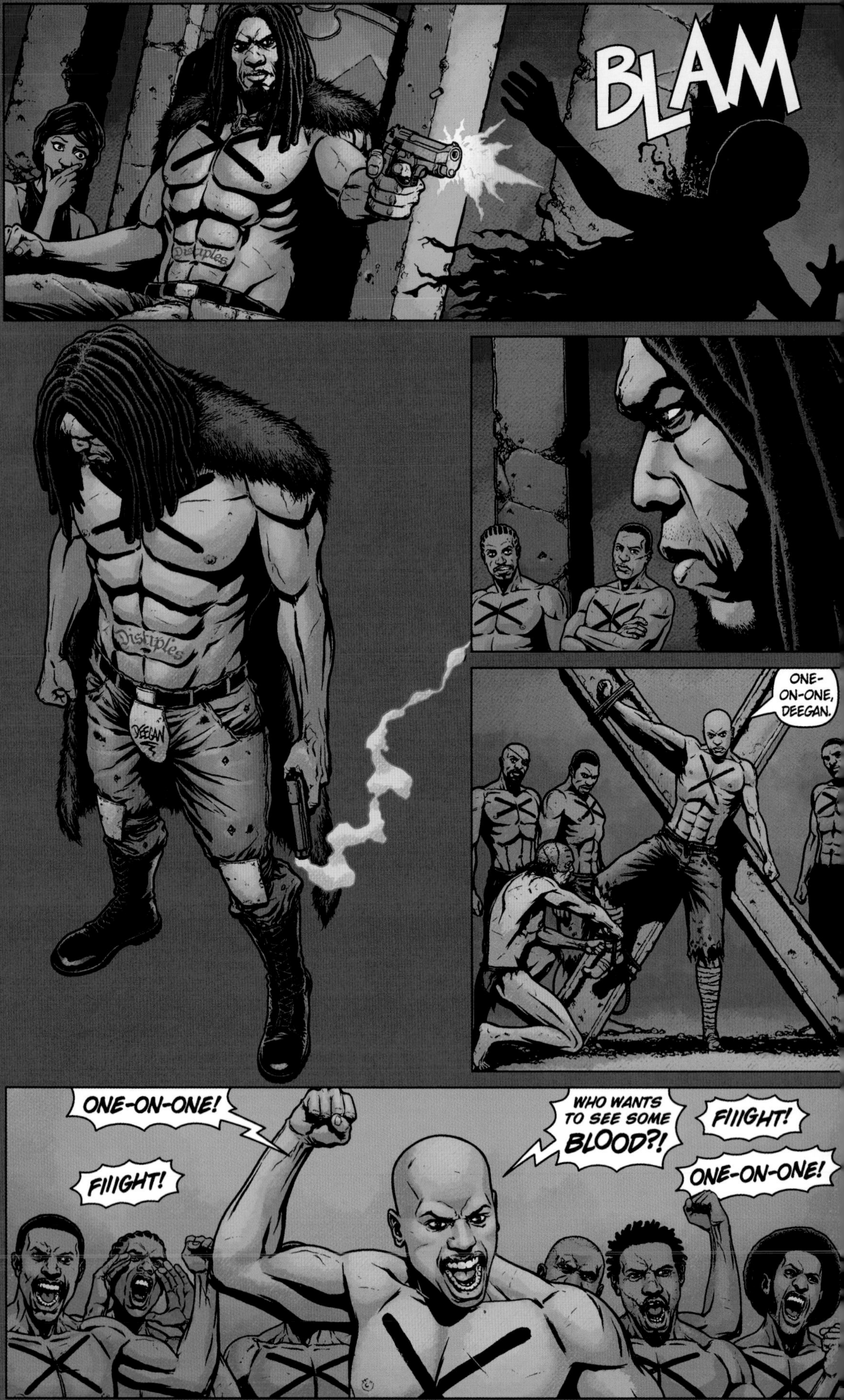
BLAM
Disciples
Disciples
DEEGAN
ONE-ON-ONE, DEEGAN.
ONE-ON-ONE!
FIIIGHT!
WHO WANTS TO SEE SOME BLOOD?!
FIIIGHT!
ONE-ON-ONE!

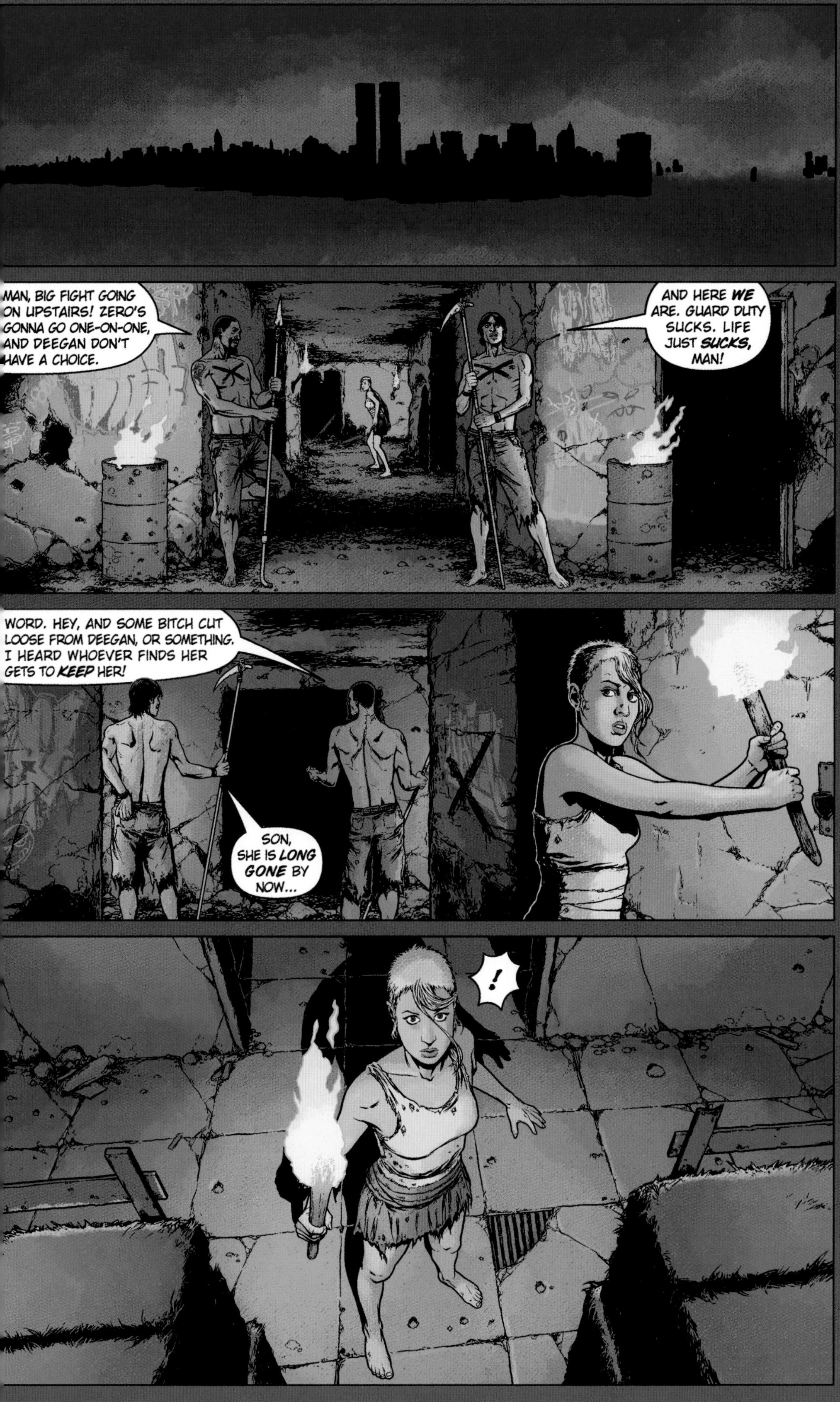
MAN, BIG FIGHT GOING ON UPSTAIRS! ZERO'S GONNA GO ONE-ON-ONE, AND DEEGAN DON'T HAVE A CHOICE.
AND HERE WE ARE. GUARD DUTY SUCKS. LIFE JUST SUCKS, MAN!
WORD. HEY, AND SOME BITCH CUT LOOSE FROM DEEGAN, OR SOMETHING. I HEARD WHOEVER FINDS HER GETS TO KEEP HER!
SON, SHE IS LONG GONE BY NOW...
!

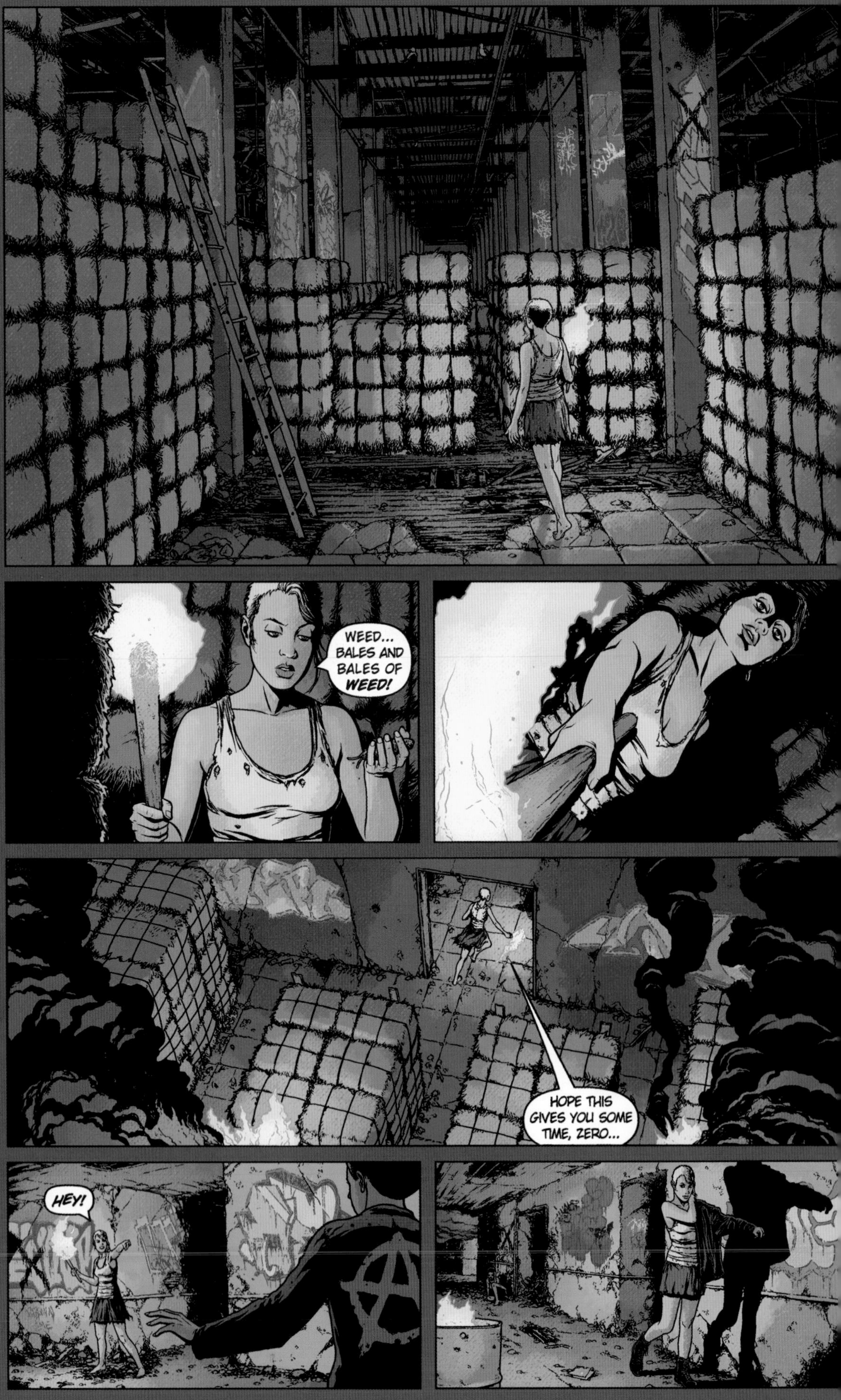
WEED... BALES AND BALES OF WEED!
HOPE THIS GIVES YOU SOME TIME, ZERO...
HEY!

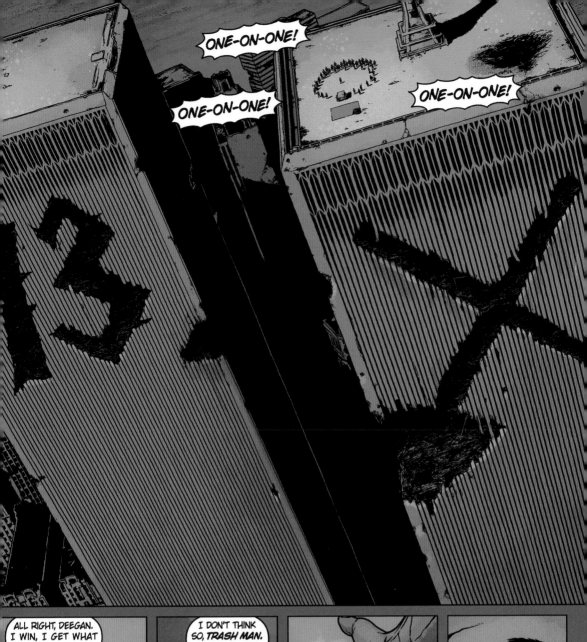

ONE-ON-ONE!

ONE-ON-ONE!

ONE-ON-ONE!

ALL RIGHT, DEEGAN. I WIN, I GET WHAT I CAME FOR. THE BRIEFCASE.

NOW GET DOWN HERE!

I DON'T THINK SO, TRASH MAN. I DECIDE WHO YOU FIGHT.

GOT A SURPRISE FOR YOU, ZERO--

!

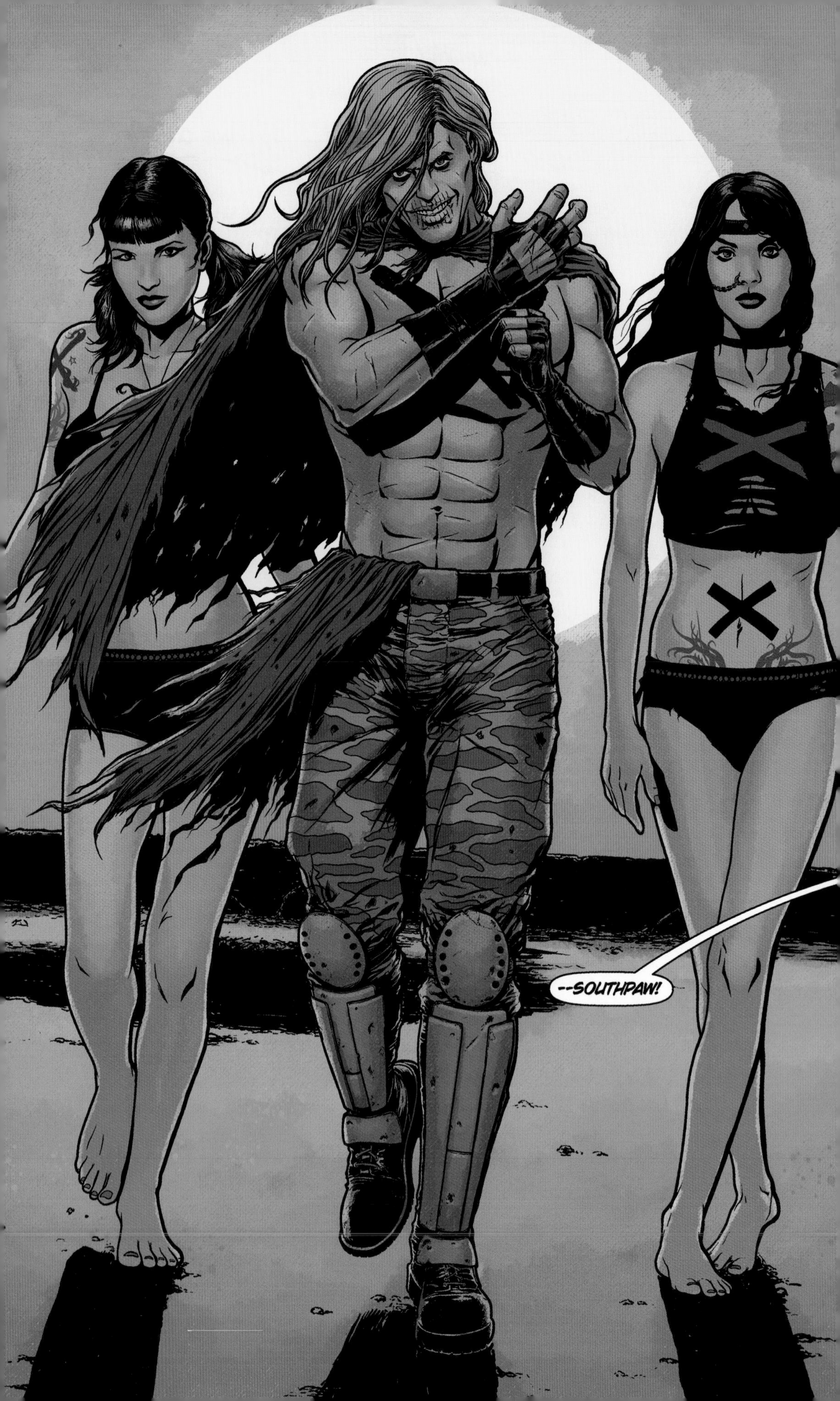
--SOUTHPAW!

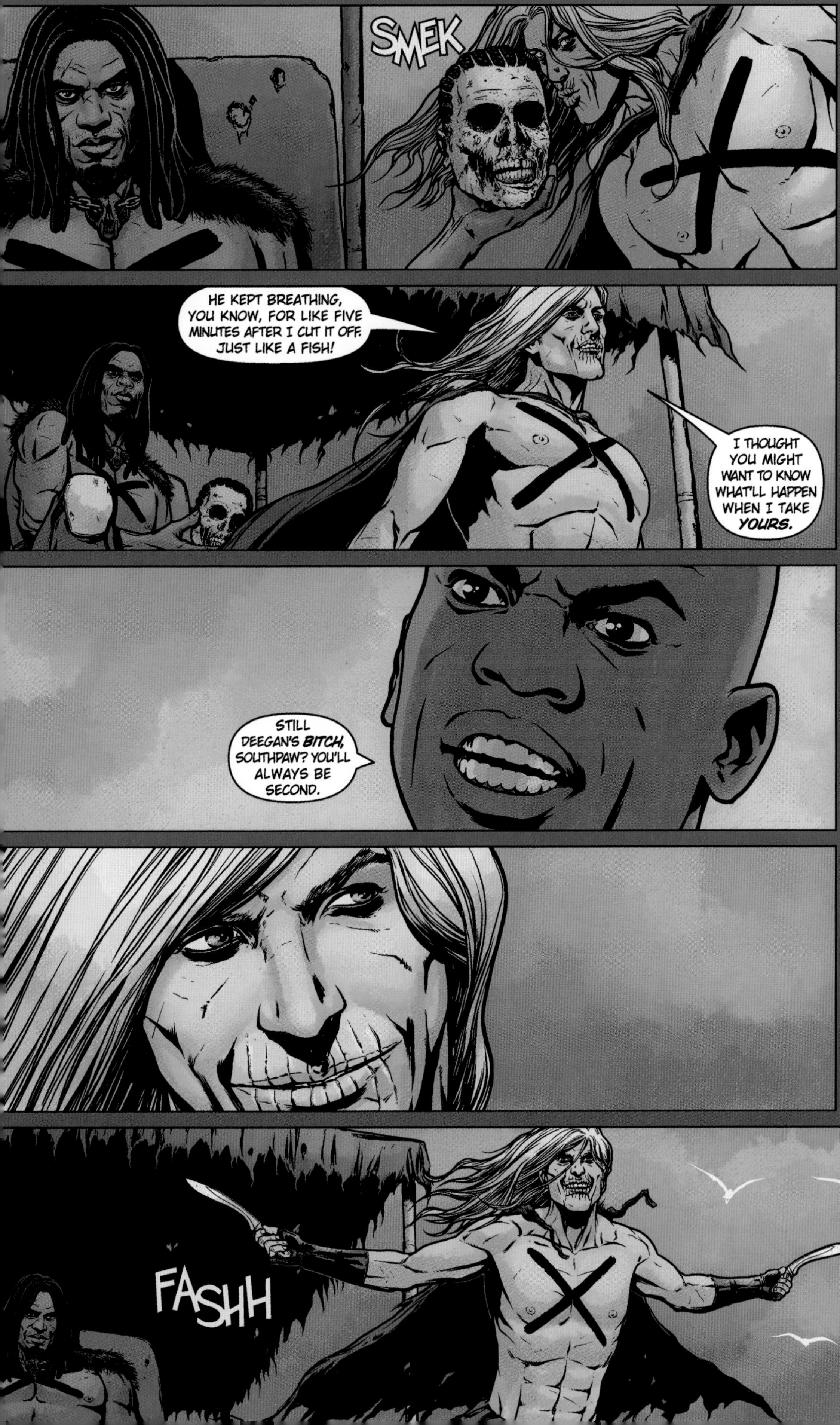

SMEK
HE KEPT BREATHING, YOU KNOW, FOR LIKE FIVE MINUTES AFTER I CUT IT OFF. JUST LIKE A FISH!
I THOUGHT YOU MIGHT WANT TO KNOW WHAT'LL HAPPEN WHEN I TAKE *YOURS.*
STILL DEEGAN'S *BITCH,* SOUTHPAW? YOU'LL ALWAYS BE SECOND.
FASHH

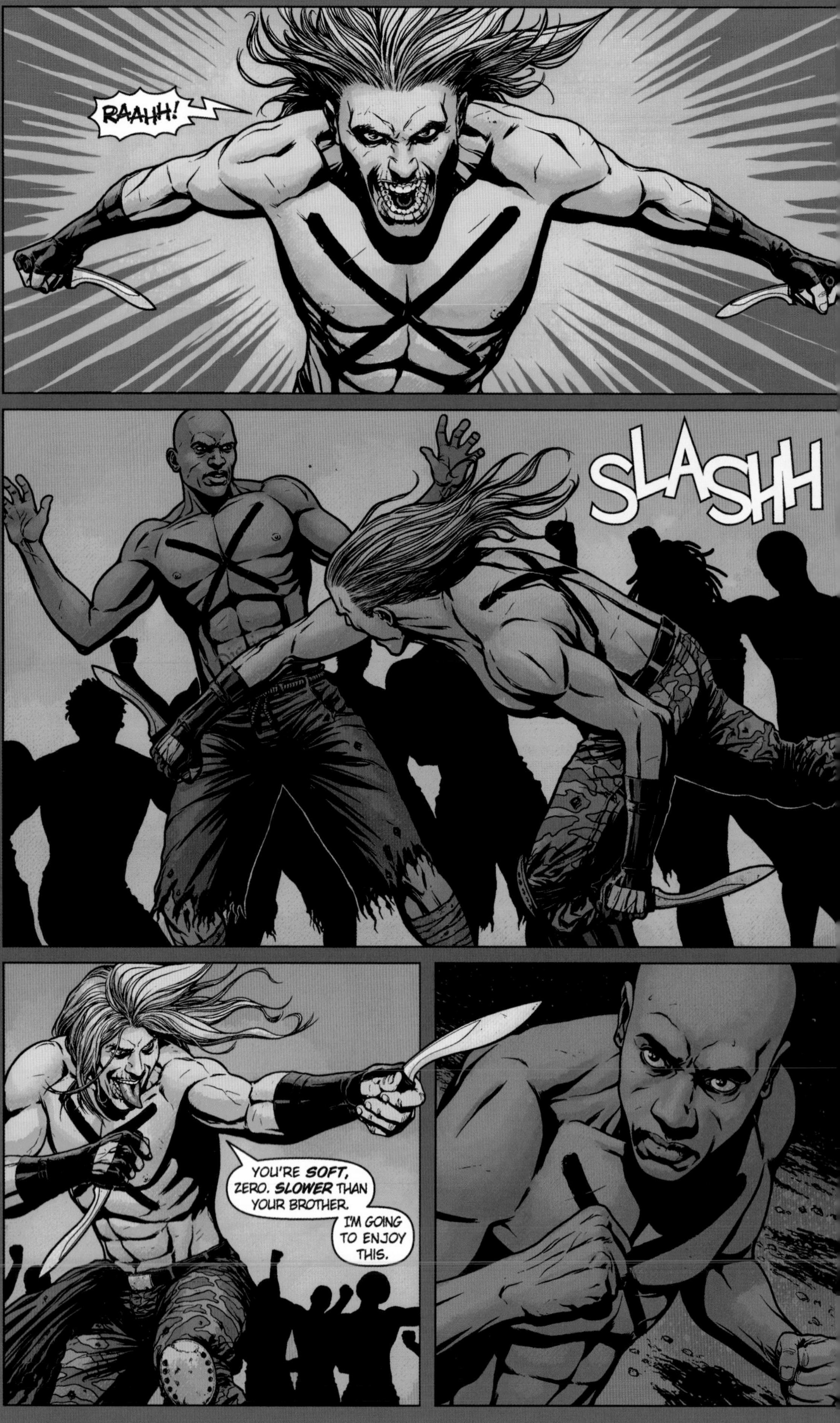
RAAHH!
SLASHH
YOU'RE SOFT, ZERO. SLOWER THAN YOUR BROTHER.
I'M GOING TO ENJOY THIS.

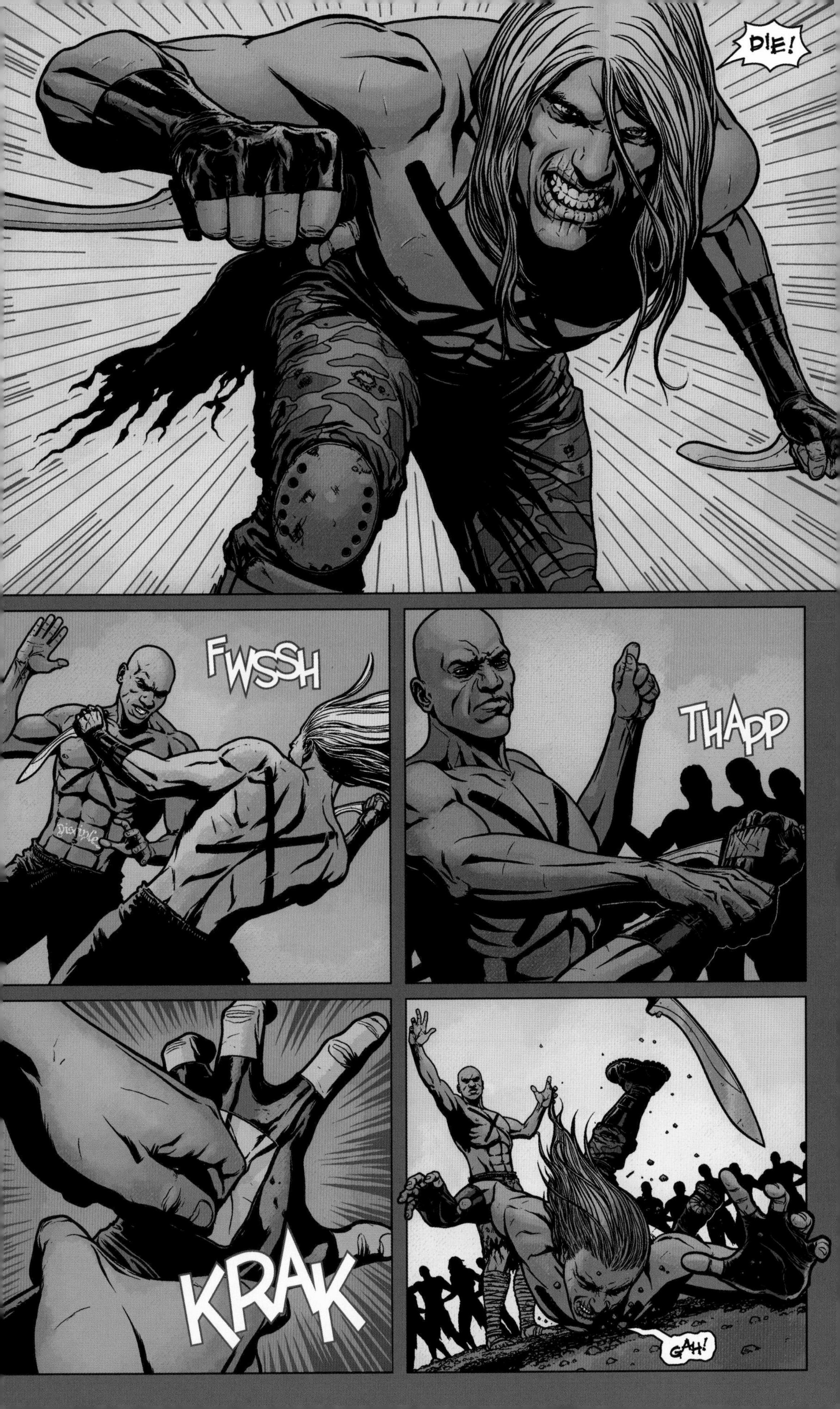
DIE!
FWSSH
THAPP
KRAK
GAH!

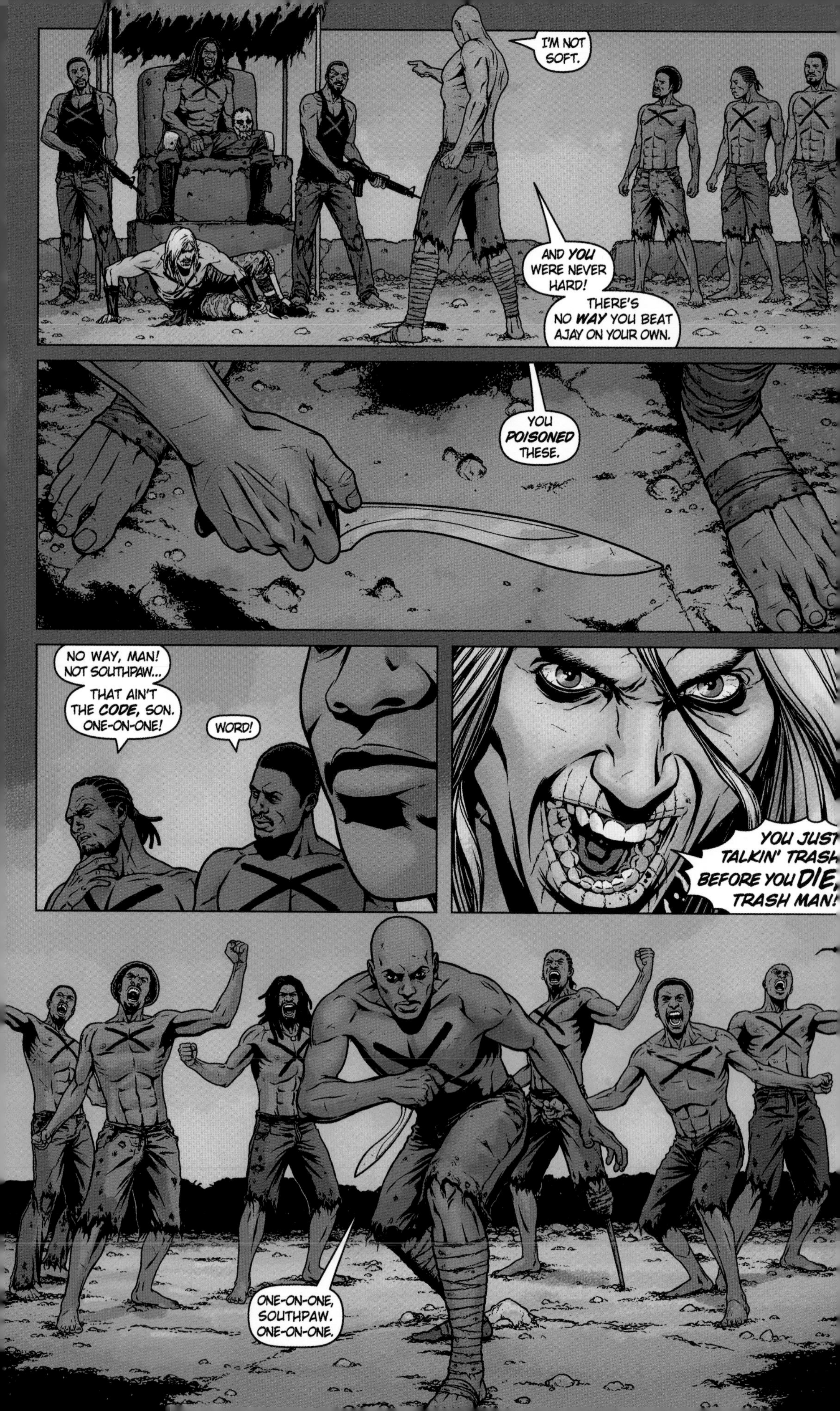
I'M NOT SOFT.
AND YOU WERE NEVER HARD!
THERE'S NO WAY YOU BEAT AJAY ON YOUR OWN.
YOU POISONED THESE.
NO WAY, MAN! NOT SOUTHPAW...
THAT AIN'T THE CODE, SON. ONE-ON-ONE!
WORD!
YOU JUST TALKIN' TRASH BEFORE YOU DIE, TRASH MAN!
ONE-ON-ONE, SOUTHPAW. ONE-ON-ONE.

The JOCOM Daily ✦ Serving Those Who Serve ✦ July 22, 2007 ✦ Vol. 66, No. 18

DAWN'S EARLY LIGHT

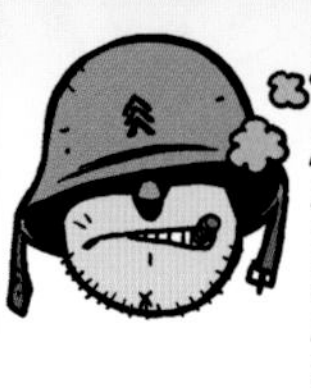

SARGE-N-CHARGE!

RUSSKIE SPIES AREN'T THE ONLY ADVERSARIES THE JOCOM WARRIOR FACES ON THE HOME FRONT. THE GANGSTERS PROWLING THE RUINS OF NEW YORK CITY ARE AN ADAPTABLE AND DETERMINED ENEMY! SARGE HAS MORE ON THE BACK PAGE.

SOVIET SPIES UNMASKED

Espionage Ring Is First Conclusive Proof USSR Survived Global Nuclear Exchange of 1973

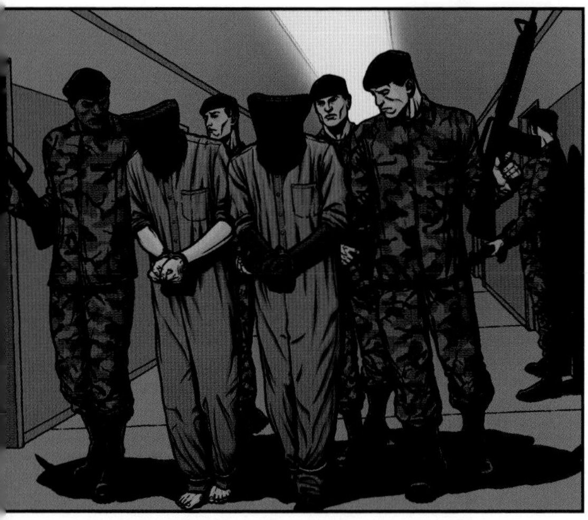

he alleged masterminds of the spy ring are brought to justice.

ligh-Ranking OJCS ;taff Indicted; "This 'ust Confirms What Ve Already Know."

)efense Intelligence Agency DIA) prosecutors announced series of arrests of high-rankng military officials yesterday 1 what they said was "concluve proof the Soviet Union is hriving and has established a etwork of spies that reaches ito the highest echelons of OCOM."

Maj. Michael Chertoff, a pecial DIA prosecutor headng the investigation, made nose explosive claims in a atement released to the press early this morning. If true, it is the first conclusive proof of the Soviet Union's continuing existence.

High-ranking officials in the Office of the Joint Chiefs of Staff (OJCS) have long argued whether the Soviet Union survived the devastation of Zero Hour. The majority held the communist state lived through the holocaust, while a vocal minority argued conclusions without concrete proof were premature.

These so-called "Skeptics" argued the lack of evidence of Soviet activity returned by transoceanic reconnaissance teams leaves room for doubt. But now it seems the Skeptics may have had sinister motives.

Many of the individuals named in yesterday's indictments are prominent Skeptics, among them Maj. Gen. Colin Powell, JOCOM-A second-in-command, and Maj. Gen. Eric Shinseki, number two at the National Security Agency.

None of the indicted individuals could be reached for comment, as they were placed under a FISA-court-imposed gag order.

Chertoff did not present any of the evidence against the accused men, but said it was "clear and compelling." He said the men would all be arraigned on multiple counts of espionage, treason, and conspiracy to commit treason.

The trials will be held in closed-door tribunals "to protect the national security interests of the United States," according to Chertoff. He offered assurances the men would receive fair hearings.

If found guilty, the accused could face the death penalty.

Many in the OJCS feel vindicated by the arrests.

"This just confirms what we already know," National Security Advisor Richard Perle said. "The Skeptics were raising doubts to throw us off the trail, so they could continue to compromise our safety with complete impunity.

"This also explains why our reconnaissance teams never uncovered anything in Europe. The Soviets were warned in advance," he said.

Indeed, the arrests raise serious questions about JOCOM's counter-intelligence capabilities.

"It's hard to wrap your head around the magnitude of this treason," Defense Intelligence Secretary William Kristol said. "This spy ring would have compromised everything if we hadn't intervened in time. But there's no immediate danger of a Soviet attack.

"Now that we've identified the threat, we'll take measures to insure these kinds of breaches never happen again."

Future War Planning Secretary Paul Wolfowitz wouldn't give specific information about what investigators had learned about the current condition of the USSR.

"The Soviets present a very clear and very grave danger to the American way of life. But we've been planning for this phase of the war for a long time. That's all anyone needs to know right now," he said.

Chertoff said more arrests were "likely, once we interrogate those already in custody." He asked all JOCOM personnel "to be vigilant, and to report any suspicious activity to a DIA officer immediately." ✦

SARGE'S TIPS 'N' TACTICS

Stay alert ✦ Stay focused ✦ Stay alive

YOU ***GRUNTS*** HAVE BEEN SENDING ME A LOT OF LETTERS RECENTLY, LIKE SPECIALIST JACK LIN, WHO WANTS TO KNOW, "SARGE, WHY DON'T WE JUST KILL EVERY LAST ONE OF THEM SONS OF BITCHES IN THE TOWERS?" ***THAT'S NOT HAPPENING ANYTIME SOON, SPECIALIST!*** THE TOWER DWELLERS ARE THE PERFECT GUINEA PIGS FOR THE BOYS IN THE WHITE COATS AT THE ***ADVANCED GENETIC RESEARCH INITIATIVE***. LIKE IT OR NOT, WE NEED THE TOWER PEOPLE... FOR NOW. BUT THE GANGSTERS FOLLOW THEIR OWN TWISTED CODE OF HONOR, WHICH ***CAN*** BE USED AGAINST THEM IN EMERGENCIES. SO PAY ATTENTION TO THE DEFINITIONS BELOW! THE INTEL JUST MIGHT SAVE YOUR BUTT ONE DAY.

TRUE BLOOD
BLACK CATS
The Jokers
Disciples
Rumblers

"THE CODE": A CRUDE FORM OF TRIBAL JUSTICE BASED ON GROUP LOYALTY. THE CODE ONLY APPLIES TO FULL-FLEDGED GANG MEMBERS, EASILY IDENTIFIABLE BY THEIR TATTOOS. SO KEEP YOUR EYES PEELED, SOLDIER! AVOID GANGSTERS AT ALL COSTS. THE VAST MAJORITY OF TOWER DWELLERS ARE EASY MARKS FOR THE GANGSTERS... ***AND*** YOUR HARVESTING QUOTAS.

THE CODE IS JUST ABOUT THE ONLY THING THE GANGSTERS RESPECT; THEY ***HAVE*** TO, SINCE IT'S THE ONLY PROTECTION THEY HAVE AGAINST EACH OTHER! THOSE WHO BREAK IT BECOME ***OUTCASTS,*** AND ARE HUNTED DOWN BY THE HATED BOUNTY HUNTERS KNOWN AS ***TRASH MEN.*** SO WHAT ***ARE*** THE RULES OF THE CODE? READ ON.

"THRASHED IN": A VICIOUS BEATING, THE RITUAL FOR GANG ADMISSION. YOUNG TOUGHS HAVE TO PROVE THEMSELVES TO JOIN A GANG, THROUGH FEATS OF CRUELTY AND STRENGTH. THE SELECTION PROCESS IS BASED ON THE WHIMS OF THE GANGSTERS AND THEIR LORD, BUT GENERALLY CULMINATES WITH SLAYING ANOTHER ASPIRING "GANG BANGER" IN HAND-TO-HAND COMBAT.

GETTING ***THRASHED IN*** IS A HUGE STEP UP THE SOCIAL LADDER FOR THE TOWER SCUM. BENEFITS INCLUDE THE PROTECTION OF THE REST OF THE GANG, A DEPENDABLE, RELATIVELY NUTRITIOUS (IF REVOLTING) DIET, AND LIVING HIGH UP IN THE TOWER, FAR AWAY FROM THE RADIOACTIVE WATER. BUT GETTING "THRASHED IN" IS SO BRUTAL, MANY DIE IN THE PROCESS. ONLY THE TOUGHEST AND MEANEST SURVIVE TO BECOME GANGSTERS. UNDERESTIMATE THEM AT YOUR OWN RISK!

"ONE-ON-ONE": ATTACKING A FELLOW GANG MEMBER IS COMPLETELY FORBIDDEN EXCEPT UNDER THE RULES OF A ***ONE-ON-ONE,*** A DUEL TO THE DEATH. ONE-ON-ONE IS THE ***ONLY*** MEANS GANGSTERS HAVE OF SETTLING DISPUTES WITH MEMBERS OF THE SAME GANG. ANY MEMBER MAY CHALLENGE ANOTHER, USUALLY BECAUSE OF AN INSULT OR GRUDGE. ANYONE WHO BACKS DOWN IS KICKED OUT OF THE GANG.

THE TWO COMBATANTS ARE OFFERED THEIR CHOICE OF HAND WEAPONS, BUT NO FIREARMS ARE ALLOWED. TRICKERY OF ANY KIND IS ALSO FORBIDDEN. IN THE RARE INSTANCES WHEN A GANG LORD IS CHALLENGED, THE LORD MAY SELECT A SECOND TO FIGHT IN HIS PLACE. THE DUELS ARE A FORM OF HIGH ENTERTAINMENT FOR GANGSTERS, OFTEN RESULTING IN THE DEATHS OF ***BOTH*** PARTIES!

"BLOOD IN, BLOOD OUT": THERE ARE TWO WAYS TO LEAVE A GANG: EXPULSION, THROUGH VIOLATION OF ***THE CODE,*** OR DEATH. THAT IS THE ESSENCE OF ***BLOOD IN, BLOOD OUT***. BUT GANG MEMBERS MUST ALWAYS CONCERN THEMSELVES WITH THEIR STANDING WITHIN A GANG. SIGNS OF WEAKNESS RESULT IN A LOSS OF FACE.

OCCASIONALLY A GANGSTER WILL SUFFER A LOSS OF FACE ***SO*** COMPLETE HIS FELLOWS LOSE ALL RESPECT FOR HIM. SUCH A PERSON IS UNABLE TO CHALLENGE A ONE-ON-ONE, YET HE ***CANNOT*** BE KILLED BECAUSE OF BLOOD IN, BLOOD OUT. THESE RARE INDIVIDUALS BECOME WANDERERS, IN A STATE OF SOCIAL LIMBO. THEY DON'T SURVIVE LONG WITHOUT THE ACTIVE SUPPORT OF THEIR GANG.

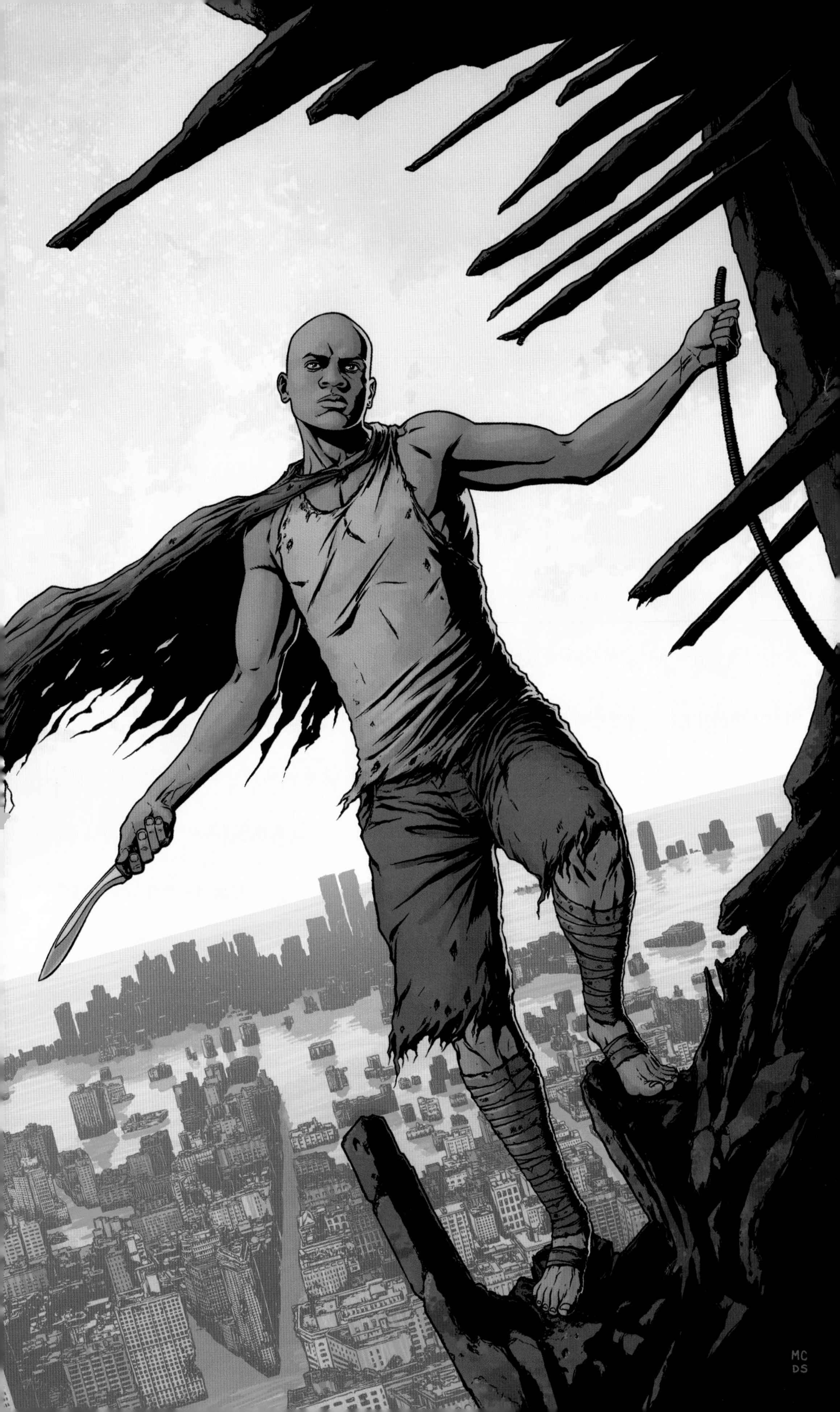
MC
DS

CHAPTER 6

LORD OF THIS WORLD

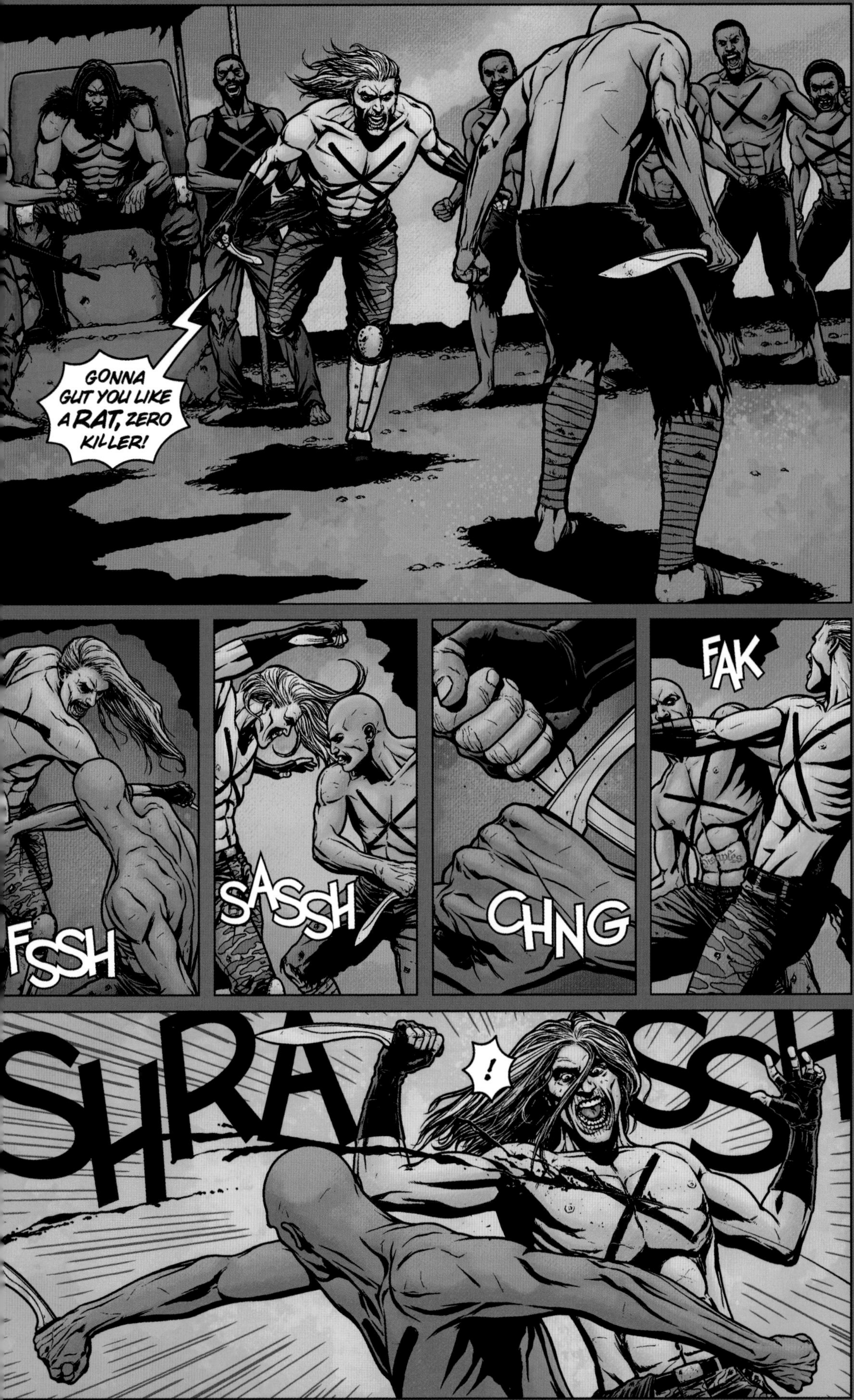
GONNA GUT YOU LIKE A RAT, ZERO KILLER!
FSSH
SASSSH
CHNG
FAK
SHRAASSH
!

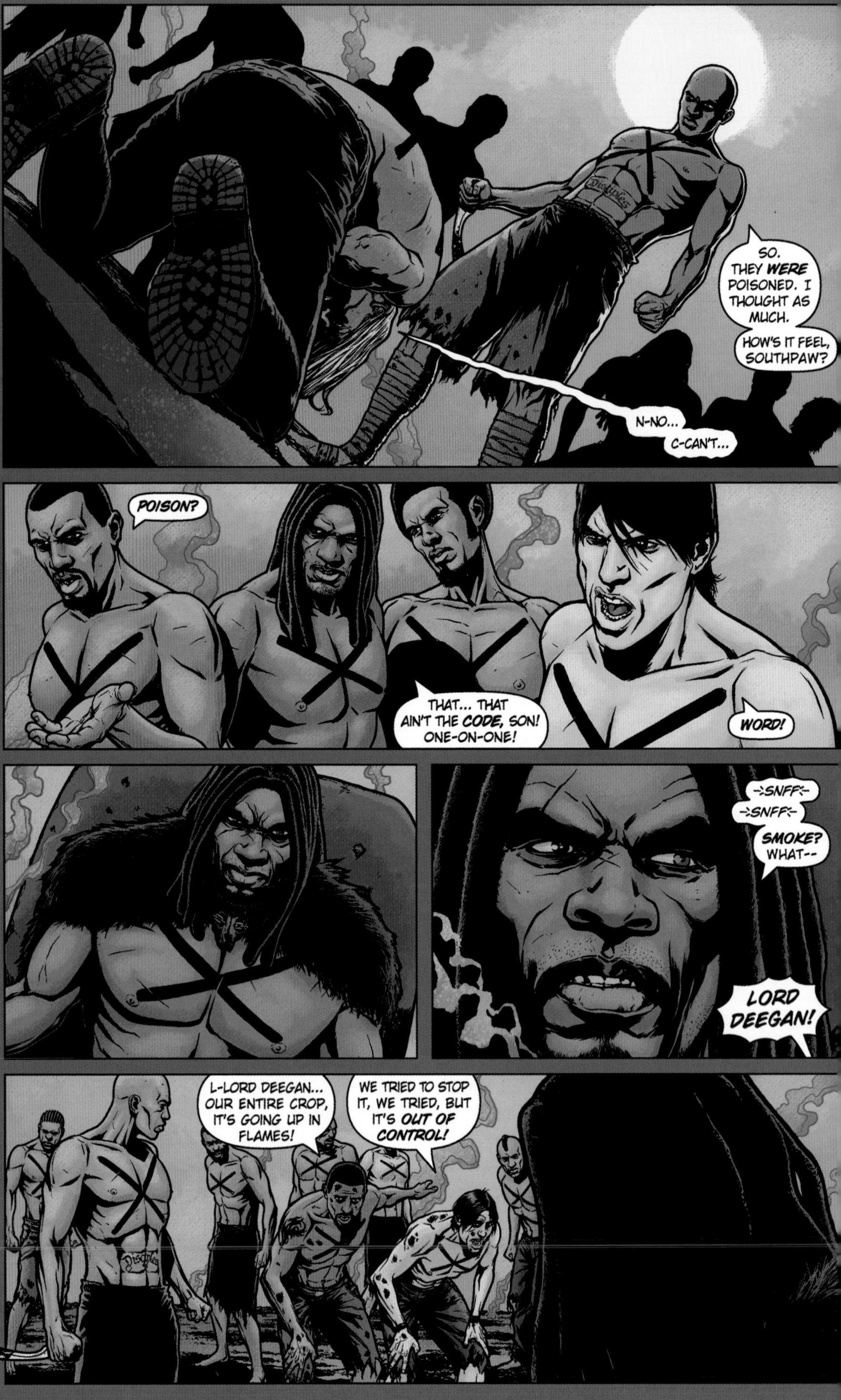
SO. THEY WERE POISONED. I THOUGHT AS MUCH.
HOW'S IT FEEL, SOUTHPAW?
N-NO...
C-CAN'T...
POISON?
THAT... THAT AIN'T THE CODE, SON! ONE-ON-ONE!
WORD!
-SNFF-
-SNFF-
SMOKE? WHAT--
LORD DEEGAN!
L-LORD DEEGAN... OUR ENTIRE CROP, IT'S GOING UP IN FLAMES!
WE TRIED TO STOP IT, WE TRIED, BUT IT'S OUT OF CONTROL!

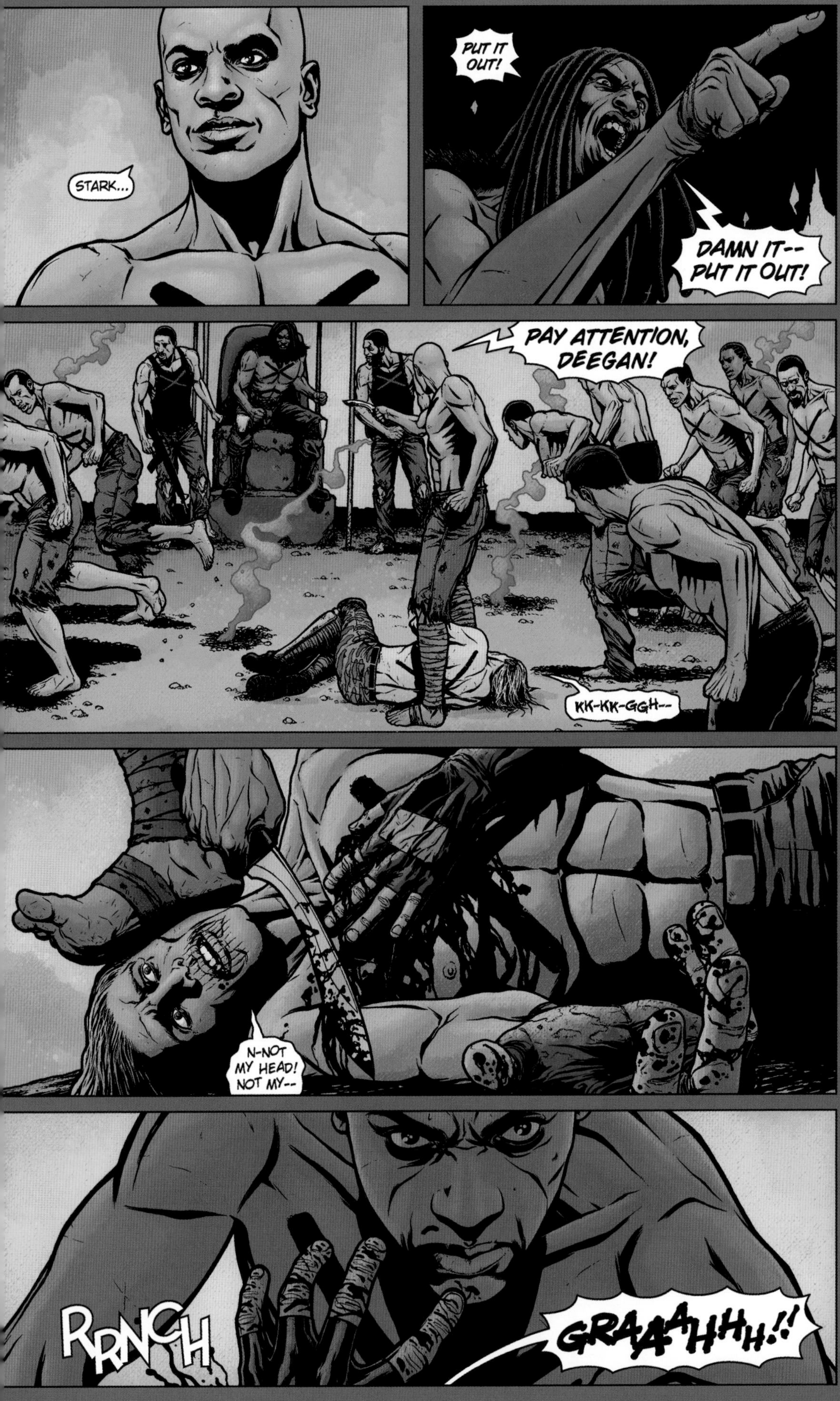
STARK...
PUT IT OUT!
DAMN IT-- PUT IT OUT!
PAY ATTENTION, DEEGAN!
KK-KK-GGH--
N-NOT MY HEAD! NOT MY--
RRNCH
GRAAAHHHH!!!

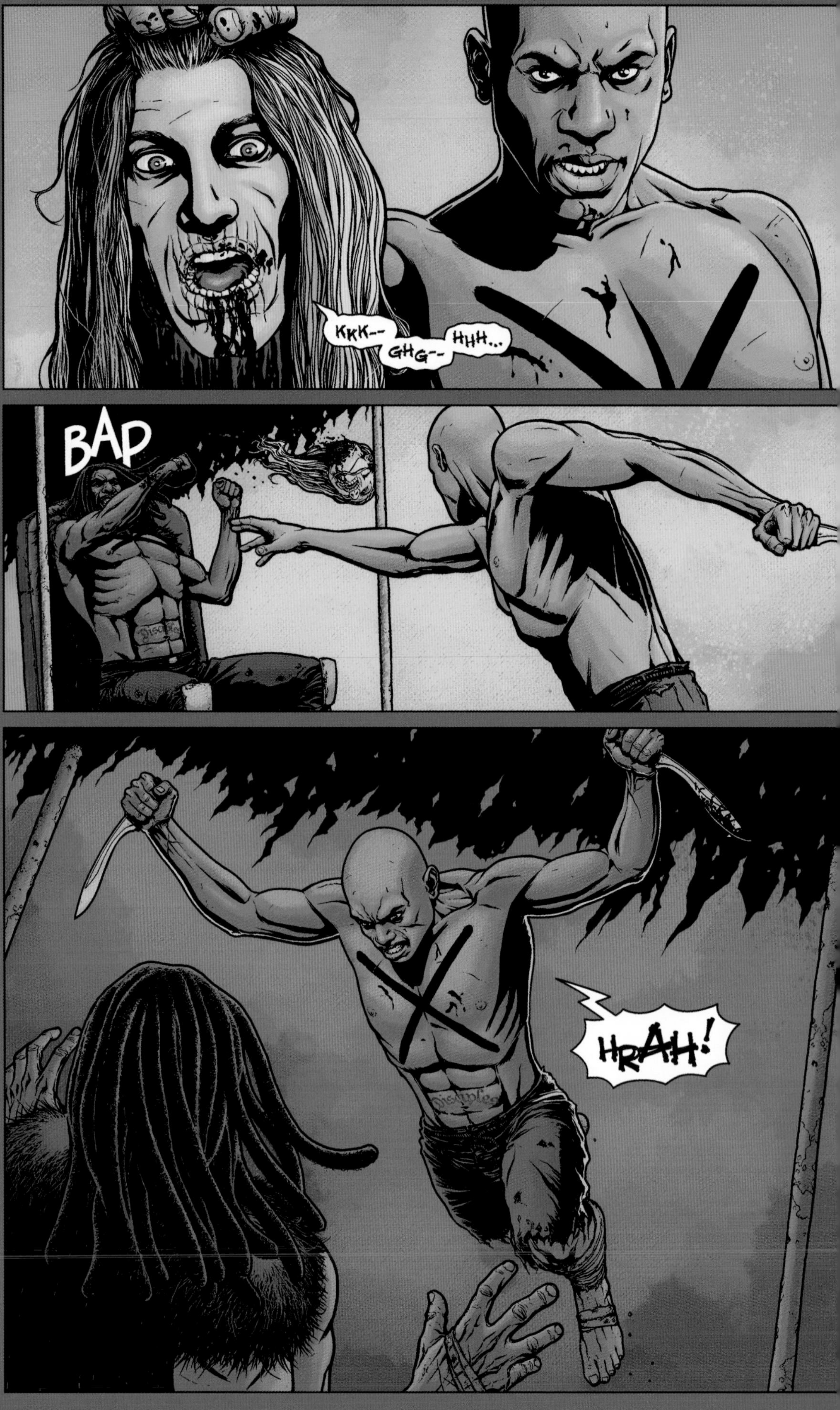
KKK-- GHG-- HHH...
BAP
HRAH!

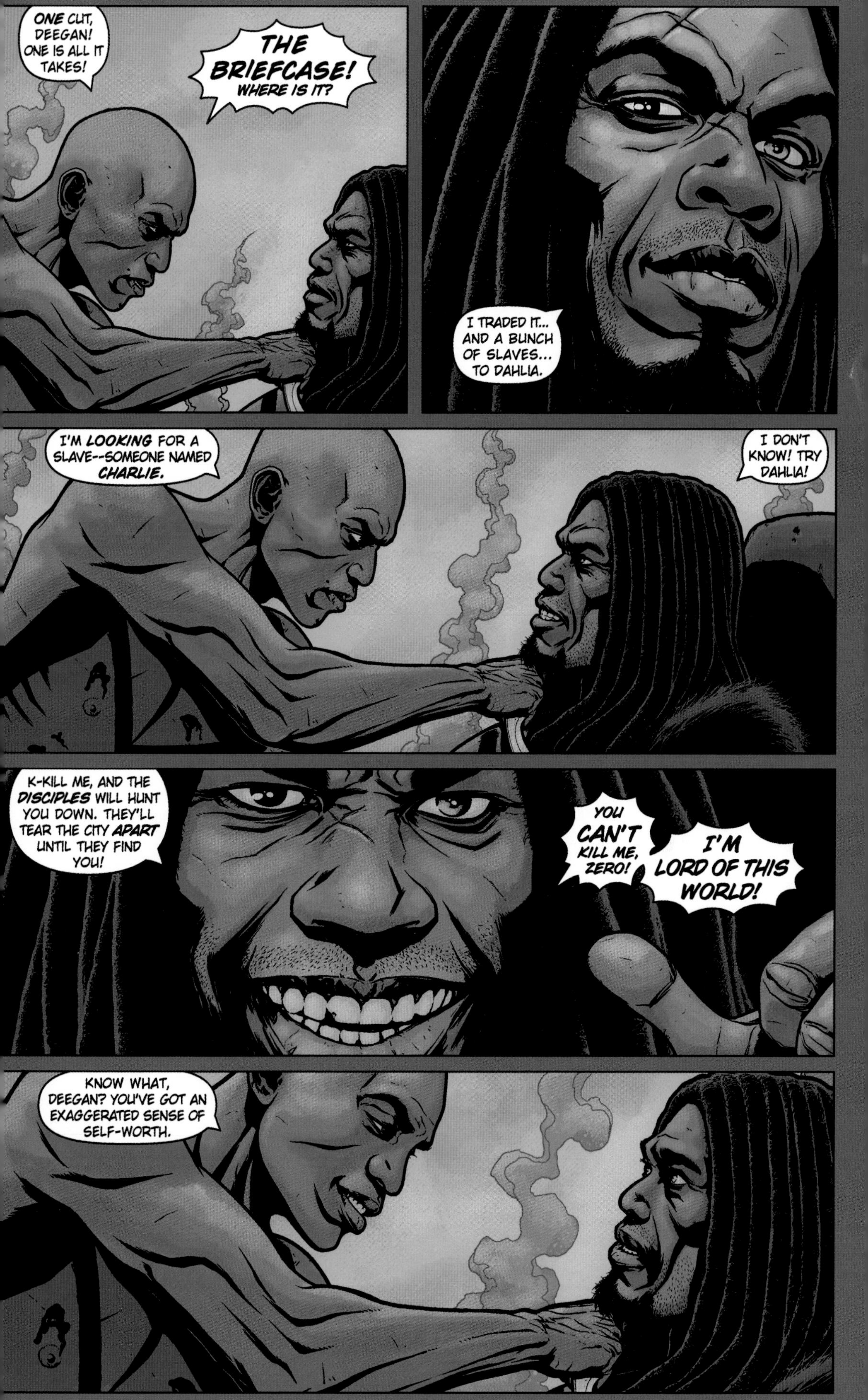
ONE CUT, DEEGAN! ONE IS ALL IT TAKES!
THE BRIEFCASE! WHERE IS IT?
I TRADED IT... AND A BUNCH OF SLAVES... TO DAHLIA.
I'M LOOKING FOR A SLAVE--SOMEONE NAMED CHARLIE.
I DON'T KNOW! TRY DAHLIA!
K-KILL ME, AND THE DISCIPLES WILL HUNT YOU DOWN. THEY'LL TEAR THE CITY APART UNTIL THEY FIND YOU!
YOU CAN'T KILL ME, ZERO!
I'M LORD OF THIS WORLD!
KNOW WHAT, DEEGAN? YOU'VE GOT AN EXAGGERATED SENSE OF SELF-WORTH.

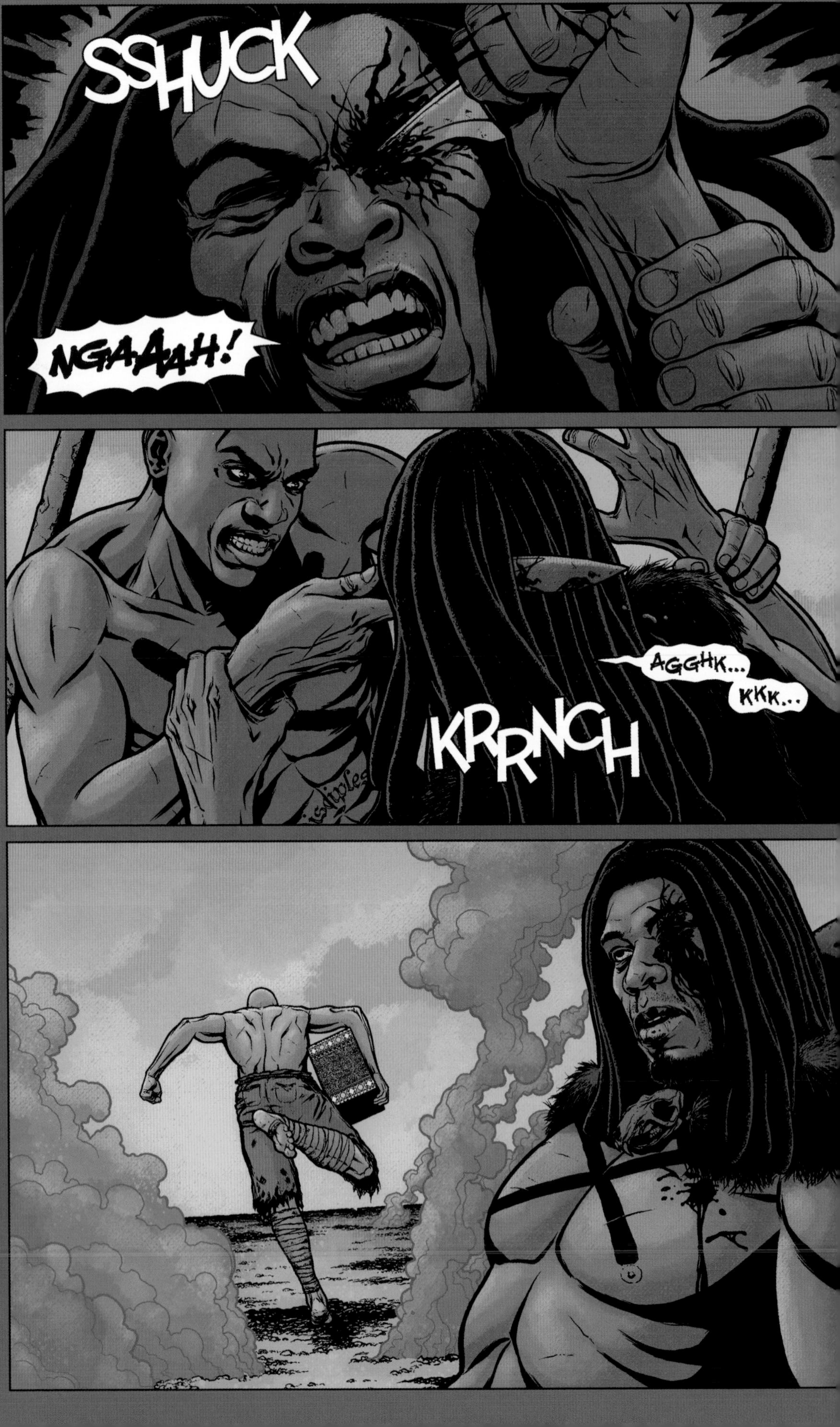
SSHUCK
NGAAAH!
AGGHK...
KKK...
KRRNCH

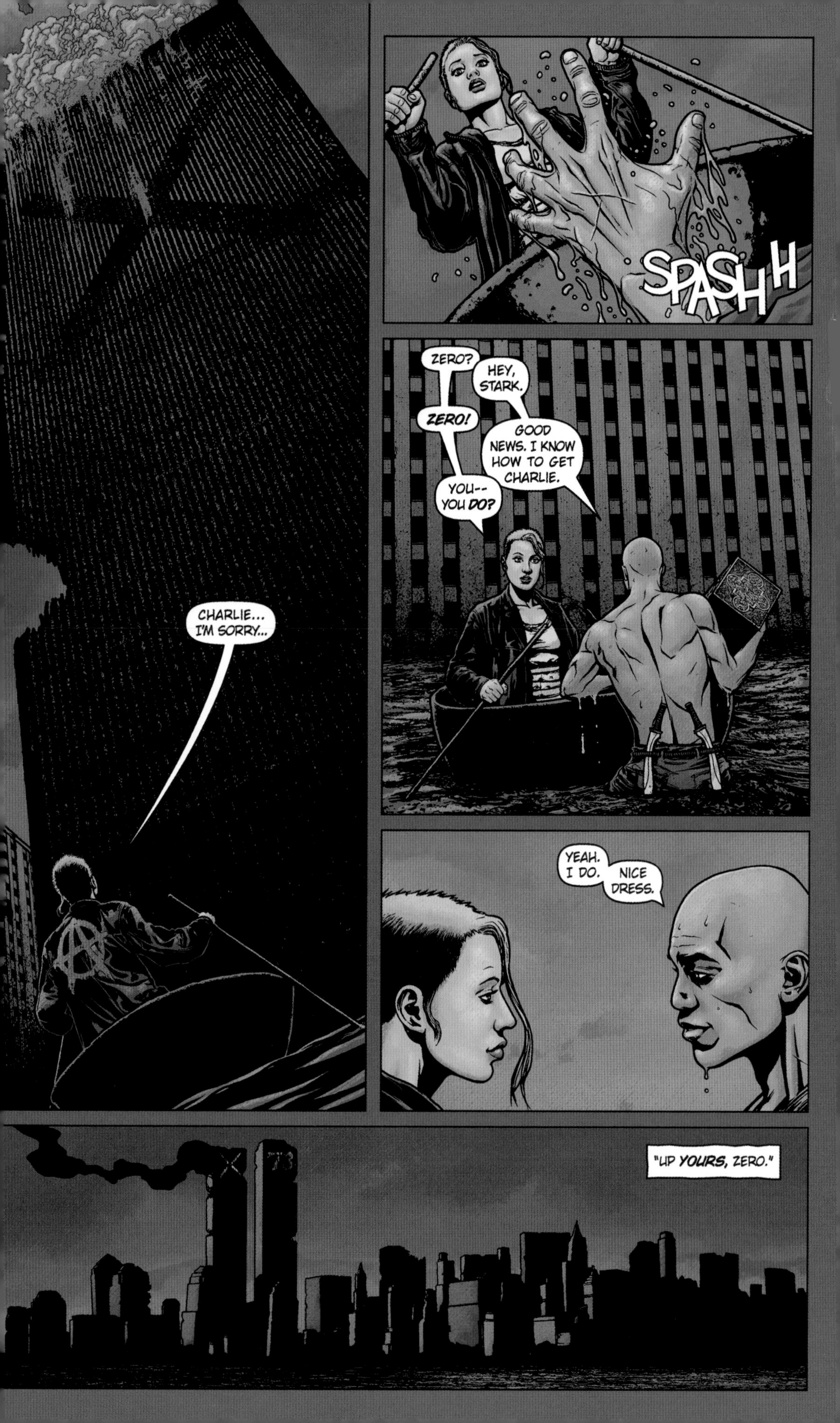
CHARLIE... I'M SORRY...
SPASHHH
ZERO?
HEY, STARK.
ZERO!
GOOD NEWS. I KNOW HOW TO GET CHARLIE.
YOU-- YOU DO?
YEAH. I DO.
NICE DRESS.
"UP YOURS, ZERO."

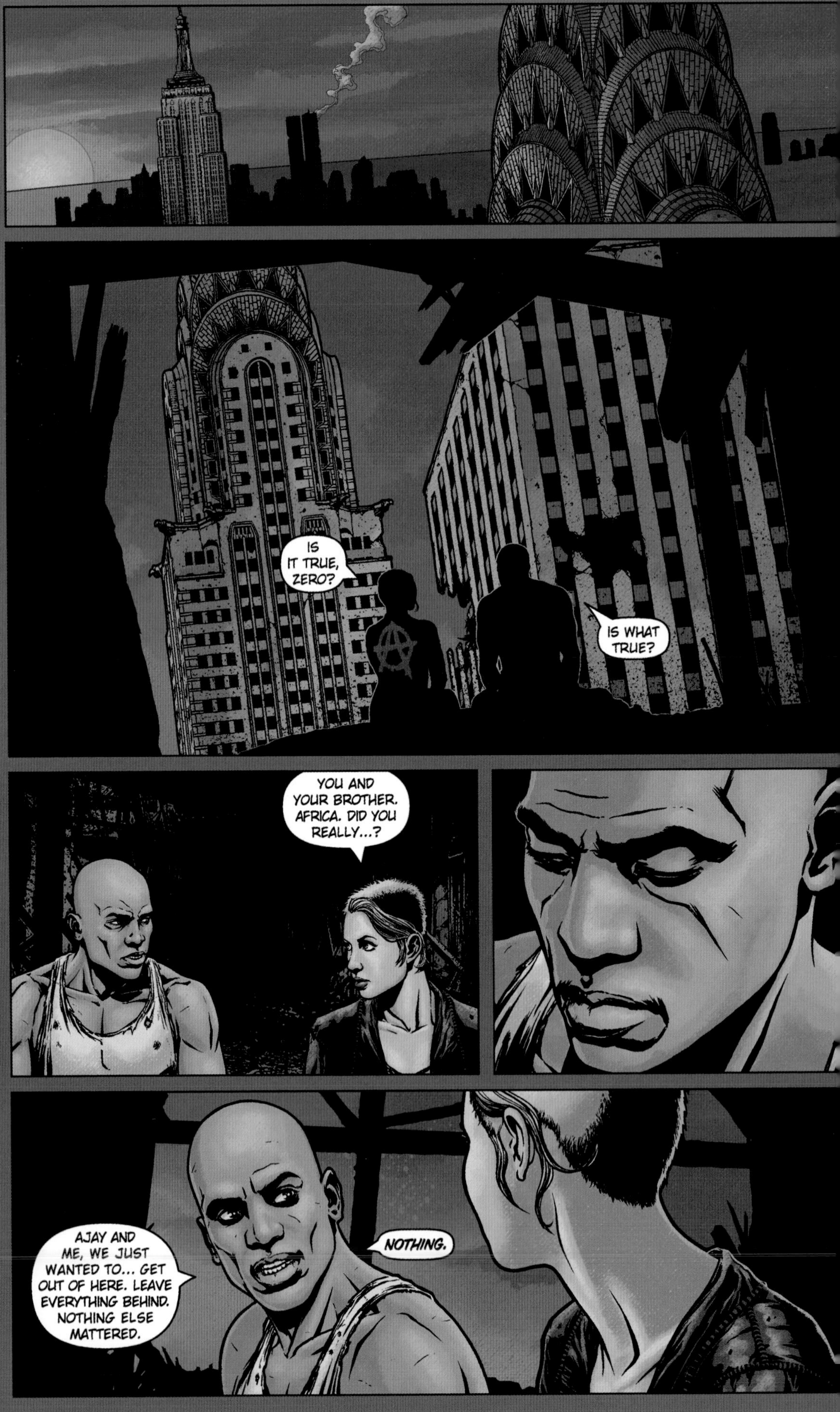
IS IT TRUE, ZERO?
IS WHAT TRUE?
YOU AND YOUR BROTHER. AFRICA. DID YOU REALLY...?
NOTHING.
AJAY AND ME, WE JUST WANTED TO... GET OUT OF HERE. LEAVE EVERYTHING BEHIND. NOTHING ELSE MATTERED.

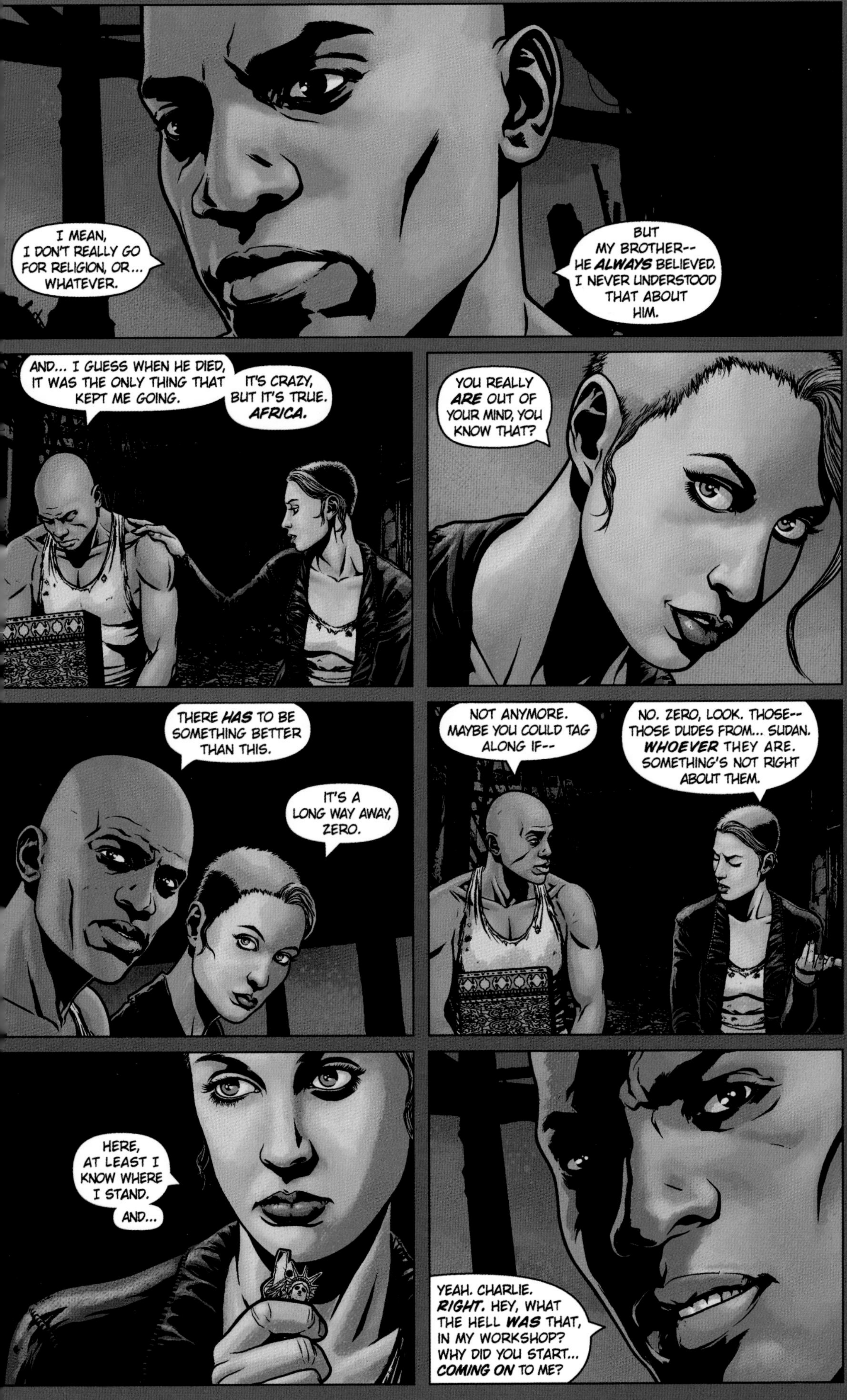

I MEAN, I DON'T REALLY GO FOR RELIGION, OR... WHATEVER.
BUT MY BROTHER-- HE ALWAYS BELIEVED. I NEVER UNDERSTOOD THAT ABOUT HIM.
AND... I GUESS WHEN HE DIED, IT WAS THE ONLY THING THAT KEPT ME GOING.
IT'S CRAZY, BUT IT'S TRUE. AFRICA.
YOU REALLY ARE OUT OF YOUR MIND, YOU KNOW THAT?
THERE HAS TO BE SOMETHING BETTER THAN THIS.
IT'S A LONG WAY AWAY, ZERO.
NOT ANYMORE. MAYBE YOU COULD TAG ALONG IF--
NO. ZERO, LOOK. THOSE-- THOSE DUDES FROM... SUDAN. WHOEVER THEY ARE. SOMETHING'S NOT RIGHT ABOUT THEM.
HERE, AT LEAST I KNOW WHERE I STAND.
AND...
YEAH. CHARLIE. RIGHT. HEY, WHAT THE HELL WAS THAT, IN MY WORKSHOP? WHY DID YOU START... COMING ON TO ME?

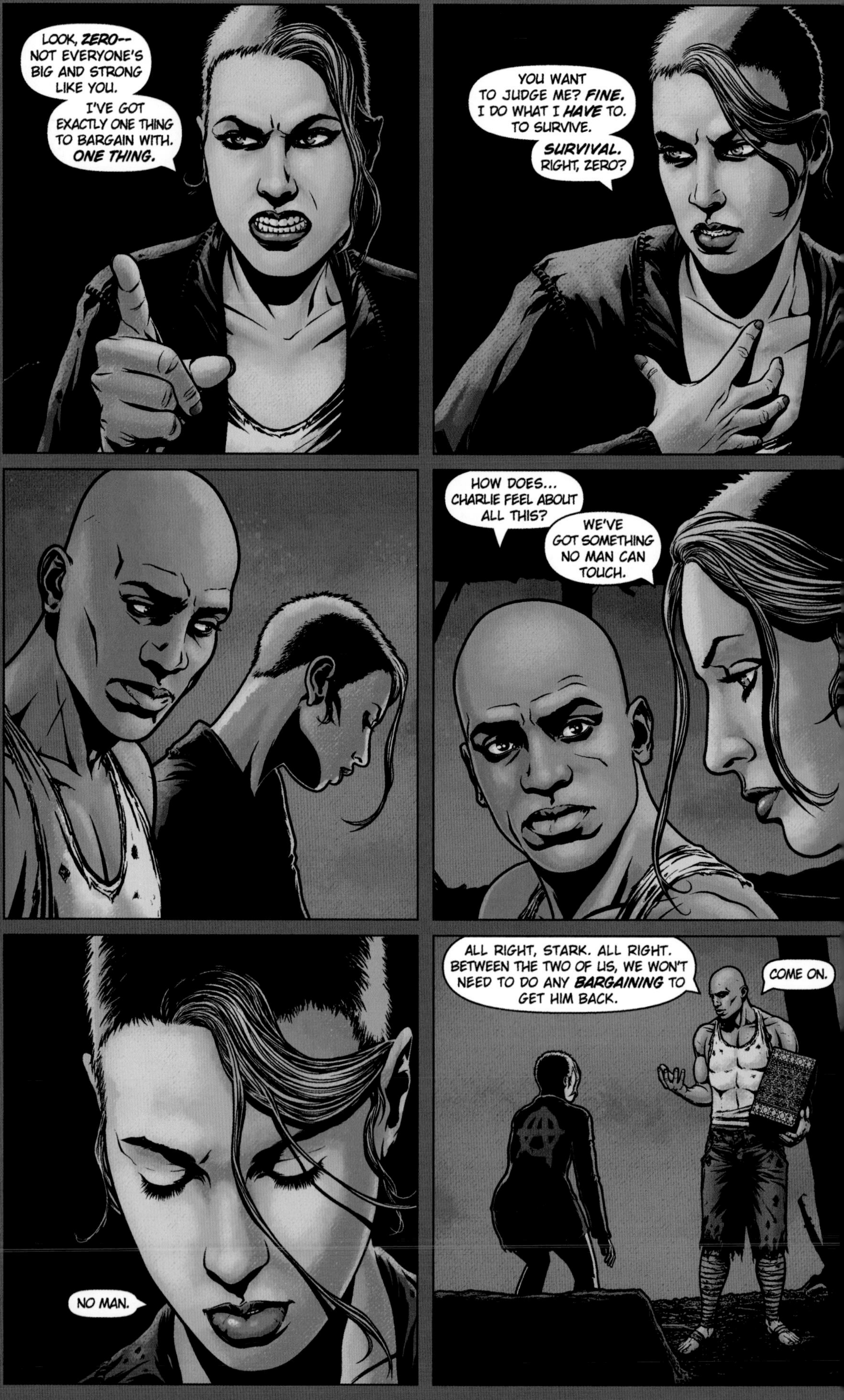
LOOK, ZERO-- NOT EVERYONE'S BIG AND STRONG LIKE YOU.
I'VE GOT EXACTLY ONE THING TO BARGAIN WITH. ONE THING.
YOU WANT TO JUDGE ME? FINE. I DO WHAT I HAVE TO. TO SURVIVE.
SURVIVAL. RIGHT, ZERO?
HOW DOES... CHARLIE FEEL ABOUT ALL THIS?
WE'VE GOT SOMETHING NO MAN CAN TOUCH.
NO MAN.
ALL RIGHT, STARK. ALL RIGHT. BETWEEN THE TWO OF US, WE WON'T NEED TO DO ANY BARGAINING TO GET HIM BACK.
COME ON.

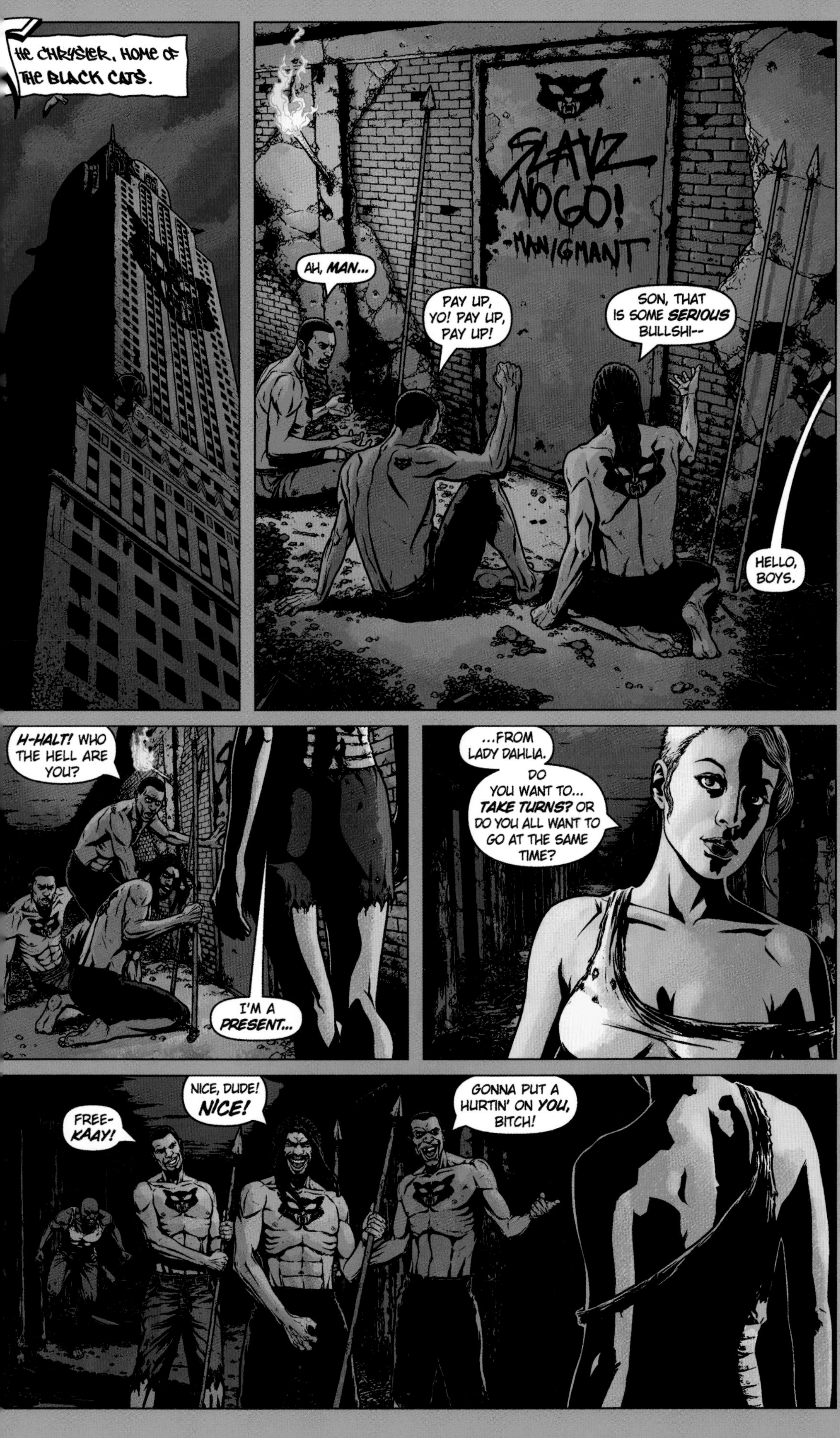

THE CHRYSLER. HOME OF THE BLACK CATS.
SLAVZ NO GO! -MANIGMANT
AH, MAN...
PAY UP, YO! PAY UP, PAY UP!
SON, THAT IS SOME SERIOUS BULLSHI--
HELLO, BOYS.
H-HALT! WHO THE HELL ARE YOU?
I'M A PRESENT...
...FROM LADY DAHLIA.
DO YOU WANT TO... TAKE TURNS? OR DO YOU ALL WANT TO GO AT THE SAME TIME?
FREE-KAAY!
NICE, DUDE! NICE!
GONNA PUT A HURTIN' ON YOU, BITCH!

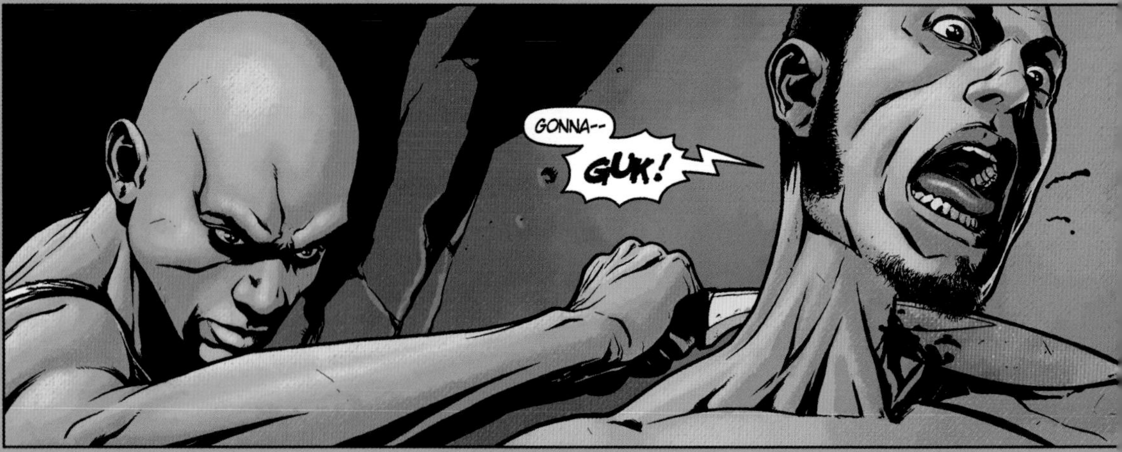
GONNA--
GUK!

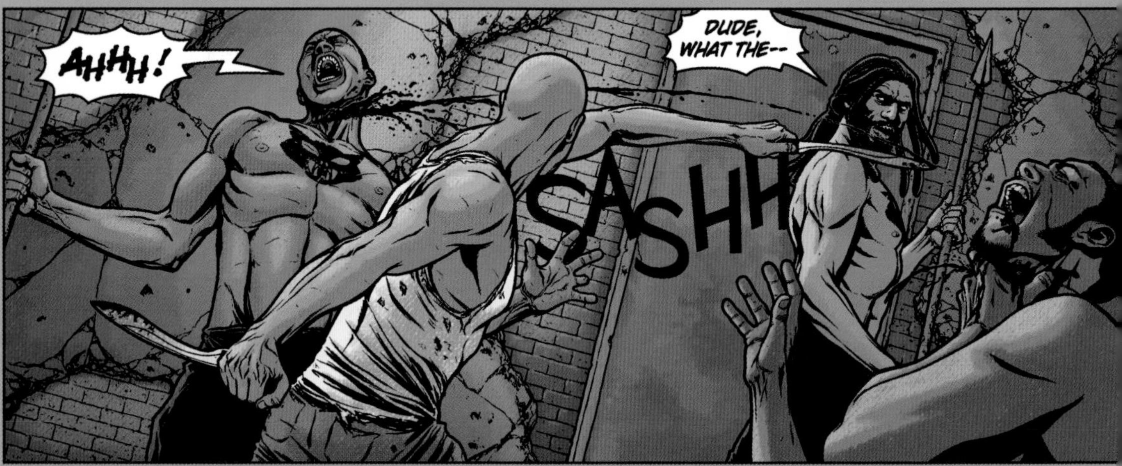
AHHH!
DUDE, WHAT THE--
SASHH

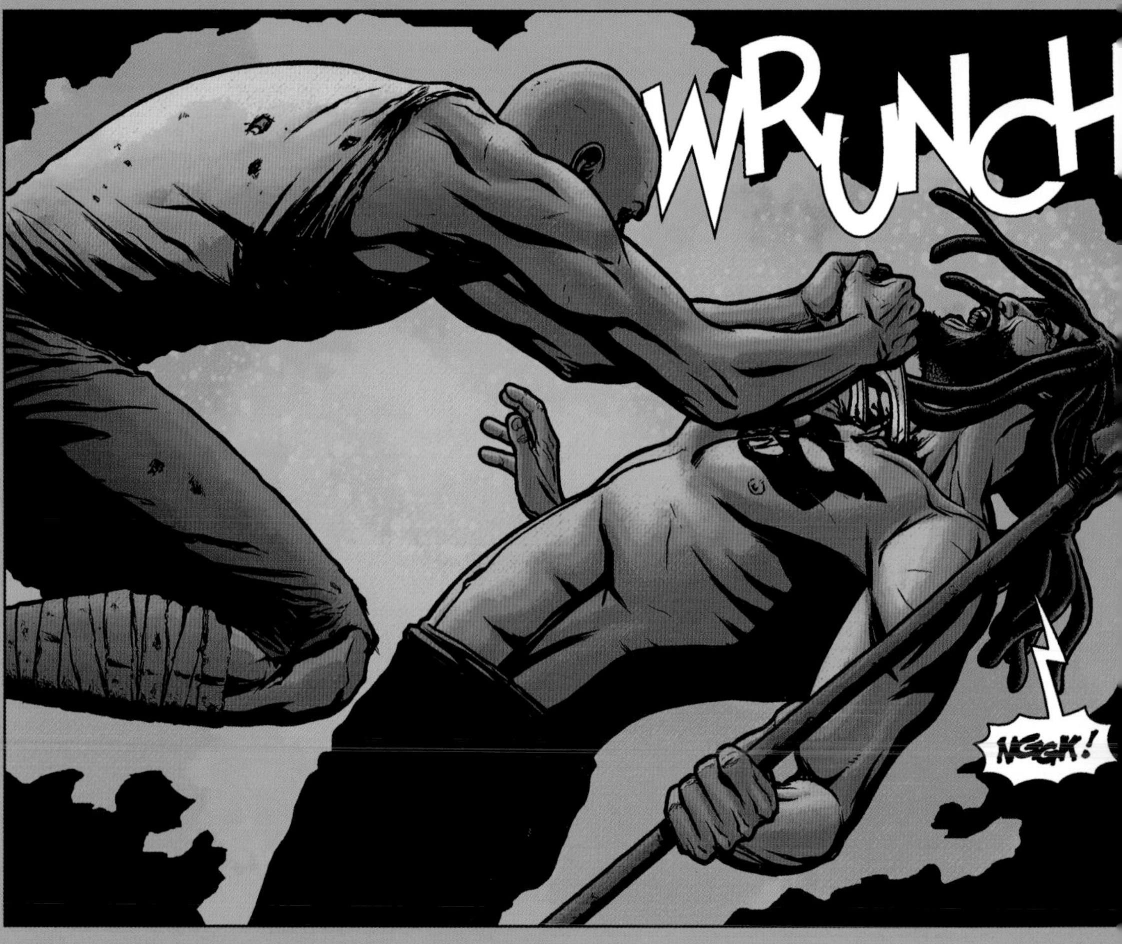
WRUNCH
NGGK!

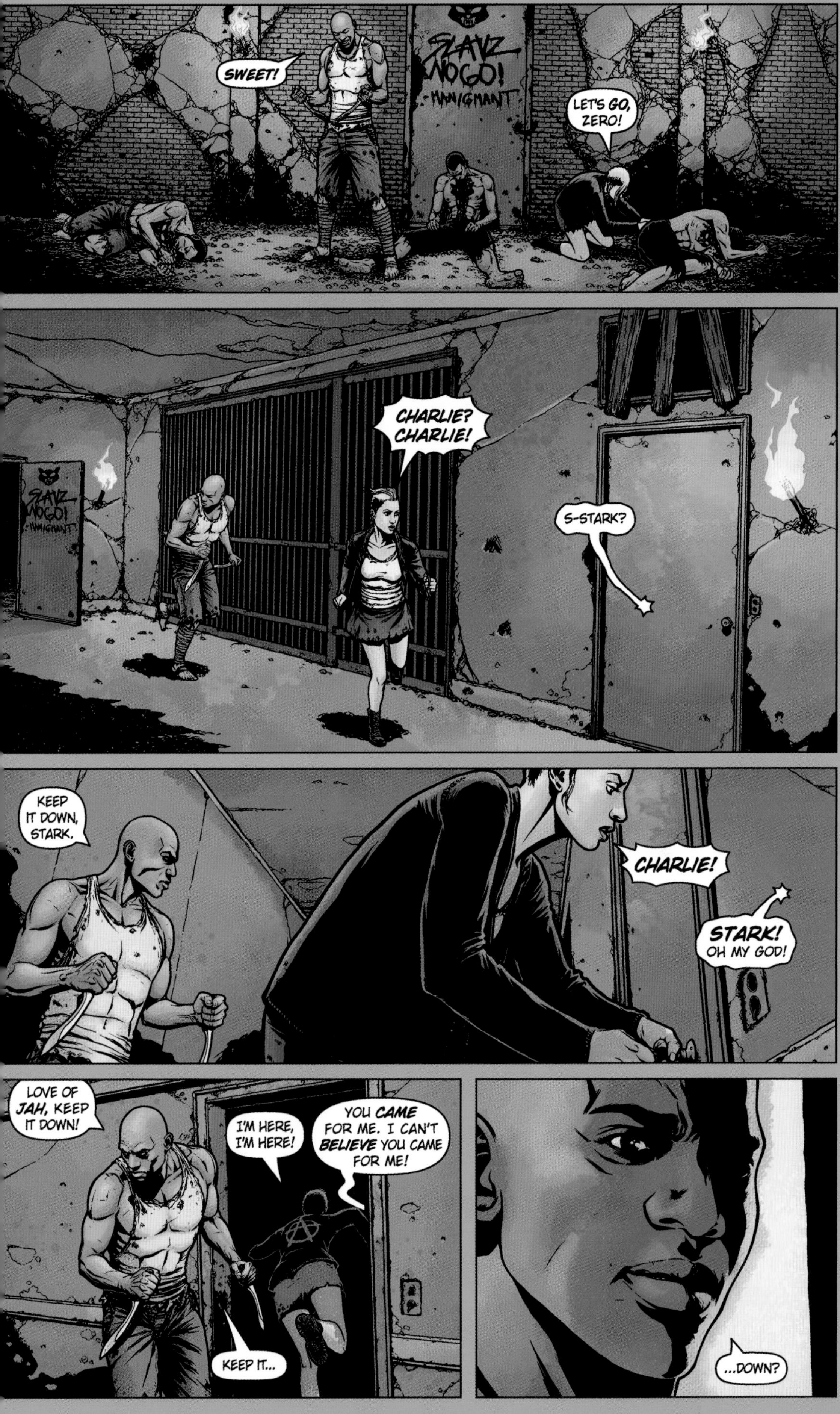
SWEET!
SLAVZ NOGO! -MANIGMANT
LET'S GO, ZERO!
CHARLIE? CHARLIE!
SLAVZ NOGO! -MANIGMANT
S-STARK?
KEEP IT DOWN, STARK.
CHARLIE!
STARK! OH MY GOD!
LOVE OF JAH, KEEP IT DOWN!
I'M HERE, I'M HERE!
YOU CAME FOR ME. I CAN'T BELIEVE YOU CAME FOR ME!
KEEP IT...
...DOWN?

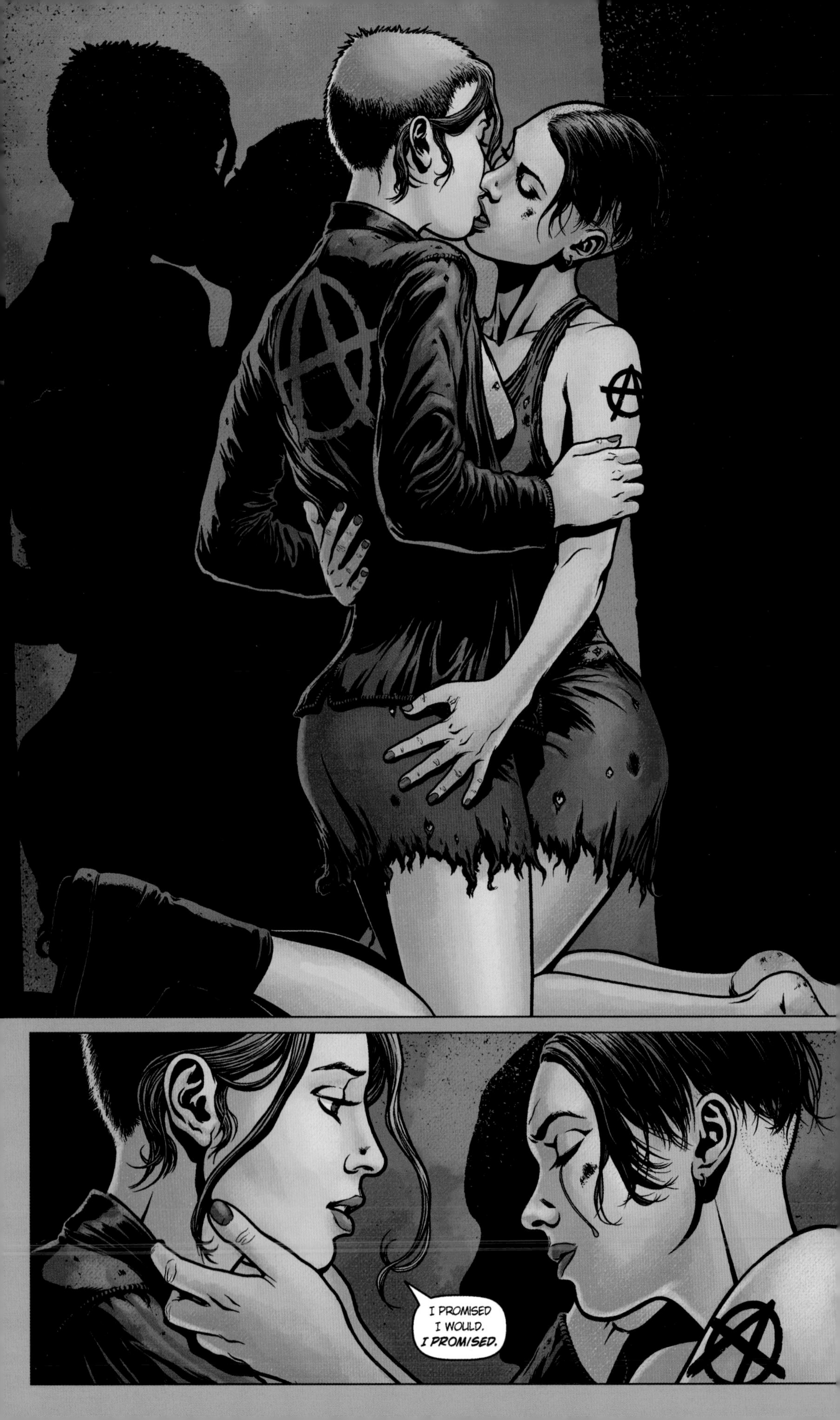
I PROMISED
I WOULD.
I PROMISED.

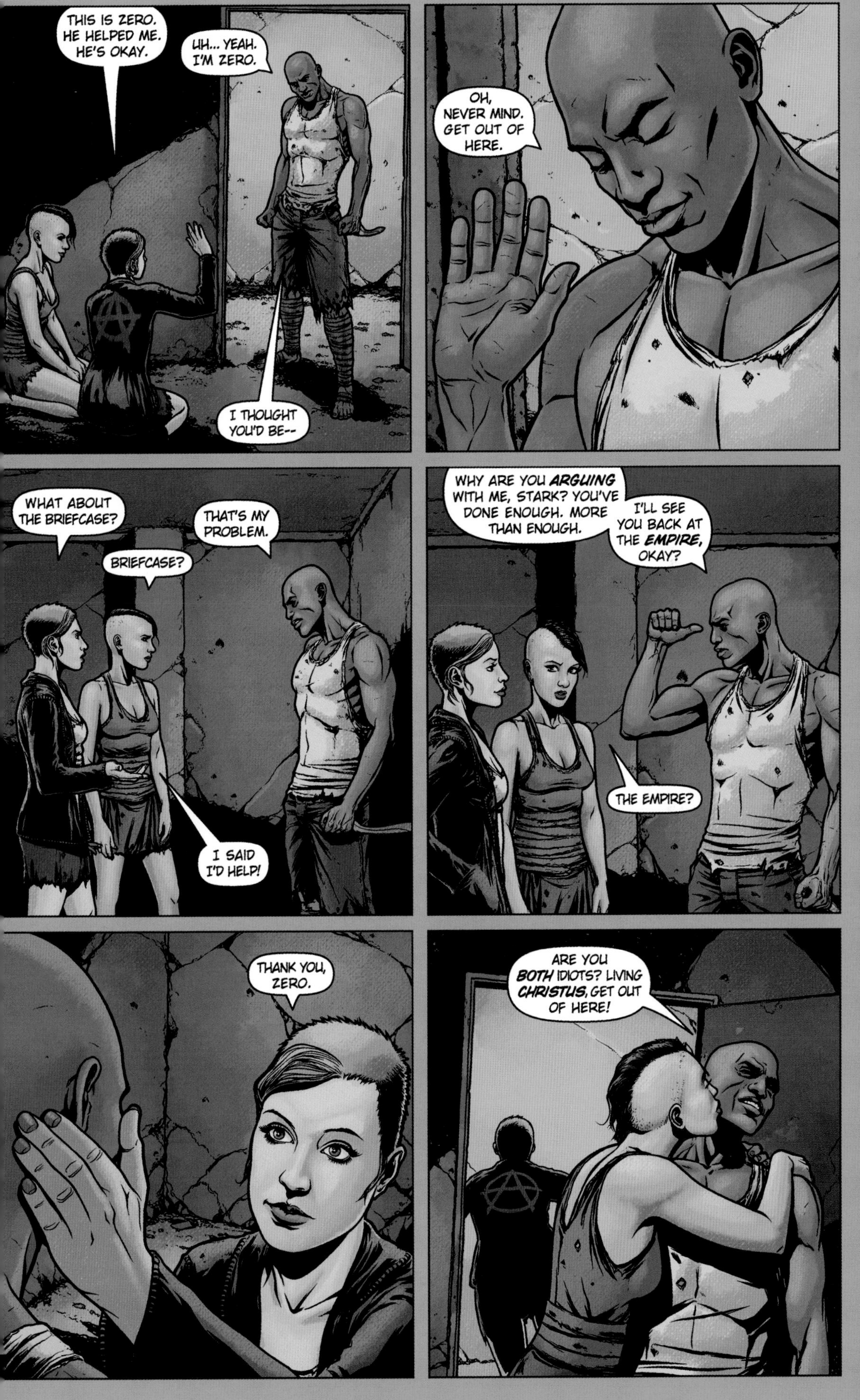
THIS IS ZERO. HE HELPED ME. HE'S OKAY.
UH... YEAH. I'M ZERO.
I THOUGHT YOU'D BE--
OH, NEVER MIND. GET OUT OF HERE.
WHAT ABOUT THE BRIEFCASE?
BRIEFCASE?
THAT'S MY PROBLEM.
I SAID I'D HELP!
WHY ARE YOU *ARGUING* WITH ME, STARK? YOU'VE DONE ENOUGH. MORE THAN ENOUGH.
I'LL SEE YOU BACK AT THE *EMPIRE,* OKAY?
THE EMPIRE?
THANK YOU, ZERO.
ARE YOU *BOTH* IDIOTS? LIVING *CHRISTUS,* GET OUT OF HERE!

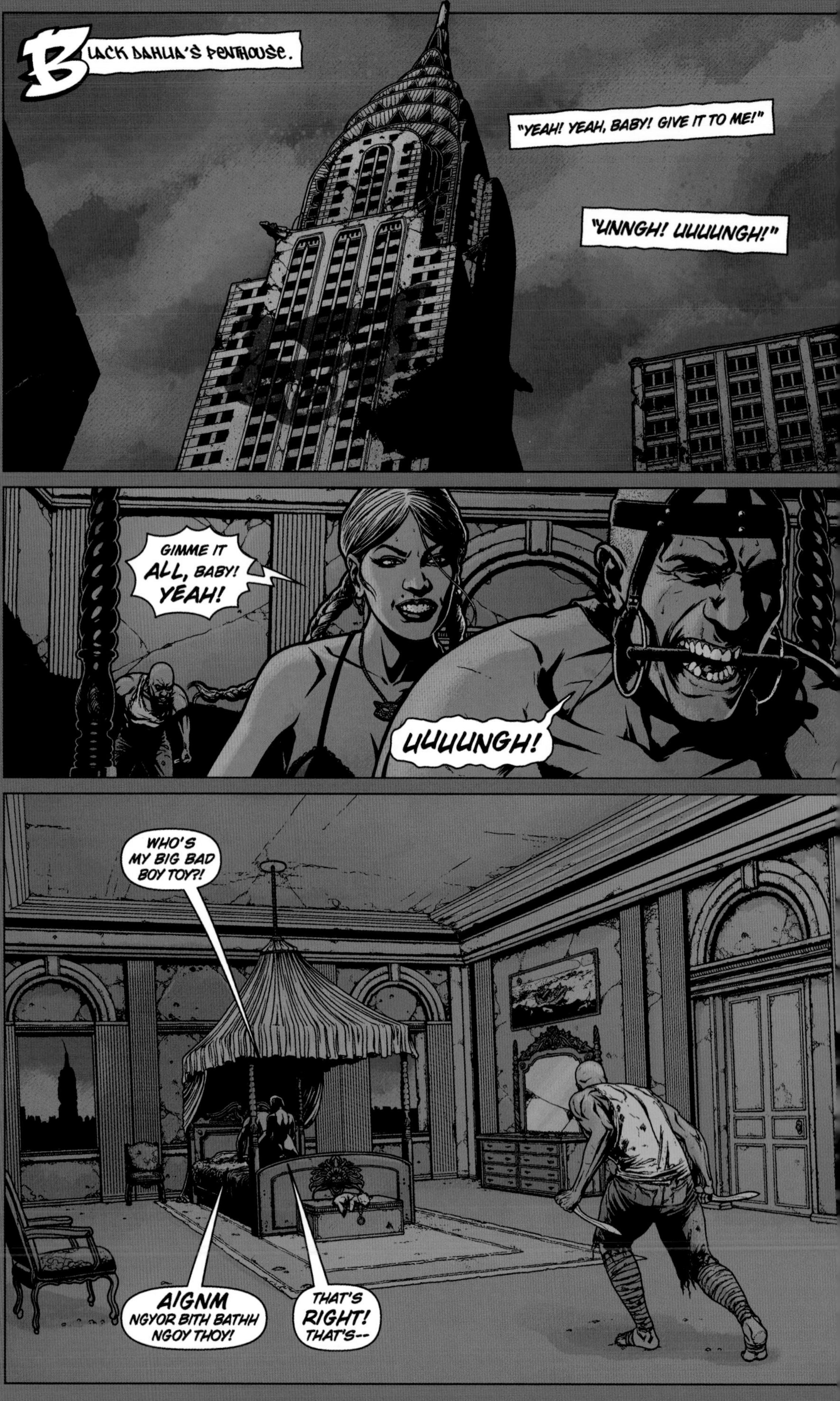
BLACK DAHLIA'S PENTHOUSE.
"YEAH! YEAH, BABY! GIVE IT TO ME!"
"UNNGH! UUUUNGH!"
GIMME IT ALL, BABY! YEAH!
UUUUNGH!
WHO'S MY BIG BAD BOY TOY?!
AIGNM NGYOR BITH BATHH NGOY THOY!
THAT'S RIGHT! THAT'S--

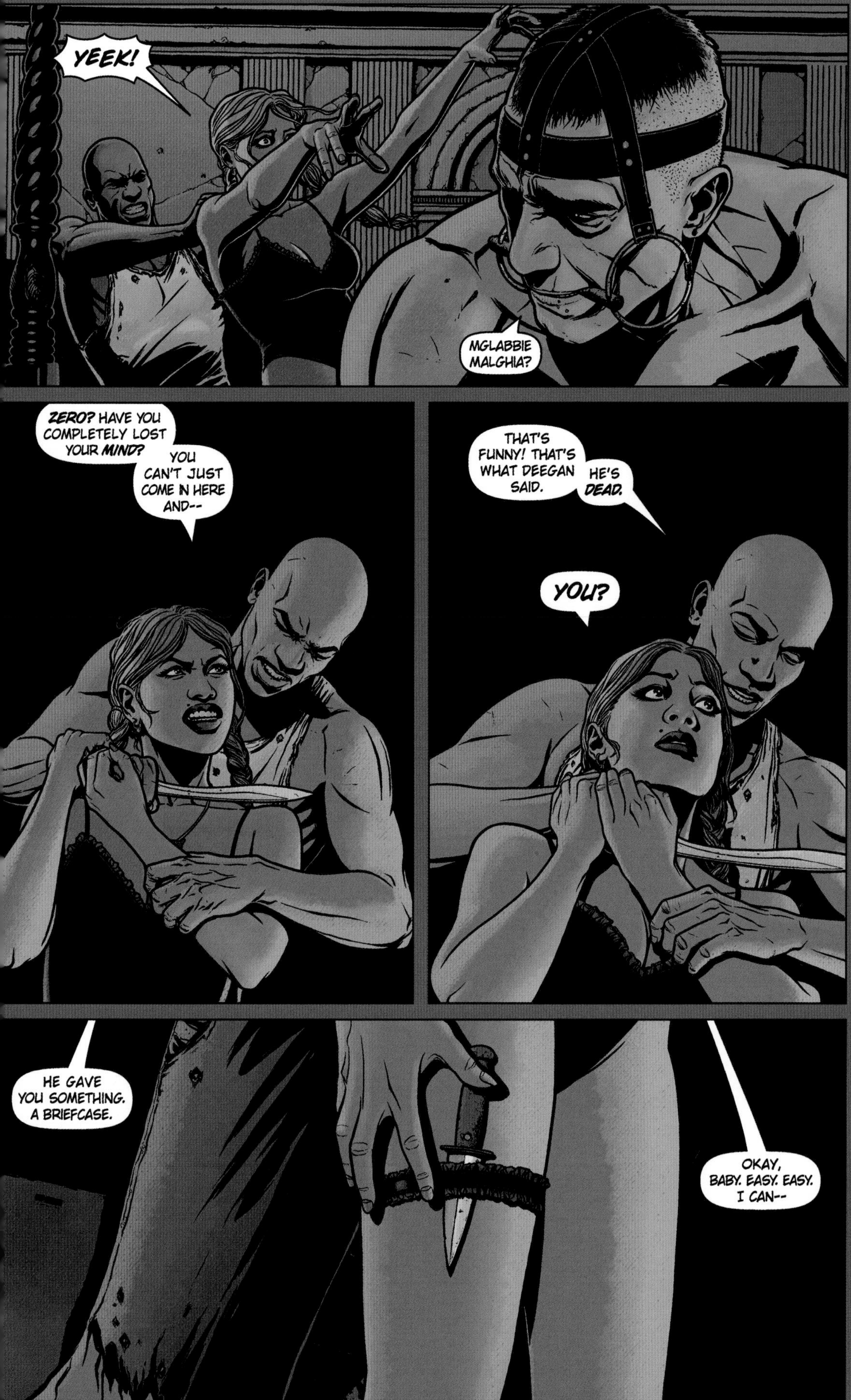
YEEK!
MGLABBIE MALGHIA?
ZERO? HAVE YOU COMPLETELY LOST YOUR MIND?
YOU CAN'T JUST COME IN HERE AND--
THAT'S FUNNY! THAT'S WHAT DEEGAN SAID.
HE'S DEAD.
YOU?
HE GAVE YOU SOMETHING. A BRIEFCASE.
OKAY, BABY. EASY. EASY. I CAN--

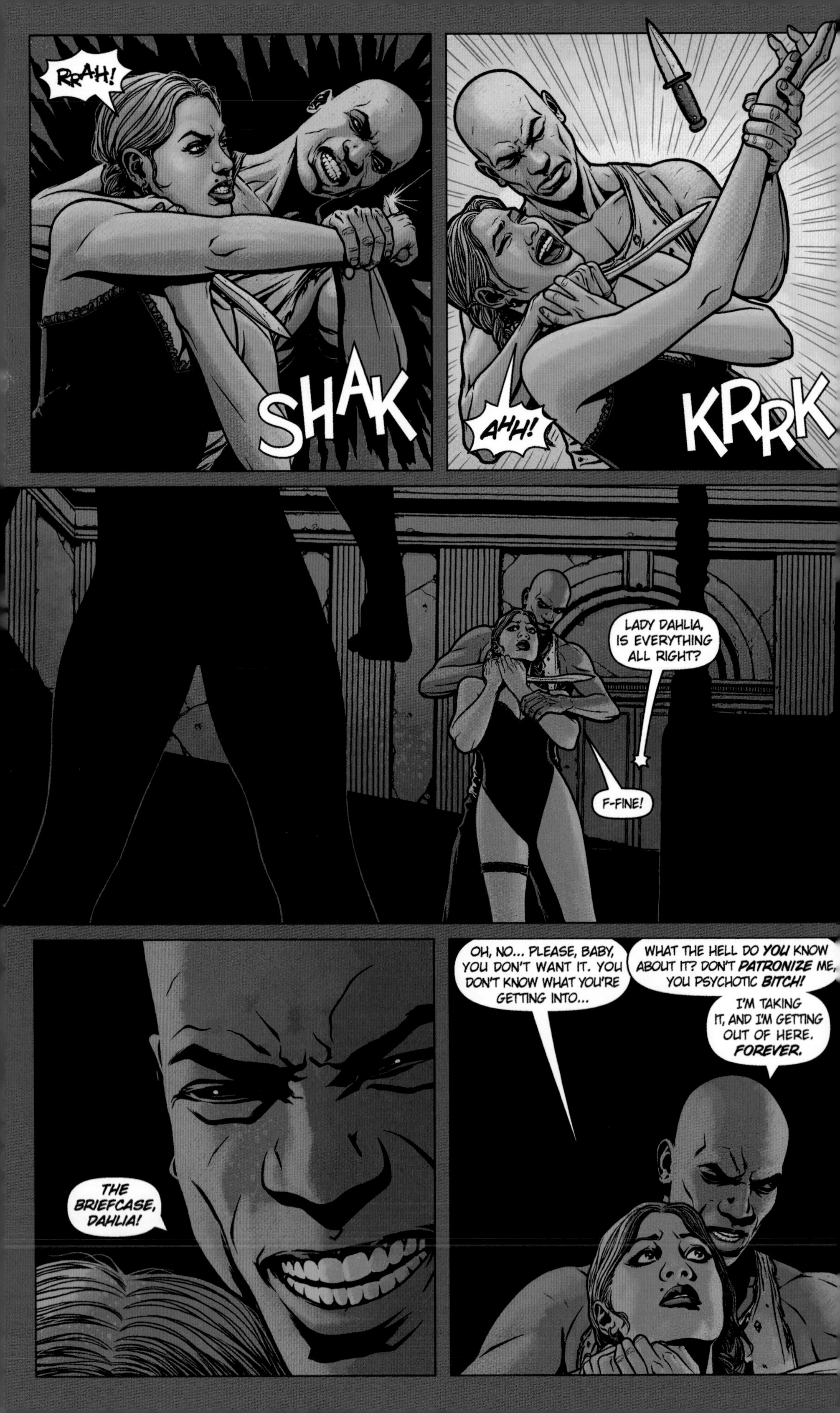
RRAH!
SHAK
AHH!
KRRRK
LADY DAHLIA, IS EVERYTHING ALL RIGHT?
F-FINE!
THE BRIEFCASE, DAHLIA!
OH, NO... PLEASE, BABY, YOU DON'T WANT IT. YOU DON'T KNOW WHAT YOU'RE GETTING INTO...
WHAT THE HELL DO YOU KNOW ABOUT IT? DON'T PATRONIZE ME, YOU PSYCHOTIC BITCH!
I'M TAKING IT, AND I'M GETTING OUT OF HERE. FOREVER.

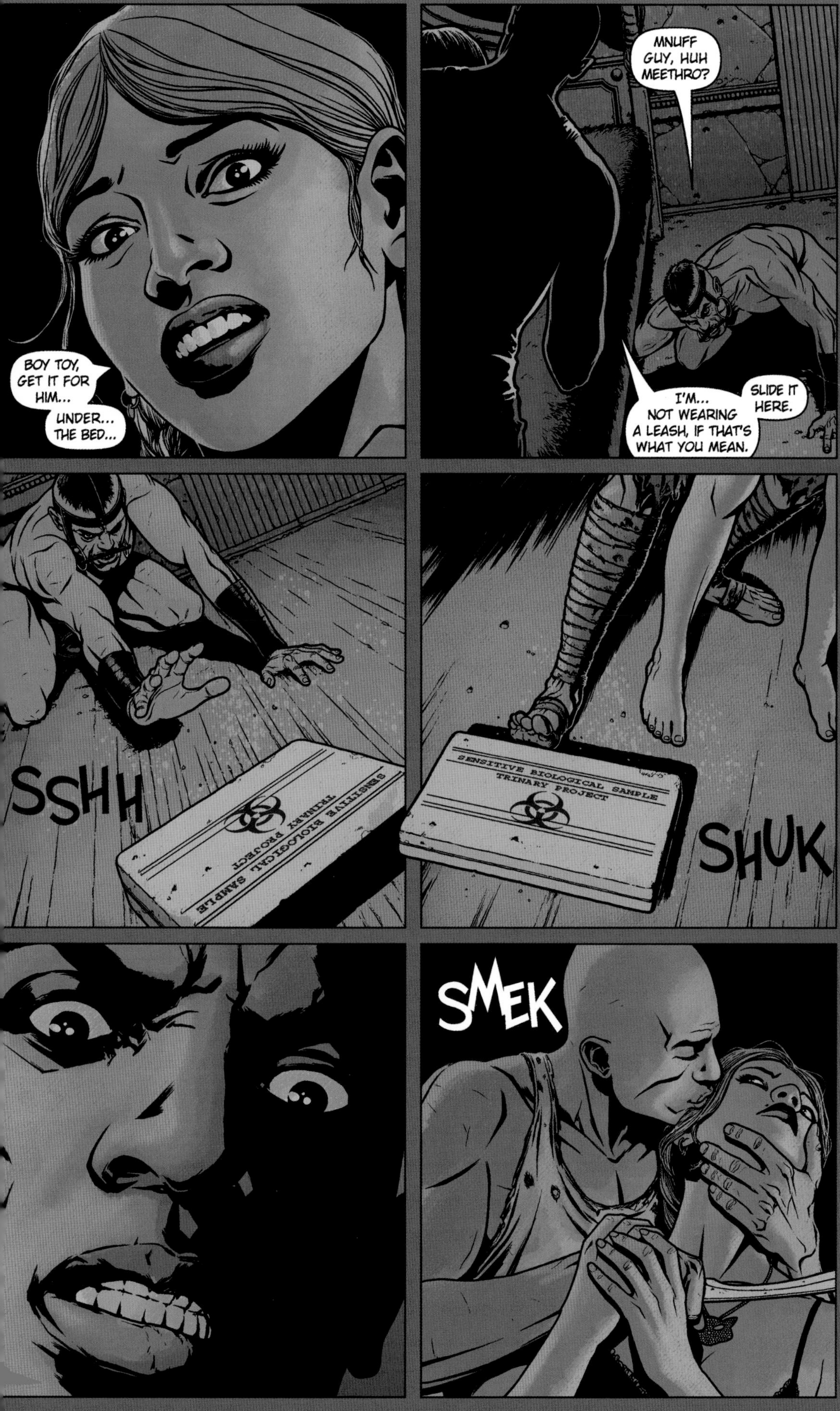
BOY TOY, GET IT FOR HIM...
UNDER... THE BED...
MNUFF GUY, HUH MEETHRO?
I'M... NOT WEARING A LEASH, IF THAT'S WHAT YOU MEAN.
SLIDE IT HERE.
SSHH
SENSITIVE BIOLOGICAL SAMPLE
TRINARY PROJECT
SENSITIVE BIOLOGICAL SAMPLE
TRINARY PROJECT
SHUK
SMEK

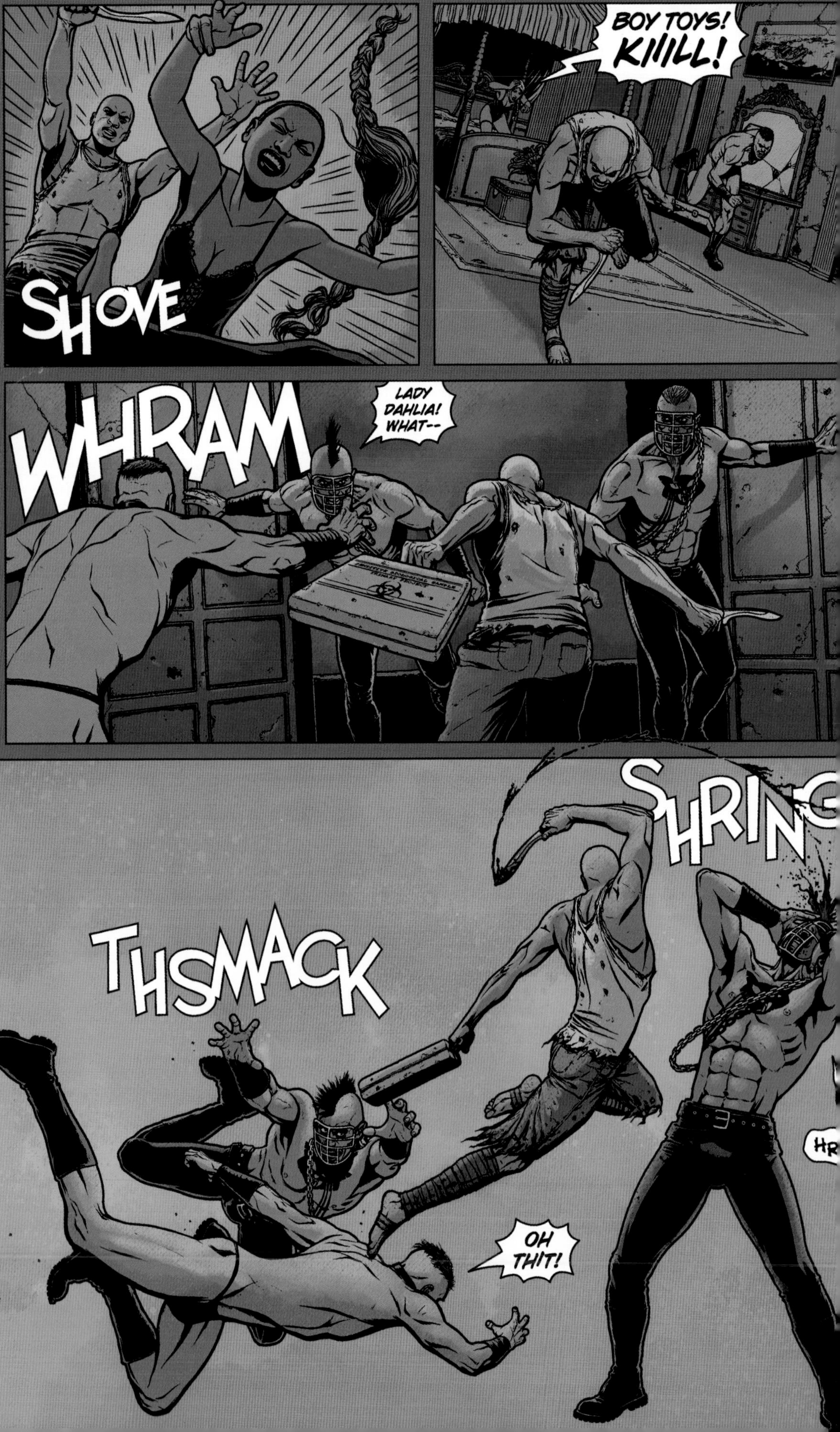
SHOVE
BOY TOYS! KIIILL!
WHRAM
LADY DAHLIA! WHAT--
SHRING
THSMACK
OH THIT!

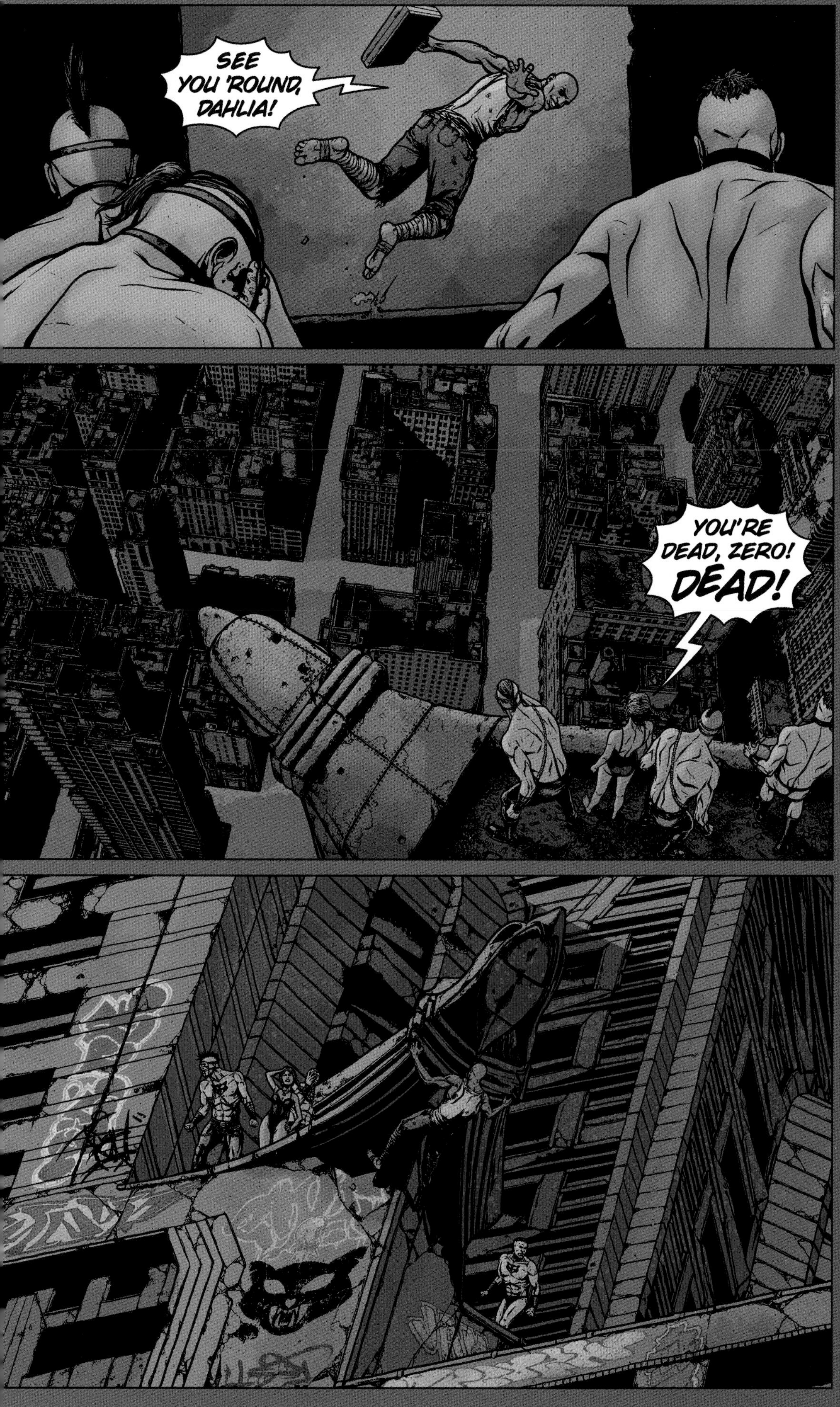
SEE YOU 'ROUND, DAHLIA!
YOU'RE DEAD, ZERO! DEAD!

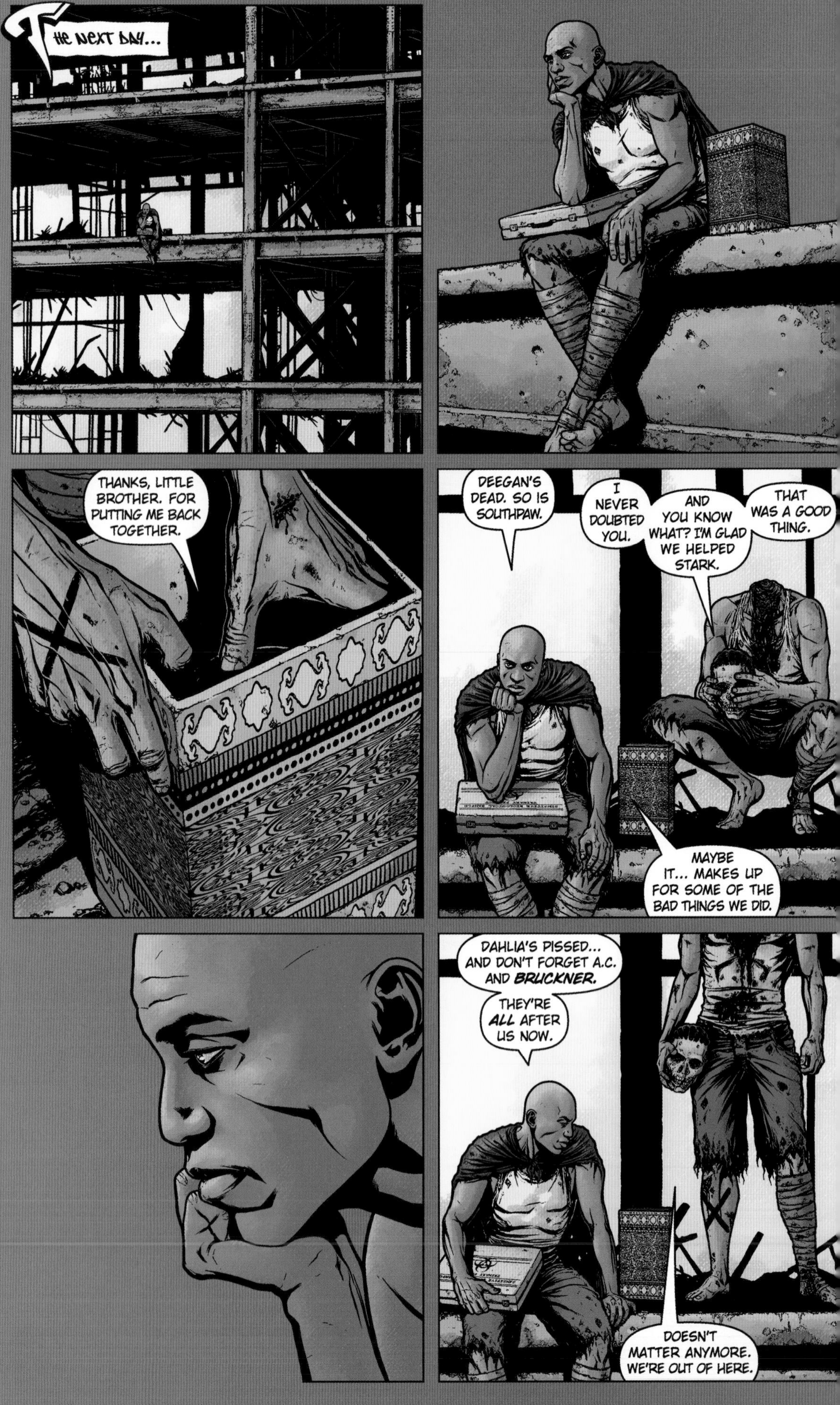
The next day...
THANKS, LITTLE BROTHER. FOR PUTTING ME BACK TOGETHER.
DEEGAN'S DEAD. SO IS SOUTHPAW.
I NEVER DOUBTED YOU.
AND YOU KNOW WHAT? I'M GLAD WE HELPED STARK.
THAT WAS A GOOD THING.
MAYBE IT... MAKES UP FOR SOME OF THE BAD THINGS WE DID.
DAHLIA'S PISSED... AND DON'T FORGET A.C. AND BRUCKNER.
THEY'RE ALL AFTER US NOW.
DOESN'T MATTER ANYMORE. WE'RE OUT OF HERE.

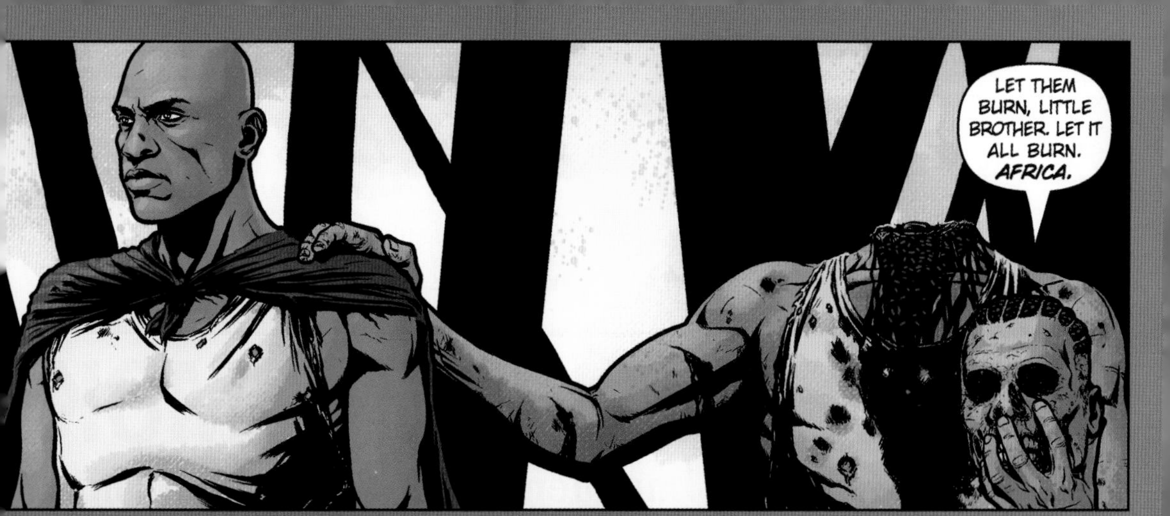
LET THEM BURN, LITTLE BROTHER. LET IT ALL BURN. *AFRICA.*

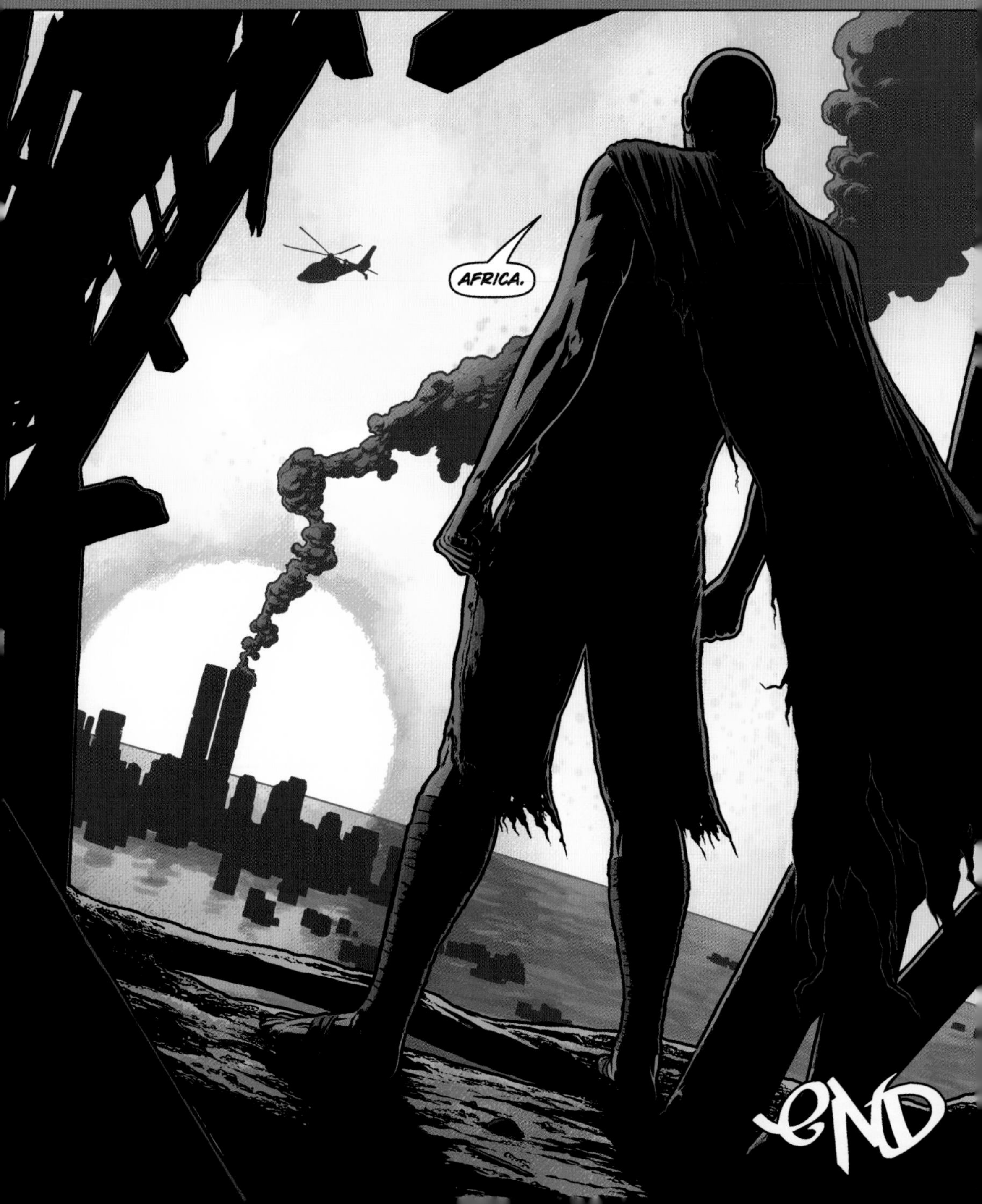
AFRICA.
END

DAWN'S EARLY LIGHT

DOWNTOWN UP IN SMOKE

Is a Major Gang War Imminent? Is It Such a Bad Thing?

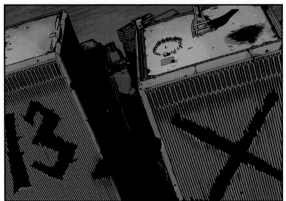

Predator UAVs observed a mass gathering on top of the North Tower yesterday.

Downtown Manhattan literally went up in flames yesterday, following weeks of simmering unrest.

The disturbances centered on the North Tower of the Twin Towers, the building dominated by the vicious Disciples gang.

Reconnaissance drones observed an unusually large crowd on top of the building around dawn in the early hours of morning. The crowd dispersed when a major fire erupted somewhere in the depths of the building.

Special Investigations Command officials say these activities, along with other recent disturbances, indicate the likelihood of a "major gang war" breaking out sometime in the next few days.

"You can just feel it out there," JOCOM-A Corporal Stephen Hicks said. "The entire city is ready to explode."

Attacks on JOCOM personnel operating in the Manhattan ruins have risen over 10 percent in the last month.

One of the most deadly incidents occurred six days ago, when ground fire from an unidentified source caused a Black Hawk helicopter to crash into the upper stories of the North Tower. Both the pilot and copilot were lost.

Ominously, the perpetrators might have used an advanced shoulder-fired missile in the attack. Defense Intelligence Secretary William Kristol said the rise in the number and the sophistication of the attacks is "cause for concern, not alarm."

"The gangster scum inhabiting the ruins of Manhattan are an adaptable and highly determined enemy. The weaponry they steal from downed JOCOM warriors enables them to conduct more am-

bushes, and therefore to gain access to increasingly sophisticated firepower," he said.

Richard Cheney, executive director of the Advanced Genetic Research Initiative, acknowledges it's a "vicious cycle," but insists the inhabitants of the New York ruins are still the "best available source of test subjects."

Future War Planning Secretary Paul Wolfowitz predicted JOCOM forces would have the gangster insurgency cleaned up "before the end of the year."

"The fact remains, we still have an overwhelming advantage in tactics and in firepower," he said.

All-out gang war could actually be a positive develop-

ment, he said.

"We can take advantag[e] of the instability, absolutely[,]" he said. "The more preoccu[-] pied they are with each othe[r] the easier they are to contro[l]. Forming temporary allianc[es] with certain gang leaders ca[n] also be productive. We he[lp] them raid a rival's strongho[ld] and in return they hand ov[er] captives for our biotechnolog[y] and reproduction research."

Wolfowitz refused to sa[y] whether his office was direct[ly] responsible for the current u[n-] rest in the towers.

"I won't comment on inte[l-] ligence operations that may [or] may not be ongoing. We hav[e] an extensive network of agen[ts] in the towers. I'll leave it a[t] that," he said.

More Fallout from Soviet Spy Ring Arrests

A second wave of arrests followed two days after the unsealing of a Defense Intelligence Agency probe into a Soviet spy ring operating in the highest levels of the Office of the Joint Chiefs.

It is the first direct evidence the Soviet Union survived Zero Hour, the nuclear war that engulfed the world in 1973.

Maj. Michael Chertoff, who is in charge of the investigation, said details about the size, strength, and disposition of the Soviet threat were "forthcoming."

The latest arrests we[re] made based on "intelligenc[e] gathered from interrogation[s] of those already in custody[,]" Chertoff said. He would n[ot] release the names of those a[r-] rested, but said all had "clo[se] links with those already i[n] custody."

He said "enhanced tech[-] niques" had been used to obtai[n] information for the new wa[r-] rants, including "kicking, spi[t-] ting, biting, slapping, smac[k-] ing, poking, stress position[s,] urinating, slamming, genit[al] *continued on page A[?]*

continued on page A[?]

WHERE EAGLES DARE

Words of wisdom from the captain ✦ Honor, duty, loyalty, pride!

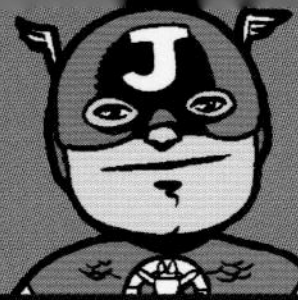

THE AFTERMATH OF THE SOVIET NUCLEAR STRIKE 34 YEARS AGO WAS GRIM: NOTHING REMAINED OF ***AMERICA*** BUT A FEW SCATTERED MILITARY PERSONNEL HIDING OUT IN UNDERGROUND FALLOUT SHELTERS. BUT THANKS TO THE UNIFYING VISION OF OUR LEADER, THE ***DIRECTOR OF THE RECONSTRUCTION OF THE UNITED STATES OF AMERICA (DURSA),*** THOSE MEN ROSE TO FORM THE ORGANIZATION KNOWN AS ***JOCOM***.

DRUSA HAS SET OUR TASK: WE MUST REBUILD THE UNITED STATES FROM THE ASHES OF THE NUCLEAR FIRES. BUT WE AREN'T DOING IT FROM THE GROUND UP--WE'RE DOING IT FROM THE GROUND ***DOWN!*** WE'VE TRANSFORMED THOSE ORIGINAL FALLOUT SHELTERS INTO EXTENSIVE UNDERGROUND ***COMPLEXES***, EACH ONE AUTONOMOUS AND SELF-SUFFICIENT.

EACH COMPLEX ALSO SERVES A UNIQUE ***OPERATIONAL ROLE*** IN THE GRAND STRATEGY FOR THE REBIRTH OF AMERICA. LET'S TAKE A LOOK AT SOME OF THE BIGGEST BASES, ONE BY ONE!

GREAT PLAINS-SARATOGA PROVING GROUNDS: NO JOCOM WARRIOR NEEDS AN INTRODUCTION TO ***THIS*** PLACE! OUR ***RECRUITERS*** CONSTANTLY SEARCH THE IRRADIATED WASTES FOR WANDERERS. THOSE DEEMED FIT ENOUGH ARE SENT TO ***SARATOGA***. THE REST EARN THEIR KEEP AS UNCOMPENSATED LABORERS OR TEST SUBJECTS FOR BIOLOGICAL RESEARCH--EVERYONE DOES THEIR PART! THE CASUALTY NUMBERS IN THE SARATOGA COMPLEX HAVE BEEN GREATLY EXAGGERATED: A MERE 17 PERCENT OF RECRUITS FAIL BOOT CAMP DUE TO FATALITIES. SUCK IT UP, WARRIOR!

SIKORSKY-VALLEY FORGE INDUSTRIAL COMPLEX: PRIOR TO ***ZERO HOUR***, THE ***SIKORSKY AIRCRAFT CORPORATION*** BUILT SECRET PRODUCTION FACILITIES BENEATH THE GROUND, IN ANTICIPATION OF A NUCLEAR ATTACK. JOCOM COMMANDEERED THESE SUBTERRANEAN FACTORIES IN THE MONTHS FOLLOWING THE SOVIET STRIKE AND HAS BEEN EXPANDING THEM EVER SINCE. TODAY ***VALLEY FORGE*** PRODUCES MUCH OF THE HEAVY GEAR JOCOM DEPENDS ON FOR ITS MISSIONS, AND IT IS THE MOST COMMON DESTINATION FOR OUR UNCOMPENSATED LABORERS.

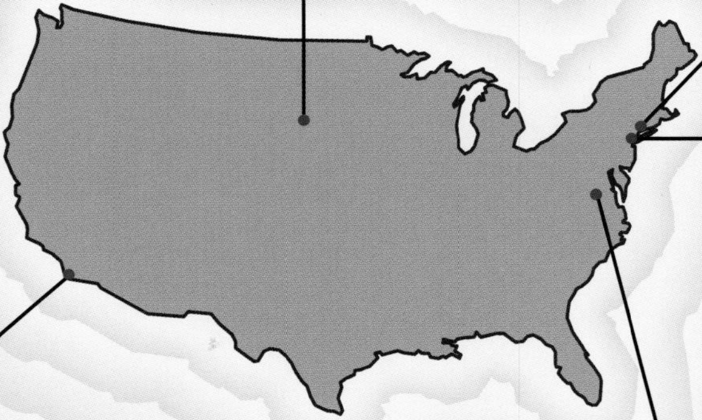

PALISADES-CONCORD RESEARCH COMPLEX: THIS IS JOCOM'S MAIN RESEARCH FACILITY, DUG DEEP INTO THE ***PALISADES CLIFFS*** ALONG THE HUDSON RIVER NEAR ***NEW YORK CITY***. A SURPRISINGLY LARGE NUMBER OF PEOPLE SURVIVED THE MULTIPLE WARHEADS THAT HIT NEW YORK. THEY ARE IDEAL TEST SUBJECTS FOR THE LAB-COAT CONTINGENT AT THE ***ADVANCED GENETIC RESEARCH INITIATIVE,*** WHICH HAS ITS HQ IN THE ***CONCORD*** COMPLEX.

THE ***REPRODUCTIVE TECHNOLOGY*** RESEARCH CONDUCTED BY ***AGRI*** SCIENTISTS IS ***CENTRAL*** TO THE PLAN FOR REPOPULATING THE UNITED STATES AND COMBATING THE SOVIET MENACE. DRUSA HAS THEREFORE DETERMINED "ETHICAL CONSTRAINTS" AND "HUMANE STANDARDS" ARE NO LONGER RELEVANT TO SCIENTIFIC RESEARCH.

THANKS TO THAT DECISION, OUR SCIENTISTS HAVE COME UP WITH MANY AMAZING TECHNOLOGIES THEY COULD ***NEVER*** HAVE DISCOVERED BEFORE THE BOMBS! TOO BAD MOST OF THESE BREAKTHROUGHS ARE CLASSIFIED, IN THE INTEREST OF NATIONAL SECURITY. BUT TRUST THE CAPTAIN, WARRIOR: ***IT'S BETTER THAT YOU DON'T KNOW!***

SAN DIEGO-YORKTOWN FERTILITY COMPLEX: REPOPULATING THE UNITED STATES IS ONE OF DRUSA'S TOP PRIORITIES. THE BOYS IN THE WHITE COATS HAVE MADE SOME REAL STRIDES IN REPRODUCTIVE TECHNOLOGY, BUT THEY STILL CAN'T MAKE BABIES IN TEST TUBES--SO FOR NOW, WE HAVE TO DO IT THE OLD-FASHIONED WAY! ASSIGNMENT TO YORKTOWN FOR A WEEK OR TWO OF ***REPRODUCTIVE DUTY*** IS A PRIVILEGE OF OFFICERS AND ENLISTED MEN WHO HAVE DISTINGUISHED THEMSELVES. REMEMBER: ***YOUR FEMALE QUOTA DEPENDS ON HOW FAITHFULLY YOU PERFORM YOUR DUTIES!***

GREENBRIER-TICONDEROGA: GREENBRIER WAS A FIVE-STAR HOTEL BEFORE ***ZERO HOUR***. IT WAS ALSO THE LOCATION OF A SECRET BUNKER FOR THE ENTIRE U.S. CONGRESS! BUT DRUSA DETERMINED CONGRESS WAS ***NOT*** A VIABLE INSTITUTION POST-ZERO HOUR. AFTER ***REMOVING*** THE SENATORS AND REPRESENTATIVES, HE TRANSFORMED GREENBRIER INTO ***TICONDEROGA***, HIS NEW WASHINGTON. TICONDEROGA IS JOCOM'S CENTRAL NERVOUS SYSTEM. DRUSA WORKS THERE DAY AND NIGHT FOR THE BENEFIT OF ALL YOU BRAVE WARRIORS!

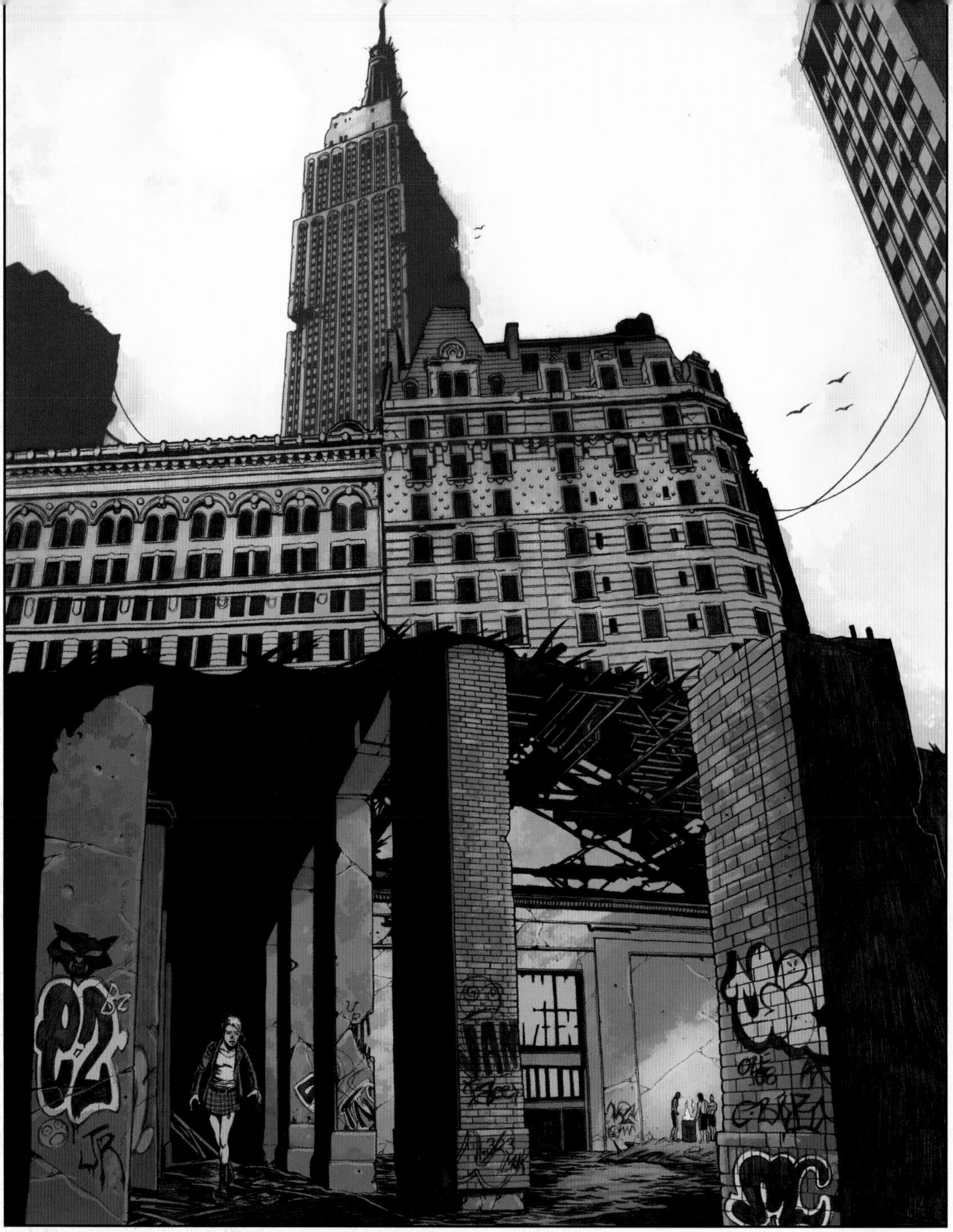

ZERO KILLER WORLD TIMELINE »»

1945: Franklin Roosevelt dies, and Harry Truman becomes president of the United States. The Yalta and Potsdam conferences are acrimonious and inconclusive. Rather than use atomic weapons on Hiroshima and Nagasaki, Truman elects to demonstrate their power on an uninhabited island in the Pacific. Emperor Hirohito plans to surrender, but hard-line fascists in the Japanese military command kidnap him. The junta vows to fight the Allies regardless of their use of atomic weapons. General Douglas MacArthur recommends an invasion of the Japanese home islands. Operation Downfall begins with the invasion of the island of Kyushu. The Soviet Union invades the island of Hokkaido in the north.

1946: The Soviet and United States invasion forces encounter brutal Japanese resistance on Kyushu and Hokkaido. 50,000 American and Soviet casualties; 300,000 Japanese, military and civilian. MacArthur convinces Truman to allow the use of atom bombs in tandem with a conventional land offensive. The plan: use a series of atom bombs to blast an irradiated corridor through Honshu Island, through which Allied troops can then march. This tactic, known as "walking the nukes," proves to be a complete disaster. The majority of the Allied troops who enter the irradiated corridor of death die from radiation poisoning. 75,000 United States casualties. MacArthur is relieved of command, replaced with Matthew B. Ridgway. Ridgway orders the eradication of Tokyo, Hiroshima, Osaka, and Nagasaki with atomic weapons. Widespread use of chemical weapons on Japanese population centers. Soviets are forced to withdraw troops from Iran to assist in the subjugation of Japan.

1947: World War II ends. 3 million Japanese dead. 300,000 Allied casualties. Emperor Hirohito is forced to abdicate, permanently ending the 1,600-year-old Japanese imperial dynasty. A communist Democratic Republic of Japan (DRJ) supported by the Soviets is formed in the north and a truly democratic South Japan supported by the United States is founded in the south. Tokyo is divided into a communist North Sector and a democratic South Sector, much like East and West Berlin. Marshall Plan initiated to rebuild Western Europe.

AFTERWORD
THE LOST CONTINENT

I lived a million miles from New York City when 9/11 went down.

I lived in Queens.

When you inhabit one of New York's outer boroughs, Manhattan becomes "The City" . . . a mythical isle populated by investment bankers stuffed into broom-closet apartments, "celebrity chef" restaurateurs, and tourists from Ohio and Japan. I have friends—friends!—who live in "The City" but refuse to travel the fifteen minutes it takes to get to us outlanders. Those few yards across the East River are as far apart as any Cold War demilitarized zone.

Hell, I slept through 9/11, even though my place was just a couple of miles from downtown Manhattan. No din of chaos; it was quiet in Queens. I only found out about the Twin Towers by calling someone in California around eleven in the morning, after both buildings had collapsed.

I went for a walk right after that. What else could I do? It was one of those perfect, golden September days. Again and again I overheard people enthusiastically recounting the footage of the towers collapsing, of the bodies flinging themselves out of the smoking sides of the doomed buildings, as if it were all a movie or a first-person shooter.

And then the smell started creeping into the air. It got stronger as the day went on, especially when the wind peeled off from the East River to the south, where the towers had been. It was never overpowering. It died down in a few days. But I'll never forget it. It was that dusty, stale tobacco smell that hangs around construction sites, mixed with gunpowder. That, and something richer, something darker.

I went home around sundown. A few blocks from my place I heard the sound of jet engines overhead . . . but weren't all airplanes supposed to be grounded? This sound, though, was different from that of an airliner. Sharper.

I looked up, and there were two F-15 fighter jets crawling across the orange yellow sky, in perfect silhouette. *Zero Killer* was born then and there.

I watched the evening news that night, for the first time in a long time. One of the first things that struck me was how quickly the entire political leadership of the United States had disappeared from view. It turns out they'd been planning for 9/11 for a long time.

And I don't mean 9/11 was "an inside job." It was not. But that doesn't mean our fearless leaders hadn't been dying to test out all the top-secret bunkers and nuclear Armageddon "contingency plans" they'd been working on ever since the early days of the Cold War. Then–Vice President Dick Cheney, when questioned about his disappearing act, smugly hinted at how he'd been covertly drilling for doomsday ever since becoming Gerald Ford's chief of staff in 1975.

In the final *Dawn's Early Light* newsletter you might have noticed the mysterious "DRUSA"—the gray eminence behind JOCOM—has his headquarters in a bunker beneath the grounds of a luxury hotel in Virginia. Both the hotel and the bunker are real. The bunker was supposed to be the secret refuge for the entire United States Congress in case of a nuclear war, but it was exposed and abandoned in 1992.

You can take tours of it now.

The Soviet political class was even more self-serving. There are rumors of an entire secret subway system called "M2" deep below Moscow, built during the communist era for the exclusive purpose of evacuating "important people" in a nuclear attack. If M2 exists, the "kleptocrats" currently running Russia are probably still using it.

There's something bigger than East and West at stake. The Cold War ripped open a chasm between "we, the people" and the political elites who govern in our name. The actions of the upper echelons of the United States government on 9/11, as cowardly and undignified as they

OPPOSITE: *Zero Killer* DH 100 cover by Matt Camp and Dave Stewart.

1948: United States helps Greek royalists defeat a communist insurgency. Truman Doctrine of supporting corrupt regimes against communist insurgencies established. Israel established in the aftermath of the Arab-Israeli war.

1949: Soviet troops block American access to West Berlin and South Tokyo. The United States responds by airlifting supplies to Berlin, ending the embargo and saving the city, but Tokyo falls to the Soviets. Mao Zedong defeats the Kuomintang nationalists and establishes the communist People's Republic of China. Kuomintang forces flee to Taiwan. Soviets explode their first atomic device and establish COMECON, their version of the Marshall Plan. East Germany formed. Reunification of Japan and Germany now politically impossible. NATO formed.

1950: Korean War begins. Because UN forces under General Ridgway are not able to use northern Japan as a base of operations, they lose the decisive battle of Pusan Perimeter. Seoul falls to the communists. The United States loses the Korean War in less than a year, without the Chinese ever entering. Treaty of Friendship and Alliance between Soviet Union and China.

1951: The Soviets and Chinese establish a Far East version of the Warsaw Pact, called the Comprehensive Asian Mutual Assistance Treaty, or CAMAT. Document is ratified in Seoul, Korea. Signatories include North Japan, Russia, China, and Korea. CAMAT becomes an important Soviet tool for projecting dominance in the Middle and Far East in the following decades. CAMAT is a major deviation from real-world history; no such organization ever existed in reality. Muhammad Mossadegh elected prime minister of Iran. Iranians nationalize the Anglo-Persian Oil Company, angering the British and Americans.

1952: United States detonates first hydrogen (thermonuclear) bomb in the remote Enewetak atoll.

1953: Dwight D. Eisenhower elected president of the United States. Stalin dies, replaced by Nikita Khrushchev. The United States and Great

were, revealed exactly what would have happened if the Cold War ever had gone nuclear. The very people responsible for plastering the earth with mushroom clouds would have saved themselves and left the rest of us to our fiery and unpleasant fates. And let's not forget who pays for all their "Strangelovian" hidey-holes and private escape jets. We do.

I'd like to think the gap between "us" and "them" has been closing since the demise of the Soviet Union, but Hurricane Katrina convinced me it's only getting wider. Wouldn't it be nice if our elected representatives spent as much time on us as they do on themselves? Whether people who seem to care so little for us can legitimately claim to govern in our name is a disturbingly open question.

But do we deserve any better? 9/11 exposed an even darker, uglier conspiracy, one I took part in without even knowing it. I stumbled onto my complicity through *Zero Killer* in a way that was personally quite shameful. But, as Emperor Claudius said, "Let all the poisons that lurk in the mud hatch out."

I originally cast the Middle East as Zero's "promised land." After all, Zero's world is the polar opposite of ours, a world in which nothing but the Twin Towers are left standing. If the United States is on the bottom, then the Middle East must be on top. What could be more logical than that?

I explained all this to a friend of mine, a friend who's a lot smarter than me. He listened politely and replied, "That's fine, Arvid, but everybody forgets Africa."

Africa.

I forgot about Africa.

The more I learned about Africa, and I still don't claim to know a lot, the more embarrassed I felt. Who am I to criticize Dick Cheney for being insensitive and self-serving? Here's a fun little fact: three thousand children die of starvation every day in Africa. That's the number of people who died in the 9/11 attacks. Every day.

Not to mention the unimaginable brutality of Darfur, of the Congolese civil wars, of Rwanda, Uganda, Sierra Leone, Ethiopia, Somalia, and Zimbabwe. Child soldiers, mass rape, genocide—huge parts of Africa are actually a lot worse than Zero's world. We said "never again" after the Nazi Holocaust, but we didn't mean it. Why is it that when three thousand people in one part of the world die,

it's a tragedy, but when three thousand children die in another part of the world, it's not worth five seconds on a twenty-four-hour cable news program?

Why are we so obsessed with the Middle East? We're like stalkers camping outside the home of a ditzy pop star. The news media, they're the sleazy paparazzi magazines, feeding on and perpetuating the sickness. It's not just about the oil; there's a religious dimension to it, too. But there's a lot more to the world than the southwestern rump of Asia.

People will look back at this period of history and scratch their heads at how catastrophically misplaced our attention was. Regardless of how well or how poorly our military enterprises fare in the Middle East, Africa will be remembered as our great, enduring failure. It is the "black hole" of our consciousness.

So it only makes sense that, if there had ever been a nuclear war between the Soviet Union and the United States, both sides would have quite simply forgotten about the Lost Continent. Now Africa is such an integral part of Zero's story, it's hard to believe he ever wanted to go anywhere else. Africa is, after all, the homeland of his ancestors. Home—that's what he's looking for. And it's not just his home; it's home for every single human being on this planet.

The world is, I hope, finally waking up to the horrors desecrating our collective homeland. I wonder what it will take for us to do the things necessary to help Africans lift themselves out of their misery. Whatever the case, I believe the words of the great reggae musician Warrior King—"Africa shall be free." Despite all the failed summits, despite all the disastrous economic policies of the World Bank and the International Monetary Fund, it shall be free.

I just hope it doesn't take a nuclear war.

—**Arvid Nelson**
Queens, New York
December 2009

ZERO KILLER WORLD TIMELINE »»

Britain orchestrate a coup against Prime Minister Muhammad Mossadegh of Iran. Muhammad Reza Pahlavi becomes shah of Iran, alienating and radicalizing large portions of Iranian society. East German uprising crushed by Soviet Union.

1954: French expelled from Indochina at the Battle of Dien Bien Phu. Vietnam divided. North Vietnam joins CAMAT. The People's Liberation Army invades Taiwan. Taipei falls in several days, reduced to smoking ruins. The battered and demoralized Taiwanese defenders retreat to the mountainous eastern side of the island, where they launch guerrilla raids on the PLA. This did not happen in reality, but the Chinese are much more confident in the world of *Zero Killer* due to the communist People's Republic of Japan and the fall of Korea to Kim Il Sung. But the mainland Chinese underestimate the resolve of the United States, still smarting over the loss of Tokyo and Korea. Eisenhower launches a "police action" to send United States troops to Taiwan without a congressional declaration of war.

1955: Warsaw Pact formed. Soviets test-detonate a 1.6-megaton hydrogen bomb. Soviet successes in the Far East have elevated the USSR's global status far above what it was at this time in reality. The fall of Tokyo and Korea also frees up Soviet resources for strategizing in the Middle East. Khrushchev capitalizes on Iranian nationalist discontentment begins funding anti-shah communist guerrilla movements, even offering them safe haven in the SSR of Turkmenistan. The Soviets also begin funding communist insurgencies in Afghanistan.

1956: Hungary spontaneously revolts against Soviet rule, but the popular rebellion is brutally repressed by the Soviets. Anti-Soviet riots in Poland viciously quelled by pro-Stalinist and Soviet forces. Egyptian president Abdel Nasser nationalizes the Suez Canal and allies himself with the Soviets. Israel, Britain, and France attack Egypt and seize the canal. Khrushchev threatens nuclear attacks on London and Paris, and Eisenhower forces Israel, France, and Britain to relent. Crisis draws Egypt closer to the Soviet Union. Syria, Iraq, Lebanon, and Iran also develop Soviet ties

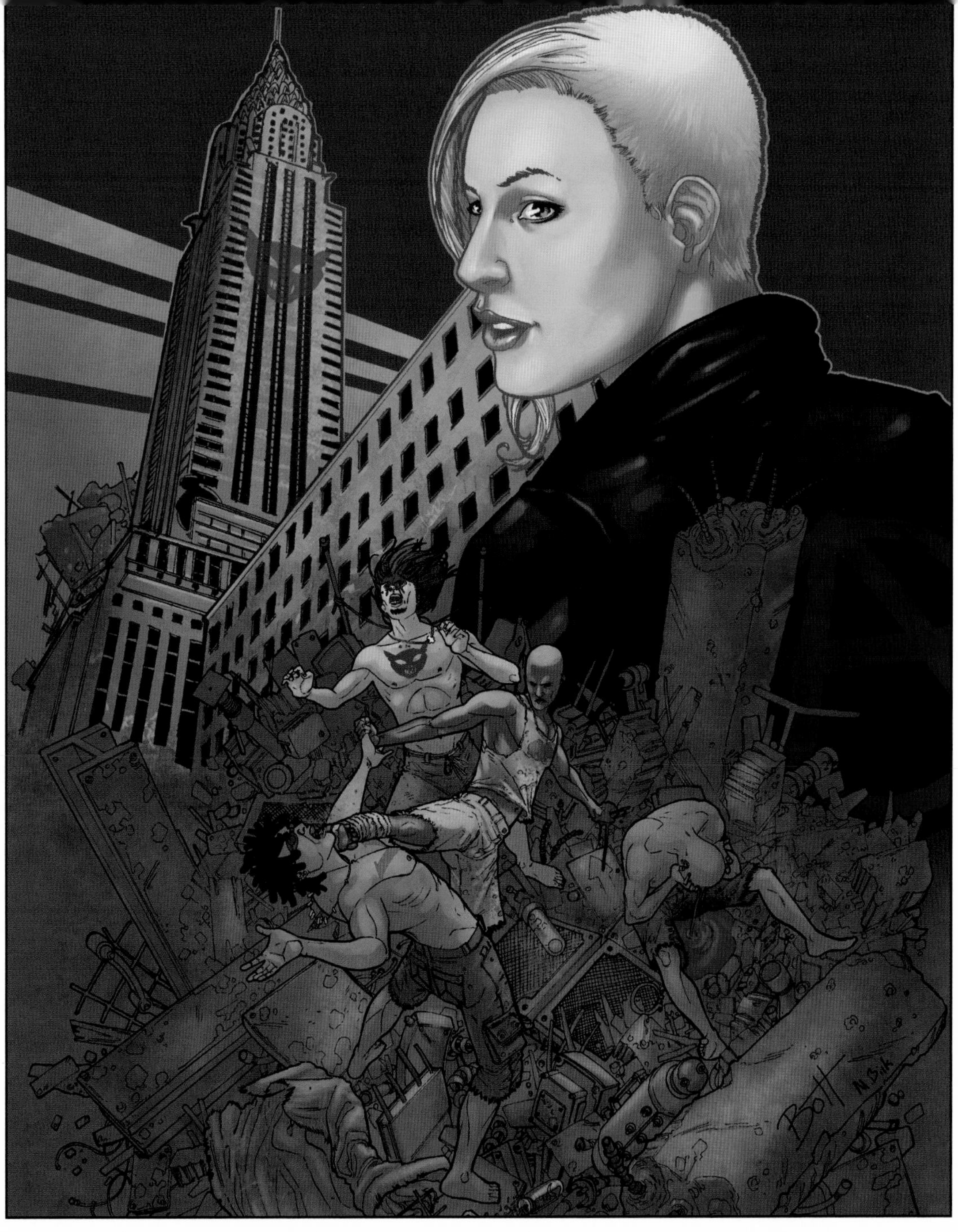

ABOVE: *Zero Killer* pinup by Jimmy Bott.

and enact socialist economic reforms. Taiwanese and US forces expel the mainland Chinese People's Liberation Army from Taiwan after two years of brutal war.

1957: Soviets launch Sputnik I, initiating the Space Race.

1958: The Great Leap Forward begins in the People's Republic of China. United States launches its first satellite, *Explorer I*.

1959: 1959 is significant in the world of *Zero Killer* because of what did *not* happen. In reality, Khrushchev tried to engage with the West in the late '50s. He even met with Eisenhower in 1959. Because of the Soviet Union's success in Asia, Khrushchev does not adopt a conciliatory attitude during this time. Moreover, the Soviets follow through on their promise to help the Chinese develop nuclear weapons again, the opposite of what happened in reality. Thus the Sino-Soviet split does not occur in *Zero Killer*. In fact, China and the Soviet Union grow closer in the late '50s and early '60s. Soviet *Luna 1* spacecraft becomes the first probe to reach the moon, and the *Luna 2* becomes the first to land (crash) on the moon. Communists seize power in Cuba.

1960: The Great Leap Forward fails, but the negative effects of the disastrous modernization program are mollified by economic support to China from CAMAT. Soviet-funded communist insurgency in Iran grows in strength, virtually controlling the mountainous northeast of the country. U-2 crisis.

1961: Berlin Wall erected. Yuri Gagarin is the first man in space. John F. Kennedy elected president of the United States, declares America will land a man on the moon and return him safely to Earth before 1970. Bay of Pigs invasion ends in disaster for US-funded anti-Castro forces.

1962: The communist North Japanese begin blocking refugees fleeing to the south, much as the East Germans do in Berlin. Communist Japanese erect the "North-South Security Fence," much like the current wall the Israelis are building around the Palestinians. The wall closes

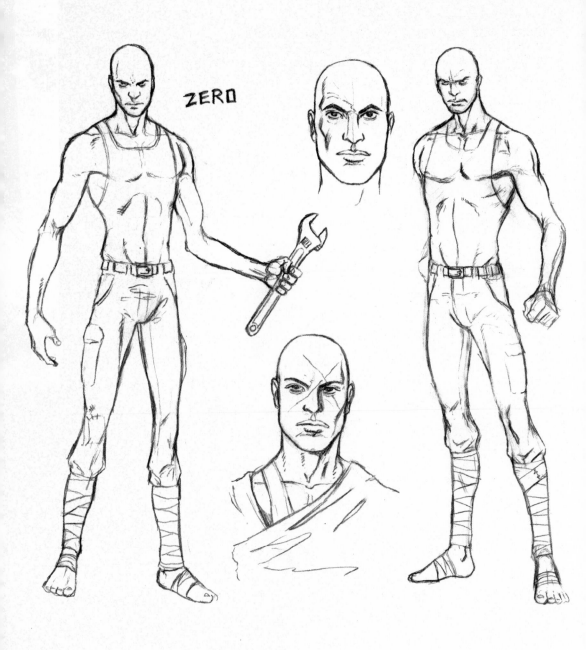

ZERO

ZERO KILLER WORLD TIMELINE »»

Tokyo off from the south completely and severs the country in half. This wall is jokingly referred to as the "Great Wall of Japan." Cuban Missile Crisis pushes the world to the brink of nuclear annihilation, but Khrushchev withdraws missile installations from Cuba. At the same time, Soviet gains in the Far East lead Khrushchev to support China in its war against India (the opposite of what happened in reality). China annexes northeastern Indian provinces. John Glenn becomes the first American to orbit the Earth.

1963: John F. Kennedy assassinated, succeeded by Lyndon Johnson. Iranian "Red Revolution" occurs. Iranian communists, armed with Soviet and Chinese weapons, seize power and depose the tottering shah of Iran. Soviet troops swiftly move into Tehran to bolster the fledgling communist government, over vigorous protests from the United States. Iran joins CAMAT.

1964: The monarchist government of Afghanistan falls to a loose coalition of communist and fundamentalist insurgents. King Muhammad

Zahir Shah is assassinated. Soviet satellite government installed, but does not join CAMAT for fear of upsetting the fundamentalist elements who helped overthrow Zahir Shah and pose a serious threat to the stability of the new communist government. Leonid Brezhnev becomes general secretary of the Communist Party of the Soviet Union. Success in Afghanistan causes Brezhnev to initiate a similar strategy of funding anti-Western insurgents in Pakistan, hoping to replicate success there. *Dr. Strangelove* debuts in theaters. Gulf of Tonkin incident opens the Vietnam War.

1965: 200,000 US troops in Vietnam. Aleksey Leonov becomes the first man to walk in space. Although the escapade nearly ends in disaster, the Soviet Union is flush with recent successes in Afghanistan and Iran. Brezhnev increases funding for the Soviet lunar-landing effort (in reality, the Soviets severely curtailed funding for space exploration at this time). Overthrow of President Sukarno in Indonesia leads to a power struggle between Soviet-supported communists and US-supported right-wing militarists.

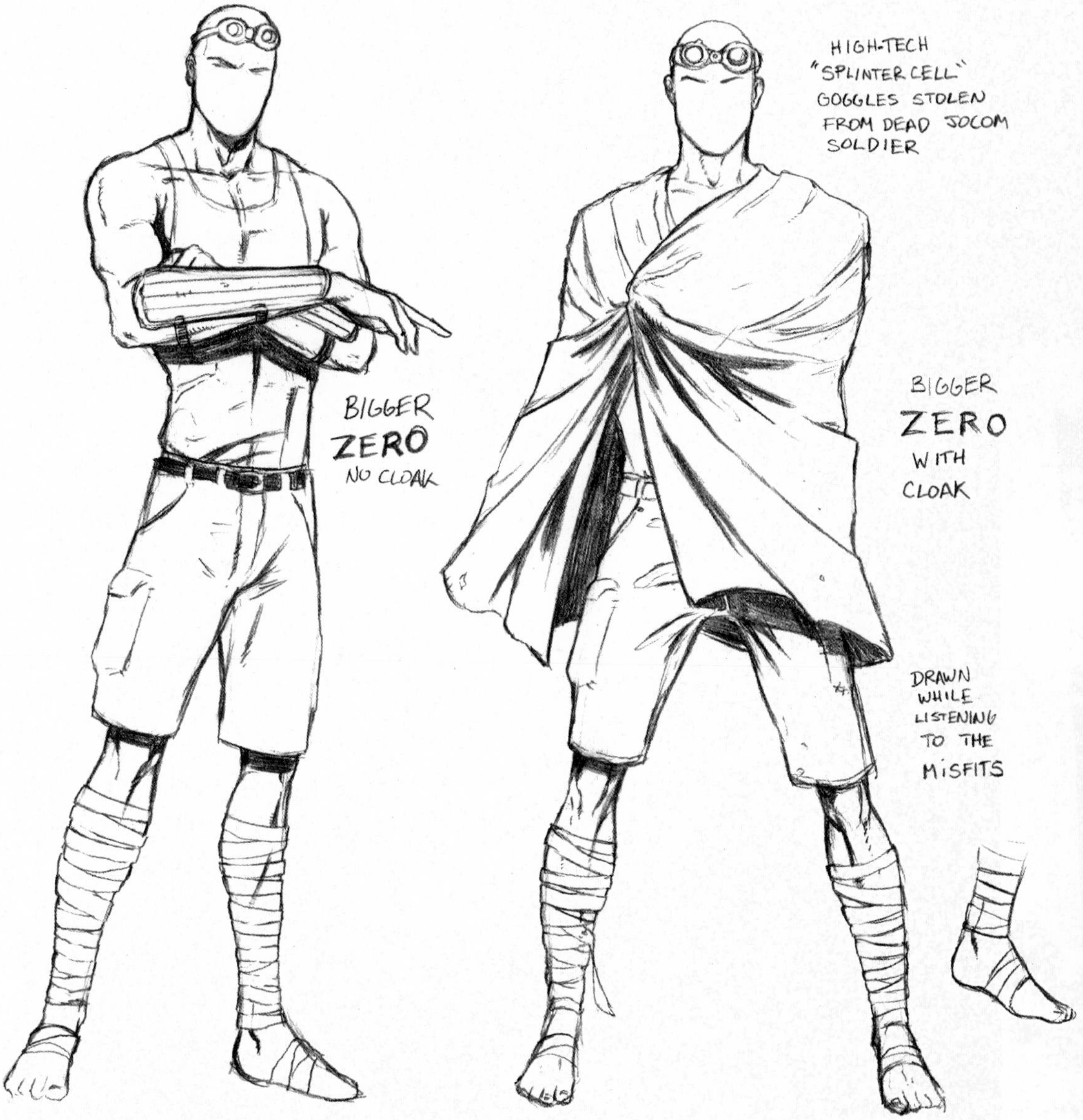
HIGH-TECH
"SPLINTER CELL"
GOGGLES STOLEN
FROM DEAD JOCOM
SOLDIER
BIGGER
ZERO
NO CLOAK
BIGGER
ZERO
WITH
CLOAK
DRAWN
WHILE
LISTENING
TO THE
MISFITS

ABOVE AND FACING PAGE: The evolution of Zero—early character designs by Matt Camp.

1966: Persistent Islamic guerrilla movements in Afghanistan and Pakistan threaten the Soviet Union's hold on those countries. Brezhnev begins supporting anti-Israeli terrorist groups as a "safety valve" to siphon religious militants away from Soviet satellite states and direct them toward Israel, the United States' key puppet in the Middle East. US-supported forces seize power in Indonesia.

1967: Egyptian president Abdel Nasser blocks the Suez Canal and the Straits of Tiran, leading to the Six-Day War. Brezhnev's strategy of directing Islamic militants away from Afghanistan and Pakistan towards Israel works only too well. Israel still wins the 1967 war, but at a far greater cost. Syria occupies northern Israel to Nazareth. Egypt permanently cuts off Israeli supplies from the Red Sea, crippling its economy. The United States secretly arms Israel with nuclear weapons. Three United States astronauts die in a fire during a ground test of the United States' *Apollo 1* lunar voyager. Setbacks in the Middle East and Asia devastate the American economy. Popular support for NASA wanes in face of economic depression at home. United States space program is severely curtailed.

1968: Soviets crush the Prague Spring in Czechoslovakia. They also send a secret manned mission to the moon, a "test run" to make sure their technology works before they make an "official" trip. Brezhnev calculates a failed mission to the moon would be disastrous for the Soviet Union's global image. Against all odds, the mission to the moon is successful. A public mission is announced for 1969. Tet Offensive in Vietnam turns American public opinion decisively against the Vietnam War. Afghanistan joins CAMAT, but the move proves disastrous, triggering religious uprisings in Pakistan and Afghanistan. The communists are restored to power by a joint Chinese, Korean, and Soviet invasion, but the insurgencies thrive and even grow in the countryside.

1969: The publicly announced Soviet manned space flight to the moon ends in disaster. Both cosmonauts die and the *Soyuz* craft is lost. It's a colossal public-relations disaster for the Soviet Union. This, plus an economic boom in the United States, revitalizes US interest in the Space Race. NASA and the Apollo program receive new life. Nixon becomes United States president. Operation Menu, the secret bombing campaign

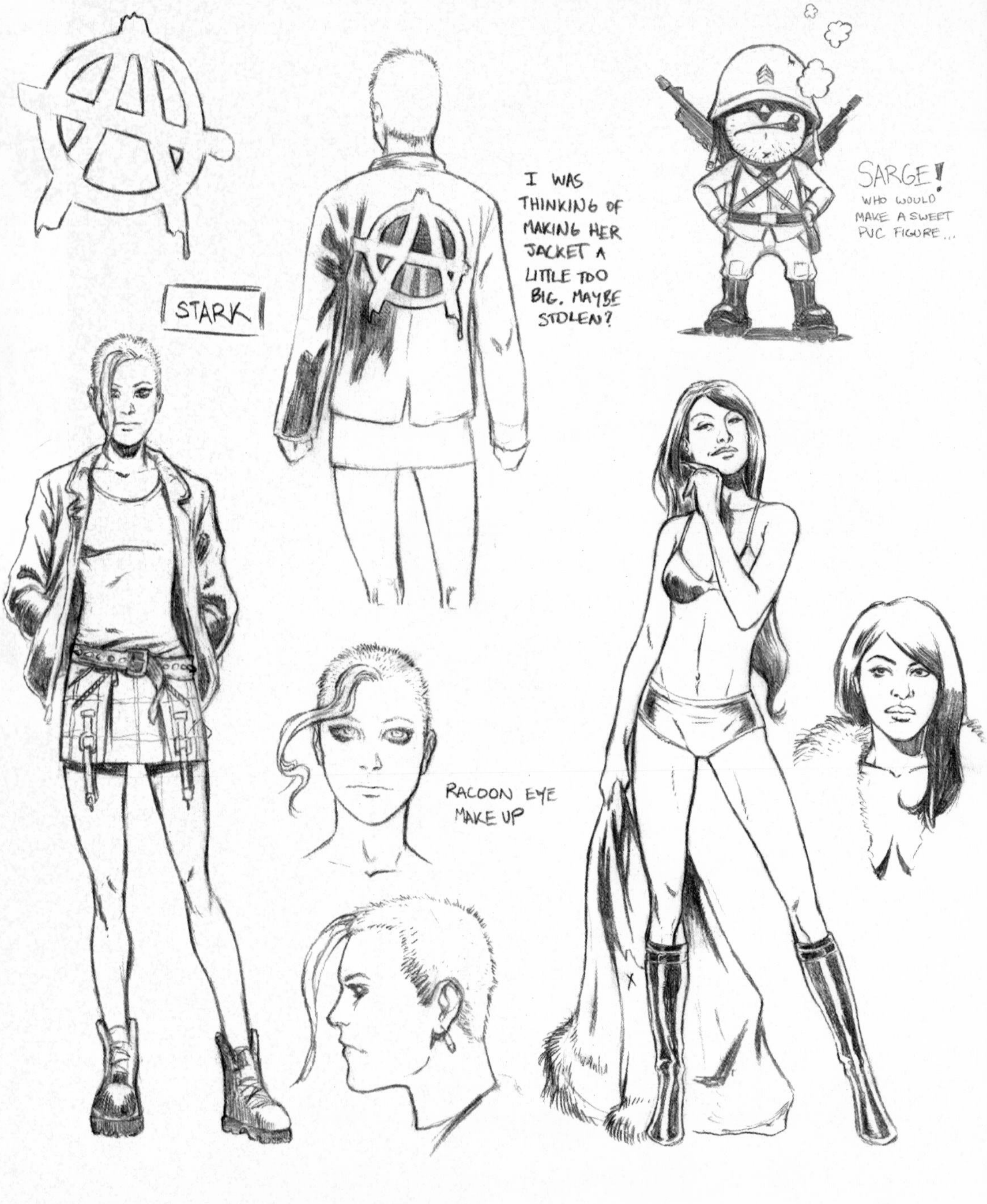
STARK
I WAS THINKING OF MAKING HER JACKET A LITTLE TOO BIG. MAYBE STOLEN?
SARGE!
WHO WOULD MAKE A SWEET PVC FIGURE...
RACOON EYE MAKE UP

ABOVE: Matt Camp's early sketches of Stark, Dahlia, and Sarge.

ZERO KILLER WORLD TIMELINE »»

of Cambodia in the Vietnam War, begins. Ussuri River skirmishes between the Soviet Union and China do not occur in the world of *Zero Killer*, as both countries are too embroiled in joint counterinsurgency operations in Pakistan and Afghanistan. Local resistance in both these countries escalates; total of 300,000 Sino-Soviet troops in the region. The presence of foreign troops only fosters popular support for the rebels.

1970: In reality, the early '70s were a time of reduced tension between the United States and the Soviet Union. President Nixon embarked on a policy of de-escalation with the Soviet Union. But in *Zero Killer*, the Soviet Union's stunning early Cold War success in the Far East and its aggressive tactics in Iran, Pakistan, and Afghanistan, as well as the absence of a Sino-Soviet split, make the Soviets more cocky and the United States less conciliatory. Nixon's secretary of state, Henry Kissinger, fearing a global victory for communism, promotes an aggressively anti-Soviet policy at this time, the exact opposite of the détente policy he advocated in reality. *Apollo 11*, the second successful manned mission to the moon (but the first the world at large is aware of; see 1968), occurs one year after its date in reality. Soviets successfully conclude the *Soyuz 9* manned mission to the moon several months after the Americans.

1971: Soviets win the Space Race, landing a man on the moon in the *Cosmos 434* lander and returning him safely to Earth mere weeks ahead of the United States. The close finish only feeds antipathy toward the Soviet Union amongst the American public. Pentagon Papers released to the *New York Times*, revealing President Lyndon Johnson's duplicity about his management of the Vietnam War. American mood on Vietnam sours further. North Japan invades South Japan, aided by China and Korea. Although the United States is already faced with a deteriorating military situation in Vietnam, Congress declares war on North Japan on the condition a drawdown of US forces in Vietnam will begin within a year. It is now clear Brezhnev's strategy of aiding religious fundamentalists in Iran, Afghanistan, and Pakistan is backfiring. While in the '60s this policy led to the expulsion of the United States and Britain from the region, it has also created a transnational movement

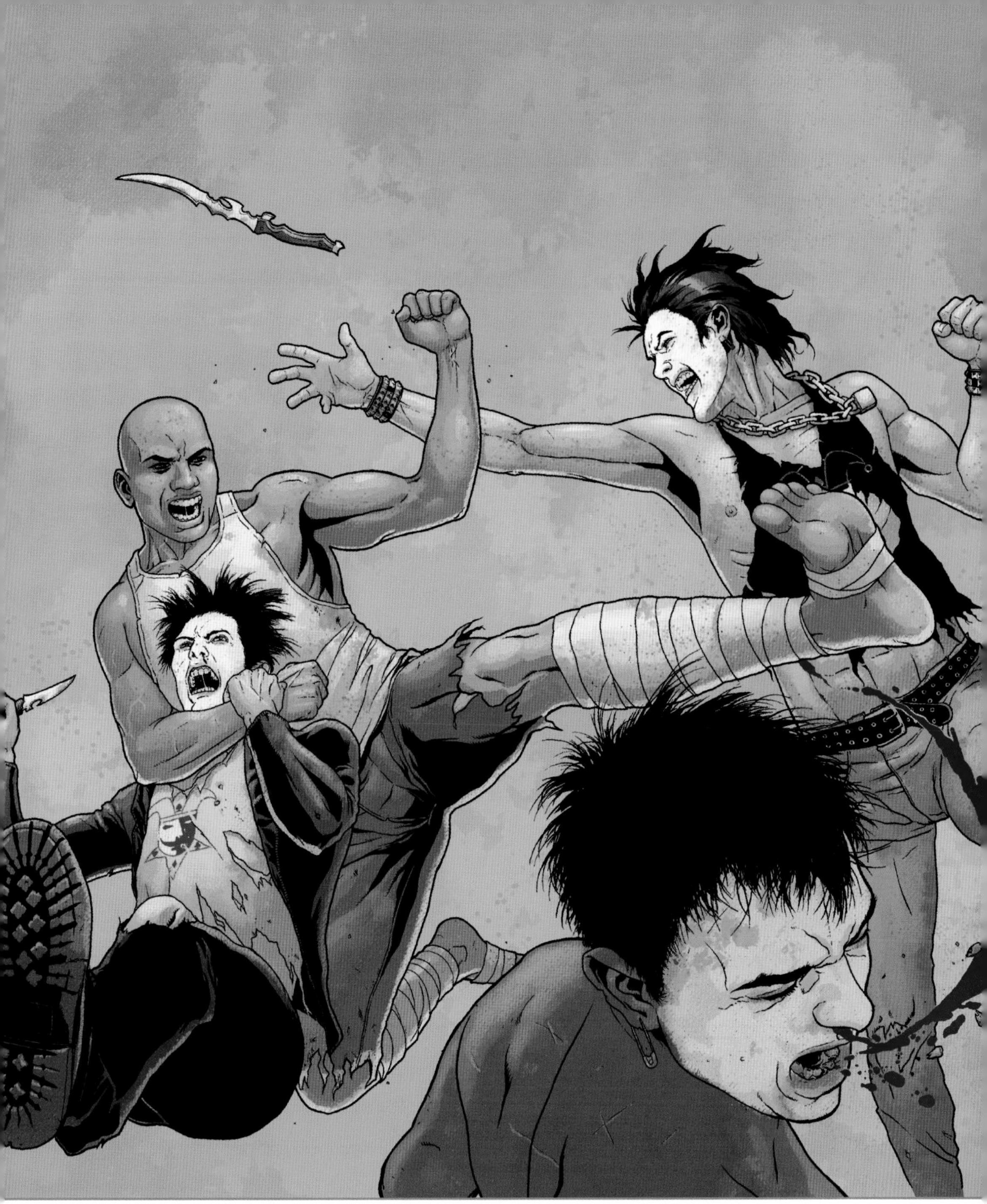

ABOVE: Dark Horse's *Free Comic Book Day 2007* back cover art by Matt Camp and Dave Stewart.

as hostile to the Soviet Union as it is to Israel and the United States. China and Russia find themselves in a debilitating counterinsurgency, much like the United States faces in Vietnam, and Israel finds itself in a very precarious position, as the United States is now embroiled in two wars in the Far East.

1972: 58,000 US servicemen and 2 to 5.7 million Vietnamese dead due to war in Vietnam. US begins withdrawing troops from Vietnam to bolster support for South Japan. Faced with limited resources, Nixon diverts arms sales from Israel to Japan. He reasons Israel's nuclear stockpile will prevent its neighbors from seeking all-out annihilation of the increasingly isolated US satellite. It proves to be the worst miscalculation ever made in human history.

1973: The United States withdraws all combat troops from Vietnam to aid in the defense of South Japan. The Yom Kippur war erupts when Egypt and Syria launch joint surprise attacks on Israel. Soviet/Iranian-backed guerrillas from Lebanon also take part. OPEC suspends oil sales to the West, triggering an economic crisis. From the start, the war goes badly for Israel—the increased Soviet influence in the Middle East and the transnational fundamentalist guerrilla movements the Soviets inadvertently created make a decisive difference in the military capability of the combatant Arab states. Within weeks the Syrians are at the gates of Tel Aviv. The Israelis launch nuclear strikes on Tehran and Damascus. The Soviet Union responds by annihilating Israel. The United States retaliates by launching a nuclear strike against Moscow. It escalates into a massive global exchange known as Zero Hour. Over 90 percent of the human population perishes in the span of twenty-four hours. Nixon and Ford are assassinated in the chaos, along with most of the Senate and the House. JOCOM is formed.

2007: Present day. The ruins of New York City are a grim necropolis of feuding gangs, although it's said Africa was spared the devastation of Zero Hour. The sinister, militaristic JOCOM persists in sprawling underground complexes. And a bounty hunter named Zero stalks the towers of New York . . .

The following story first appeared in Dark Horse's *Free Comic Book Day 2007* offering, as a preview of our creative team and Zero's world. This story takes place before the events in *Zero Killer* #1.

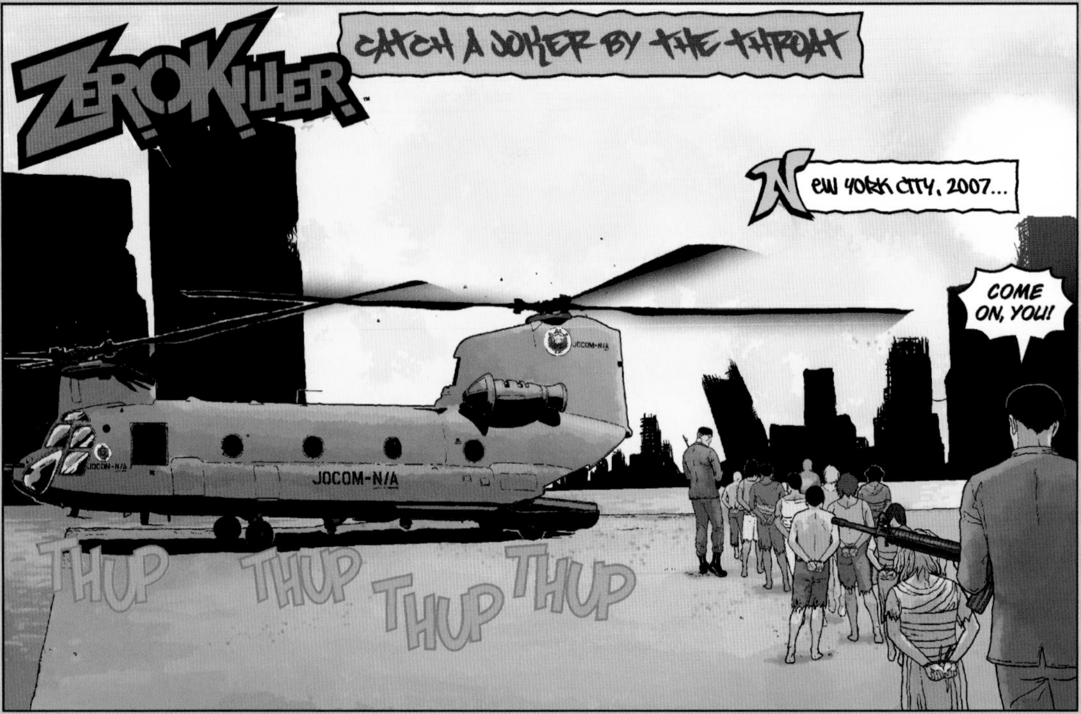
ZERO KILLER
CATCH A JOKER BY THE THROAT
NEW YORK CITY, 2007...
COME ON, YOU!
JOCOM-N/A
THUP THUP THUP THUP

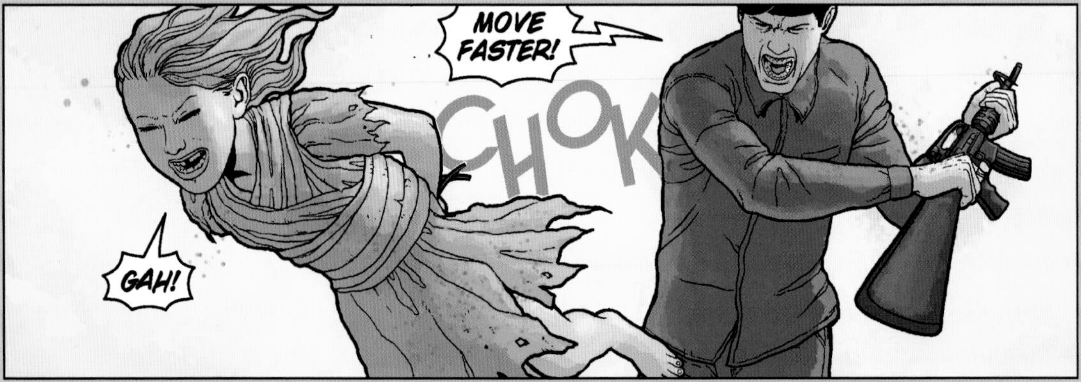
MOVE FASTER!
CHOK
GAH!

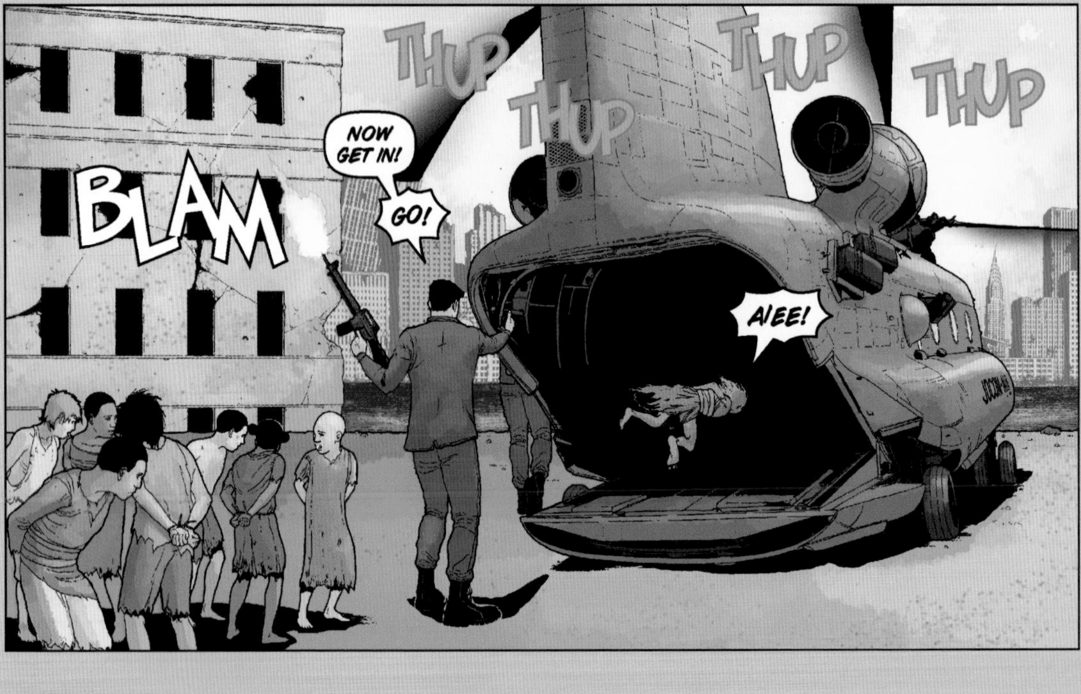
THUP THUP THUP THUP
NOW GET IN!
GO!
BLAM
AIEE!

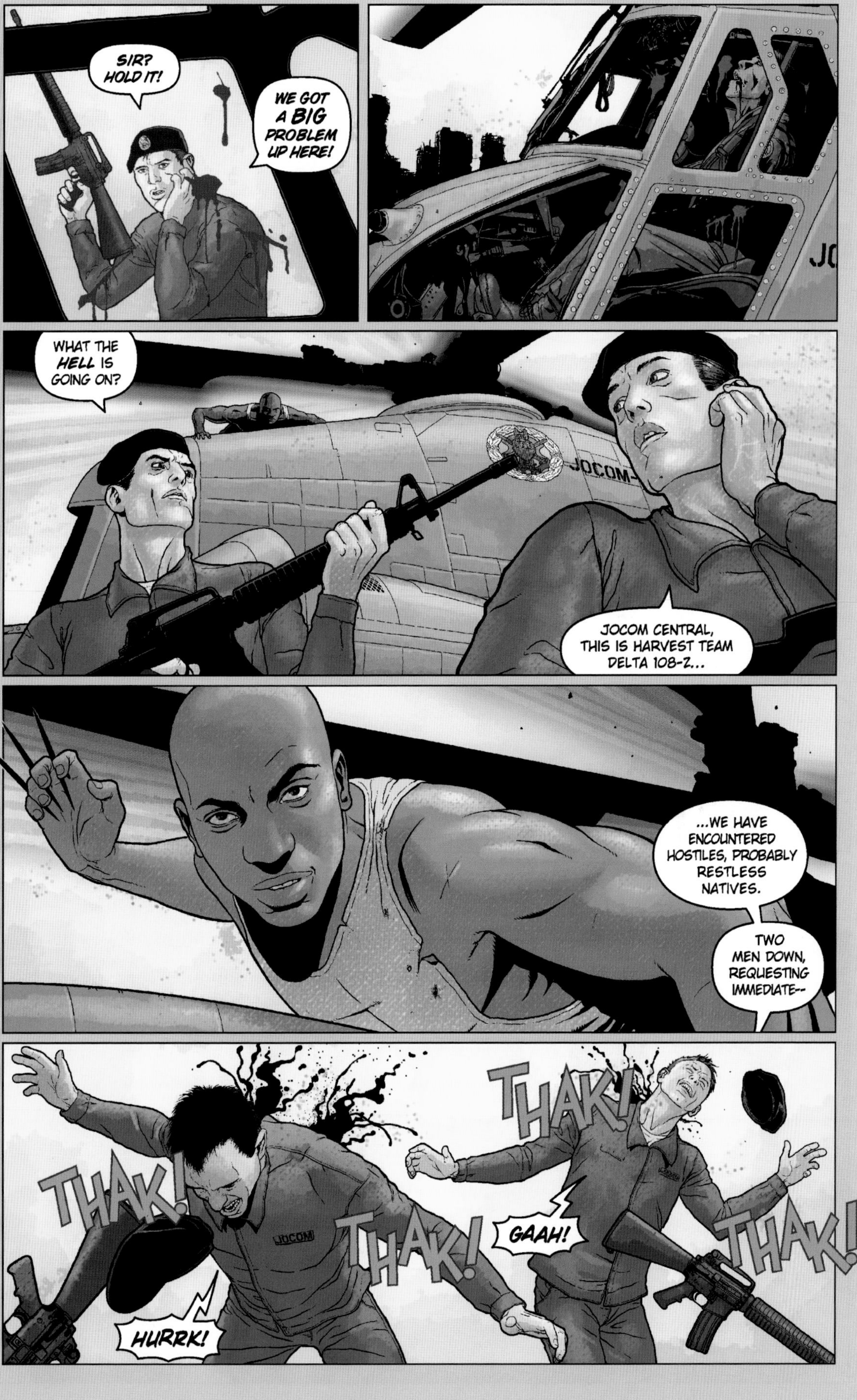
SIR? HOLD IT!
WE GOT A BIG PROBLEM UP HERE!
JOC
WHAT THE HELL IS GOING ON?
JOCOM-
JOCOM CENTRAL, THIS IS HARVEST TEAM DELTA 108-2...
...WE HAVE ENCOUNTERED HOSTILES, PROBABLY RESTLESS NATIVES.
TWO MEN DOWN, REQUESTING IMMEDIATE--
THAK!
THAK!
JOCOM
THAK!
GAAH!
THAK!
HURRK!

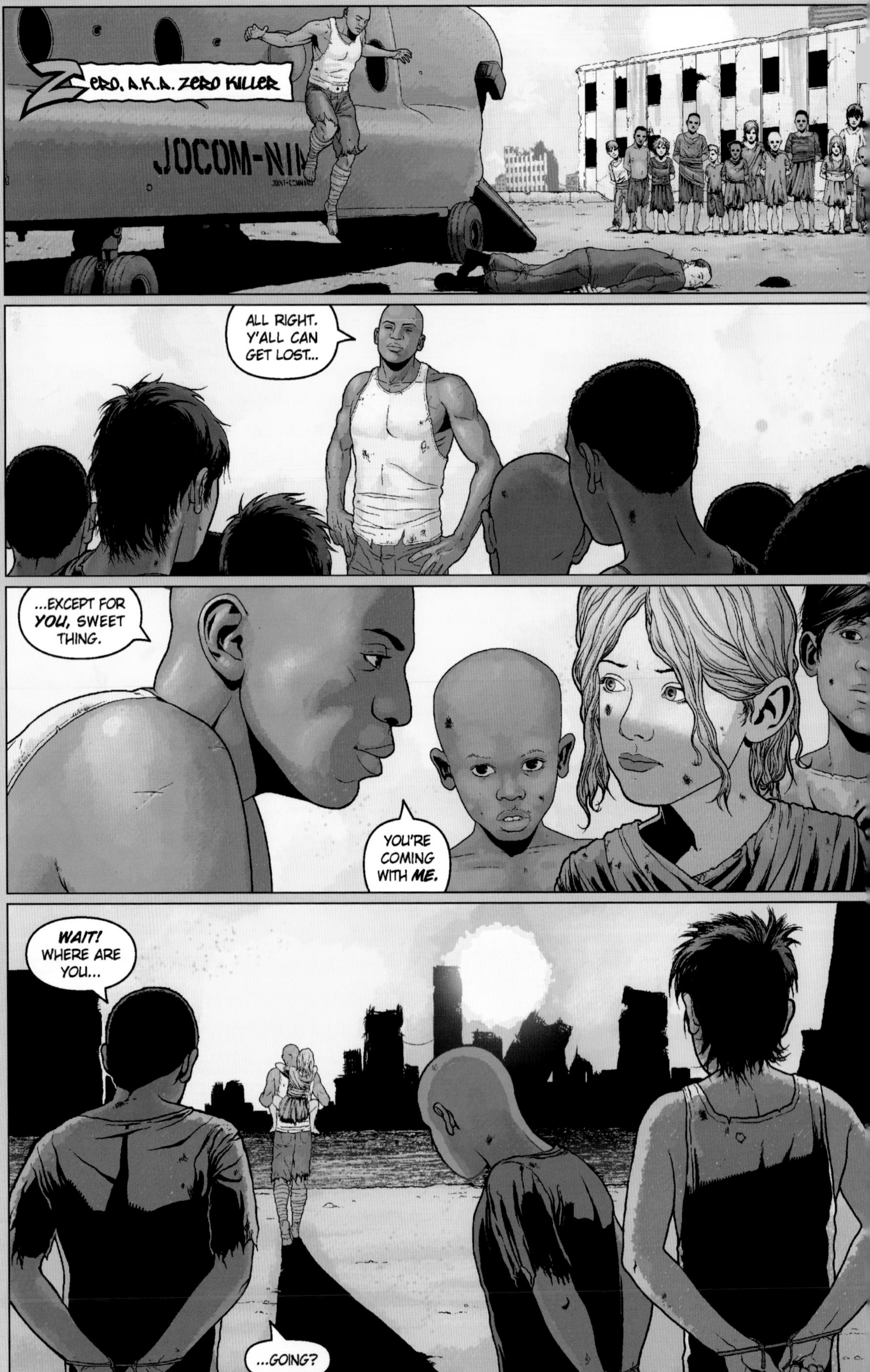

ZERO, A.K.A. ZERO KILLER
JOCOM-NI
ALL RIGHT. Y'ALL CAN GET LOST...
...EXCEPT FOR YOU, SWEET THING.
YOU'RE COMING WITH ME.
WAIT! WHERE ARE YOU...
...GOING?

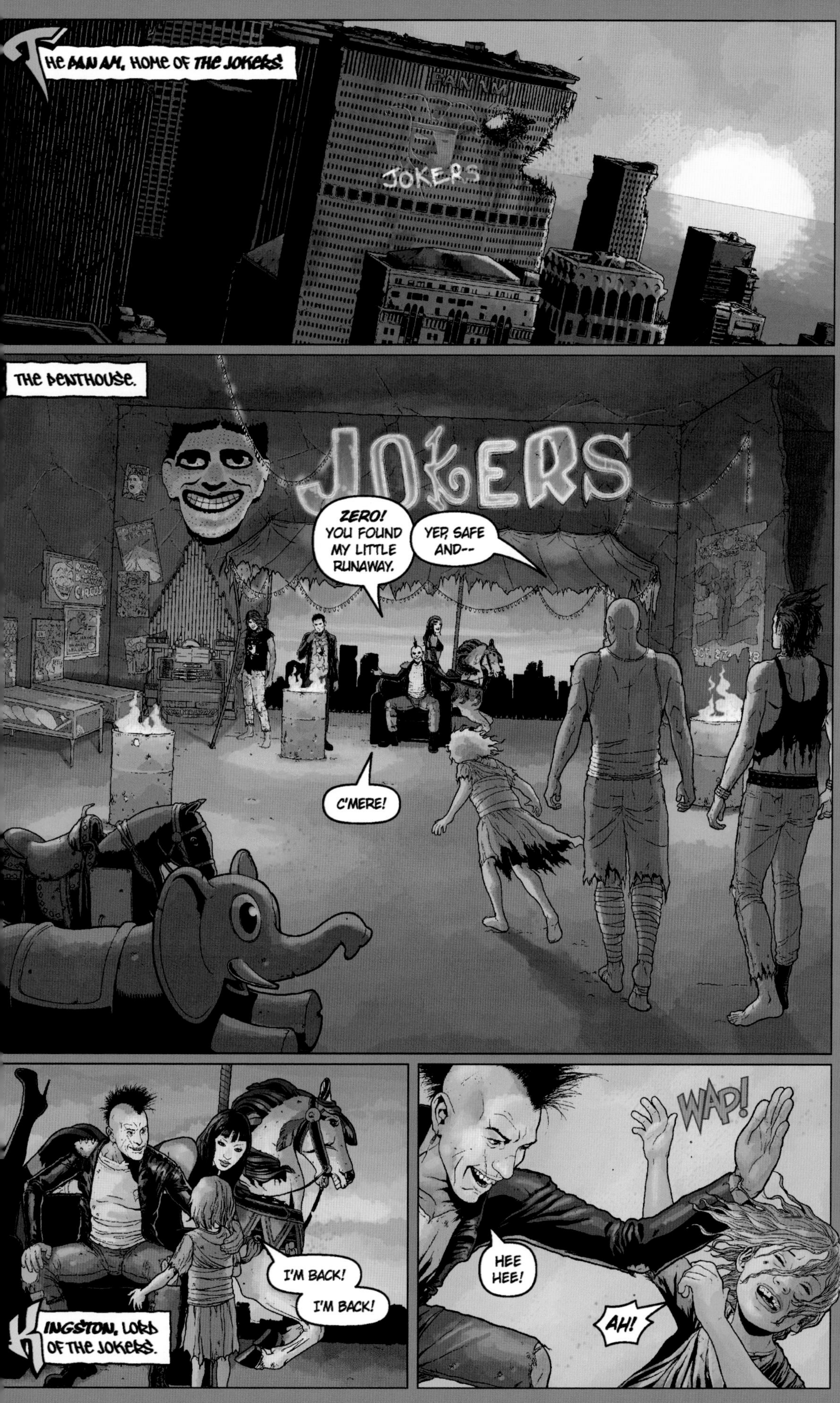
THE PAN AM, HOME OF THE JOKERS.
PAN AM
JOKERS
THE PENTHOUSE.
JOKERS
CIRCUS
ZERO! YOU FOUND MY LITTLE RUNAWAY.
YEP, SAFE AND--
C'MERE!
I'M BACK!
I'M BACK!
KINGSTON, LORD OF THE JOKERS.
WAP!
HEE HEE!
AH!

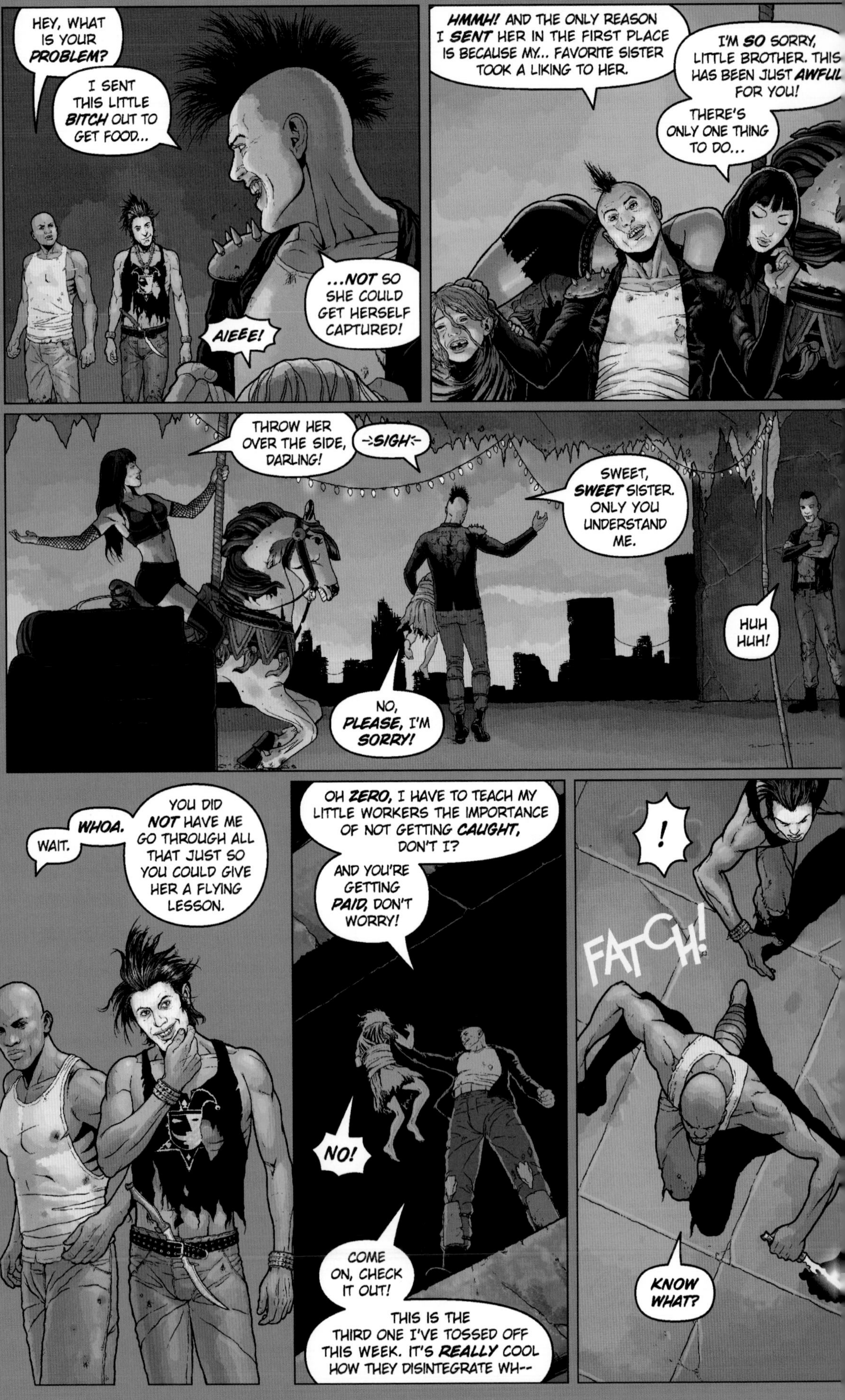
HEY, WHAT IS YOUR PROBLEM?
I SENT THIS LITTLE BITCH OUT TO GET FOOD...
...NOT SO SHE COULD GET HERSELF CAPTURED!
AIEEE!
HMMH! AND THE ONLY REASON I SENT HER IN THE FIRST PLACE IS BECAUSE MY... FAVORITE SISTER TOOK A LIKING TO HER.
I'M SO SORRY, LITTLE BROTHER. THIS HAS BEEN JUST AWFUL FOR YOU!
THERE'S ONLY ONE THING TO DO...
THROW HER OVER THE SIDE, DARLING!
-SIGH-
SWEET, SWEET SISTER. ONLY YOU UNDERSTAND ME.
HUH HUH!
NO, PLEASE, I'M SORRY!
WAIT.
WHOA.
YOU DID NOT HAVE ME GO THROUGH ALL THAT JUST SO YOU COULD GIVE HER A FLYING LESSON.
OH ZERO, I HAVE TO TEACH MY LITTLE WORKERS THE IMPORTANCE OF NOT GETTING CAUGHT, DON'T I?
AND YOU'RE GETTING PAID, DON'T WORRY!
NO!
COME ON, CHECK IT OUT!
THIS IS THE THIRD ONE I'VE TOSSED OFF THIS WEEK. IT'S REALLY COOL HOW THEY DISINTEGRATE WH--
!
FATCH!
KNOW WHAT?

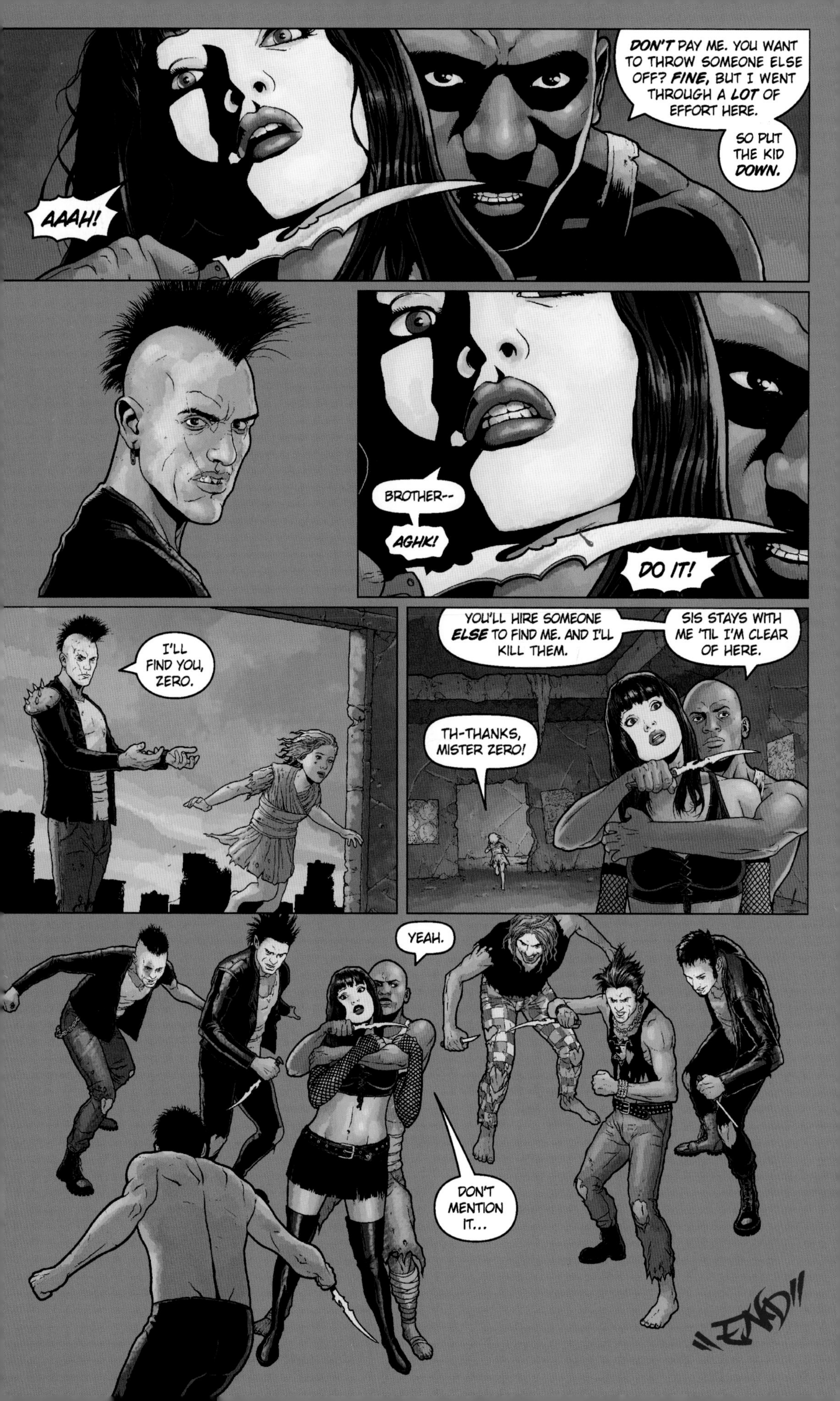
DON'T PAY ME. YOU WANT TO THROW SOMEONE ELSE OFF? FINE, BUT I WENT THROUGH A LOT OF EFFORT HERE.
SO PUT THE KID DOWN.
AAAH!
BROTHER--
AGHK!
DO IT!
I'LL FIND YOU, ZERO.
YOU'LL HIRE SOMEONE ELSE TO FIND ME. AND I'LL KILL THEM.
SIS STAYS WITH ME 'TIL I'M CLEAR OF HERE.
TH-THANKS, MISTER ZERO!
YEAH.
DON'T MENTION IT...
END

"*Rex Mundi* is priceless."
Brian K. Vaughan

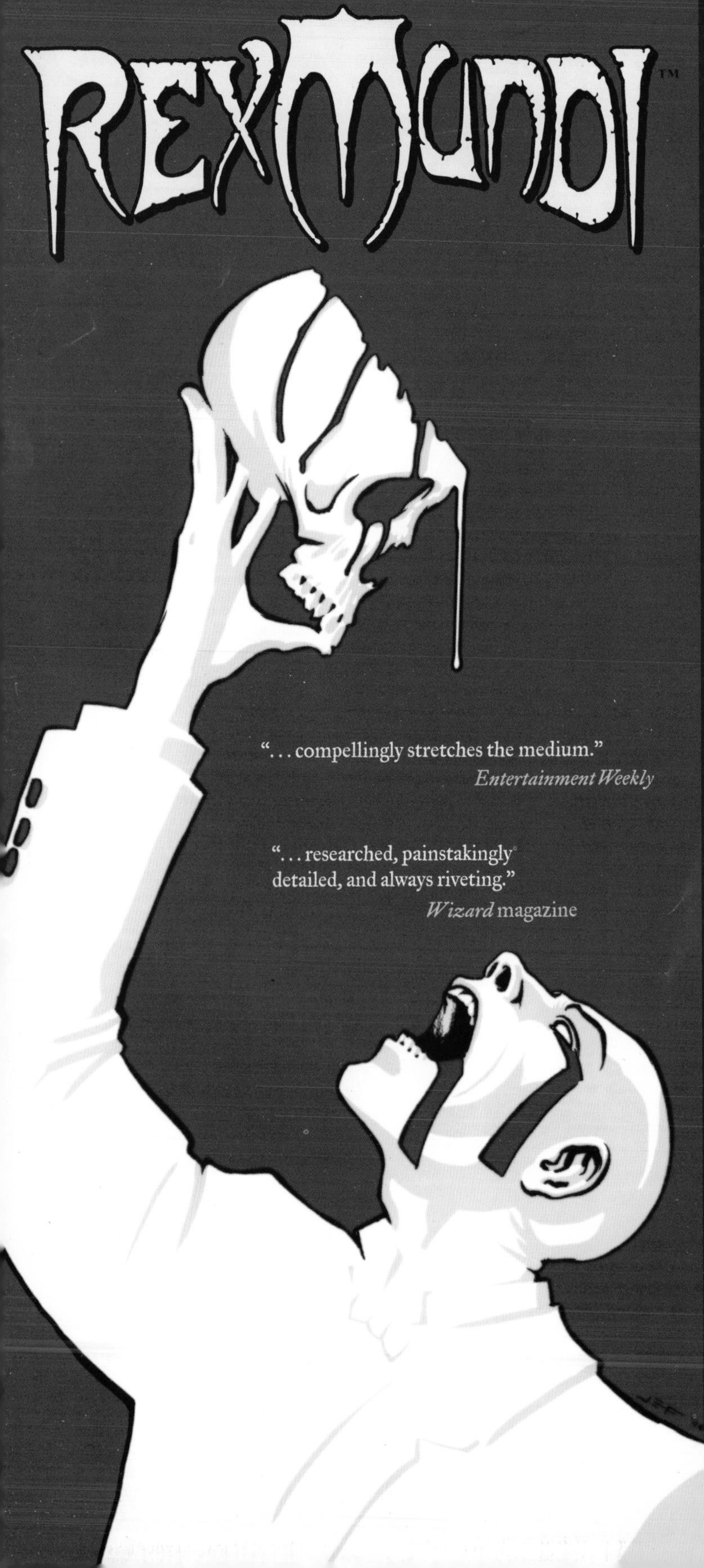
REX MUNDI™

"...compellingly stretches the medium."
Entertainment Weekly

"...researched, painstakingly detailed, and always riveting."
Wizard magazine

ARVID NELSON
JUAN FERREYRA
ERICJ

AVAILABLE NOW

THE GUARDIAN OF THE TEMPLE
ISBN 978-1-59307-652-8
$16.99

THE RIVER UNDERGROUND
ISBN 978-1-59307-682-5
$16.99

THE LOST KINGS
ISBN 978-1-59307-651-1
$16.99

CROWN AND SWORD
ISBN 978-1-59307-824-9
$16.99

THE VALLEY AT THE END OF THE WORLD
ISBN 978-1-59582-192-8
$17.99

GATE OF GOD
ISBN 978-1-59582-403-5
$17.99

DARK HORSE BOOKS

AVAILABLE AT YOUR LOCAL COMICS SHOP OR BOOKSTORE

TO FIND A COMICS SHOP IN YOUR AREA, CALL 1-888-266-422

For more information or to order direct: •On th web: darkhorse.com •E-mail: mailorder@darkhors com •Phone: 1-800-862-0052 Mon.-Fri. 9 AM to PM Pacific time.